Teacher Preparation Classroom

TEACHER PREP

**MERRILL
PRENTICE HALL**

**See a demo at
www.prenhall.com/teacherprep/demo**

Your Class. Their Careers. Our Future. Will your students be prepared?

We invite you to explore our new, innovative and engaging Web site and all that it has to offer you, your course, and tomorrow's educators! Preview this site today at www.prenhall.com/teacherprep/demo. Just click on "go" on the login page to begin your exploration.

Organized around the major courses pre-service teachers take, the Teacher Preparation site provides media, student/teacher artifacts, strategies, research articles, and other resources to equip your students with the quality tools needed to excel in their courses and prepare them for their first classroom.

This ultimate online education resource will provide you and your students access to:

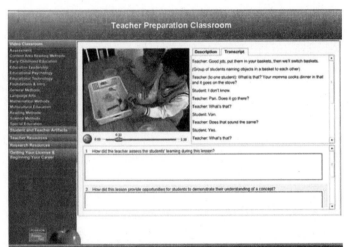

Online Video Library. More than 250 video clips—each tied to a course topic and framed by learning goals and Praxis-type questions—capture real teachers and students working in real classrooms.

Student and Teacher Artifacts. More than 200 student and teacher classroom artifacts—each tied to a course topic and framed by learning goals and application questions—provide a wealth of materials and experiences to help your students observe children's developmental learning.

Lesson Plan Builder. Step-by-step guidelines and lesson plan examples to support students as they learn to build high-quality lesson plans.

Articles and Readings. Over 500 articles from ASCD's renowned journal *Educational Leadership* are available. The site also includes Research Navigator, a searchable database of additional educational journals.

Strategies and Lessons. Over 500 research-supported instructional strategies appropriate for a wide range of grade levels and content areas.

Licensure and Career Tools. Resources devoted to helping your students pass their licensure exam; learn standards, law, and public policies; plan a teaching portfolio; and succeed in their first year of teaching.

Access Code previously been used?
Students:
◆ To purchase or renew an access code, go to www.prenhall.com/teacherprep and click on the "Register for Teacher Prep" button.
Instructors:
◆ Email Merrill.marketing@pearsoned.com and provide the following information:
  ◆ Name and Affiliation
  ◆ Author/Title/Edition of Merrill text
Upon ordering *Teacher Prep* for their students, instructors will be given a lifetime *Teacher Prep* Access Code.

Teaching and Learning K–8
A Guide to Methods and Resources

Ninth Edition

RICHARD D. KELLOUGH
Professor Emeritus, California State University,
Sacramento

JOHN JAROLIMEK
Professor Emeritus, University of Washington, Seattle

PEARSON

Merrill
Prentice Hall

Upper Saddle River, New Jersey
Columbus, Ohio

Library of Congress Cataloging-in-Publication Data
Kellough, Richard D. (Richard Dean)
    Teaching and learning K–8 : a guide to methods and resources / Richard D.
Kellough, John Jarolimek. — 9th ed.
        p. cm.
    Rev. ed. of: Teaching and learning in the elementary school / John Jarolimek,
Clifford D. Foster, Sr., Richard D. Kellough. 8th ed. ©2005.
    Includes bibliographical references and index.
    ISBN-13: 978-0-13-158962-9
    ISBN-10: 0-13-158962-8
    1. Elementary school teaching.   2. Lesson planning.   I. Jarolimek, John.   II. Jarolimek, John. Teaching
and learning in the elementary school.   III. Title.
    LB1555.J34 2008
    372.1102—dc22   2007015946

Vice President and Executive Publisher: Jeffery W. Johnston	**Design Coordinator:** Diane C. Lorenzo
Senior Editor: Darcy Betts Prybella	**Cover Designer:** Janna Thompson-Chordas
Development Editor: Christina Robb	**Cover Image:** SuperStock
Project Manager: Kris Roach	**Production Manager:** Susan Hannahs
Production Coordination: Shelley Creager/ Aptara, Inc.	**Director of Marketing:** David Gesell
Photo Coordinator: Valerie Schultz	**Marketing Coordinator:** Brian Mounts

This book was set in Dutch823 BT by Aptara, Inc. It was printed and bound by
R.R. Donnelley & Sons Company/Harrisonburg. The cover was printed by
R.R. Donnelley & Sons Company/Harrisonburg.

Chapter Opener Photo Credits: Anne Vega/Merrill, pp. 1, 290; Anthony Magnacca/Merrill, pp. 43, 110,
199; Scott Cunningham/Merrill, p. 84; Kathy Kirtland/Merrill, p. 143; Pearson Learning Photo Studio, p. 259;
Barbara Schwartz/Merrill, p. 352.

Pearson Education Ltd.	Pearson Education Australia Pty. Limited
Pearson Education Singapore Pte. Ltd.	Pearson Education North Asia Ltd.
Pearson Education Canada, Ltd.	Pearson Educación de Mexico, S.A. de C.V.
Pearson Education—Japan	Pearson Education Malaysia Pte. Ltd.

10 9 8 7 6 5 4 3 2
ISBN: 13: 978-0-13-158962-9
ISBN: 10:   0-13-158962-8

Our intent for this ninth edition is to provide a contemporary source of appropriate and relevant pedagogy, learning activities, and resources for people preparing to teach elementary grade children.

We believe that exemplary educational programs are rooted in celebrating and building on the diverse characteristics and needs of America's youth. To become and to remain exemplary, teachers in such programs must be in a continual mode of inquiry, reflection, and transformation. It is no different for us as authors. In an effort to prepare a comprehensive and exemplary book for elementary school teaching, we find ourselves in a *continual mode of inquiry* into the latest findings in research and practice, in *constant reflection* as we listen to and assess the comments from practitioners in the field and from users and reviewers of previous editions of the book, and in *steady transformation* as we respond to the challenge of continuing to provide relevant and appropriate coverage for integrating methods and resources. As a result, here are some changes we have made for this edition.

New to This Ninth Edition

Although the primary organization and number of chapters (9) has not changed, we rewrote to add clarity, update, and more closely reflect the new title of the book, most extensively in Chapters 5, 6, 8, and 9. In addition, we made the following enhancements to this edition:

- **A collection of suggestions for motivational teaching strategies with ideas for lessons, interdisciplinary teaching, transcultural studies, and student projects.** Chapter 8 offers an annotated list to coincide with our interest in promoting the use of project-centered, discipline-integrated learning.
- **Additional active learning activities.**
- **Additional vignettes and scenarios.**
- **Attention to the ongoing effects of the No Child Left Behind Act of 2001**.
- **Increased attention to matters of student diversity, with consideration for that diversity and concomitant personalized instruction, a central theme throughout this edition** (see Chapter 8).
- **References are now listed at the end of the book.**
- **Video Classroom video clips from the Prentice Hall Teacher Prep Web site (TPW) are referenced throughout.** Watch for the icon in the margins of the text.

We recognize that competent elementary-school teaching is a kaleidoscopic, multifaceted, eclectic process. When preparing and writing a book to prepare one to teach, by necessity its authors must separate that kaleidoscopic process into separate topics, which is not always possible to do in a way that makes equal sense to all users of the book. So, here, as an overview, is our plan and advice for you.

An Overview of This Edition

Chapter 1 introduces the influences and challenges of elementary-school teaching today, and is followed by Chapter 2 which discusses basic teaching responsibilities and behaviors. Chapter 3 discusses assisting children in the development of two important skills needed for learning—thinking and questioning—without which all else would be irrelevant. Chapter 4 then discusses the establishment and maintenance of an effective classroom environment for learning.

Chapters 5 and 6 address instructional planning. Chapter 5 covers the necessary planning of the curriculum followed by Chapter 6, which covers the detailed instructional planning necessary to bring the planned curriculum to fruition. Because becoming a competent teacher is not nearly as linear a process as might be implied by our chapter by chapter arrangement, as you proceed through Chapters 5 and 6 and begin to develop your own instructional plans, you will want to occasionally refer to particular topics in both chapters.

Chapter 7 discusses assessing the progress and results of the implementation of the instructional plans. Chapter 8 covers ways of grouping children for instruction and optimal learning. Finally, Chapter 9 explores additional strategies for teaching and the integration of strategies.

Features of the Text

Previous users of the book will find most of its features familiar; however, we have made a major effort to increase content comprehensiveness, conciseness, reader friendliness, as well as include more engaging activities. Features include

- **Activities for active learning.** This edition includes three dozen activities that require the student user to deal in some descriptive, analytical, or self-reflective manner with text concepts and real practice. Several of the activities are new to this edition, most notably are 8.1 (preparing of a self-instructional module) and 9.3 (a final performance assessment).
- **Activities for inclusion in the developing professional portfolio.** Some activities might be suitable for inclusion in the student-user's developing professional portfolio. To start, we recommend Activities 4.2, 5.3, 6.2, 6.3, 8.1, and 9.3.
- **Advance organizers.** To establish an appropriate mind-set we have included Anticipated Outcomes at the beginning of each chapter.
- **Study questions and additional activities for class discussion and suggestions for further reading.** Each chapter concludes with a list of questions for class discussion, followed by a listing of additional sources, mostly current and some that are significant classics.

- **Teaching vignettes and classroom scenarios.** Distributed throughout, each is designed to stimulate reflective thought and discussion.
- **Internet resources.** The end of each chapter lists Internet sites and Internet references that we recommend. We visited and checked each site in 2007 immediately before publication but because the Internet is ever changing, some of these Web addresses may have changed.
- **Glossary, references, and index.** The text concludes with an updated glossary of terms, a listing of references, and a subject index.

ACKNOWLEDGMENTS

Although teaching and learning have become increasingly complex—with many new and exciting things happening as schools continue to restructure their efforts to provide the best learning for today's children—we strive to keep the text at a reasonable length and user friendly. We thank everyone who helped in its development. We thank those who contributed and who are acknowledged at appropriate places throughout. We also thank our friends and efficacious professionals at Merrill/Prentice Hall, who have maintained their belief in and support for this book since its first appearance more than 30 years ago.

Although we take full responsibility for any errors or omissions in this book, we are deeply grateful to others for their cogent comments and important contributions that led to the development of this ninth edition. We express our appreciation to the reviewers:

Janet M. Fever (recently deceased), Lindenwood University; Marilyn S. Howe, Clarion University of Pennsylvania; Sue R. Abegglen, Culver-Stockton College; and Kris Sloan, Texas A&M University.

We are indeed indebted and grateful to all the people in our lives, present and past, who have interacted with us and reinforced what we have known since the day we began our careers as teacher: Teaching is the most rewarding profession of all.

R.D.K.
J. J.

Brief Contents

Contents

Chapter 4
Planning and Managing the Classroom Learning Environment   110

Chapter 7
Assessing and Evaluating Student Performance   259

Chapter 1

Elementary School Teaching Today:
An Overview of Influences and Challenges

INTASC Principles	PRAXIS III Domains	NBPTS Standards
• The teacher fosters relationships with colleagues, parents, and agencies in the community to support students' learning and well-being. (Principle 10)	• Teacher Professionalism (Domain D)	• Respect for Diversity
• The teacher plans instruction based on knowledge of subject matter, students, community, and curriculum goals. (Principle 7)	• Organizing Content Knowledge for Student Learning (Domain A)	• Family Involvement

Nearly a century ago the author H. G. Wells described the teacher as that "sower of unseen harvests" because the results of what the teacher sows in students' young minds may not be apparent until long after the teacher is gone, or perhaps even forgotten. But good teachers are rarely forgotten. They put their imprint on the students they teach just as surely as artists put their unique mark on their work. Your great challenge as an elementary school teacher, therefore, lies precisely in determining the kind of imprint you will leave on the character, sensitivity, curiosity, love of learning, and moral values of the children whom you are given the privilege and responsibility of teaching. Regardless of the long-term and positive imprint you leave on your students, however, there is today considerable pressure on teachers and schools for more immediate and measurable results to determine how well children are learning.

Welcome to the exciting, ever-changing world of elementary school teaching. In most teacher education programs, students become familiar with the various techniques and strategies needed to conduct classroom instruction—how to teach reading, mathematics, science, social studies, and other subjects and skills. All of that is important to know if you are to become a competent professional, and we deal with some of these fundamentals in this text. More important, however, at this early point in your professional development, you should be thinking seriously about what it means to be an elementary school teacher and about the kinds of responsibilities associated with the profession. You should be formulating intellectually some vision of the future for the children you will teach. As the Greek philosopher Aristotle noted, "The character of the speaker is more important than the content of his speech." The same may be said about the elementary school teacher. Your character is a critical variable in determining the kinds of "unseen harvests" that your teaching is likely to produce.

In all of society, no other professionals are given as much wide-ranging responsibility for shaping the development of young citizens as are elementary school teachers. Only parents and legal guardians spend more time with children between the ages of 5 and 12 than do teachers. Unfortunately, for some children the teacher is the *only* adult whose behavior has any possibility of affecting their lives in a positive way. Far too often, home and neighborhood influences are working at cross-purposes with what schools are attempting to achieve. Today's efforts with such positive approaches as forging home–school–community partnerships and mentoring programs hopefully are correcting that reality. Still, and regrettably, teachers and other school personnel have little to no control over many of the social forces that directly affect their work.

Despite the plethora of blue-ribbon commissions, authors, and politicians who doggedly vilify what they perceive as the failures of America's public schools, thousands of committed teachers, administrators, parents, guardians, and community members struggle daily, year after year, to provide young people with a quality education. In this chapter we focus your attention on contemporary influences and challenges that often are central to the concerns held by educators, parents and guardians, and the public about their schools.

ANTICIPATED OUTCOMES

After completing this chapter, you should be able to do the following:

1. Explain why the authors refer to the teaching profession as a "call to social service."
2. Describe today's concept of *literacy* as a purpose of formal education in this country.
3. Describe today's concept of *citizenship education* as a purpose of formal education in this country.
4. Describe today's concept of *personal development* as a purpose of formal education in this country.
5. Describe today's concept of *quality education for each child* as a purpose of formal education in this country.
6. Identify factors in and out of school that affect children's achievement in school.
7. Identify specific ways in which elementary schools are attempting to help each child succeed in school.
8. Describe variations common to today's elementary-school grade organization.
9. Identify arguments for and against the *graded school* concept.
10. Describe the concept of "school choice" and the extent to which it likely affects the work of today's elementary-school classroom teacher.
11. Describe steps a classroom teacher should take when suspecting child abuse, illicit drug use, or gang involvement.
12. Describe the status of bilingual education and English as a second language education.
13. Describe efforts made by today's schools to involve parents, guardians, and the community in the children's education.
14. Describe the concept of *student rights* and how the concept will affect your work as an elementary-school classroom teacher.
15. Describe the basic principles of the No Child Left Behind Act and how that act is likely to affect your work as a classroom teacher.

FUNDAMENTAL PURPOSES OF ELEMENTARY EDUCATION

We begin with an examination of the fundamental purposes that are central to the elementary-school educational enterprise: literacy, citizenship education, personal development, and quality education for each and every child.

Literacy

At its most basic, *literacy* is the ability to read and write. Since colonial times, schools have had the responsibility of developing basic literacy in children. Colonial schools often were little more than schools for reading, a skill taught mainly for religious purposes. Reading has been an important component of the elementary school curriculum throughout our nation's history. Indeed, at the early levels, more time is spent on teaching reading than on anything else.

Dissatisfaction with school programs often focuses on what has come to be called "the basics." Used in this context, "the basics" refer to fundamental academic skills—reading, writing, and mathematical operations, also called the "three Rs." These skills are considered *basic* in the sense that without them, individuals would be handicapped in being able to learn other things. They are *tools for learning*, and without them we are stymied in learning how to learn. Without command of these basic skills, adults would also be handicapped in ordinary living in a society that relies so heavily on written communication and quantitative operations.

Although the three Rs are basic to literacy, these alone cannot be considered adequate for life in our society today. When people have attended school, we assume that they have gained a general background of information about the world and its inhabitants, that they are familiar with basic scientific information, and that they have a modicum of cultural awareness. Beyond that, functional literacy is to some degree situation specific. Thus, educators today speak of "cultural literacy," "language literacy," "prose literacy," "economic literacy," "scientific literacy," "computer literacy," "quantitative literacy," "media literacy," and so on. Functional literacy does not mean the same thing for everyone, nor is it the same in all circumstances. The job of the elementary school is to focus on those aspects of literacy that are a part of the common culture and presumed to be a part of the intellectual background of all citizens.

Citizenship Education

A second purpose of elementary education, also having a long tradition in our nation's schools, is citizenship education. Education for intelligent and loyal citizenship was introduced in the school curriculum early in the nation's history to ensure self-government at an enlightened level. Citizenship education was to take place through the formal study of such subjects as history, government (civics), and geography and through the indoctrination of such values as freedom, human dignity, responsibility, independence, individualism, democracy, respect for others, and love of country. Informally, citizenship education was promoted through an educational setting that included learners from a broad social and economic spectrum of society. Unlike its European counterparts, the American dream of the "common" school was to provide an institution that would serve all the children of all the people. Although that ideal has not been reached completely, it comes close to being realized in the elementary school. Today, the mix of schoolchildren includes members of many cultural, racial, and ethnic groups. Teachers are thus challenged, perhaps as never before, to prepare children for citizenship in a dynamic multicultural society whose economic and political involvement is international in scope and global in influence.

> At the grades K–5 John Stanford International School (Seattle, WA), children receive three levels of multicultural experience.
> 1. Beginning with kindergarten, children spend half of each day immersed in the study of either Japanese or Spanish.
> 2. Global topics are interweaved throughout all areas of the curriculum.
> 3. The school operates a Bilingual Orientation Center, where immigrant children learn English until they're ready for regular school.
>
> *Source:* Grace Rubenstein (2006, p. 23)

Citizenship education in elementary school should include developing affective attachments to this nation and its democratic heritage. Pageants, plays, creative stories, poems, and creative dramatics, under the direction of an imaginative and stimulating teacher, can make the struggle for freedom and the history of the United States' development unforgettable experiences for young children. It is through activities of this type that the social values of classroom life are realized. These are powerful tools in building appreciations, ideals, and values. When sensibly used, the folklore and legends associated with the development of this nation are important and valuable vehicles for teaching citizenship. When not overly depended on, and when not a substitute for more thoughtful approaches to citizenship education, a certain amount of symbolism, such as saluting the flag and reciting the Pledge of Allegiance, is an important component of citizenship education, especially in engendering feelings of fidelity.

Today's citizenship education focuses on citizens as thinking, decision-making individuals. In a democracy, citizens are, on one hand, expected to be loyal, faithful, and law-abiding members of the community, state, and nation. On the other hand, citizens are expected to think independently and to be thoughtful critics of the system itself. Moreover, the charge of citizenship goes beyond being critical; it includes responsibility for taking action to improve the system. It is through the actions of responsible citizens, as individuals or with others, that we have seen the blessings of liberty and the privileges of democracy extended to increasing numbers of people. With each new generation of citizens the process continues.

Engaging a New Generation of Citizens

Immigrant students might find the U.S. concept of democracy difficult to grasp. How can a school make students with different languages, ethnicities, races, and complex personal histories understand the importance of the democratic tradition even as they pursue individual dreams of achievement?

> The answer: Make learning student-centered and activity- and project-based. Allow immigrant students to communicate in both English and native languages and work in small groups to create a play, collaborate on a work of art, or hash out a mathematical concept.
>
> *Source:* Rick Allen (2003, p. 8)

Personal Development

The personal growth of individual children, concern about each individual's potential for development, and the inclusion of school goals to include emotional, social, and physical growth as well as intellectual development are seen as major purposes of elementary education. The nation expects its elementary schools to be concerned about *individual* children, to help children develop a sense of self-identity, to learn to feel good about themselves, to learn what their individual talents are, and to be able to set attainable goals for themselves. Out of necessity, schools must teach aggregates of children in what we call classes, but as a teacher your concern is and must always be the individual human beings within those groups.

The dimension of personal development that *has* had a long tradition in elementary education is something that might be called *character education* or *moral education*. Wynne and Ryan (1997) refer to this as "the great tradition" in education, meaning that the transmission of moral values has been and is a high-priority educational goal of most cultures of the world.

Elementary schools are not simply information supermarkets—they are shapers of human beings. The earliest schools in this country recognized this reality; schools for young children were to extend and reinforce the moral and character education begun in the family's home and religious life. As schools became public, secular institutions, moral and character education became separated from religious orientation. Schools, nonetheless, were expected to continue to concern themselves with principles of right and wrong under the assumption that such knowledge would serve the betterment of society. Teachers continue to create classroom settings that encourage children to develop a sense of fair play, do what is right, live up to verbal agreements, show consideration and respect for others, and be trustworthy. The fact is that a society cannot survive unless a majority of its people internalize common values and live their lives in accordance with them.

Reminiscent of the 1930s and the late 1960s, in the 1990s a resurgence of interest began in the development of students' values, especially those of honesty, kindness, respect, and responsibility. Stimulated perhaps by a perceived need to act to reduce students' antisocial behaviors and to produce more respectful and responsible citizens, many schools and districts today have developed or are developing curricula in character education with the ultimate goal of "developing mature adults capable of responsible citizenship and moral action" (Burrett and Rusnak, 1993, p. 15). A report by the late Ernest L. Boyer (1995), president of the Carnegie Foundation for the Advancement of Teaching, entitled *The Basic School: A Community of Learning*, lists commitment to character as one of the four key priorities for a model elementary school. (The other three priorities are The School as Community, A Curriculum with Coherence, and A Climate for Learning.) In promoting character, the report suggests, schools should affirm the following virtues: honesty, respect, responsibility, compassion, self-discipline, perseverance, and giving. See sites listed at the end of this chapter for Internet resources on character education.

Quality Education for Each and Every Child

School organization has a direct effect on what students learn; if it didn't, educators wouldn't be spending so much valuable time trying to organize and reorganize their schools to effect the most productive (and cost-effective) delivery of the curriculum. Exemplary schools establish and maintain a climate of constant modification in a continual process of inquiry, reflection, and change.

Organizational changes are often referred to as *school restructuring*, a term with a variety of connotations, including site-based management, collaborative decision making, school choice, personalized learning, integrated curricula, and collegial staffing. School restructuring has been defined as "activities that change fundamental assumptions, practices, and relationships, both within the organization and between the organization and the outside world, in ways leading to improved learning outcomes" (Conley, 1993, p. 12). No matter how it is defined, educators agree on the following point: The design and functions of schools should reflect the needs of young people of the 21st century rather than embodying a 19th-century factory model. The movement to year-round operation and the redesigning of schools into smaller cohorts or "houses" represents an increasingly common movement across the country. The intention of this redesign is that schools will better address the needs and capabilities of each unique student, that is, provide a quality education for every child so that no child is left behind. Undoubtedly, you will be involved with and will help accomplish many of these changes. Today's exemplary educators are making major efforts to enhance the connections between home, school, and local and global communities to promote the academic and personal successes of each child. Indeed, enhanced connections between home and school is a key provision of the No Child Left Behind (NCLB) Act of 2001, a massive federal education policy initiative (a revised version of the Elementary and Secondary Education Act, the central federal law in precollegiate education first enacted in 1965) that affects nearly all aspects of public education. It has been called the most significant and controversial change in federal education policy since the federal government assumed a major role in American education nearly half a century ago (Sunderman & Kim, 2004). Highlights of the NCLB Act are shown in Figure 1.1.

A revolt has been happening to certain aspects of NCLB and/or to its cost, with some school districts refusing federal funding rather than complying with NCLB mandates. At least 40 states have requested federal waivers on certain requirements

Signed into Law by President Bush in 2002, highlights of the NCLB Act of 2001 include:

- Annual reporting of school-by-school data that show a range of information
- Annual testing must demonstrate all groups of disadvantaged children making substantial progress every year in every school, thus narrowing the gap between advantaged and disadvantaged students and between all subgroups of students.
- Annual testing of children in reading and mathematics in grades 3 through 8 with tests that are aligned with state academic standards
- Dialogue between schools and families, especially in low-income communities, and for states, districts, and schools to notify parents/guardians about their children's progress and about their options for transferring out of low-performing schools. (Note: The number of parents/guardians opting to transfer their children to better schools has been quite low; for example just 215 out of 204,000 eligible in Los Angeles; 1,097 out of 279,000 in Chicago; 6828 out of 230,000 in New York City [Helfand & Rubin, 2004]. In fact, just the opposite seems to be happening—the ones who are transferring schools are the higher-achieving students [Glod, 2004].)
- Federal school funding changes
- Higher learning expectations for kindergarten children
- Paraprofessionals hired with Title I funds must have completed at least two years of college, obtained an associate's degree or higher, or passed an evaluation to demonstrate knowledge and teaching ability
- Scientific, research-based reading programs for children in grades K–3
- States must bring all students up to the "proficient" level on state tests by the year 2013–14
- Teachers in core content areas must be highly qualified. (Note: As defined by NCLB, core content areas are English, reading or language arts, mathematics, science, foreign languages, civics and government, economics, art, history and geography. Although each state can determine its own definition of "the arts," it most likely will include music, visual arts, and dance. As defined by NCLB, "highly qualified" means the teacher has (1) full state certification, which can be "alternative certification," as defined by a state; (2) at least a bachelor's degree; and (3) demonstrated subject matter competence in the core academic subjects taught.)
- Content standards in science were to be in place by the 2005–06 school year, and beginning in the year 2007–08 states must test students in science once in each of three grade spans, 3–5, 6–9, and 10–12. The NCLB act, however, does not specify that states must include science-test results in measuring adequate yearly progress.

FIGURE 1.1
Highlights of the No Child Left Behind Act of 2001

(Brown, 2005). It is probable that modifications to the NCLB Act of 2001 will occur for years to come.

Today's elementary school reforms, used alone or in varying combinations and with varying degrees of success, include the following:

1. *Alternative schools*—charter schools, theme or magnet schools, Montessori schools, year-round schools.

2. *Looping*—also referred to as multiyear grouping, multiyear instruction, multi-year placement, and teacher–student progression. Looping is when a cohort of students and teachers remain together as a group for several or all of the years students are at that school.

3. *Multiage classrooms*—use of nongraded classrooms with mixed-age children, known also as continuous promotion, open education, and heterogeneous grouping (Carter, 2005).

4. *School-within-a-school* (SWAS) concept, also called the small school, house, village, pod, academy, family, or sometimes just plain team concept, where a teaching team is assigned each day to the same cohort of students for a common block of time.

One of the most absurd vestiges of yesteryear in the public schools is the widely accepted practice of moving students to different teachers and grade levels every year.
—Patricia A. Lennon & David Middlemas (2005)

Self-Contained Classroom The most common arrangement for at least the primary grades, that is, the K–3 level organization, is the self-contained classroom. A *self-contained classroom* is one in which one teacher is assigned to a group of children of approximately the same age for an academic year, and that teacher has primary responsibility for implementing the program of instruction for those children. She or he is the teacher of record for those children for an entire school year, even though other teachers of special subjects, such as music, art, physical education, or computers, may work with them part of the time. Within the self-contained classroom, we can find incorporated many if not all the characteristics common to research findings on exemplary teaching:

- Classrooms rich in materials for children to experience choices, challenges, social interaction, and success
- Classrooms with provisions for a variety of types of group settings, including one-on-one, dyad, small-group, and large-group instruction
- Climate of community, respect, and cooperation
- Climate of expectations for work and achievement
- Emphasis on skill development
- Instructional experiences designed to foster the construction of meaning
- Interdisciplinary thematic instruction
- Multilevel (differentiated) instruction
- Opportunities for peer tutoring and cross-age mentoring

Elementary school teachers must be prepared not only to teach several subjects, but also to do it effectively with students of different cultural backgrounds, diverse linguistic abilities, and different learning styles, and also with children who have educationally relevant differences: for example, students with disabilities, students who live in extreme poverty, and those who are significantly influenced by variations in religion or gender.

Anthony Magnacca/Merrill

DIVERSITY IN THE CLASSROOM

The bell rings, and your students enter your classroom, a kaleidoscope of personalities, all peerless and idiosyncratic, each a packet of energy with different focuses, experiences, dispositions, and learning capacities, differing proficiencies in the English language—each one a different challenge. And what a challenge this is—to understand and to teach 20 or more unique individuals, all at once, and to do it for 6 hours a day, 5 days a week, 180 days a year! What a challenge, indeed, it is to be a public elementary-school classroom teacher. To succeed, you must become familiar with the diverse characteristics and needs of childhood, for the quality of children's academic achievement will depend on how well you understand and satisfy their other developmental needs.

Starting with children in the earliest grades, teachers are challenged by the variety of needs of students who are not only demographically but also developmentally diverse. Primary-grade teachers must maintain the interest and promote the growth of children who have already demonstrated signs of early literacy and numeracy while simultaneously encouraging the emergence of basic skills in children who have not yet acquired them. In like fashion, as with all teachers, they must meet the needs of students with learning difficulties while reserving sufficient attention and effort for those with few or no difficulties and for those others who have in some way or another shown signs of giftedness.

Children differ in physical characteristics, interests, home life, intellectual ability, learning capacities, motor ability, social skills, aptitudes and talents, language skills, experience, ideals, attitudes, needs, ambitions, hopes, and dreams. Furthermore, for a variety of reasons (e.g., learning styles and learning capacities, modality preferences, information-processing habits, motivational factors, physiological factors), all people learn in their own ways and at their own rates. Interests, background, innate and acquired abilities, and myriad other influences shape how and what a person will learn. From any particular learning experience no two persons ever learn exactly the same thing. But all can learn!

The variety of individual differences among students requires that teachers use teaching strategies and tactics that accommodate those differences. To most effectively teach children who are different from you, you must develop skills in the following areas, and the process of building your skills in these categories begins now and will continue throughout your professional career.

- Establishing a classroom climate in which *all* children feel welcome, that they can learn, and that you support them in doing so (Chapter 4)
- Using techniques that emphasize cooperative and social-interactive learning (Chapter 8)
- Building on students' individual experiences, conceptions, learning styles, learning capacities, and learning modalities (Chapter 6)
- Using techniques that have proven successful for students of specific differences (Chapter 8)

A wealth of information is available to help you meet this challenge. As a professional you are expected to know it all, or at least to know where you can find all necessary information—and to review it when needed. Certain information you have stored in memory will surface and become useful at the most unexpected times. Although you are concerned about all students' safety and physical well-being, you will want to remain sensitive to each student's attitudes, values, social adjustment, emotional well-being, and cognitive development. You must be prepared not only to teach several subjects but also to do it effectively with students of different cultural backgrounds, diverse linguistic abilities, and different learning styles, as well as with children who have other educationally relevant differences, such as students with disabilities, students who live in extreme poverty, and those who are significantly influenced by variations in religion or gender. It is, indeed, a challenge, as the following statistics make even clearer.

Approximately 18 percent of today's children in the United States live in poverty. Approximately one half of the children in the United States will spend some years being raised by a single parent. Between one third and one fourth of U.S. children go home after school to places devoid of any adult supervision. And on any given day, it is estimated that 120,000 children have no place at all to call home (National Law Center on Homelessness and Poverty, 2003), and although "homelessness may be more visible in big cities . . . it is not exclusively an urban problem: 21 percent of the nation's homeless live in the suburbs, and 9 percent live in rural areas or small towns" (Vail, 2003, p. 13). At least 40 schools are now operating that are designed especially for homeless children (see, for example, the Web site of the Thomas J. Pappas School).

The United States is a multilingual, multiethnic, multicultural country—perhaps the most diverse nation in the world. Of kindergarten-age children, ages 5–7, approximately one of six speaks a language other than English at home, and that percentage is increasing every year. In many large school districts, as many as 100 or

*Classroom teachers who tradition-
ally have used direct instruction
as their dominant mode of instruction have done so on the assumption that their students were
relatively homogeneous in terms
of experience, background, knowledge, motivation, way of learning,
and facility with the English language. However, no such assumption can be made today in classrooms of such cultural, ethnic,
and linguistic diversity.*

David Mager/Pearson Learning Photo Studio

more languages are represented, with as many as 20 or more different primary
languages found in some classrooms. Increasing ethnic, cultural, and linguistic
diversity is affecting schools across the country, not only in large urban areas but
also in traditionally homogeneous suburbs and small rural communities. Indeed,
the steady increase in interracial marriages and childbirths may challenge traditional conceptions of multiculturalism and race.

The overall picture that emerges is of a rapidly changing, diverse student population that challenges teaching skills. Teachers who traditionally have used direct
instruction (discussed in Chapter 8) as their dominant mode of instruction have
done so on the assumption that their students were relatively homogeneous in
terms of experience, background, knowledge, motivation, way of learning, and facility with English. However, no such assumption can be made today in classrooms of such cultural, ethnic, and linguistic diversity. *As a classroom teacher
today, you must be knowledgeable and skilled in using teaching strategies that recognize, celebrate, and build on that diversity.* In a nutshell, this is your challenge.
Some guidelines are provided in Figure 1.2. Additional guidelines are found
throughout this book.

TPW Video Classroom

Series: General Methods

Module 2: Student Learning in Diverse Classrooms

Video 1: Incorporating the Home Experiences of Culturally
Diverse Students

Supporting Multiracial Children and Countering Racism

- Address directly the history of and reasons for racism against groups of people, including the multiracial population.
- Among the toys for younger children, include dolls with multiracial characteristics.
- Celebrate many different heritages, stressing their interplay in life and the ways that different cultures have similar commemorations.
- Demonstrate how people in the United States have successfully mixed languages, cultures, and religions throughout the nation's history, and how the country has always been a home to multiethnic people (for example, early settlers, whose parents comprised different European heritages).
- Discuss the current status of multiracial people around the world, such as Mestizos, Creoles, and Brazilians.
- Encourage the development and sharing of family trees.
- Facilitate age-appropriate discussions that foster open and supportive questioning about race in ways that build student self-concepts and educate the questioner.
- Identify multiracial historical heroes such as Frederick Douglass and James Audubon and cultural figures like ballerina Maria Tallchief and singer and *American Idol* star Paula Abdul.
- Include curriculum study units in art, music, and literature that transcend ethnic boundaries instead of focusing on specific groups, such as "Indians."
- Include multiracial persons as role models when selecting assembly speakers and other resource persons.
- Provide children with information and pictures of people of many racial and ethnic groups, including those of mixed heritage.
- Study monoracial groups to promote an understanding of the role of race in society by exploring why some people need to belong to an exclusive group or need to feel superior to others, and what the societal and personal consequences of such attitudes are.
- Use children's books that depict multiracialism.

FIGURE 1.2

Suggestions for teachers and schools to support multiracial children and to counter racism

Source: W. Schwartz, *The Schooling of Multiracial Students,* ERIC/CUE Digest, Number 138 (New York: ERIC Clearinghouse on Urban Education, 1998).

These are the realities that confront beginning teachers in varying degrees of intensity in virtually every school district in the United States. To succeed, you must perceive these realities as challenges and opportunities. Your challenges lie in seeing that every child succeeds in school, so no child is left behind. Your opportunities can be found in making sure that the lives of *all* children are enriched through contact with classmates whose cultural and ethnic backgrounds may be quite different from their own. Responding to these challenges and grasping these opportunities underscore the idea that the teaching profession is basically a call to social service.

FAMILY LIFE

Before children have formal contact with school, they have, of course, been receiving early education from their families. There can be little doubt that these family experiences are among the most powerful and pervasive influences on human development. A family that is doing its child-rearing job properly will help children learn some of the most important, fundamental things they need to know in life. Children learn language and basic linguistic skills in the home. Here, too, children learn to give and receive emotional support. The family should provide security and reassurance, thereby supplying the psychological support needed to face life and to function confidently and competently. In the process, children develop feelings of personal worth and positive self-concept. It is in the family that children first learn what is right and wrong, what things are prized and valued, and what standards of conduct are expected. Lifetime ambitions and aspirations are planted and germinate in early family life. The extent to which the family has responded to these responsibilities will reflect itself in children's life in school. For example, a child reared in a linguistically rich home environment where elaborative language is used daily is bound to have many advantages in learning language-related skills in school.

Extended families have obvious advantages in terms of bringing up children within the expectations of a family. Children have more contact with closely related adults and consequently have available a greater range of adult role models. Similarly, concerned and caring adults can more closely and constantly monitor child behavior. There is also likely to be a more elaborate family culture or set of rituals that provides emotional stability and roots for growing children, such as the gathering of the entire family for holidays, anniversaries, birthdays, and other special events. In structures of this type, children are hardly ever out of range of the supervision of some member of the immediate family.

Many factors have contributed to changes in the traditional extended-family pattern. People tend to move in the direction of increased economic opportunity. Thus, a young couple may locate hundreds of miles away from many of their relatives. Children growing up in such nuclear families today may hardly know relatives other than their parents. Babysitters replace grandparents in part-time care of children. Neighbors and friends may help supervise children in the neighborhood. Preschool children may spend the better part of their waking hours in a daycare center.

Student mobility, that is, students moving from one school to another, is common in the United States. Whether frequent movement is a symptom or a cause of poor school performance is not known, but studies (Rumberger, 2002) indicate that children who move three or more times during elementary-school years have a greater tendency for lower achievement and diminished prospects for high-school graduation than do students who are less mobile.

Undoubtedly, the most common exception to the conventional family arrangement is the one-parent family (which includes both unmarried and previously married individuals). Death, separation, and, most commonly, divorce not only dissolve a marriage but leave one or the other of the partners with the responsibility of carrying on as a family. Even though joint custody arrangements are becoming more common, the custody of children is usually given to the mother in the case of divorce, and the one-parent family for the most part means a mother and her children. Divorce rates in the United States have continued to rise for the past century, after having peaked during the years immediately following World War II, receded during the 1950s and early 1960s, risen sharply again in the 1970s, and continued at a high level through the 1990s and into the 2000s.

The problem of children left unattended and unsupervised after school continues to be a serious one. The behavior problems or low achievement of children from one-parent families is explained away on the basis of their being products of "broken homes." This, of course, ignores the fact that many children from one-parent families achieve at high levels and present no behavior problem in school, and that many from so-called intact families are low achievers and do present behavior problem. It also ignores the psychological and emotional damage to a young child that results from growing up in a dysfunctional family of whatever structure: one filled with conflict, hostility, and abuse.

Dramatic changes are occurring within family lifestyles. With increasing numbers of parents and guardians employed outside the home, greater numbers of children are enrolled in daycare centers, are placed in the care of persons other than parents for several hours each day, or are "latchkey kids" who are on their own before and after school. When compared with young children of previous generations, children today are more accustomed to being away from home much of the day and to spending much of the day with peers and are more aware of the world around them. In many communities those factors have led to full-day kindergarten and, to a lesser extent, *full-service schools*, which offer quality education and comprehensive social services under one roof (Black, 2004).

SOCIOECONOMIC INFLUENCES

Social stratification occurs because others rank individuals as being higher or lower on some standard of preference. When a segment of society is set apart as having characteristics different from others, we have the beginning of a social class. If a group of individuals has particular characteristics a society values, the group so identified will enjoy high status. The reverse is also true. In time, a hierarchy of groups develops in accordance with societal preferences, and a social-class structure emerges, one that usually correlates with socioeconomic status.

There can be no question that one variable separating the "haves" from the "have-nots" in this or any other society is level of education. Those who are the decision makers, who have good jobs, who contribute in significant ways to the health and welfare of their fellow citizens, and who have power and wealth are almost always better educated than the balance of the population. It is patently clear from research, as well as from the personal experiences of countless thousands of individuals, that limited education forecloses many social and economic options and thereby severely restricts opportunity for upward social mobility. It does not follow, of course, that improved education will alleviate all socioeconomically related problems. Restricted or foreshortened education, for whatever reason, simply means limited opportunities to exercise alternatives and options for self-development.

Evidence abounds that the largest number of educational casualties comes from the lower socioeconomic levels. These children often come from educationally impoverished environments, and such an atmosphere conditions nearly every aspect of their lives. Today, these and other members of our school population are among those referred to as *at-risk children*, that is those who are the most likely candidates for school failure and for facing multiple social and/or personal problems. Their family lifestyles contribute to the perpetuation of educational deprivation. Traditional school programs simply have not been able to deal successfully with the educational needs of these socioeconomically disadvantaged children. We are likely to have large numbers of miseducated children until we as a society hold the highest expectations for *all* students and commit ourselves to eradicating those underlying conditions that produce children for whom the school experience is meaningless. The education of children who are at risk is discussed more fully in Chapter 6.

> *Some school districts are integrating students by socioeconomic status—and narrowing achievement gaps.*
>
> —**Richard D. Kahlenberg (2006)**

EQUALITY OF EDUCATIONAL OPPORTUNITY

Equality of educational opportunity has traditionally been interpreted to mean equal *access* to education, and the nation has made a substantial effort to make schooling available to all its children. No area of the country is so remote as to preclude the opportunity for children who live there to go to school. Children of all racial and ethnic groups, children of migrants, children of the poor, children with physical or mental disabilities—all of these are not only encouraged but also required to attend school. But does school attendance in itself ensure equality of educational opportunity? Many think not, because there are social, psychological, and economic inequities that both condition the quality of schooling provided from place to place and also affect individuals' abilities to take full advantage of what is offered.

Inequities in educational opportunity do exist in this country. Educational inequity is usually thought of in terms of differences in the dollar amounts spent on education from one place to another. Because communities differ in both their *ability* and their *willingness* to support education, the average amount spent per student varies significantly from one district to another, even within the same state.

Variations in educational spending do not, however, fully explain prevailing inequities in educational opportunity. The quality of education tends to follow the pattern of power and wealth in a community. Those parents and guardians who are reasonably well educated themselves and who have average or above-average incomes, regardless of ethnic identity, most often choose to reside in areas that provide well for their children's education. Poorly educated, low-income families, whose range of choice is much more limited, tend to live in areas that provide less well for children's education. It is not so much a matter of actual dollars spent on education in the more favored areas as it is a combination of economic and social forces that coalesce to produce better-quality education. Education, and most especially early education, must be concerned with the way it either opens or forecloses subsequent opportunities for learning. Teachers and schools should be greatly concerned about children who do not learn to read because this deficiency severely limits their later options. Similarly, children who grow to dislike school or to dislike particular subjects create self-imposed limiting conditions on their continued educational achievement. Any experience that children have that discourages or terminates their continued ability or motivation for further learning restricts equality of educational opportunity. This is why early intervention programs are so important for those children who are products of poverty and impoverished environments. The documented success of the Head Start program is a case in point. Children who come from low-socioeconomic-status families face a high risk of failure in school unless steps are taken very early to counteract the profound effects of poverty on their education. To the maximum extent possible, teachers and schools must accommodate learner needs, whatever their background may be.

Equity is the approach. Equality is the goal.

—**Enid Lee**

Student Rights

You probably already know that as a result of legislation of more than a quarter-century ago (Federal law Title IX of the Education Act Amendments of 1972, PL 92-318) a teacher is prohibited from discriminating among children on the basis of gender. In all aspects of school, male and female students must be treated the same. This means, for example, that a teacher must not pit males against females in a subject content quiz game—or for any other activity or reason. Further, no teacher, student, administrator, or other school employee should make sexual advances toward a student (i.e., touching or speaking in a sexual manner).

Each school or district should have a clearly delineated statement of steps to follow in the process of protecting students' rights. Many schools provide students (or parents and guardians) with a publication of these rights.

Learning Styles

Although some students may begin to learn a new idea in the abstract (e.g., through visual or verbal symbolization), most need to begin concretely (e.g., learning by actually doing it). Many children prosper while working in groups, whereas others

Activity 1.1: Teach But Don't Touch

Pat Blake, attorney for the local teachers' professional association, is addressing the teachers at their fall preschool meeting:

> Last year in this country, we had an alarming number of cases of parents and school officials taking teachers to court for touching children in ways considered inappropriate. In Arizona, a music teacher with 16 years' experience faced charges of sexual harassment and unprofessional conduct and a recommendation of dismissal because of a hugging incident. For the past three decades, this society has given social approval to hugging and other forms of physical contact for purposes of comfort and support. We say to people in distress, "Is there anything I can do?" And the reply could very well be, "I need a warm and fuzzy hug."
>
> On Sunday in church you might hug your neighbor and her 10-year-old daughter and wish them "peace," but don't try it the next day in school without putting yourself in jeopardy! My advice to you is to teach but don't touch. Don't hug kids. Don't put your arms around them. Don't hold hands with them on the playground. Don't pat them on the back. Don't have any physical contact with them in any way. Period.

1. Do you think this attorney's advice is sound or extreme?
2. Can elementary school teachers do their jobs without having *any* physical contact with children?
3. How can teachers project feelings of affection and genuine caring without touching children?
4. Research shows that physical contact with other human beings is a critical requirement for children's normal development. If children are caressed neither at home nor at school, how can we expect them to develop normally? Is this a teacher's responsibility?
5. Using a selected specific occurrence, discuss this issue with others in your class in terms of *context* variables such as the following: (1) the age of the student; (2) the gender of the teacher and the child; (3) whether the contact is in a public, open place with others around or in an isolated area; (4) whether the contact is a pattern of the teacher's behavior; and (5) the *intent* of the teacher's behavior.

prefer to work alone. Some are quick in their studies, whereas others are slow, methodical, cautious, and meticulous. Some can sustain attention on a single topic, becoming more absorbed in their study as time passes. Others are slower starters and more casual in their pursuits but are capable of shifting with ease from subject to subject. Some can study in the midst of music, noise, or movement, whereas others need quiet, solitude, and a desk or table. The point is this: *Children vary not only in their skills and preferences in the way they receive information, but also in how they mentally process that information once they receive it.* This mental processing is a person's style of learning. The topic as well as that of the related topic, *learning capacities* (multiple intelligences), is discussed more fully in Chapter 6. For now, the point is this: We must learn how to teach children in ways that they learn best.

Race and Racism

It is perfectly obvious that human beings differ in their physical characteristics. Some are fair skinned; others are dark. Some have curly hair and others straight hair, which may be light or dark. Through the centuries, groups of people who occupied certain geographical areas of the world and who have some physical traits in common have been identified as subgroups of *Homo sapiens* and have been called *races*. These physical traits are inherited, but because their presence or absence varies so greatly *within* these groups, it is sometimes impossible to assign an individual to any one group on the basis of unique characteristics. Consequently, anthropologists and sociologists have not found the use of race to be a meaningful way of grouping human beings, preferring instead the concept of *ethnicity*, which describes people on the basis of their *cultural identity* and may include geographical and physical components. Be that as it may, the fact that groups of human beings have differing physical characteristics and that we designate these groups as races does not *in itself* give rise to social and educational problems.

Problems of race arise when nonphysical, social, or cultural qualities are assigned to individuals only because they are members of such a group. When this happens, race becomes defined socially. *Racism* is the practice of associating significant (usually pejorative) cultural abilities and/or characteristics with groups that are defined socially as races. Racism becomes institutionalized when these associations, whether overt or subtle, are given legitimacy and social approval.

Racism, particularly institutionalized racism, is difficult to deal with because of the tendency to associate it with overt and conscious acts of prejudice. It has been referred to as the "disease of hate." Thus, individuals who generally have humanitarian attitudes toward others may be shocked and outraged if accused of racist behavior. The practices may have become so thoroughly institutionalized that awareness of their racist dimensions has been hidden.

Institutionalized racism consists of practices that have been *legitimized* by society and that result in *systematic* discrimination against members of *specific* groups. Practices that have been legitimized are accepted. Few question them. Until recently, even those against whom the discrimination was directed have accepted these practices. The word *systematic* in this definition is also important. This means that the discrimination is not a random occurrence; the discrimination is practiced with consistency and regularity, rather than being whimsical or capricious. It is directed against specific groups (perhaps not even by design) because members of those groups have certain characteristics or qualities.

Following are examples of practices that would qualify as institutionalized racism, some of which are often so subtle that they go undetected:

1. Unnecessary and irrelevant references, especially in social studies and current events, to an individual's or group's racial or ethnic identity, such as "the black mayor of . . . ," "the Hispanic candidate from . . . ," "Asian parents gathered . . . ," or "the driver, an Indian from Forks, was charged with drunken driving." Such references are almost never used when the individual or group is White.

2. Optional "free choice" educational programs that require one to have a certain level of affluence to be able to participate. For example, attending a particular magnet or charter school or participating in enrichment opportunities (e.g., music, dance, sports, art, clubs) may depend on one's ability to afford transportation, supplies, or other expenses. Such demands have a disproportionate adverse effect on low-income families, many of whom are members of ethnic minorities.

3. Homogeneous grouping. This practice discriminates against ethnic minorities because it often results in their being placed in low-achieving groups.

4. Expectations that children of color are more likely to misbehave, combined with harsher and more frequent punishment for those children when they do misbehave.

5. Social acceptance of a higher incidence of failure and a higher dropout rate among certain ethnic minorities.

6. Curriculum content unrelated to the life and culture of certain groups. This circumstance discriminates against those who are not represented in the subject matter of the school.

7. Curriculum content that places certain groups in a negative light; for example, introducing such study topics as "Indians as savages during the Westward Expansion" or "Pancho Villa as an outlaw."

8. Neglecting or ignoring the contributions of individuals of color to humankind in social studies, mathematics, and science classes, or wherever else it is relevant.

9. Accepting implicitly the assumption that nonwhites are less capable than whites in any field of study or endeavor or, conversely, that nonwhites have specific aptitudes but are limited to those areas of achievement.

10. Bias against the use of a language other than English or against a child who speaks a dialect of English or with a non-English accent.

11. References that portray black as bad and white as good.

Gender Equity

Just as racism is the practice of ascribing certain abilities and characteristics to individuals on the basis of their identification with groups socially defined as races, *sexism,* or *gender bias,* does the same thing on the basis of one's gender (*Note:* It is important to distinguish between sex and *gender.* Sex has to do with differences attributed to genetics; that is, one is born either male or female. Gender, on the other hand, has to do with the differences attributed to the roles males and females play in a society. A society defines its idealized role behavior of males and females—what is masculine and what is feminine—and these differences are properly called *gender* differences.) Historically, female roles tended to be stereotyped along the lines of domestic and child-rearing responsibilities, whereas male roles were stereotyped in the world of work outside the home. Also, women frequently were portrayed in art and literature in subservient roles, roles in which they served, waited on, picked up after, and took orders from men.

There can be little doubt that such stereotyping works to the disadvantage of women by restricting their range of significant opportunities for self-development (perhaps less obviously, it has a similar restrictive influence on men). In addition, it has led to manifestly unfair discrimination against women. Changing attitudes, the growing independence of women, and legislative reforms have aided in combating the invidious distinctions between males and females that result from sex-role stereotyping.

Educational programs, particularly the part that teachers play in them, are vitally important in shaping young children's images of gender roles. If children always see males rather than females in preferred, prestigious occupational and social roles, they are bound to conclude that the male is superior: Because these positions are obviously not available to women, women must not be capable of holding them. It hardly seems necessary to add that when gender roles are presented this way, both boys *and* girls come to believe them, which does grave disservice to *all* children.

What follows are some common teacher behaviors that violate the concept of gender equity:

1. Consistently using generic terms such as *man, mankind, early man,* and *common man* when the reference is to humanity. It is always better to substitute inclusive terms such as *people, human beings, ordinary people, humankind,* and *early people.*

2. Exaggerating the emphasis on the socialization of children into traditional gender roles: neatness, conformity, docility, and fastidiousness for females; competitiveness, aggressiveness, and physical activity and strength for males. It is important to maintain a balanced emphasis.

3. Segregating children on the basis of gender, such as in the seating arrangement in the classroom, in playground games, and in classroom learning activities.

4. Allowing or ignoring humor that ridicules one gender or the other, such as that directed toward the behavior of "nonmacho" males or women drivers.

5. Neglecting or ignoring the contributions of women to humankind in social studies, mathematics, and science classes, or wherever else it is relevant.

6. Accepting implicitly the assumption that females are less capable than males in such fields as mathematics, science, and athletics and, conversely, that males have less aptitude for art, literature, music, and dance.

7. Expressing a preference for teaching either males or females.

8. Displaying charts or graphs that compare the achievement of individuals according to gender.

9. Identifying certain leadership positions or specific activities in the classroom as being solely for one gender or the other.

10. Making light of, ignoring, or even ridiculing social movements or individuals associated with movements to secure equity for women.

11. Administering harsher consequences to males than to females for the same rule infraction.

12. Interacting more with males than with females in class discussions.

If the social goal of gender equity is to be achieved, we must present a range of role models to young children as a part of their formal education. Children must learn that it is just as appropriate for a woman to be a business executive, judge, mayor, senator, astronaut, bus driver, carpenter, or any of a variety of occupations as it is for a man. They also must learn that it is equally appropriate for a man to take care of and feed his young children, to do household duties or secretarial work, to be a nurse or a dancer, or to engage in any tasks or occupations traditionally associated with women.

What is important is that, as a teacher, you must present gender-role models in ways that provide your students with maximum opportunity for choice. Perhaps many will want to conduct their lives according to more or less traditional gender role definitions. Some may wish to exercise other choices, and they should not be prevented from or handicapped in doing so because of prejudicial attitudes or ridicule. Removing gender barriers should create almost unlimited opportunity for choice.

Inclusion

During the last half of the 20th century, the Congress of the United States passed only a few statutes pertaining to education, with none perhaps as powerful an agent for change as Public Law 94-142, the Education for All Handicapped Children Act (EAHCA) of 1975. Passage of that legislation marked the beginning of free and appropriate public education services to all school-age children and youth, regardless of disability (Hewit & Whittier, 1997). PL 94-142 mandates that all children have the right to such educational services, as well as to nondiscriminatory assessment. (The law was amended in 1986 by PL 99-457; in 1990 by PL 101-476, at which time its name was changed to the Individuals with Disabilities Education Act [IDEA]; and again in 1997 by PL 105-17.) Emphasizing normalizing the educational environment for students with disabilities, this legislation requires provision of the "least restrictive environment" (LRE) for these students. A *least restrictive environment* is one that offers the fewest restrictions and the greatest opportunities in the context of a particular disability or limiting condition.

Students with disabilities (referred to also as "exceptional" and "special-needs" students) include those with disabling conditions or impairments in any one or more of the following categories: mental retardation, hearing, speech or language, visual, emotional, orthopedic, autism, traumatic brain injury, other health impairment, or specific learning disabilities. To the extent possible, students with special needs must be educated with their peers in the regular classroom.

Students identified as having special needs may be placed in the regular classroom for the entire school day, called *full inclusion* (as is the trend). Those students may also be in a regular classroom the greater part of the school day, called *partial inclusion*, or only for designated periods. Although there is no single, universally accepted definition of the term *inclusion*, it is generally understood to mean that students with disabilities should be integrated into general education classrooms regardless of whether they can meet traditional academic standards (Tiegerman-Farber & Radziewicz, 1998). Indications are that when students with disabilities are integrated into general education classrooms, as opposed to pulled out into segregated special education classrooms, they earn higher grades, achieve higher or comparable standardized test scores, attend more days of school, and draw fewer discipline referrals (Krank, Moon, & Render, 2002; Rea, McLaughlin, & Walther-Thomas, 2002). Inclusion has largely replaced the earlier term *mainstreaming*.

As a classroom teacher you will need information and skills specific to teaching children with special needs who are included in your classroom. The law does provide for help to the regular classroom teacher in the form of paraprofessionals and aides in addition to special education teachers, although the degree of assistance and support varies widely among districts and states. Generally speaking, teaching children who have special needs requires more care, better diagnosis, greater skill, more attention to individual needs, and an even greater understanding of the children. The challenges of teaching children with special needs in the regular classroom are great enough that to do it well you need specialized training, which you are likely to receive at some point in your teacher preparation.

It is unlikely that there will ever be one model of inclusion that is the solution for all children. It is enough to say that when a child with special needs is placed in your classroom, your task is to deal directly with the differences between this child and your other students. To do this, you should develop an understanding of the general characteristics of different types of special-needs learners, identify the child's unique needs relative to your classroom, and design lessons that teach to different needs at the same time. Remember also that because a person has been identified as having one or more special needs, this does not preclude that person from being gifted or talented. As a matter of fact, often left unidentified is the cognitive giftedness of a student who has a disabling condition because the focus and attention is given to accommodating the child's disability (Willard-Holt, 1999).

Congress stipulated in PL 94-142 that an Individualized Educational Program (IEP) be devised annually for each special-needs child. According to that law, an IEP is developed for each student each year by a team that includes special education teachers, the child's parents or guardians, and the classroom teachers. The IEP contains a statement of the student's present educational levels, the educational goals for the year, specifications for the services to be provided and the extent to which the student will be expected to take part in the regular education program, and the evaluative criteria for the services to be provided. Consultation by special and skilled support personnel is essential in all IEP models. A consultant works directly with teachers or with students and parents. As a classroom teacher, you may play an active role in preparing the specifications for the special-needs children assigned to your classroom, as well as a major responsibility for implementing the program.

Newcomers to the English Language

From early colonial America to the present, people from every ethnic and cultural group of the world have arrived at the borders of this nation and, of course, brought their own languages with them. Often, they have settled in communities inhabited by immigrants from the same part of the world. Consequently, throughout the United States are geographic locations in which people commonly speak a language other than English.

By the early 1900s, the use of languages other than English was so widespread that in some cases those languages were used for instructional purposes in public schools. All this changed, however, in the period during and after World War I, when adverse feelings toward immigrant groups in general and German-speaking people in particular were so great that several states passed legislation prohibiting instruction in languages other than English in public schools. At the federal level, legislation was enacted to severely restrict immigration from southern and eastern Europe and from Asia. The suppressive legislation at the state and federal levels was destructive of foreign-language learning in America. Adverse feelings were so widespread that to speak in a language other than English was considered by many to be un-American. This attitude persists today.

There have been some positive changes in attitudes and practices in recent years, in part as a result of a growing ethnic awareness, multicultural enlightenment, and our increasing global interdependency. However, the movement to legitimize bilingual education as a part of the curriculum of the public schools has been only partially successful.

One argument against bilingual education has been the observation that people have succeeded without it. However, such people are usually those who have had the advantages of good early education in their country of origin. Children who arrive in the United States with a good education in their primary language have already gained two objectives of a good bilingual education program: literacy and subject matter development. Research indicates that the ability to read transfers across languages, even when the writing systems are different.

Although there are many variations, bilingual education programs can be grouped into four categories: (1) transitional, (2) immersion, (3) English as a second language (ESL), and (4) bilingual/bicultural. A fifth category, submersion, is direct placement of non-English-speaking (NES) and limited-English-speaking (LES) children into all English-speaking classes without any sort of special help whatsoever. Submersion is simply a sink-or-swim situation and is not a bilingual program at all (Pai & Adler, 2001).

Transitional bilingual education, less widely used today than it used to be, provides instruction for some subjects in the students' language but with some time each day spent on developing English skills. Classes are made up of students who share the same native language.

Immersion involves teaching English to children by a teacher who is proficient in the learners' primary language, although the teacher uses only English for instruction. The English used for instruction is simplified so the children learn English and the academic subject content. Maintaining children's primary language is not an objective of either transitional or immersion programs.

Unlike transitional and immersion programs, teaching *English as a second language* (ESL) involves placing English-language learners (ELLs) with NES and LES children in all-English-speaking classes that are taught by instructors who have special training in ESL methods, but who may or may not have second-language proficiency. ESL programs are usually transitional, but may also be used as bilingual maintenance programs.

Bilingual/bicultural programs, which are sometimes called *maintenance* programs and may also be the same as immersion, are those in which the bilingual instruction continues for several years in an effort to maintain students' fluent command of both languages. Advocates of maintenance programs argue that it makes no sense to allow the knowledge of an alternate language, already partially mastered, to deteriorate. Many experts now are encouraging the use of *two-way programs*, where both language groups, the monolingual and the bilingual students, remain together throughout the school day, serving as peer tutors for each other. Research studies indicate that after 5 or 6 years in a two-way program, English learners can demonstrate both English and native-language proficiency and also outperform monolingual students on academic tests (Thomas & Collier, 1997–1998). The two-way approach is also sometimes called *dual-immersion* or *dual-language* and is one of the fastest growing in elementary education, where children are placed in dual-language classrooms starting with kindergarten with the goal to have them completely bilingual by the time they reach at least the sixth grade (Senesac, 2002; Thomas & Collier, 2003).

Regardless, as the debates continue and we await further research evidence, certain facts stand out as significant requirements for the successful application of any program for English-language learners. At a minimum, for these students in particular, teachers must be committed to (a) holding and instilling high expectations; (b) fostering a sense of community identity; and (c) seeking and holding strong parental and guardian involvement and support.

School Choice and Organizational Change

Traditionally, elementary-school children in the public schools were required to attend their local neighborhood school. It was often difficult for parents and guardians to get school district permission to send children to a public school outside the designated attendance area. To attend school in another district meant that parents had to pay the tuition cost required by the host district. Parents could, of course, send their children to a private or parochial school but also at additional cost. In recent years, however, many of these policies regarding attendance have changed. The federal courts called for a racial balance in schools, and that required the movement of some children to schools outside their neighborhood school attendance area. This had the effect of making school district administrations less rigid with respect to the specific schools children could attend. This trend may, however, be once again in the process of reversing.

There is a feeling among many that the public school system has a monopoly on the education of the nation's children and that this condition works to the detriment of quality education. The business community, oriented to the concept of competition, believes that better school programs would result if individual schools had to rely on the quality of their programs for their students. This idea has also been attractive to some governors and federal officials. Some go so far as to suggest that parents or guardians should be able to select *any* school, public or private, for their children through the use of tax credits or *vouchers* to cover at least partial tuition costs. The basic idea is that schools, much like business institutions, should obtain their "clients" (i.e., students) on a competitive basis. The most effective schools would initially have the most students, whereas the least effective schools would be forced to improve their effectiveness to become and remain competitive.

One of the strongest arguments against this plan is that it discriminates against the very students that it is intended to help: low-income students. It might be that parents and guardians can choose any school in the district for their children, but the children still have to be able to get to the school. Low-income parents/guardians often cannot afford the transportation costs involved. Thus, more affluent parents and guardians will select the best schools for their children, whereas lower income families will tend to keep their children in local schools. Because income, socioeconomic level, and school achievement are such closely related variables, this usually means that the local schools in low socioeconomic areas will have a disproportionate number of low-achieving children, just as they do now.

The concept of a "charter school" is another option on the menu of school choices. A *charter school* is "an autonomous educational entity operating under a charter, or contract, that has been negotiated between the organizers, who create and operate the school, and a sponsor, who oversees the provisions of the charter" (Mulholland & Bierlein, 1995, p. 7). Once a school is granted a charter, it qualifies for state and local funding on the same basis and at the same formula-based rate as regular public schools. Since the first in Minnesota in 1991, charter school legislation has been passed in at least 40 states, the District of Columbia, and Puerto Rico, reflecting a general dissatisfaction with centralized state or district control, bureaucratic inflexibility, and uneven progress in student performance. As stated in *A Study of Charter Schools: First-Year Report,*

> The charter school movement grew out of a belief that a carefully developed competition among existing public schools and new kinds of schools developed by local educators, parents, community members, school boards and other sponsors could provide both new models of schooling and the incentive to improve the current system of public education. (U.S. Department of Education, 1997)

There can be no doubt that school choice motivates school faculties to be concerned about the quality of their programs. The idea has certainly proved to be effective in the private-school sector. Moreover, choice encourages schools to provide enrichment programs that are attractive to children with special abilities in the academic areas, music, art, drama, or physical education. Such *magnet schools* within the public school system have an enthusiastic clientele in several large school districts across the nation. The North Dade Center for Modern Languages (Miami, FL), for example, is a public elementary magnet school that focuses on international studies and provides students with the opportunity to become bilingual, biliterate, and multicultural. Chollas Elementary School (San Diego, CA) is a math/science magnet school. Some schools, such as Paul Revere Charter/LEARN Middle School (Los Angeles, CA), are both charter and magnet schools.

Efficiency and *standardization,* two concepts from the industrial world, have had a profound effect on education in recent years. In their name the number of school districts has been reduced from more than 100,000 in 1940 to fewer than 15,000 today. These large school districts can have central curriculum personnel to plan programs for the entire district and can purchase books and materials in huge quantities, and thus at discounted prices. Record keeping, payrolls, and school maintenance can be performed more efficiently because the procedures are standardized and centralized. But, of course, what also happens is that much significant decision making concerning students, the curriculum, teachers, and the learning process takes place farther and farther away from the classroom.

Accountability for students' progress, or lack of it, however, remains with the individual teacher at the classroom level. Charter schools are designed to combat some of the limitations of a large, centralized system.

With school redesigns and other trends, shown in Figure 1.3, some of which are discussed in subsequent chapters (see index for topic locations), the purpose is to better address the needs and capabilities of each unique student. As a teacher in this 21st century, you will undoubtedly help accomplish many of these changes.

Grade-Level Organization

The elementary school usually enrolls children between the ages of 5 and 11 (Figure 1.4); converting these ages to grades, we get kindergarten (K) through 6. In some places, the elementary school is a primary school, with grades K–4, followed by a 4-year middle school, and then a high school. In some places, the elementary-school grade ranges are K through 8, an arrangement in which there is a rekindled interest in the United States (Pardini, 2002). The K–8 elementary schools ordinarily are followed by a 4-year high school (K–8–4). The K–6 elementary schools are usually followed by a 3-year junior high school, or a middle school, followed by a 3-year senior high school (K–6–3–3). However, a K–6 elementary school with a 2-year middle school and a 4-year high school is not uncommon.

The Graded School Concept

Schools in colonial America and those of the early national period did not use the age-sorting system we call *grades*. Children of varying ages were assigned to a single teacher, who tutored them individually or taught them in small cross-age groups. It was not until the middle of the 19th century that the practice of grouping children according to age (i.e., age grading) became widespread. This practice was developed in Germany in the 8-year *Volkschule*. It appealed to American educators as an efficient way of managing the teaching of a large number of children.

Following the Civil War, there was rapid acceptance of the practice of grouping children of a similar age and keeping those groups intact from one year to the next as they progressed through school. Schools were therefore *graded* by age, and communities and states used that term in curriculum documents and school regulations and names. Even today, it is possible to find etched into the stonework of some remaining old school buildings such names as "Frederic Graded School." The expression *grade school* is common parlance when speaking of the elementary school.

Proponents of the graded-school concept argue the following:

- It reduces variability within instructional groups by keeping the age of children constant within the groups.
- It equalizes educational opportunity by exposing all children to the same curriculum.

- A rapid influx of immigrant and language-minority students throughout the United States, rural, suburban, and urban
- Dividing the student body and faculty into smaller cohorts, the school-within-a school concept
- Increasing enrollment from 2005, with an additional 1.8 million pre-K–8 children expected in public schools by the year 2013
- Encouraging habits of healthy living
- Encouraging the practices of reflective thinking and self-discipline
- Establishing and maintaining high expectations for all students by establishing goal or target standards and then assessing the achievement of each student against those standards
- Facilitating students' social skills as they interact, relate to one another, solve meaningful problems, develop skills in conflict resolution, and foster peaceful relationships and friendships
- Facilitating the developing of students' values as related to their families, the school and community, and the nation
- Finding productive ways to reduce the so-called summer setback, which is the loss of students' skills and content knowledge due to the traditional summer layoff
- Focusing on the use of strategies that have been proven to work, such as heterogeneous small-group learning, peer coaching, and cross-age tutoring
- Increased movement to the one-school elementary, that is a school with grades K–8 (sometimes referred to as an "elemiddle" school), rather than an elementary school with grades K–4, K–5, or K–6, and a middle school of grades 4–8, 5–8, 6–8, or 7–8
- Individualizing (personalizing) the instruction
- Integrating the subjects of the curriculum
- Involving parents, guardians, and communities in the education of the children
- Involving students in self-assessment of their learning
- Making multicultural education work for all children
- Providing students with the time and opportunity to think and be creative, rather than simply memorizing and repeating information
- Redefining giftedness to include nonacademic as well as traditional academic abilities
- School-based community social centers providing family services
- Statewide accountability systems for all students
- Teaching and assessing for higher order thinking skills
- Transformation of large schools into smaller learning communities
- Using nontraditional scheduling, such as modified year-round scheduling, extended school day, and half-day Saturday school
- Using the Internet and other modern technological resources (such as iPods and laptop computers) in the classroom

FIGURE 1.3
Key trends and practices affecting today's elementary schools

Age 5	Age 6	Age 7	Age 8
Arkansas	Arizona	Alabama	Pennsylvania
Delaware	California	Alaska	Washington
Maryland	Florida	Connecticut	
New Mexico	Georgia	Idaho	
Oklahoma	Hawaii	Illinois	
South Carolina	Iowa	Indiana	
Virginia	Kentucky	Kansas	
	Massachusetts	Louisiana	
	Michigan	Maine	
	Mississippi	Minnesota	
	New Hampshire	Missouri	
	New Jersey	Montana	
	New York	Nebraska	
	Ohio	Nevada	
	Rhode Island	North Carolina	
	South Dakota	North Dakota	
	Tennessee	Oregon	
	Texas		
	Utah		
	West Virginia		
	Wisconsin		
	Wyoming		

FIGURE 1.4

Age by state for beginning compulsory school attendance

For Colorado, no ages were listed on this table, but earlier data from 1996 listed the compulsory age at 7.

Source: Digest of Education Statistics, 2004 (Washington, DC: National Center for Education Statistics, 2004).

- Textbooks, instructional materials, and achievement tests can be constructed on the basis of age-grade norms.
- Children's social development, to some extent, relates to age, and therefore, age groups tend to be natural social groups.
- It is an efficient way to accommodate the large number of children who are required to attend school.
- It allows teachers to specialize their teaching skills in terms of the age of the children with whom they work best.
- It is possible to require set standards of achievement for the various grades.

Opponents of the graded-school concept argue the following:

- It is too lockstep, encouraging teachers to disregard individual differences in children and in their developmental patterns.
- It sets unrealistic standards for children and is especially unfair to low achievers.
- It encourages mechanical teaching, analogous to assembly-line production in industry.
- It encourages traditional recitation-response teaching practices, ignoring what has been learned in recent years about learning.
- It encourages a rigid and undifferentiated curriculum.
- The competitive and comparative system of determining grades (marks of achievement) and promotion are educationally dysfunctional and psychologically unsound.
- It encourages an authoritarian classroom atmosphere that is antagonistic to what is now known about how children best learn.

Activity 1.2: Graded vs. Nongraded School: Study, Debate, and Vote

Organize a debate among your class members, those who tend to favor the traditional graded-school concept versus those who tend to favor a nongraded organization. Establish rules for the debate, a time period for study of the issues, then a time limit for the debate. After completion of the debate, hold a secret vote to determine the number who favor versus the number who do not favor the graded school.

CURRICULUM STANDARDS AND ACHIEVEMENT TESTING

Curriculum standards are definitions of what students should know (content) and be able to do (process and performance) as a result of instruction. National curriculum standards did not exist in the United States until those developed and released for mathematics education in 1989. Shortly after the release of the mathematics standards, the National Governors Association supported national goals in education, and the National Council on Education Standards and Testing recommended that in addition to those for mathematics, national standards for subject matter content in K–12 education be developed for the arts, civics/social studies, English/language arts/reading, geography, history, and science. The U.S. Department of Education provided initial funding for the development of national standards. In 1994 the U.S. Congress passed the Goals 2000: Educate America Act, amended in 1996 with an Appropriations Act, encouraging states to set standards. Long before this, however, national organizations were defining standards, as the National Council for Teachers of Mathematics had already done for mathematics.

The national standards for a given discipline represent the best thinking by expert panels, including teachers from the discipline, about what are the essential elements of a basic core of subject knowledge that all students should acquire. They serve not as national mandates but rather as voluntary guidelines to encourage curriculum development to promote higher student achievement. State and local curriculum developers may decide the extent to which they use the standards. Strongly influenced by the national standards, nearly all 50 states have completed or are presently developing state standards for the various disciplines. The topic of curriculum standards is discussed more fully in Chapter 5.

> *We don't need more testing. What we need is fewer bad tests and more good tests.*
> —W. James Popham (2006)

Preparing Students for High-Stakes Achievement Testing

The adoption of tougher K–12 learning standards throughout the United States, coupled with an emphasis on increased high-stakes competency testing to assess how schools and teachers are doing with respect to helping their students meet those standards, has provoked considerable debate, actions, and reactions among educators, parents/guardians, politicians, and people from the world of business. Some argue that this renewed emphasis on testing means too much "teaching to the test" at the expense of more meaningful learning, and that it ignores the leverage that home, community, and larger societal influences have over the education of children and young people today. For example, in the words of Lauren Sosniak (2001),

> We need to find ways to ask what our communities, corporations, media, and all of our organizations and institutions are doing to promote the development of readers, writers, historians, scientists, artists, musicians, designers and craftspersons. Schools cannot do this work alone, in the 9% of [a child's K–12 lifetime in school] allotted to them. If this is only "school work," it is hard to imagine that our students will see it as a meaningful part of their lives and their futures. . . . For too long our schools have been held accountable for too much, with too little acknowledgement of the responsibilities of the rest of society.

Nevertheless, responding to the call for increased accountability, especially although certainly not exclusively when state and federal funding may be withheld and/or jobs are on the line for schools, teachers, and administrators where students do not score well, teachers in some schools put aside the regular curriculum for several weeks in advance of the testing date and concentrate on the direct preparation of their students for the test. As stated by Carol Ann Tomlinson (2000),

> for many teachers, curriculum has become a prescribed set of academic standards, instructional pacing has become a race against a clock to cover the standards, and the sole goal of teaching has been reduced to raising student test scores on a single test, the value of which has scarcely been questioned in the public forum.

Although interest in this practice, often called "drill and kill," has been rekindled in recent years, it is certainly not new. When comparing standardized achievement testing of today with that of about a half century ago, it is probably safe to conclude (a) the purpose for statewide standardized testing remains unchanged—it is to determine how well children are learning, at least to the extent determined by the particular test instrument; (b) although alignment of tests with curriculum standards is an expensive and time-intensive challenge, test design is accomplished today with much greater precision and accuracy; but (c) today's focus on testing is taking precious time away from the most creative aspects of teaching and learning; and (d) the manner today in which test results are being used and the long-term results of that use may have ramifications considerably more serious than at any time before.

> *As we think about testing policies, we should remember the wisdom in the farmer's comment that weighing a pig every day won't ever make the pig any fatter. Eventually, you have to feed the pig.*
>
> **—Audrey L. Amrein and David C. Berliner (2003, p. 22)**

SOCIAL TRAGEDIES

The discussion of professional challenges to today's schools and teachers would not be complete without some attention to HIV/AIDS, illicit drug use, child abuse, and youth gangs, but their scope extends far beyond the school and the classroom. These topics are not exhaustive of the nation's social tragedies that deeply affect youth, nor are they necessarily related to one another except that each represents a major social tragedy of our time. It is *not* the purpose of this text to provide extensive coverage of these problems. It *is* our purpose to alert you to the need to be prepared psychologically and professionally to in some way deal with these and the other social tragedies—such as eating disorders in young people (Black, 2002), youth pregnancies, and gay and lesbian taunting and bashing (Sadowski, 2006)—that affect children and, in some way or another, activities in the classroom.

Acquired Immune Deficiency Syndrome (AIDS): The Threat Continues

Acquired immune deficiency syndrome (AIDS), first identified in 1981, is the final stage of a viral infection caused by the human immunodeficiency virus (HIV). Since that beginning, it has become one of the deadliest epidemics in human history, killing more than 25 million people worldwide, including a half million Americans. In the United States, AIDS has been a major cause of death among 1- to 4-year-olds, 15- to 24-year-olds, and 25- to 44-year-olds.

Although new annual infections in this country have been declining from an estimated 150,000 at the peak of the epidemic to about 40,000 per year in recent years, the problem is far from over. The transmission of HIV from mother to child has been nearly eliminated, but still it is estimated by the U.S. Centers for Disease Control and Prevention that many new infections in the United States are transmitted by people who do not even know they are infected with HIV.

HIV prevention is complex and requires a continued commitment from people at risk, people who are infected, and society in general. It's important to realize there are now new generations of Americans who may not remember the deadly, early years of the epidemic. Evidence indicates the epidemic is now migrating into our poor and minority communities, where it may be difficult for victims to get the help they need. Most experts believe that schools and parents should begin teaching children about HIV/AIDS as early as kindergarten so that children can grow up knowing how to protect themselves from exposure to the virus. As a matter of fact, the risk of elementary-school children contracting HIV is greater than many people realize because a significant number of them have sex before they finish elementary school (Schonfeld & Quackenbush, 2000).

In addition to the question of when and how to educate children about the disease are the questions of how to educate children who have the disease and how best to work with children who do not have the disease but nevertheless are AIDS victims.

Illicit Drug Use

It is generally acknowledged that since the 1960s the United States has had a serious drug-abuse problem, and that it seems to steadily worsen. Most experts agree that drug education should begin by at least the third grade, perhaps even as early as kindergarten. Moreover, a number of states have had regulations calling for the teaching of "the evils of narcotics, alcohol, and tobacco" for many years. The problem is not in finding agreement concerning the *need* for such education but in the nature of the education provided. Information is important, of course, but it is clearly inadequate as an absolute deterrent to drug abuse.

Schools can educate children about drug use in at least four ways. First, schools can provide accurate information about drugs and their effects on the human mind and body. Second, schools can stress the individual's responsibility to keep her or his own body in good physical condition. Third, the school must provide a drug-free environment. There must be a *zero-tolerance attitude* for any drug use, possession, or trafficking anywhere in the school or on the playground, day or night. Fourth, teachers can be sensitive to the behavior of individual children to identify signs of possible illicit drug use. Teachers must be aware of and follow school policy in reporting matters of illicit drug use.

Child Abuse and Neglect

Child abuse and neglect (e.g., physical abuse, incest, malnutrition, being improperly clothed, and inadequate dental care) have become grave matters of pressing national concern. Teachers in all states are legally mandated to report any suspicion of child abuse. It is a serious moral issue to not report such suspicion; lawsuits have been brought against educators for negligence in not doing so. If for any reason you suspect child abuse, follow school policy or telephone toll-free 1-800-4-A-CHILD (1-800-422-4453, the National Child Abuse Hotline) or use the hotline from your state. Proof of abuse is not necessary.

Although physical abuse and certain kinds of neglect, such as improper clothing and inadequate dental care, may be easiest to spot, other types of abuse such as

Apathy, short attention span, and lack of interest in school

Apparent lack of supervision

Bruised or swollen lip; mouth, lip, or tongue lacerations

Difficulty walking or sitting

Evidence of drug or alcohol abuse

Expression of little to no emotion when hurt

Fear of everyone and everything

Fear of going home after school

Fear of parent/guardian and other adults

Frequent absence from school

Frequent depression, sudden crying, evidence of poor self-image, extreme withdrawal

Frequent expression of and extreme hunger

Frequently tired and often falls asleep in class

Inappropriate interest in or knowledge of sexual acts

Strong and unpleasant body odor

Sudden and dramatic changes in behavior

Undue craving for attention or affection

Unexplained bites, fractures, lacerations, burns, welts, bruises, and/or scars in various stages of healing

FIGURE 1.5
Characteristics of children who may be abused or neglected

sexual, emotional, and malnutrition can be just as serious. Characteristics of children who are abused or neglected are shown in Figure 1.5. An abused or neglected child in your classroom needs to feel welcome and secure while in the classroom. For additional guidance in working with such a child, contact experts from your local school district and obtain guidelines from your state department of education or from the local children's protective services (CPS) agency.

Youth Gangs

Another serious threat to the safety and future of the nation's youth is the preponderance of youth gang activity. Although children in at least the early elementary grades are not ordinarily eligible for hardcore gang membership, a considerable amount of readiness for gang life takes place during these formative years. Although gang members may be as young as 12, the average age is 17 or 18 (Egley, 2002). One multicity survey of eighth graders found that 38 percent of gang members were female (Esbensen & Osgood, 1997). It is imperative that elementary school teachers be aware of the gang movement and have the knowledge and courage to assist in thwarting its negative effects.

Associated with gang life is unrestrained violence of the most vicious kind. Drive-by shootings, assaults, maiming, robberies, burglaries, intimidation, and murder characterize gang activity. Since the 1970s, youth gangs have been strongly connected with drug sales, especially crack cocaine. Although once considered to be an inner-city problem, perhaps no community today is immune to the havoc and terror of criminal youth gangs (Miller, 2001).

Generally, young people are not forced to join a gang; they may refuse without fear of retaliation (Howell, 2000). So then, why do young people join gangs? Among the reasons most often given are seeking a sense of excitement to relieve feelings of boredom, prestige, protection, opportunity to make money, and a sense of belonging (Howell, 1998). In other words, they find that gang life fills personal nurturing needs not met by their home, school, or other support groups in the neighborhood. Acceptance seems to be a major factor—gang members want to know that somebody cares about them.

Gangs develop their own colors, dress codes, trappings, icons, handshakes, and signals that help establish their identity. These are perceived as almost sacred rituals, and a violation of them or their appropriation by others can result in serious retribution and even death. Regrettably, many young children find these symbols attractive and may be drawn to them long before they are eligible for gang membership. For example, when a gang member walks through a neighborhood decked out in colorful gang regalia, little children may literally follow him around out of a sense of admiration. A young child may emulate some of that behavior in the classroom. When this happens, it is a clear sign of the need for intervention.

It is important to recognize the warning signs of gang activity. Teachers and parents/guardians should be suspicious of gang involvement if a *pattern of behavior* is observed that consistently includes a combination of the following: extended absences from school or home; unexplained wealth; abrupt change in personality; withdrawing from family; decline in school grades; lack of school involvement; radical change in friends; signs of alcohol or drug abuse; keeping late hours; associating with gang members; hand signals, symbolism, and graffiti; using excessive gang verbiage; change in vocabulary, especially high use of nicknames; dress code—style, color, or specific items such as a scarf; and increased violence.

How should you intervene if you have reason to believe that a child is involved in gang activity? The best course of action seems to be to come down very hard at the first sign of gang involvement. Schoolteachers at all levels are in a strategic position to observe such signs and should report their sightings and suspicions to the school principal.

Bullying and Violence

In many ways, teaching is clearly different from how it used to be.

> About a decade ago, an elementary school principal calling for a security assessment of his or her school would have been the exception, not the rule. But in light of high-profile school violence in recent years, and especially since September 11th [2001], parents have been demanding to know what principals are doing to improve their schools' security and crisis planning. (Trump, 2002)

More and more often today, starting as early as kindergarten, teachers are confronted with major problems that have ramifications beyond the classroom or that begin elsewhere and spill over into the classroom. If this happens, you may need to ask for help and should not hesitate to do so. As a teacher, you must remain alert. The words of Johnson and Johnson (1995, p. 1), of more than a decade ago, have only increased in their significance today.

> Fifty years ago, the main disciplinary problems were running in halls, talking out of turn, and chewing gum. Today's transgressions include physical and verbal violence, incivility, and in some schools, drug abuse, robbery, assault, and murder. The result is that many teachers spend an inordinate amount of time and energy managing classroom conflicts. When students poorly manage their conflicts with each other and with faculty, aggression results. Such behavior is usually punished with detentions, suspensions, and expulsions. As violence increases, pressure for safe and orderly schools increases. Schools are struggling with what to do.

Today's schools are adopting a variety of types of schoolwide and classroom instructional programs designed to reduce or eliminate violent, aggressive student behaviors and to help all students succeed in school. The most effective school programs for antiviolence use four strategies. They (a) teach social competence; (b) create a positive, calm environment; (c) establish behavior standards; and (d) establish rules and regulations for responding to violence (Schwartz, 1999).

Ever since the 1999 massacre at Columbine High School in Littleton, Colorado, where two students shot and killed a dozen classmates and a teacher before taking their own lives, parents and teachers are abandoning old notions of bullying as a kind of rite of passage and, across the nation, are launching unprecedented efforts to protect children from each other, aiming not just at physical intimidation but also at more subtle forms of emotional harassment. The most successful efforts at reducing bullying, clearly a marker for more serious violent behaviors (Nansel et al., 2003), begin with kindergarten and includes establishing and consistently enforcing a "no taunting policy." For example, at Seeds University Elementary School in Los Angeles, students and their parents or guardians sign contracts at the beginning of the school year acknowledging they understand it is unacceptable to ridicule, taunt, or attempt to hurt other students (Lumsden, 2002).

PARENTS, GUARDIANS, AND THE COMMUNITY

One of the exciting recent developments in elementary education has been the increased involvement of parents and guardians as partners in their children's education. Historically, parents and guardians have been involved in parent–teacher associations (PTAs), parent–teacher organizations (PTOs), or parent–student–teacher organizations (PSTOs), in fund-raisers for the schools, as assistants on field trips, as guests at an annual school open house, or as audiences for their children's pageants and plays. But parents and guardians have not really been centrally involved in instructional programs as knowledgeable partners with teachers, and it is this relationship that seems to be emerging today. Quite different from

Activity 1.3: Neighborhood Violence

Maria Garcia (all names are fictional) stands watching the front door of Emeryville Elementary School, located in an inner-city neighborhood of a large midwestern city, waiting for her 6-year-old son, Emilio, to emerge. At last he appears, flashing a gap-toothed smile. The first-grader skips along the wall of waiting parents and guardians to his mother and hands her his backpack.

Garcia is here to make sure her son gets home safely. She's concerned about gang activity in the area. A recent police alert about attempted child abductions in the neighborhood also worries her, as well as a violent fight between older children that she witnessed recently one day after school.

1. What are your initial thoughts after reading this real scenario?
2. Does this scenario sound familiar or realistic to you? Discuss why or why not with your classmates.
3. Some communities have established Neighborhood Watch programs designed to protect children while traveling from home to school (Salcido, Ornelas, & Garcia, 2002). Are similar programs operating in your geographic area?

most parental involvement to date, this newer relationship between parents, guardians, and schools is best described as a *partnership*.

It is well known that parents' and guardians' and even older siblings' involvement in their children's education can have a positive impact on their children's achievement at school. For example, when parents/guardians of at-risk students get involved, the children benefit with more consistent attendance at school, more positive attitudes and actions, better grades, and higher test scores (National PTA, 1997).

Although not all schools have a parent organization, when elementary school principals are asked to assess the influence each extant group has exerted on their school, the one likely to have the most influence is the parent–teacher organization. In recognition of the positive effect that parent and family involvement has on student achievement and success, in 1997 the National PTA published *National Standards for Parent/Family Involvement Programs.*

Many schools have adopted formal policies about home and community connections. These policies usually emphasize that parents and guardians should be included as partners in the educational program, and that teachers and administrators will inform parents and guardians about their children's progress, about the school's family involvement policy, and about any programs in which family members can participate. Some schools also are members of the National Network of Partnership 2000 Schools. Efforts to foster parent/guardian and community involvement are as varied as the people who participate and include the following:

- Student–teacher–parent/guardian contracts and assignment calendars, sometimes available via the school's Web site
- Home visitor programs
- Involvement of community leaders in the classroom as mentors, aides, and role models (see, for example, the *Hand in Hand* Web site)
- Newsletters, workshops (see, for example, Whiteford, 1998), and electronic hardware and software for parents and guardians to help their children

- Homework hotlines
- Regular phone calls (Gustafson, 1998) and personal notes home about a child's progress
- Involvement of students in community service learning (see examples in the list of motivational strategies in Chapter 8)

SERVICE LEARNING

Through service learning students learn and develop during active participation in thoughtfully organized and curriculum-connected experiences that meet community needs (see, for example, McCarthy & Corbin, 2003). Community members, geographic features, buildings, monuments, historic sites, and other places in a school's geographic area constitute one of the richest instructional laboratories that can be imagined. To take advantage of this accumulated wealth of resources, as well as to build school–community partnerships, once hired by a school district you should start a file of community resources as related to subject areas in which you work (see Figure 1.6). For instance, you might include files about the skills of the students' parents and other family members, noting those that could be resources for the study occurring in your classroom. You might also include files on various resource people who could speak or present to the class, on free and inexpensive materials, on sites for field trips, and on what other communities

A professional resources file is a project you could begin now and continue throughout your professional career. Begin your resources file either on a computer database program or on color-coded file cards listing: (1) name of resource, (2) how and where to obtain the resource, (3) description of how to use the resource, and (4) evaluative comments about the resource.

Organize the file in a way that makes sense to you. Cross-reference or color-code your system to accommodate the following categories of resources.

- CD/DVD titles
- Community resources
- Free/inexpensive materials
- Games
- Guest speakers/presenters
- Internet resources
- Media sources
- Motivational ideas
- Print resources

- Printed visuals
- Resources to order
- Software titles
- Student worksheets
- Test items
- Thematic units/ideas
- Unit/lesson plans/ideas
- Video titles
- Miscellaneous/other

FIGURE 1.6
Beginning my professional resources file

of teachers, students, and adult helpers have done. Many resource ideas and sources are mentioned and listed throughout this book. See, for example those among the motivational strategies listed in Chapter 8.

SUMMARY

Meeting the educational and developmental needs of all children in an increasingly diverse society presents challenges to teachers and schools. As never before, teachers are challenged to prepare children for citizenship in a dynamic multicultural society whose economic and political involvement is international in scope and global in influence.

American education continues to be dramatically affected by changes occurring in the lifestyles of families, pernicious attitudes of racism, economic and educational inequities, and other issues, including the threats of terrorism and war. Because the elementary school is so close to the most formative years of young human beings, these matters are of special relevance to those who teach at that level. School policies and professional concerns of teachers emerge from the social context within which the school operates.

No one who was knowledgeable about the matter ever said that good elementary-school teaching was easy. As a matter of fact, it is not easy. However, the good news is that you have many valuable resources at your disposal and that the intrinsic rewards are well worth the effort needed to become and to remain a knowledgeable and effective classroom teacher. Regardless of all else, in the end the dedication, commitment, and nature of the understanding of the teacher and other adults remain the decisive elements that determine whether a child succeeds in school or is left behind and drops out somewhere along the way.

As a classroom teacher you must acknowledge that the children of your classroom have different ways of receiving information and different ways of processing that information—different ways of knowing and of constructing their knowledge. These differences are unique and important and are central considerations in curriculum development and instructional practice as discussed in Chapters 5 and 6. Although you cannot cure all the woes of society, you can ensure that each child feels welcome, accepted, respected, safe, and successful while in your classroom.

Involvement of parents and guardians in the school experiences of their children is one of the few educational issues on which there is universal accord. The importance of such involvement may rival that of family income or family education as a variable contributing to children's success in school.

In beginning your plan to develop your professional competencies, you have read in this chapter an overview of some of the issues and problems that will affect both that development and your work and effectiveness as a classroom teacher. Despite various society-wide efforts to more effectively and efficiently educate children, it is still the classroom teacher, working mostly alone in a self-contained classroom, who bears responsibility for implementing the program to meet all children's educational and developmental needs. In Chapter 2, we look more closely at the teacher's specific professional responsibilities.

STUDY QUESTIONS AND ADDITIONAL ACTIVITIES

1. This chapter calls attention to changes in the demographics of U.S. society. What major ethnic, racial, and/or cultural groups live in the area in which you plan to teach? Have the percentages of represented groups changed in the past 25 years? What implications are there in these social realities for your work as a teacher?

Newspaper Headlines

All kindergarten students will be divided by age into junior kindergarten and kindergarten classes beginning with the upcoming school year. (*The Kauai Garden Island*, June 3, 2006)

Jumping into the rigors of learning: As number of full-day kindergartens increases, reading and math lessons supplant playtime. (*Washington Post*, October 26, 2004)

Boston kindergartners to receive report cards. (*Boston Globe*, November 10, 2004)

Kindergarten cramming: Schools pushing kids beyond naps, crackers. (*Sacramento Bee*, April 7, 2005)

---

2. What were your immediate thoughts when you read the newspaper headlines in the preceding box? In your opinion, should kindergarten, all day, with a more standardized curriculum, replace first grade as the official start of school? Are 5-year-olds ready for that sort of academic thrust? Some say that we are asking too much too soon of young children. Find support for your opinion, and share it with members of your class.
3. Literacy, citizenship, and moral education have been important goals of education since the time of colonial America. Research and discuss the importance of the teaching methods used to achieve these goals. Speculate on how such methods have changed through the years.
4. Think back and recall your most vivid pleasant memories of your own elementary school experience. Do you think children today still enjoy similar experiences or activities? Explain.
5. In terms of today's ethnic and cultural diversity of our society, explain why you believe that goals related to the common culture are more or less important than they were a century ago.
6. Other than those discussed in this chapter, what additional social realities influence children's learning and the subject matter or methods of teaching that

teachers select? Are any unique to a specific geographic area or areas of the United States?

7. What opportunity costs are sacrificed when students and their parents/ guardians select a school outside the usual attendance area? What might the positive or negative long-term effects of this practice be on society as a whole if it becomes widespread?

8. Some people believe that the primary function of our schools is to transmit societal values. Others believe that schools should be agents of social reform (transformation). Still others argue that schools should be agents of *both* cultural transmission and transformation. Prepare a one-page position paper in favor of one of these positions. Present and defend your position before your classmates.

9. Some say that the ability of United States to cope with an explosion of religious, ethnic, socioeconomic, and political diversity will determine the future of the nation in much the same way as the American Revolution and the Civil War did. Explain why you agree or disagree with this position. If you agree, explain what you see to be an elementary-school classroom teacher's responsibility toward making the successful changes of society.

10. Express your opinion on the following statement: It is not important that a child might complete his or her elementary-school education without ever having had a male or an ethnic minority teacher.

WEB SITES RELATED TO CONTENT OF THIS CHAPTER

- Blendedschools (K–8 online curriculum) *www.blendedschools.net*
- Blueprint for Violence Prevention: Book Nine *www.colorado.edu/cspv/publications/ blueprints/BP-009.html*
- Character Counts Coalition *www.charactercounts.org*
- Character Education Partnership *www.character.org/resources/search*
- Educators for Social Responsibility *www.esrnational.org/about-rccp.html*
- Federal Citizen Information Center *www.pueblo.gsa.gov*
- John Stanford International School *www.jsisweb.com*
- Making Schools Work *www.sreb.org*
- Northeast Foundation for Children *www.responsiveclassroom.org*
- Rand study on obesity and school performance available *www.nihcm.org*
- Safe and Responsive Schools Project *www.indiana.edu/~safeschl*
- Second Step: A Violence Prevention Curriculum *www.cfchildren.org/ssf/ssf/ssindex*
- Teachers Helping Teachers *www.pacificnet.net/~mandel*
- Thomas J. Pappas School *www.tjpappasschool.org*
- Yahoo! Education Directory *www.yahoo.com/Education*

FOR FURTHER READING

Abrams, J., & Ferguson, J. (2005). Teaching students from many nations. *Educational Leadership, 62*(4), 64–67.

Canter, A. S. (2005). Bullying at school. *Principal, 85*(2), 42–45.

Checkley, K. (2006). Social studies jockeys for position in a narrowing curriculum. *Education Update, 48*(5), 1–2, 6, 8.

Chen, M. (2005). Go year-round. *Edutopia, 1*(5), 51.

Christian, D., Pufahik, I. U., & Rhodes, N. C. (2005). Language learning: A worldwide perspective. *Educational Leadership, 62*(4), 24–30.

DeCicca, P. (2007). Does full-day kindergarten matter? Evidence from the first two years of schooling. *Economics of Education Review, 26*(1), 67–82.

Friend, M., & Pope, K. L. (2005). Creating schools in which all students can succeed. *Kappa Delta Pi Record, 41*(2), 56–61.

Hadi-Tabassum, S. (2005). The balancing act of bilingual immersion. *Educational Leadership, 62*(3), 66–69.

Hamilton, J., Johnson, S., Marshall, J., & Shields, C. (2006). Making the most of time. *Educational Leadership, 63*(8), 72–73.

Harvard Education Letter. (2006). Recent research on the achievement gap: Interview with Ronald Ferguson. *Harvard Education Letter, 22*(6), 4–6.

Herman, B. E. (2004). *The revival of K–8 schools.* Fastback 519. Bloomington, IN: Phi Delta Kappa Educational Foundation.

Joseph, P. B, & Efron, S. (2005). Seven worlds of moral education. *Phi Delta Kappan, 86,* 525–533.

Klump, J., & McNeir, G. (2005). *Culturally responsive practices for student success: A regional sampler.* Portland, OR: Northwest Regional Educational Laboratory.

Lindeman, B. (2001). Reaching out to immigrant parents. *Educational Leadership, 58*(6), 62–66.

Magnuson, K. A., Ruhm, C., & Waldfogel, J. (2007). Does prekindergarten improve school preparation and performance? *Economics of Educational Review, 26*(1), 33–51.

Merisuo-Storm, T. (2007). Pupils' attitudes toward foreign-language learning and the development of literacy skills in bilingual education. *Teaching & Teacher Education, 23,* 226–235.

Neuman, S. B., & Roskos, K. (2005). The state of state pre-kindergarten standards. *Early Childhood Research Quarterly, 20,* 125–145.

Parrett, W. H. (2005). Against all odds: Reversing low achievement of one school's Native American students. *School Administrator, 62*(1), 26.

Schibsted, E. (2006). Fighting for fitness. *Edutopia, 1*(9), 30–35.

Sussman, G. L. (2006). The violence you don't see. *Educational Leadership, 63,* 1–7. In *Helping All Students Succeed,* ASCD online journal at www.ascd.org:80/portal/site/ascd

Chapter 2

The Teacher's Professional Responsibilities

INTASC Principles	PRAXIS III Domains	NBPTS Standards
• The teacher is a reflective practitioner who continually evaluates the effects of his/her choices and actions on others (students, parents, and other professionals in the learning community) and who actively seeks out opportunities to grow professionally. (Principle 9)	• Teaching Professionalism (Domain D)	• Instructional Resources
• The teacher fosters relationships with school colleagues, parents, and agencies in the larger community to support students' learning and well-being. (Principle 10)	• Teaching for Student (Learning (Domain C)	• Reflection

- The teacher uses knowledge of effective verbal, nonverbal, and media communication techniques to foster active inquiry, collaboration, and supportive interaction in the classroom. (Principle 6)

Why do people select teaching as a career? Why have *you* decided to become a teacher? More specifically, why did you elect to become an elementary-school teacher? What responsibilities and teaching behaviors do you expect to be held accountable for? Which responsibilities and behaviors do you feel most competent about? Which do you feel least competent about?

You will be interested to know that a number of research studies have addressed precisely the question of why individuals select elementary-school teaching as a career. The reasons people most frequently give are that they like working with children, and they like the social service aspect of teaching (Cruickshank, 1990).

As you study this chapter, think about your own motivations for selecting elementary-school teaching as a career. What are your expectations in terms of personal and material rewards? To what extent do you have a sense of social service and a desire to work with children? Your study of this chapter will guide you as you reflect on these important questions.

The primary expectation of any teacher is to facilitate student learning. As an elementary-school classroom teacher, however, your professional responsibilities will extend well beyond the ability to work effectively in a classroom from approximately 8:00 a.m. until midafternoon. In this chapter, you will learn about the many responsibilities you will assume and the competencies and behaviors necessary for fulfilling them. Much has been learned in recent years about exemplary teacher behaviors. From that research we identify three categories of responsibilities and competencies and elaborate on specific teacher behaviors that will promote your students' learning.

The three categories of professional responsibilities are (a) responsibility as a reflective decision maker; (b) commitment to children and to the profession; and (c) fundamental teaching competencies. Our presentation of these categories and competencies will guide you through the reality of these expectations as they exist for today's elementary school classroom teacher. Our discussion of strategies will enhance your teaching effectiveness by providing you with a set of tools you will find useful throughout your career.

Finally, as a teacher you will be a learner among learners. Long after you finish the course for which you are using this textbook, after you have obtained your credentials and your first teaching job, you will continue to learn about teaching. Your learning will never cease; at least, it should not. You will not automatically maintain your teaching effectiveness forever; you will need constantly to work at maintaining and improving your teaching effectiveness. This moment is or should be

Activity 2.1: Is This a Typical Day for a Fifth-Grade Teacher?

Kristin is a fifth-grade teacher in a low SES school in a moderately large city of Texas. Her 34 students include 10 limited-English speakers and 10 with identified learning problems. Some of the children have reading and comprehension skills as low as first grade. In any given week, Kristin recycles newspapers and sells snacks to pay for field trips because the school and the children can't. On a typical school day recently, Kristin began her work at school at 7:00 a.m. with three parent conferences. The children arrived and school started at 8:15 and ran until 2:45 p.m. Kristin then tutored children until 3:45, conducted four more parent conferences, and entered data into her classroom desktop computer before going home at 6 p.m. In the evening she planned lessons and graded papers for another 2 hours before retiring.

Questions for individual thought and class discussion:

1. What were your immediate thoughts and feelings after reading this synopsis of Kristin's day?
2. Do you think that Kristin's day is typical for many or most elementary school teachers? Why or why not?

much closer to the start of your learning about teaching than it is to the end of that learning process.

ANTICIPATED OUTCOMES

After completing this chapter, you should be able to do the following:

1. Demonstrate your understanding of the magnitude of responsibilities of being an elementary-school classroom teacher.
2. Describe the decision-making and thought-processing phases of instruction and the types of decisions a teacher must make during each phase.
3. Describe the importance of the concept of locus of control and its relationship to the teacher's professional responsibilities.
4. Compare and contrast facilitating behaviors with instructional strategies.
5. Demonstrate your understanding of the importance of reflection to the process of constructing skills and understandings, including to becoming a competent teacher.
6. Compare and contrast minds-on and hands-on learning.
7. Compare and contrast the teacher's use of praise versus encouragement.
8. Identify and describe the results of the exemplary execution of the basic teacher behaviors as identified and described in this chapter.
9. Describe how one can determine the effectiveness with which a teacher executes the basic teacher behaviors.
10. Describe with examples how a teacher's incongruent behavior would send children a negative message via the covert curriculum.
11. Identify and describe ways technology is used for teaching and learning in today's elementary school classrooms.
12. Begin the development of a professional development portfolio.
13. Demonstrate an understanding of the importance of helping children develop impulse control, and of ways of doing it.

THE TEACHER AS A REFLECTIVE DECISION MAKER

During any single school day you will make hundreds, perhaps thousands, of decisions. You will make some decisions prior to meeting your students for instruction, others during instructional activities, and still others later as you reflect on the day's instruction. Let's now consider further the decision-making and thought-processing phases of instruction.

You Can Be the Reason

You can be the reason some student gets up and comes to school when his life is tough. You can be the reason some student "keeps on keeping on" even though her parents are telling her that she can't succeed. You can inspire your at-risk students. Remember that as long as you are a teacher, even on your worst day on the job, you are still some student's best hope.

—Larry I. Bell

Source: L. I. Bell, "Strategies That Close the Gap," *Educational Leadership* 60(4): 34 (December 2002/January 2003).

Decision-Making Phases of Instruction

Instruction may be divided into four decision-making and thought-processing phases: (1) the planning or *preactive phase*, (2) the teaching or *interactive phase*, (3) the analyzing and evaluating or *reflective phase*, and (4) the application or *projective phase* (Costa, 1991).

The planning phase consists of all those intellectual functions and decisions you will make prior to actual instruction. This includes decisions about relevant curriculum standards, goals and objectives, homework assignments, what children already know and can do, appropriate learning activities, questions to ask (and possible answers), and selecting and preparing instructional materials.

The interactive phase includes all decisions made during the immediacy and spontaneity of your actual teaching. This includes maintaining student attention, asking questions, types of feedback given, and ongoing adjustments to the lesson plan. As noted before, decisions made during this phase are likely to be more intuitive, unconscious, and routine than those made during planning.

The reflective phase is the time you will take to reflect on, analyze, and judge the decisions and behavior that occurred during the interactive phase (see questions for self-reflection in Figure 2.1). It is during reflection that you make decisions about student learning, student grades, feedback given to parents and guardians, and adjustments on what to teach next.

As emphasized by Schon (1983) a quarter century ago, it is not that we learn so much from our experience, but from our reflection on our experience. As a result of this teacher self-reflection, decisions are made to use what was learned in subsequent teaching actions. At this point, you are in the projective phase, abstracting

- What is my overall opinion about today's lesson—good, fair, or bad? What specifically made me feel this way?
- Did students seem to enjoy the lesson? What specifically makes me think so?
- Were I a student in my class today would I look forward to returning tomorrow? Why?
- Did the objectives seem to be met? What evidence is there?
- What aspects of the lesson went well? What makes me believe so?
- Were I to repeat the lesson, what changes might I make?
- Which students seemed to do well? Which ones didn't? What should I do about that?
- To what extent was this lesson personalized for the students? Could I do more in this regard? If so, what? If not, then why not?
- To what extent did this lesson engage various learning modalities? Should more have been done in this area? Why or why not?
- Did the students seem to have sufficient time to think and apply? Why or why not?
- Would I have wanted my own child present as a student in this class? Why or why not?
- Would I have been proud had the school district superintendent been present to observe this lesson? Why or why not?

FIGURE 2.1
Questions for self-reflection

from your reflection and projecting your analysis into subsequent teaching behaviors. It is suggested that one reason some teachers are not as effective as they might be is because of their lack of attention to any sustained self-reflection (Danielson & McGreal, 2000). What is the characteristic of a "sustained self-reflection"? It is when a teacher asks herself or himself questions like those of Figure 2.1, thoughtfully answers the questions, and then acts accordingly.

Reflection, Locus of Control, Sense of Self-Efficacy, and Teacher Responsibility

During the reflective phase, teachers have a choice of whether to assume full responsibility for the instructional outcomes or to assume responsibility for only the positive outcomes of the planned instruction while placing the blame for the negative outcomes on outside forces (e.g., district, state, or federal requirements, parents and guardians or society in general, colleagues, administrators, textbooks, or lack thereof). Where the responsibility for outcomes is placed is referred to as *locus of control*. A person with an internal locus of control typically is more likely to persist against formidable odds (see "intelligent behaviors" in Chapter 3). Furthermore, a teacher who believes he or she can, generally will, a characteristic called *efficacy*. Teachers who have a strong sense of self-efficacy (feeling of "I can") are more likely to instill in their students the same sense of empowerment (Ashton & Webb, 1986).

However, just because a teacher thinks he or she "can" teach doesn't mean he or she "will." If many of a teacher's students are not learning, then that teacher is not competent. In the words of the late Madeline Hunter, "To say that I am an effective teacher, and acknowledge that my students may not be learning is the same as saying I am a great surgeon, but most of my patients die" (Villa & Thousands, 1995). Teachers who are intrinsically motivated and competent tend to assume full responsibility for instructional outcomes, regardless of whether or not the outcomes are as intended from the planning phase.

Of course every teacher realizes there are factors that the teacher cannot control, such as the negative effects on children from poverty, bullying, gangs, alcohol, and drug abuse, so they must do what they can within the confines of the classroom and resources of the school and district.

> History brims with examples of how a relatively few, but positive, moments with a truly caring and knowledgeable adult can drastically change for the better the life of a young person whom until then had a history of mostly negative experiences.

COMMITMENT AND PROFESSIONALISM

Our second category of professional responsibility is that of commitment and professionalism. As teacher you are expected to demonstrate commitment to the personal as well as the intellectual development of all your students. Not only do the most effective teachers expect, demand, and receive positive results in learning from their students while in the classroom, they are also interested and involved in their students' activities outside the classroom and willing to sacrifice personal time to provide attention and guidance.

IDENTIFYING AND BUILDING YOUR INSTRUCTIONAL COMPETENCIES

A major purpose of this book is to assist you in understanding and beginning to build your instructional competencies, and this is where we begin. We begin with the identification of specific teacher behaviors that have been identified from years of research that clearly promote student learning. You will continue to reflect and build on these competencies through your study of the remaining chapters of this book and, indeed, throughout your professional career.

Your ability to perform your instructional responsibilities effectively directly depends on your knowledge of students and how they best learn and on your knowledge of and the *quality* of your teaching skills. As we frequently state, development of your strategy repertoire along with your skills in using specific strategies should be ongoing throughout your teaching career. To be most effective, you need a large repertoire from which to select a specific strategy for a particular goal with a distinctive group of children. In addition, you need skill in using that strategy. As with intelligences, teaching style is neither absolutely inherited nor fixed, but continues to develop and emerge throughout one's professional career. This section is designed to help you begin building your specific strategies repertoire and to develop your skills in using these strategies.

Fundamental Assumptions

The concept of building a strategies repertoire rests on three fundamental assumptions. First, you must know why you have selected a particular strategy. An unknowing teacher is likely to use the teaching strategy most common in college classes—the lecture. However, as many student teachers have discovered the hard way, lecturing is seldom an effective or appropriate way to instruct elementary-school children. As a rule, unlike many college and university students, not many K–8 students are strong auditory learners by preference and by adeptness. Learning by sitting and listening is difficult. Instead, they learn best when physically (*hands-on*) and intellectually (*minds-on*) active—that is, when using tactile and kinesthetic experiences, touching objects, feeling shapes and textures, moving objects, and talking about and sharing what they are learning.

Second, basic teacher behaviors create the conditions needed to enable students to think and to learn, whether the learning is a further understanding of concepts, internalizing attitudes and values, developing cognitive processes, or actuating the most complex behaviors. These basic behaviors are those that produce the following results: (a) students are physically and mentally engaged in learning activities; (b) instructional time is efficiently used; and (c) classroom distractions and interruptions are minimal. Your choice of a particular *strategy* in a given situation will in part be determined by what particular *behaviors* will, in that situation, produce these results.

Third, one can measure the effectiveness of a teacher's basic behaviors and choice of strategies by how well students learn (the topic of Chapter 7).

In the remainder of this section we discuss the following basic teacher behaviors and strategies to facilitate student learning: (a) structuring the learning environment; (b) accepting and sharing instructional accountability; (c) demonstrating withitness and overlapping; (d) providing a variety of motivating and challenging activities; (e) modeling appropriate behaviors; (f) facilitating student acquisition of data; (g) creating a psychologically safe environment; (h) clarifying whenever necessary; (i) using periods of silence; and (j) questioning thoughtfully.

Facilitating Behaviors and Instructional Strategies: A Clarification

Clearly at least some of these 10 "behaviors" are also instructional "strategies"—questioning, for example. The difference is that while behaviors must be in place for the most effective teaching to occur, strategies are more or less discretionary—that is, they are pedagogical techniques from which you may select but may not be obligated to use. For example, questioning and the use of silence are fundamental teaching behaviors, whereas giving demonstrations and showing videos are not. So, you see, your task is twofold: (1) to develop your awareness of and skills in using fundamental teaching behaviors, and (2) to develop your repertoire of and skills in selecting and using appropriate instructional strategies.

Starting now and continuing throughout your teaching career, you will want to evaluate your developing competency for each of the 10 fundamental facilitating behaviors and work to improve in those areas in which you need help. Consider the following descriptions and examples, and discuss them in your class. (*Note:* In some instances, a specific component of the facilitating behavior is the focus of a particular chapter of this book, in which case that chapter is so identified. Some are discussed more fully later in this chapter, whereas in other instances the behavior is discussed in many places throughout the book, in which case you may refer to the index for a specific location.)

Structuring the Learning Environment

Structuring the learning environment means establishing an intellectual, psychological, and physical environment that enables all students to act and react productively. Specifically, you

- Attend to the organization of the classroom as a learning laboratory to establish a positive, safe, and efficient environment for student learning (the focus of Chapter 4).
- Establish and maintain clearly understood classroom procedures, definitions, instructions, and expectations. Help students clarify learning expectations and

The successful teacher structures the learning environment in such a way that encourages and enables all students to act and react productively.

establish clearly understood learning objectives. (These are principally the top-ics of Chapters 4 and 5, respectively.)

- Help students assume tasks and responsibilities, thereby empowering them in their learning.
- Organize students, helping them to organize their learning. Help students in iden-tifying and understanding time and resource constraints. Provide *instructional scaffolds*, such as building bridges to learning by helping students connect what they are learning with what they already know or think they know and have experienced.
- Plan and implement techniques for schema building, such as providing content and process outlines, visual diagrams, and opportunities for concept mapping (discussed in Chapter 9).
- Use techniques for students' metacognitive development, such as *think–pair–share*, in which students are asked to think about an idea, share thoughts about it with a partner, and then share the pair's thoughts with the entire class.
- Plan units and lessons that have clear and concise beginnings and endings. Do at least some planning collaboratively with students. (Unit and lesson planning is the focus of Chapter 6.)
- Provide frequent summary reviews, often by using student self-assessment of what they are learning. Structure and facilitate ongoing formal and informal discussion based on a shared understanding of the rules of discourse.

Accepting and Sharing Instructional Accountability

While holding students accountable for their learning, you must be willing to be held accountable for the effectiveness of the learning process and outcomes (the "locus of control" discussed earlier in this chapter). Specifically, you

- Assume a responsibility for professional decision making and the risks associated with that responsibility. Share some responsibility for decision making and risk taking with students. A primary goal in the education of children must be to see that they become accountable for themselves as learners and as citizens. To some degree, then, you are advised to work with students as *partners* in their learning and development. One dimension of that partnership is sharing accountability; one effective way of doing this is by using student portfolios (discussed in Chapter 7).
- Communicate clearly to parents, guardians, administrators, and colleagues.
- Communicate to students that they share with you the responsibility for accom-plishing learning goals and objectives.
- Plan exploratory activities that engage students in learning.
- Provide continuous cues for desired learning behaviors and incentives contin-gent on desired performance, such as grades, points, rewards, and privileges; also establish a clearly understood and continuous program of assessment that includes reflection and self-assessment.
- Provide opportunities for students to demonstrate their learning, to refine and explore their questions, and to share their thinking and results.

Demonstrating Withitness and Overlapping

In *School Begins at Two* (New York: New Republic, 1936), Harriet Johnson wrote of the early childhood educator's need to be "with it," by which she was referring to the teacher's awareness of each child's emotions and needs as well as those of the whole group. Years later, Jacob Kounin (1970) wrote of another kind of teacher withitness. As described by Kounin, withitness and overlapping are two separate but closely related behaviors. *Withitness* is your awareness of the whole group. *Overlapping* is your ability to attend to several matters simultaneously, what today is usually referred to as *multitasking*. Although these are discussed later, especially in Chapters 4 and 6, specifically, you

- Attend to the entire class while working with one student or with a small group of students, communicating this awareness with eye contact, hand gestures, body position and language, and clear but private verbal cues.
- Continually and simultaneously monitor all classroom activities to keep students at their tasks and to provide them with assistance and resources.
- Continue monitoring the class during any distraction, such as when a visitor enters the classroom.
- Demonstrate understanding of when comprehension checks and instructional transitions are appropriate or needed.
- Dwell on one topic only as long as necessary for students' understanding.
- Quickly intervene and redirect potentially undesirable student behavior.
- Refocus or shift activities for a student or students when their attention begins to fade.

Providing a Variety of Motivating and Challenging Activities

Elementary school teachers who are most effective use a variety of activities that motivate and challenge all students to work to the utmost of their abilities and that engage and challenge the preferred learning styles and learning capacities of more of the students more of the time. Specifically, you

- Demonstrate optimism and enthusiasm toward each child's ability.
- Demonstrate an unwavering expectation that all students will work to the best of their ability.
- Demonstrate pride, optimism, and enthusiasm in learning, thinking, and teaching.
- View teaching and learning as an organic and reciprocal process that extends well *beyond the traditional* "2 by 4 by 6 curriculum"—that is, a curriculum bound by the two covers of the textbook, the four walls of the classroom, and the six hours of the school day.
- Plan exciting and interesting learning activities with students, including those that engage their natural interest in the mysterious and the novel. (These last two are the principal foci of Chapters 5, 6, and 8.)

TPW Video Classroom

Series: Classroom Management

Module 2: Fostering Student Accountability

Video 1: Modeling Mutual Respect, Routines, and Transitions

Modeling Appropriate Behaviors

As emphasized throughout this book, effective teachers model the very behaviors expected of their students. Specifically, you

- Arrive promptly in the classroom and demonstrate on-task behaviors for the entire class meeting, just as you expect the children to do.
- Demonstrate respect for all students. For example, do not interrupt when a student is showing rational thinking, even though you may disagree with the direction of the thinking.
- Demonstrate that making "errors" is a natural event in learning and during problem solving, and readily admit and correct any mistakes you may make.
- Promptly return student papers and offer comments that provide positive, instructive, and encouraging feedback.
- Model and emphasize the skills, attitudes, and values of higher-order intellectual processes. Demonstrate rational problem-solving skills and explain to students the processes involved (Chapter 5).
- Model professionalism by spelling correctly, using proper grammar, and printing or writing clearly and legibly.
- Practice communication that is clear, precise, and to the point. For example, use "I" when you mean "I"; use "we" when you mean "we."
- Practice moments of silence (see "Using Periods of Silence" later in this section), thus modeling thoughtfulness, reflectiveness, and restraint of impulsiveness.
- Realize that your students are also models for other children. Reinforce appropriate student behaviors, and promptly intervene when behaviors are inappropriate (Chapter 4).

Facilitating Student Acquisition of Data

The teacher makes sure that data are accessible to students as input that they can process. Specifically, you

- Ensure that sources of information are readily available to students for their use. Select books, media, and materials that facilitate student learning. Ensure that equipment and materials are readily available for students to use. Identify and use resources beyond the classroom walls and the boundaries of the school campus (discussed further later in this chapter and in Chapter 5).

- Create a responsive classroom environment (Chapter 4) with a variety of direct learning experiences (Chapter 6).
- Ensure that major ideas receive proper attention and emphasis.
- Provide clear and specific instructions.
- Provide feedback about each student's performance and progress. Encourage students to organize and maintain devices, such as learning portfolios, to self-monitor their progress in learning and thinking (Chapter 7).
- Select and display bridge examples that help learners connect what they are learning with what they already know and have experienced (Chapter 6).
- Serve as a resource person, and use cooperative learning and peer tutoring, thus regarding your students as resources, too (Chapter 8).

Creating and Maintaining a Psychologically Safe Environment

To encourage positive development of student self-esteem, to provide a psychologically safe learning environment, and to encourage the most creative thought and behavior, the teacher provides an attractive and materials-rich classroom environment and makes appropriate nonevaluative and nonjudgmental responses. Specifically, you

- Avoid negative criticism. Criticism is often a negative value judgment, and "when a teacher responds to a student's ideas or actions with such negative words as 'poor,' 'incorrect,' or 'wrong,' the response tends to signal inadequacy or disapproval and ends the student's thinking about the task" (Costa, 1991, p. 54).
- Frequently use minimal reinforcement (that is, nonjudgmental acceptance behaviors, such as nodding your head, writing a student's response on the board, or saying "I understand"). Whereas elaborate or strong praise is generally unrelated to student achievement, using minimal reinforcement, saying such words as "right," "okay," "good," "uh-huh," and "thank you," does correlate with achievement.

However, be careful with too-frequent and thereby ineffective and even damaging use of the single word "good" following student contributions during class discussion. Use the word only when the contribution was truly good; better yet, say not only "good" but tell what specifically *was* good about the contribution. This provides a more powerful reinforcement by demonstrating that you truly heard and understood the student's contribution.

- Be sparing with your use of elaborate or strong praise, especially with older children. By the time students are beyond the primary grades, teacher praise (a positive value judgment) has little or no value as a form of positive reinforcement. In fact, the use of strong praise can be counterproductive to your intent (Hitz & Driscoll, 1989). Especially when teaching children of grade 4 and above, praise should be mild, private, and for student accomplishment, rather than for effort, and for each child you should gradually reduce the frequency with which you use praise. When praise is reduced, a more diffused sociometric pattern develops, that is, more children become directly and productively involved in learning. As emphasized by Good and Brophy (2003), praise should be simple and direct, delivered in a natural voice without dramatizing. Students see overly done theatrics as insincere.

Let us take pause to consider this point. Probably no statement in this book raises more eyebrows than the statement that praise for most children beyond primary years especially has little or no value as a form of positive reinforcement. After all, praise may well motivate some people. However, at what cost? Praise and encouragement (sometimes referred to as "effective praise") are often confused and considered to be the same, but they are not, and they do not have the same long-term results. This is explained as follows:

> For many years there has been a great campaign for the virtues of praise in helping children gain a positive self-concept and improve their behavior. This is another time when we must "beware of what works." Praise may inspire some children to improve their behavior. The problem is that they become pleasers and approval "junkies." These children (and later these adults) develop self-concepts that are totally dependent on the opinions of others. Other children resent and rebel against praise, either because they don't want to live up to the expectations of others or because they fear they can't compete with those who seem to get praise so easily. The alternative that considers long-range effects is encouragement. The long-range effect of encouragement is self-confidence. The long-range effect of praise is dependence on others. (Nelsen, 1987, p. 103)

In summary, then, our advice to you is while being cautious with the use of praise, do reinforce student efforts by recognizing specific personal accomplishments (see Figure 2.2).

- Perceive your classroom as the place where you work, where students learn, and make that place of work and the tools available a place of pride—as stimulating and useful as possible.
- Plan within your lessons behaviors that exhibit respect for the experiences and ideas of individual students, regardless of their differences (Chapter 8).

Statement of Praise	Statement or Act of Encouragement
I love your drawing of a cart.	I see you have drawn a cart. What will you put in your cart?
Terrific job!	I notice you put all the crayons and scissors back in their appropriate storage bins.
I like the way you behaved on the field trip.	[nothing, as proper behavior is expected]
I love the way you have cleaned your table.	[nothing; perhaps give a smile]
You're so smart!	I see you've figured out how to turn the pieces to put that puzzle together.

FIGURE 2.2
Statements of Praise versus Statements or Acts of Encouragement

TPW Video Classroom

Series: General Methods
Module 1: The Effective Teacher
Video 1: Using Student Ideas and Contributions

- Provide positive individual student attention as often as possible. Write sincere reinforcing personalized comments on student papers. Provide incentives and rewards for student accomplishments (Chapter 4).
- Use nonverbal cues to show awareness and acceptance of individual students. Use paraphrasing and reflective listening. Use empathic acceptance of a student's expression of feelings, that is, demonstrating by words and gestures that you understand the student's position.

Clarifying Whenever Necessary

The teacher's responding behavior seeks further elaboration from a student about that student's idea or comprehension. Specifically, you

- Help students to connect new content to that previously learned. Help students relate lesson content to their other school and nonschool experiences. Help students make learning connections among disciplines (Chapters 5, 6, and 8).
- Politely invite a responding student to be more specific and to elaborate on or rephrase an idea or to provide a concrete illustration of an idea (Chapter 3).
- Provide frequent opportunity for summary reviews.
- Repeat or paraphrase students' responses, allowing them to correct any misinterpretations of what they said or implied (Chapter 3).
- Select instructional strategies that help students correct their prior and naïve notions about a topic.

Using Periods of Silence

The effective teacher uses periods of silence in the classroom. Specifically, you

- Actively listen (such as by using facial expressions and body language) when students are talking.
- Model silence when silence and thinking are wanted. Keep silent when students are working quietly or are attending to a visual display, and maintain classroom control by using nonverbal signals and indirect intervention strategies (Chapter 4).
- Pause while talking to allow for thinking and reflection (Chapter 8).
- Use your silence to stimulate group discussion (Chapter 3).
- Allow sufficient think time (also called *wait time*), longer than 2 and as long as 9 seconds, after asking a question or posing a problem (Rowe, 1974; Wilen, 1991) (Chapter 3).

Questioning Thoughtfully

The effective teacher asks thoughtfully worded questions to induce learning, to stimulate thinking, and to develop students' thinking skills. Specifically, you

- Assist students in the development of their own questioning skills, providing opportunities for them to explore their own ideas, to obtain data, and to find answers to their own questions and solutions to their problems (Chapter 9).
- Encourage students' questioning without judging the quality or relevancy of questions (Chapter 3). Attend to questions, and respond and encourage other students to respond, often by building on the content of a student's questions and on student responses.
- Plan questioning sequences that elicit a variety of thinking skills and that maneuver students to higher levels of thinking and doing. (Questioning and its relationship to thinking is discussed further in Chapter 3.)
- Use a variety of types of questions (Chapter 3).
- Use questions to help children to explore their knowledge, to develop new understandings, and to discover ways of applying their learning.

You begin now to develop your instructional competencies and refine your basic teaching behaviors, drawing inspiration from every aspect of your professional and personal life. This development will continue throughout your professional career, as we discuss in the next section.

CHARACTERISTICS OF THE COMPETENT CLASSROOM TEACHER: AN ANNOTATED LIST

The overall purpose of this textbook is to assist you in the start of building your instructional competencies so you can be an effective professional. In order to do that, we need a starting place, and this is it: the identification and presentation of 22 specific competencies. (*Note:* The following list of 22 competencies has evolved from its earliest inception as a simple [not annotated] listing of 20 "Characteristics of the Competent Teacher" [Kim & Kellough, 1991; Kellough & Roberts, 1994; Kellough, 1994; Kellough & Kellough, 1999].) Please do not feel overwhelmed by the list; it may well be that no teacher expertly models all the characteristics that follow. The characteristics do, however, represent an ideal to strive for. (*Note:* You may want to identify other competencies. You may also want to compare the 22 here with the NBPTS Standards and the INTASC Principles that are listed in this book at the start of each chapter, and with Danielson's [1996] 22 "components of professional practice.") We advise you that this section is well suited to frequent rereading during the next few years of your teaching career.

The teacher is knowledgeable about the subject matter content expected to be taught. You should have both historical understanding and current knowledge of the structure of those subjects and content standards you are expected to teach, and of the facts, principles, concepts, and skills needed for those.

The teacher is an "educational broker." You will learn where and how to discover information about content you are expected to teach. You cannot know everything there is to know about each subject—indeed, you will not always be able to predict all that your students will learn—but you should become knowledgeable about where and how to best research it, and how to assist students in developing those same skills. Among other things, this means that you should be computer literate, that is, have the ability to understand and use computers for research and writing, paralleling reading and writing in verbal literacy.

The teacher is an active member of professional organizations, reads professional journals, confers with colleagues, maintains currency in methodology and about students, subject content, and skills to be taught. Although this book offers valuable information about teaching and learning, it is much closer to the start of your professional career than it is to the end. As a teacher you are a learner among learners; you will be perpetually learning.

The teacher understands the processes of learning. You will ensure that students understand the lesson objectives, classroom procedures, and your expectations; that they feel welcomed to your classroom and involved in learning activities; and that they have some control over the pacing of their own learning. Furthermore, when preparing your lessons, you will (1) consider the unique learning characteristics of each child; (2) present content in reasonably small doses and in a logical and coherent sequence while utilizing visual, verbal, tactile, and kinesthetic learning activities, with opportunities for guided practice and reinforcement; and (3) frequently check student comprehension to ensure they are learning.

> *Students learn a lot from the company they keep—including the intellectual habits of their teachers.*
>
> **—Deborah Meier (2005, p. 7)**

The teacher uses effective modeling behavior. Your own behavior must be consistent with what you expect of your students. If, for example, you expect your students to demonstrate regular and punctual attendance, to have their work done on time, to have their learning materials each day, to demonstrate cooperative behavior and respect for others, to maintain open and inquisitive minds, to demonstrate critical thinking, and to use proper communication skills, then you must do likewise, modeling those same behaviors and attitudes for them. As a teacher, you serve as a role model for your students. Whether you realize it or not, your behavior sends important messages to students that complement curriculum content. Those messages are important components of the hidden or covert curriculum (discussed in Chapter 5). You serve your students well when you model inclusive and collaborative approaches to learning. We present specific guidelines for effective modeling later in this chapter.

The teacher is open to change, willing to take risks and to be held accountable. If there were no difference between what is and what can be, then formal schooling would be of little value. To be a competent teacher, you must not only know historical and traditional values and knowledge, but you must also know the value of change and be willing to carefully plan and experiment, to move between the known and the unknown. Realizing that little of value is ever achieved without a certain amount of risk, and out of personal strength of convictions, competent teachers stand ready to be held accountable, as they undoubtedly will be, for assuming such risks.

No coward ever got the Great Teacher Award.

—**Selma Wassermann (1999)**

The teacher is nonprejudiced toward gender, sexual preference, ethnicity, skin color, religion, physical disability, socioeconomic status, learning disability, and national origin (as discussed in Chapter 1). Among other things, this means making no sexual innuendoes, religious or ethnic jokes, or racial slurs. It means being cognizant of how teachers, male and female, knowingly or unknowingly, historically have mistreated female students, and of how to avoid those same errors in your own teaching. It means learning about and attending to the needs of individual students in your classroom. It means having high, not necessarily identical, expectations for all students.

The teacher organizes the classroom and plans lessons carefully. You must prepare long-range plans and daily lessons thoughtfully, and reflect on, revise, and competently implement them with creative, motivating, and effective strategies and skill.

The teacher is a capable communicator. You will learn to use thoughtfully selected words, carefully planned questions, expressive voice inflections, useful pauses, meaningful gestures, and productive and nonconfusing body language. Some of these you carefully and thoughtfully plan during the preactive phase of your instruction; others will, through practice and reflection, become second-nature skills.

The teacher can function effectively as a decision maker. The elementary-school classroom is a complex place, busy with fast-paced activities. In a single day you may engage in a thousand or more interpersonal exchanges with children, to say nothing of the numerous exchanges possible with other adults. As a competent teacher you will initiate, rather than merely react, and be proactive and in control of your interactions, having learned how to manage time to analyze and develop effective interpersonal behaviors.

The teacher is in a perpetual learning mode, striving to further develop a repertoire of teaching strategies. As an effective teacher you also will be a serious student, continuing your own learning by reflecting on and assessing your work, attending workshops, studying the work of others, and talking with students, parents and guardians, and colleagues, sometimes over Internet bulletin boards.

The teacher demonstrates concern for children's safety and health. The competent teacher consistently models safety procedures, ensuring precautions necessary to protect the mental and physical health and safety of all students. You must strive to

The elementary school classroom is a complex place, busy with fast-paced activities. In a single day you may engage in a thousand or more interpersonal exchanges with children. No wonder you may feel exhausted at the end of your teaching day!

Scott Cunningham/Merrill

maintain a comfortable room temperature with adequate ventilation and to prevent safety hazards in the classroom. You should encourage students who are ill to stay home and to get well. If you suspect that a student may be ill or may be suffering from neglect or abuse (see Chapter 1), you must appropriately and promptly act on that suspicion by referring it to the school nurse, an appropriate administrator, or the Children's Protective Services (CPA).

The teacher demonstrates optimism for the learning of every child, while providing a constructive and positive environment for learning. Both common sense and research tell us clearly that students enjoy and learn better from a teacher who is positive and optimistic, encouraging, nurturing, and happy, rather than from a teacher who is negative and pessimistic, discouraging, uninterested, and grumpy.

Anyone who has spent time with a good teacher knows that content knowledge and classroom management skills are only two of the skills needed. Being able to connect with students is the critical third skill needed for effective teaching.

Source: Nancy Protheroe (2005, p. 51)

The teacher demonstrates confidence in each child's ability to learn. For a child, nothing at school is more satisfying than a teacher who demonstrates confidence in that student's abilities. Unfortunately, for some children, a teacher's show of confidence may be the only positive indicator that child ever receives. Each of us can recall with admiration a teacher (or other significant person) who expressed confidence in our ability to accomplish seemingly formidable tasks. As a competent teacher, you will demonstrate this confidence with each and every child.

The teacher is skillful and fair in employing strategies to assess student learning. You must become knowledgeable about the importance of providing immediate intensive intervention when learning problems become apparent and of implementing appropriate learning assessment tools, while avoiding the abuse of power afforded by the assessment process. (Assessment of student learning is the topic of Chapter 7.)

The teacher is skillful in working with parents and guardians, colleagues, administrators, and the support staff and maintains and nurtures friendly and ethical professional relationships. Teachers, parents and guardians, administrators, cooks, custodians, secretaries, and other adults of the school community all share one common purpose, and that is to serve students' education. This, of course, happens best when everyone cooperates. An exemplary school staff and skillful teachers work together to ensure that parents or guardians are involved in their children's learning.

The teacher demonstrates continuing interest in professional responsibilities and opportunities in the learning community. Knowing that ultimately each and every school activity has an effect on the classroom, the competent teacher assumes an active interest in the school community. The purpose of the school is to serve children's education, and the classroom is the primary, but not the only, place where this occurs. Every committee meeting, school event, faculty meeting, school board meeting, office, program, and any other planned function related to school life shares in the school's ultimate purpose. Unfortunately, involved adults sometimes forget and must be reminded of that fact.

The teacher exhibits a range of interests. This includes interest in students' activities and the many aspects of the school and its surrounding community. You are interesting in part because of your interests; a variety of interests more often motivates and captures the attention of more students. If you have few interests outside your subject and classroom, you will likely seem exceedingly dull to your students.

The teacher shares a healthy sense of humor. The positive effects of appropriate humor (humor that is not self-deprecating or disrespectful of others) on learning are well established: increased immune system activity and decreased stress-producing hormones; drop in the pulse rate; reduction of feelings of anxiety, tension, and stress; activated T-cells for the immune system, antibodies that fight against harmful microorganisms, and gamma interferon, a hormone that fights viruses and regulates cell growth; and increased blood oxygen. Because of these effects, humor is a stimulant to not only healthy living, but also to creativity and higher-level thinking. As they should, students appreciate and learn more from a teacher who shares a sense of humor and laughs with them. (Humor is one of the intelligent behaviors discussed in Chapter 3.)

The teacher is quick to recognize a child who may be in need of special attention. A competent teacher is alert to recognize any child who demonstrates behaviors indicating a need for special attention. For example, patterns of increasingly poor attendance or of steadily negative attention-seeking behavior are two of the more obvious early signals of a student who is potentially at risk of dropping out of

Activity 2.2: Are Teachers Prepared to Deal with the Severe Social and Emotional Problems Many Children Bring to School? If Not, Who Is?

Recently, in one metropolitan elementary school, 13 of the 20 students in a classroom had witnessed a drive-by shooting the previous day. The children could not stop talking about it, and the classroom teacher was having a difficult time settling them down. The school's full-time social worker stepped in to help counsel the children. The principal told the teacher that many of the kids at the school had seen the worst that life has to offer, including rape, physical abuse to the women in their lives, people being shot, fights, and home invasions.

1. How available are social workers to schools in your geographic area?
2. If social workers are not readily available, are teachers then expected to make home visits to prod chronically absent children to school and to help families obtain medicine, shoes, clothing, or whatever it is that has prevented the child from coming to school?
3. What, if anything, have you learned from this activity? What aspect of this problem would you like to learn more about?

school. You must know how and where to refer such a student, and how to do so with minimal class disruption and without embarrassment to the student.

The teacher makes specific and frequent efforts to demonstrate how the subject content may relate to students' lives. With effort, you can make a potentially dry and dull topic seem significant and alive. Regardless of the topic, somewhere there are competent teachers teaching that topic, and one of the significant characteristics of their effectiveness is they make the topic alive to themselves and their students, helping students make relevant connections. Time and again studies point out what should be obvious: Students don't learn much from dull, meaningless exercises and assignments. Such bland teaching may be a major cause of student disaffection with school. You may obtain ideas from professional journals, attend workshops, communicate with colleagues either personally or via electronic bulletin boards and Web sites, and use interdisciplinary thematic instruction to discover how to make a potentially dry and boring topic interesting and alive for students (and for yourself).

The teacher is reliable. The competent teacher can be relied on to fulfill professional responsibilities, promises, and commitments. If you cannot be relied on, you will quickly lose credibility with students (as well as with colleagues and administrators). Regardless of your potential for effectiveness, if you are an unreliable teacher you are an incompetent teacher. Also, teachers who are chronically absent from their teaching duties for whatever reason are "at-risk" teachers.

SELECTING AND USING MEDIA AND OTHER RESOURCES AND TOOLS FOR INSTRUCTION

This final section of this chapter focuses your attention on the important responsibility you have for using the cognitive tools available for helping students construct their understandings. You will be pleased to know that there is a large variety of useful and effective educational media, aids, and resources—electronic, print, and objects—from which to draw as you plan your instructional experiences. On the other

Activity 2.3: Is Technology Changing the Role of the Classroom Teacher?

In 1922 Thomas Edison predicted that "the motion picture is destined to revolutionize our educational system and . . . in a few years it will supplant largely, if not entirely, the use of textbooks." William Levenson of the Cleveland public schools' radio station claimed in 1945 that "the time may come when a portable radio receiver will be as common in the classroom as is the blackboard." In the early 1960s B. F. Skinner believed that with the help of the new teaching machines and programmed instruction, students could learn twice as much in the same time and with the same effort as in a standard classroom. Did motion pictures, radio, programmed instruction, and television revolutionize education? Will computers become as much a part of the classroom as writing boards? What do you predict the public school classroom of the year 2050 will be like? Will the teacher's role be different in any way than it is today?

hand, you could also become overwhelmed by the variety and sheer quantity of materials available for classroom use. You could spend a lot of time reviewing, sorting, selecting, and practicing with these materials and tools. Although nobody can make the job easier for you, information in this final section of this chapter may expedite the process. As you peruse this final topic in this chapter we remind you again, as we did in Chapter 1 (Figure 1.6), about starting your professional resources file.

The Internet

Originating from a Department of Defense project (called ARPAnet, named after the federal government's Advanced Research Projects Agency) at the University of California, Los Angeles, computer science department in 1969, to establish a computer network of military researchers, the federally funded Internet (also known as the "Information Superhighway" and "cyberspace" or just simply the "net") has, as you undoubtedly know, become an enormous, steadily expanding, worldwide system of connected computer networks. The Internet provides literally millions of resources to explore, with thousands more added nearly every day. Today you can surf the Internet and find many sources about how to use it, and you can walk into most any bookstore and find hundreds of recent titles, most of which give their authors' favorite Web sites. However, new technologies are steadily emerging, and the Internet changes every day, with some sites and resources disappearing or not kept current, others having changed their location and undergone reconstruction, and still other new ones appearing. Therefore, it would be superfluous for us in this book, which will be around for several years, to get too enthused about sites that we personally have viewed and can recommend as teacher resources. Nevertheless, recommended sites are listed at the end of each chapter.

There is such a proliferation of information today, from both printed materials and from information on the Internet, how can a person determine the validity and currency of a particular piece of information? When searching for useful and reliable information on a particular topic, how can one be protected from wasting valuable time sifting through all the information? Students need to know that just because information is found on a printed page or is published on the Internet doesn't necessarily mean that the information is accurate or current.

Teaching all students how to access and assess Web sites adds to their repertoire of skills for lifelong learning. Consider allowing each student or teams of students to become experts on specific sites during particular units of study. It might be useful to start a chronicle of student-recorded log entries about particular Web sites to provide comprehensive long-term data about those sites.

When students use information from the Internet, require that they print copies of sources of citations and materials so you can check for accuracy. These copies may be maintained in their portfolios.

Student work published on the Internet should be considered intellectual material and protected from plagiarism by others. Most school districts post a copyright notice on their home page. Someone at the school usually is assigned to supervise the school Web site to see that district and school policy and legal requirements are observed.

> *No generation has ever had to wait so little to get so much information.*
>
> —Lisa Renard (2005)

Professional Journals and Periodicals

Figure 2.3 lists examples of the many professional periodicals and journals that can provide useful teaching ideas and Web site information and that carry information about instructional materials and how to get them. Some of these may be in your university or college library and accessible through Internet sources. Check there for these and other titles of interest to you.

Copying Printed Materials

Remember that although on many Web pages there is no notice, the material is still copyrighted. Copyright law protects original material; that is just as true for the intellectual property created by a minor as it is for that of an adult.

Although space here prohibits full inclusion of U.S. legal guidelines, your local school district should be able to provide a copy of current district policies for compliance with copyright laws. District policies should include guidelines for teachers and students in publishing materials on the Internet. If no district guidelines are available, adhere to the guidelines shown in Figure 2.4 when using printed materials.

When preparing to make a copy, you must find out whether the law under the category of "permitted use" permits the copying. If not allowed under "permitted use," then you must get written permission to reproduce the material from the holder of the copyright. If the address of the source is not given on the material, addresses may be obtained from various references, such as *Literary Market Place*, *Audio-Visual Market Place*, and *Ulrich's International Periodical's Directory*.

American Biology Teacher	*Modern Language Journal*
American Educational Research Quarterly	*NEA Today*
American Music Teacher	*Negro Educational Review*
Childhood Education	*New Advocate, The*
Computing Teacher, The	*OAH Magazine of History*
Educational Horizons	*Phi Delta Kappan*
Educational Leadership	*Physical Education*
Edutopia	*Reading Teacher*
English Journal	*Reading Today*
English Language Teaching Journal	*School Arts*
Hispania	*School Library Journal*
History Teacher	*School Science and Mathematics*
Horn Book	*Science*
Instructor	*Science Activities*
Journal of Adolescent and Adult Literacy	*Science and Children*
Journal of Geography	*Science Scope*
Journal of Learning Disabilities	*Social Education*
Journal of Physical Education and Recreation	*Social Studies*
Journal of Teaching in Physical Education	*Teacher Magazine*
Language Arts	*Teaching Pre K–8*
Language Learning	*TESOL Quarterly*
Learning and Instruction	*Voices from the Middle*
Mathematics Teacher, The	*Young Children*
Middle School Journal	

FIGURE 2.3
Selected professional journals and periodicals for teachers

The Classroom Writing Board

As is true for an auto mechanic or a brain surgeon or any other professional, a teacher's professional responsibility is to know when and how to use the tools of the trade. One of the tools available to almost every elementary-school classroom teacher is the writing board. Can you imagine a classroom without a writing board? In this section, you will find guidelines for using this important tool.

They used to be, and in some schools still are, slate blackboards (slate is a type of metamorphic rock). In today's classroom, however, the writing board is more likely to be either a board that is painted plywood (chalkboard), which, like the blackboard, is also becoming obsolete, to some extent because of the need to be concerned about the dust created from using chalk; or a white or colored (light

PERMITTED USES: YOU MAY MAKE

1. Single copies of:
   - A chapter of a book
   - An article from a periodical, magazine, or newspaper
   - A short story, short essay, or short poem whether or not from a collected work
   - A chart, graph, diagram, drawing, cartoon
   - An illustration from a book, magazine, or newspaper

2. Multiple copies for classroom use (not to exceed one copy per student in a course) of:
   - A complete poem if less than 250 words
   - An except from a longer poem, but not to exceed 250 words
   - A complete article, story, or essay of less than 2,500 words
   - An excerpt from a larger printed work not to exceed 10 percent of the whole or 1,000 words
   - One chart, graph, diagram, cartoon, or picture per book or magazine issue

PROHIBITED USES: YOU MAY *NOT*

1. Copy more than one work or two excerpts from a single author during one class term (semester or year).

2. Copy more than three works from a collective work or periodical volume during one class term.

3. Reproduce more than nine sets of multiple copies for distribution to students in one class term.

4. Copy to create, replace, or substitute for anthologies or collective works.

5. Copy "consumable" works (e.g., workbooks, standardized tests, or answer sheets).

6. Copy the same work year after year.

FIGURE 2.4
Guidelines for copying printed materials that are copyrighted
Source: Section 107 of the 1976 Federal Omnibus Copyright Revision Act.

green and light blue are common) *multipurpose dry-erase board* on which you write with special marking pens and erase with any soft cloth. In addition to providing a surface on which you can write and draw, the multipurpose board can be used as a projection screen and as a surface to which figures cut from colored transparency film will stick. It may also have a magnetic backing.

Extending the purposes of the multipurpose board and correlated with modern technology is an *electronic whiteboard* that can transfer information that is written on it to a connected computer and monitor, which in turn can save the material as a computer file. The electronic whiteboard uses dry-erase markers and special erasers that have optically encoded sleeves that enable the device to track their position on the board. The data are then converted into a display for the computer monitor, which may then be printed, cut and pasted into other applications, sent as an e-mail or fax message, or networked to other sites.

Each day, each class, and even each new idea should begin with a clean board, except for announcements that have been placed there by you or another teacher. At the end of each class, clean the board, especially if another teacher follows you in using that room (professional courtesy).

Use colored chalk or marking pens to highlight your board talk. This is especially helpful for students with learning difficulties. Beginning at the top left of the board, print or write neatly and clearly, with the writing intentionally positioned to indicate content relationships (e.g., causal, oppositional, numerical, comparative, categorical, and so on). Use the writing board to acknowledge acceptance and to record student contributions. Print instructions for an activity on the board, in addition to giving them orally. At the top of the board frame, you might find clips for hanging posters, maps, and charts.

Learn to use the board without having to turn your back entirely on the children and without blocking their view of the board. When you have a lot of material to put on the board, do it before class and then cover it, or better yet, put the material on transparencies and use the overhead projector or use a PowerPoint presentation rather than the board, or use both. Be careful not to write too much information.

The Classroom Bulletin Board

Bulletin boards also are found in nearly every classroom, and although sometimes poorly used or not used at all, they can be relatively inexpensively transformed into attractive and valuable instructional tools. Among other uses, the bulletin board is a convenient location to post reminders, assignments and schedules, and commercially produced materials, and to celebrate and display model student work and anchor papers. To plan, design, and prepare bulletin board displays, some teachers use student assistants or committees, giving those students guidance and responsibility for planning, preparing, and maintaining bulletin board displays.

When preparing a bulletin board display, keep these guidelines in mind: The display should be simple, emphasizing one main idea, concept, topic, or theme, and captions should be short and concise; illustrations can accent learning topics; verbs can vitalize the captions; phrases can punctuate a student's thoughts; and alliteration can announce anything you wish on the board. Finally, as in all other aspects of the classroom learning environment, remember to ensure that the board display reflects gender and ethnic equity.

Community Resources

One of the richest resources for learning is the local community and the people and places in it. You will want to build your own file of community resources— speakers, sources for free materials, and field trip locations. Your school may already have a community resource file available for your use. However, it may need updating. A community resource file should contain information about (a) possible field trip locations; (b) community resource people who could serve as guest speakers, presenters, or mentors; and (c) local agencies that can provide information and instructional materials. See Figure 2.5.

Airport	Highway patrol station
Apiary	Historical sites and monuments
Aquarium	Industrial plant
Archeological site	Legislature session
Art gallery	Levee and water reservoir
Assembly plant	Library and archive
Bakery	Native American Indian reservation
Bird and wildlife sanctuary	Mass transit authority
Book publisher	Military installation
Bookstore	Mine
Broadcasting and TV station	Museum
Building being razed	Newspaper plant
Building under construction	Observatory
Canal lock	Oil refinery
Cemetery	Park
Chemical plant	Poetry reading
City or county planning commission	Post office and package delivery company
Courthouse	Police station
Dairy	Recycling center
Dam and flood plain	Retail store
Dock and harbor	Sanitation department
Factory	Sawmill or lumber company
Farm	Shopping mall
Fire department	Shoreline (stream, lake, wetland, ocean)
Fish hatchery	Telecommunications center
Flea market	Town meeting
Foreign embassy	Utility company
Forest and forest preserve	Universities and colleges
Freeway under construction	Warehouse
Gas company	Water reservoir and treatment plant
Geological site	Wildlife park and preserve
Health department and hospital	Weather bureau and storm center
Highway construction site	Zoo

FIGURE 2.5
Community resources for speakers, materials, and field trips

There are many ways of using community resources, and a variety is demonstrated by the schools specifically mentioned throughout this book (see Schools in the index). Here the discussion is limited to two often used, although sometimes abused, instructional tools: (a) guest speakers or presenters and (b) out-of-classroom and off-campus excursions, commonly called field trips.

Guest Speaker or Presenter   Bringing outside speakers or presenters into your classroom can be a valuable educational experience for students, but not automatically so. In essence, guest speakers can be classified within a spectrum of four types, two of which should not be considered: (a) Ideally, a speaker is both informative and inspiring; (b) a speaker may be inspiring but with nothing substantive to offer, except for the possible diversion it might offer from the usual rigors of classroom work; (c) the speaker might be informative but boring to students; (d) at the worst end of this spectrum is the guest speaker who is both boring and uninformative. So, just like any other instructional experience, to make a guest speaking experience most effective takes your careful planning. To make sure that the experience is beneficial to student learning, consider the following guidelines.

- If at all possible, meet and talk with the guest speaker in advance to inform him or her about your students and your expectations for the presentation and to gauge how motivational and informative he or she might be. If you believe the speaker might be informative but boring, then perhaps you can help structure the presentation in some way to make the presentation a bit more inspiring. For example, stop the speaker every few minutes and involve the students in questions and discussions of points made.
- Prepare students in advance with key points of information that you expect them to obtain.
- Prepare students with questions to ask the speaker, things the students want to find out, and information you want them to inquire about.
- Follow up the presentation with a thank-you letter to the guest speaker and perhaps further questions that developed during class discussions subsequent to the speaker's presentation.
- Be sure you have a backup lesson plan in the eventuality the guest is late or fails to show.
- Consider briefing the guest ahead of time about any dos and don'ts and any particular sensitivities among your students.

Field Trips   What is the most memorable field trip that you were ever on as a student? Do you recall what made it memorable? You may want to discuss these questions and others like them and their responses with your classmates or members of your teaching team.

Today's schools often have very limited funds for the transportation and liability costs for field trips. In some cases, there are no funds at all (for example,

As with the use of any other instructional activity, to be successful a field trip needs careful planning.

Anthony Magnacca/Merrill

see the Standen entry in the suggested readings at the end of this chapter), in which case student field trips are electronic, online only. At times, parent–teacher groups and business and civic organizations help by providing financial resources so that children get valuable firsthand experiences that field trips so often afford.

To prepare for and implement a successful field trip, there are three important stages of planning—before, during, and after—and critical decisions to be made at each stage. Consider the following guidelines.

Before the Field Trip   When the field trip is your idea (and not the students), discuss the idea with your teaching team or principal (especially when transportation will be needed) *before* mentioning the idea to your students. Also you may discover that the place you had in mind is in fact an overused site for field trips, and many or most of your students have already been there. Also carefully consider the worth of the proposed field trip; don't use valuable resources for field trips for trivial learnings. The bottom line is that there is no cause served by getting students excited about a trip before you know if it is feasible.

Once you have obtained the necessary, but tentative, approval from school officials, take the trip yourself (or with team members), if possible. A previsit allows you to determine how to make the field trip most productive and what arrangements will be necessary. If a previsit is not possible, you still will need to arrange for travel directions, arrival and departure times, parking, briefing by the host, if there is one, storage of students' personal items, such as coats and lunches, provisions for eating and restrooms, and fees, if any.

If there are fees, you need to talk with your administration about who will pay the fees. If the trip is worth taking, the school should cover the costs. If that is not possible, perhaps students can plan a fund-raising activity or financial assistance can be obtained from some other source. If this does not work, you might consider an alternative that does not involve financial costs.

Arrange for official permission from the school administration. This usually requires a form for requesting, planning, and reporting field trips. After permission has been obtained, you can discuss the field trip with your students and arrange for permissions from their parents or guardians. You need to realize that although parents or guardians sign official permission forms allowing their children to participate in the trip, these only show that the parents or guardians are aware of what will take place and give their permission for their child to participate. Although the permission form should include a statement that the parent or guardian absolves the teacher and the school from liability should an accident occur, it does not lessen the teacher's and the school's responsibilities should there be negligence by a teacher, driver, or chaperone.

If relevant, arrange for students to be excused from their other classes while on the field trip. Using an information form prepared and signed by you and perhaps by the principal, the students should then assume responsibility for notifying their other teachers of the planned absence from classes and for assuring them that whatever work is missed will be made up. In addition, you may need to make arrangements for your own teaching duties to be covered. In some schools, teachers cooperate by filling in for those who will be gone. In other schools, substitute teachers are hired. Unfortunately, sometimes teachers must hire their own substitute.

Arrange to have a cell phone available for your use during the trip. Some schools have a cell phone available for just that purpose. If not, and you don't have your own, perhaps one of the drivers or other adult chaperones does have one. Check it out.

Arrange for whatever transportation is needed. Your principal, or the principal's designee, will help you with the details. In many schools, someone else is responsible for arranging transportation. In any case, the use of private automobiles is ill advised, because you and the school could be liable for the acts of the drivers.

Arrange for the collection of money that is needed for fees. If there are out-of-pocket costs to be paid by students, this information needs to be included on the permission form. No students should ever be excluded from the field trip because of a lack of money. This can be a tricky issue, because there may be some students who would rather steal the money for a field trip than admit they don't have it. Try to anticipate problems; hopefully the school or some organization can pay for the trip so that fees need not be collected from students, and therefore potential problems of this sort are avoided.

Plan details for student safety and the monitoring of their safety from departure to return. Included should be a first-aid kit and a system of student control, such as a buddy system, whereby students must remain paired throughout the trip. The pairs sometimes are given numbers that are recorded and kept by the teacher and the chaperones, and then checked at departure time, periodically during the trip, at the time of return, and again upon return. Use adult chaperones. As a general rule, there should be one adult chaperone for every 10 children. Some districts have a policy regarding this. While on a field trip, at all times all children should be under the direct supervision of a dependable adult.

Plan the complete route and schedule, including any stops along the way. If transportation is being provided, you will need to discuss the plans with the provider.

Establish and discuss, to the extent you believe necessary, the rules of behavior your students should follow. Included in this might be details of the trip, its purpose, directions, what they should wear and bring, academic expectations of them (for example, consider giving each student a study guide), and follow-up activities. Also included should be information about what to do if anything should go awry, for example, if a student is late for the departure or return, loses a personal possession along the way, gets lost, is injured, becomes sick, or misbehaves. For the latter, never send a misbehaving student back to school alone. Involve the adult chaperones in the previsit discussion. All of this information should also be included on the parental/guardian permission form.

If a field trip is supposed to promote some kind of learning, as undoubtedly will be the case unless the sole purpose is something like an end-of-term or end-of-unit celebration, then to avoid leaving it to chance, the learning expectations need to be clearly defined and the students given an explanation of how and where they may encounter the learning experience. Before the field trip, students should be asked questions such as, What do we already know about _____? What do we want to find out about _____? How can we find out? and then, with their assistance, an appropriate guide can be prepared for the students to use during the field trip.

To further ensure learning and individual student responsibility for that learning, you may want to assign different roles and responsibilities to students, just as would be done in cooperative learning, ensuring that each student has a role with responsibility.

You may want to take recording equipment so the field trip experience can be relived and shared in class on return. If so, roles and responsibilities for the equipment and its care and use can be assigned to students as well.

During the Field Trip   If your field trip has been carefully planned according to the preceding guidelines, it should be a valuable and safe experience for all. Enroute, while at the trip location, and on the return to school, you and the adult chaperones should monitor student behavior and learning just as you do in the classroom.

After the Field Trip   Plan the follow-up activities. As with any other lesson plan, the field trip lesson is complete only when there is both a proper introduction and a well-planned and executed closure. All sorts of follow-up activities can be planned as an educational wrap-up to this educational experience. For example, a bulletin board committee can plan and prepare an attractive display summarizing the trip. Students can write (or draw) about their experiences in their journals or as papers. Small groups can give oral reports to the class about what they did and learned. Their reports can then serve as springboards for further class discussion and perhaps further investigations. Finally, for future planning, all who were involved should contribute to an assessment of the experience.

Media Tools

Media tools are instructional devices that project light and sound and focus images on screens. Included are projectors of various sorts, computers, CD-ROMs, DVDs, sound recorders, and video recorders. The aim here is not to provide instruction on how to operate equipment but to help you develop a philosophy for using it and to provide strategies for using media tools in your teaching. Consequently, to conserve space in this book, except for the overhead projector, which in some respects is more practical than the writing board, we devote no attention to traditional AV equipment, such as film projectors, VCRs, opaque projectors. There are staff members on any school faculty who gladly will assist you in locating and using those tools if you so desire or need.

It is important to remember that the role of media tools is to aid student learning, not to teach for you. You must still select the objectives, orchestrate the instructional plan, assess the results, and follow up the lessons, just as you learn to do with various other instructional strategies. If you use media tools prudently, your teaching and students' learning will benefit. Like a competent brain surgeon or a competent auto mechanic, a competent teacher knows when and how to select and use the right tools at the right time. Would you want to be operated on by a surgeon who was unfamiliar with the tools used in surgery? The education of children should be no less important.

TEACHING IN PRACTICE What Is Mr. Klutz's Problem and How Can It Be Resolved?

Although Mr. Klutz is considered to be a good beginning teacher, things rarely work well for him when he uses materials and media. Right in the middle of a lesson, he often discovers that he is missing some important piece of equipment or material he needs to complete the lesson or a machine breaks down. On the very first day of school, with all the children sitting attentively to his initial greeting and presentation, as he was about to write their first assignment on the chalkboard he realized he had no chalk. Once, he was going to demonstrate to the children how a candle extinguishes when covered with a glass jar. He had the candles and the jar all right, but he forgot to bring matches. Another time, he planned to use an overhead projector, only to find at the last minute that the electrical cord was too short to reach the wall outlet, and he had no extension cord. Yesterday, while giving a PowerPoint presentation, the computer froze. Such situations always seemed to happen at the worst unexpected time to surprise Mr. Klutz and spoil his plans and lesson presentations.

Questions for Class Discussion

1. Does Mr. Klutz remind you of any teacher you have known?
2. Is it possible for Mr. Klutz' carelessness to result in other, more serious, problems?
3. What action would you take to avoid such unexpected and unwanted outcomes?
4. Is it possible for a teacher while classed "highly qualified" to also be grossly incompetent?

When Equipment Malfunctions   When using media equipment, it is nearly always best to set up the equipment and have it ready to go before students arrive. That helps avoid problems in classroom management that can occur when there is a delay because the equipment is not ready. After all, if you were a surgeon ready to begin an operation and your tools and equipment weren't ready, your patient's life would likely be placed in extra danger. Like any other competent professional, a competent teacher is ready when the work is scheduled to begin.

Of course, delays may be unavoidable when equipment malfunctions. Recall Murphy's law, which says if anything can go wrong, it will? It is particularly relevant when using media equipment. You want to be prepared for such emergencies. Effectively planning for and responding to this eventuality is an important element of your system of movement management and takes place during the planning phase of instruction. That preparation includes consideration of a number of factors.

When equipment malfunctions, three principles should be in mind: (a) avoid dead time in the instruction; (b) avoid causing permanent damage to equipment; and (c) avoid losing content continuity of a lesson. So, what do you do when equipment breaks down? Again, the answer is: Be prepared for the eventuality.

If an overhead projector bulb expires, quickly insert another. That means you should have an extra bulb on hand and know how to replace it. If the computer screen freezes during direct, whole-class instruction you should probably quickly move to an alternate activity. If it is during multilevel instruction, then while maintaining your classroom withitness, you can probably take the time to treat this as a teachable moment and show the student who is working on the computer what to do, which probably would be simply how to restart the computer. If it occurs during a PowerPoint presentation, then you might be able to continue simply by moving to an available overhead projector or to the writing board.

If, during surgery, a patient's cerebral artery suddenly and unexpectedly ruptures, the surgeon and the surgical team are ready and make the necessary repair. If while working on an automobile a part breaks, the mechanic obtains a replacement part. If, while teaching, a computer program freezes or aborts on the screen, or if a fuse blows or for some other reason you lose power and you feel that there is going to be too much dead time before the equipment is working again, that is the time to go to an alternate lesson plan. You have probably heard the expression "Go to Plan B." It is a useful phrase; what it means is that without missing a beat in the lesson, to accomplish the same instructional objective or another objective, you immediately and smoothly switch to an alternate learning activity. For you, the beginning teacher, it does not mean that you must plan two lessons for every one, but that when planning a lesson that uses media equipment, you should plan in your lesson an alternative activity, just in case. Then, you move your students into the planned alternative activity quickly and smoothly. Your state of preparedness and smoothness in your action will impress your students, with them seeing you as a competent and well-prepared teacher.

The Overhead Projector In addition to a writing board and a bulletin board, nearly every elementary-school classroom is equipped with an overhead projector. The overhead projector is a versatile, effective, and reliable teaching tool. Except for the bulb burning out, not much else can go wrong. There is no film to break or program to crash.

The overhead projector projects light through objects that are transparent. A properly functioning overhead projector usually works quite well in a fully lit room. Truly portable overhead projectors are available that can be carried easily from place to place in their compact cases.

Other types of modern-day overhead projectors include rear-projection systems that allow the teacher to stand off to the side rather than between students and the screen and overhead video projectors that use video cameras to send images that are projected by television monitors. Some schools use overhead video camera technology that focuses on an object, pages of a book, or a demonstration, while sending a clear image to a video monitor with a screen large enough for an entire class to clearly see.

In some respects, the overhead projector is more practical than the writing board, particularly for a teacher who is nervous. Using the overhead projector rather than the writing board can help avoid tension by decreasing the need to pace back and forth to the board. And by using an overhead projector rather than a writing board, you can maintain both eye contact and physical proximity with your students, both of which are important for maintaining classroom control.

Guidelines for Using the Overhead Projector As with any projector, find the best place in your classroom to position it. If there is no classroom projection screen, you can hang white paper or a sheet, use a white multipurpose board, or use a white or near-white wall.

Have you ever attended a presentation by someone who was not using an overhead projector properly? It can be frustrating to members of an audience when the image is too small, out of focus, partially off the screen, or partially blocked from view by the presenter. To use this teaching tool in a professional manner:

- Place the projector so the projected white light covers the entire screen and hits the screen at a 90-degree angle, and then focus the image to be projected.
- Face the students while using the projector. The fact that you do not lose eye contact with your students is a major advantage of using the overhead projector rather than a writing board. (A PowerPoint presentation provides the same advantage.) What you write as you face your students will show up perfectly (unless out of focus or off the screen).

- Lay the pencil directly on the transparency with the tip of the pencil pointing to the detail being emphasized rather than using your finger to point to detail or pointing to the screen (thereby turning away from your students).
- To lessen distraction, turn the projector off when you want student attention shifted back to you.

For writing on overhead projector transparencies, ordinary felt-tip pens are not satisfactory. Select a transparency-marking pen available at an office supply store. The ink of these pens is water-soluble, so keep the palm of your hand from resting on the transparency, or you will have ink smudges on your transparency and on your hand. Non-water-soluble pens—permanent markers—can be used, but the transparency must be cleaned with an alcohol solvent or a plastic eraser. When using a cleaning solvent, you can clean and dry with paper toweling or a soft rag. To highlight the writing on a transparency and to organize student learning, use pens in a variety of colors. Transparency pens tend to dry out quickly, and they are relatively expensive, so the caps must be taken on and off frequently, which is something of a nuisance when working with several colors. Practice writing on a transparency, and also practice making overlays. You can use an acetate transparency roll or single sheets of flat transparencies. Flat sheets of transparency come in different colors—clear, red, blue, yellow, and green—which can be useful in making overlays.

Some teachers prepare lesson outlines in advance on transparencies, which allows more careful preparation of the transparencies and means that they are then ready for reuse at another time. Some teachers use an opaque material, such as a 3 × 5 note card, to block out prewritten material and then uncover it at the moment it is being discussed. For preparation of permanent transparencies, you will probably want to use permanent marker pens, rather than those that are water soluble and easily smudged. Heavy paper frames are available for permanent transparencies; marginal notes can be written on the frames. Personal computers with laser printers and thermal processing (copy) machines, probably located in the teacher's workroom or in the school's main office, can be used to make permanent transparencies.

Another function of the overhead projector is made possible by the fact that transparent objects can be placed on the platform and displayed on the screen, objects such as transparent rulers, protractors, and Petri dishes for science activities; even opaque objects can be used if you want simply to show silhouette, as you might in math and art activities. The overhead projector can also be used for tracing transparent charts or drawings into larger drawings on paper or on the writing board. The image projected onto the screen can be made smaller or larger by moving the projector closer or farther away, respectively, and then traced when you have the size you want. An overhead projector can be used also as a light source (spotlight) to highlight demonstrations.

The Document Camera   Although more expensive than overhead projectors, document cameras are increasing in popularity in classrooms across the country. When connected to a computer and projector, the document camera becomes a very versatile presentation tool. In addition to displaying text you can project 3-D objects, slides, and other microscopic objects, and you can zoom in on objects.

Multimedia Program   A multimedia program is a collection of teaching and learning materials involving more than one type of medium and organized around a single theme or topic. The types of media involved vary from rather simple kits—perhaps including CDs, games, activity cards, student worksheets, and manuals of instructions for the teacher—to sophisticated packages involving building-level site-licensed computer software, student handbooks, reproducible activity worksheets, classroom wall hangings, and online subscriptions to telecommunication networks. Some kits are designed for teacher use, others by individual or small groups of students; yet many more are designed for the collaborative use of students and teachers. Teachers sometimes incorporate multimedia programs with learning activity centers.

Computers and Computer-Based Instructional Tools

As a teacher, the computer can be valuable to you in several ways. For example, the computer can help you manage the instruction by obtaining information, storing and preparing test materials, maintaining attendance and grade records, and preparing programs to aid in the academic development of individual students. This category of uses of the computer is referred to as *computer-managed instruction (CMI).*

The computer can also be used for instruction by employing various instructional software programs, and it can be used to teach about computers and to help students develop their metacognitive skills as well as their skills in computer use.

Computers in the elementary school classroom are becoming increasingly common and when used properly are valuable tools for teaching and learning.

Patrick White/Merrill

When the computer is used to assist students in their learning, it is called *computer-assisted instruction (CAI)* or *computer-assisted learning (CAL)*.

TPW Video Classroom

Series: General Methods

Module 3: Unit and Lesson Planning

Video 1: Computers in the Classroom

The Placement and Use of Computers: The Online Classroom   Teachers looking to make their classrooms more student centered, collaborative, and interactive continue to increasingly turn to telecommunications networks. Webs of connected computers allow teachers and students from around the world to reach each other directly and gain access to quantities of information previously unimaginable. Students using networks learn new inquiry and analytical skills in a stimulating environment, and they can also gain an increased awareness of their role as world citizens. Just imagine, for example, students in a classroom in Kansas in direct online communication with scientists working at the North Pole or at the bottom of the Pacific Ocean, possibilities only dreamed of just a generation ago.

How you use the computer for instruction and learning is determined by several factors, including your knowledge of and skills in its use, the number of computers that you have available for instructional use, where computers are placed in the school, the software that is available, printer availability, and the telecommunications capabilities (that is, wiring and phone lines, modems, and servers).

Schools continue to purchase or to lease computers and to upgrade their telecommunications capabilities. Regarding computer placement and equipment and technological support available, here are some possible scenarios and how classroom teachers work within each.

SCENARIO 1. With the assistance of a computer lab and the lab technician, computers are integrated into the whole curriculum. In collaboration with members of interdisciplinary teaching teams, in a computer lab students use computers, software, and sources on the Internet as tools to build their knowledge, to write stories with word processors, to illustrate diagrams with paint utilities, to create interactive reports with hypermedia, and to graph data they have gathered using spreadsheets.

SCENARIO 2. In some schools, students take a computer class as an elective or exploratory course. Students in your classes who are simultaneously enrolled in such a course may be given special computer assignments by you that they can then share with the rest of the class.

SCENARIO 3. Some classrooms have a computer connected to a large-screen video monitor. The teacher or a student works the computer, and the entire class can see the monitor screen. As they view the screen, students can verbally respond to and interact with what is happening on the computer.

Presentation software, such as Microsoft's PowerPoint, can help teachers, and students, create powerful on-screen presentations. First developed for use in the world of business for reports at sales meetings and with clients, educators quickly became aware of the power provided by presentation software to display, illustrate, and elucidate information. From the world of business, presentation software made its way into university classrooms and then into K–12 classrooms to where today it is not uncommon for it to be used even by kindergarten children in their own presentations. Whenever students are using modern presentation software, it is the teacher's responsibility to ensure that students don't become so fixated on fonts and formats and other aspects of the technology that insufficient thinking is given to the content of their presentation. Of course, that is not more a concern for electronic presentations than when students are using any other format to display their work, such as an interactive, student-created bulletin board.

SCENARIO 4. You may be fortunate to have one or more computers in your classroom for all or a portion of the school year, computers with Internet connections and CD-ROM playing capabilities, an overhead projector, and a LCD (liquid crystal display) projection system. Coupled with the overhead projector, the LCD projection system allows you to project onto your large wall screen (and TV monitor at the same time) any image from computer software or a videodisc. With this system, all students can see and verbally interact with the multimedia instruction.

SCENARIO 5. Many classrooms have at least one computer with telecommunications capability, and some have many. In some schools there is one laptop or one handheld for each student. When the former is the case in your classroom, then you most likely will have one or two students working at the computer station while others are doing other learning activities (multilevel teaching). When the latter is the case, many new exciting avenues of opportunity for learning exist as well as opening up new management challenges for the teacher. Whichever of these is the case in your classroom, computers can be an integral part of a learning center and an important aid in your overall effort to personalize the instruction within your classroom.

Using Copyrighted Video, Computer, and Multimedia Programs

You have a responsibility to be knowledgeable about the laws on the use of copyrighted videos and computer software materials. Although space here prohibits full inclusion of U.S. legal guidelines, your local school district undoubtedly can provide you with a copy of current district policies to ensure your compliance with all copyright laws. As was discussed earlier in the discussion about the use of printed materials that are copyrighted, when preparing to make any copy, you must find out whether the law under the category of "permitted use" permits the copying. If not allowed under "permitted use," then you must get written permission to reproduce the material from the holder of the copyright. Figure 2.6 presents guidelines for the copying of computer software.

Usually, when purchasing CD-ROMs, DVDs, and other multimedia software packages intended for schools' use, you are also paying for a license to modify and

---

PERMITTED USES—YOU MAY:

1. Make a single back-up or archival copy of the computer program.
2. Adapt the computer program to another language if the program is unavailable in the target language.
3. Add features to make better use of the computer program.

PROHIBITED USES—YOU MAY *NOT*:

1. Make multiple copies.
2. Make replacement copies from an archival or back-up copy.
3. Make copies of copyrighted programs to be sold, leased, loaned, transmitted, or given away.

FIGURE 2.6
Copyright law for use of computer software
Source: December, 1980, Congressional amendment to the 1976 Copyright Act.

use its contents for instructional purposes. However, not all CD-ROMs and DVDs include copyright permission, so always check the copyright notice on any package you purchase and use. Whenever in doubt, don't use it until you have asked your district media specialists about copyrights or have obtained necessary permissions from the original source.

A general rule of thumb for use of any copyrighted material is to treat the work of others as you would want your own material treated were it protected by a copyright (see Figure 2.7).

---

1. For portions of copyrighted works used in your own multimedia production for use in teaching, follow normal copyright guidelines (e.g., the limitations on the amount of material used, whether it be motion media, text, music, illustrations, photographs, or computer software).

2. You may display your own multimedia work using copyrighted works to other teachers, such as in workshops. However, you may *not* make and distribute copies to colleagues without obtaining permission from copyright holders.

3. You may use your own multimedia production for instruction over an electronic network (e.g., distance learning) provided there are limits to access and to the number of students enrolled. You may *not* distribute such work over any electronic network (local area or wide area) without expressed permission from copyright holders.

4. You must obtain permissions from copyright holders before using any copyrighted materials in educational multimedia productions for commercial reproduction and distribution or before replicating more than one copy, distributing copies to others, or for use beyond your own classroom.

FIGURE 2.7
Fair use guidelines for using multimedia programs

SUMMARY

You have reviewed the realities of the responsibilities of today's elementary school classroom teacher. Becoming and remaining a good teacher takes time, commitment, concentrated effort, and just plain hard work. Anyone who ever said that good teaching was easy work didn't know what he or she was talking about.

You have learned that your professional responsibilities as a classroom teacher will extend well beyond the four walls of the classroom, the 6 hours of the school day, the 5 days of the school week, and the 180 days of the school year. You learned of the many expectations: to demonstrate effective decision making; to be committed to young people, to the school's mission, and to the profession; to develop facilitating behaviors; and to provide effective instruction. As you have read and discussed these behaviors and responsibilities, you should have begun to fully comprehend the challenge and reality of being a competent elementary-school classroom teacher.

Today, there seems to be much agreement that the essence of learning is a combined process of self-awareness, self-monitoring, and active reflection. Children learn these skills best when exposed to teachers who themselves effectively model the same behaviors. The most effective teaching and learning is interactive and involves not only learning, but also thinking about learning and learning how to learn.

Throughout your teaching career you will continue improving your knowledge and skills in all aspects of teaching and learning. Through experience, workshops, advanced coursework, coaching, and training; through acquiring further knowledge by reading and study; and through collaborating with and role-modeling by significant and more experienced colleagues, you will be in a perpetual learning mode.

> A long, successful, and personally satisfying career does not just happen via entitlement, but from intelligent, persistent, and arduous focus.

Now that you perceive the magnitude of the professional responsibilities of the elementary school classroom teacher, Chapter 3 focuses your attention on how to help your students develop their skills in thinking and questioning.

STUDY QUESTIONS AND ADDITIONAL ACTIVITIES

1. Select a teacher whom you admired when you were an elementary-school student. What characteristics did this person possess? Do you see any of those qualities in yourself?
2. Describe the behavioral differences you would expect to see in a teacher who operates essentially as a reflective practitioner as opposed to one who is mainly a technician.
3. Explain the meaning of each of the following concepts and why you agree or disagree with each: (a) The teacher should hold high, although not necessarily identical, expectations for all students and never waver from those expectations.

(b) The teacher should not feel compelled to "cover" the content of the text-book or adopted curriculum program by the end of the school term.

4. In some schools, kindergartners and English language learners use iPods to help master vocabulary, while children of all grades use PlayStations for math games. Share with others in your class what you can find about the use and impact of these and other modern technological tools on student learning.

5. Talk with experienced teachers and find out how they remain current in their teaching fields. Share your learning with others in your class.

6. Are modern learning theory and the concept of mandatory competency testing compatible ideas, or do they create a dilemma for the classroom teacher? Explain your response.

7. Distinguish the use of *praise* and of *encouragement* for student work; for a specific grade level (identify it) describe specific classroom situations in which each is more appropriate.

8. In *Educating the Reflective Practitioner* (San Francisco: Jossey-Bass, 1987), Donald Schon speaks of "reflection-on-action," "reflection-in-action," and "reflection-for-action." Read about and compare Schon's three types of reflections with Costa's four phases of decision making and thought processing discussed at the beginning of this chapter.

9. Refer to the section in this chapter, "Modeling Appropriate Behaviors." From the list of teacher behaviors there, identify no less than five ways a teacher's inappropriate behavior would send a negative message via the covert curriculum. What effect, if any, do you believe a teacher's incongruent behavior has on children in the classroom?

10. Explain how you feel today about being a classroom teacher—for example, are you motivated, excited, enthusiastic, befuddled, confused, depressed? Explain and discuss your current feelings with your classmates. Sort out common concerns and design avenues for dealing with any negative feelings you might have.

WEB SITES RELATED TO CONTENT OF THIS CHAPTER

- Answers.com *www.answers.com*
- California Instructional Technology Clearinghouse *clrn.org/home*
- Center for Children and Technology *www2.edc.org/CCT/index.asp*
- Children's Partnership *www.childrenspartnership.org*
- ClassNotesOnline *www.ClassNotesOnline.com*
- Consortium for School Networking *www.cosn.org*
- Copyright guidelines and information *www.lib.washington.edu/help/guides/copyright.html*
- Deep Web information source *www.deepweb.com*
- Document camera *www.elmousa.com*
- Electronic boards: *www.cogsystech.com*; *www.gtcocalcomp.com*; *interactivewhiteboards.com*; *www.smarttech.com*
- Electronic Reference Formats *www.apa.org*
- Finding information on the Internet *www.lib.berkeley.edu/TeachingLib/Guides/Internet/FindInfo.html*

- Free government materials *www.ed.gov/free*
- Gateway to Educational Materials (GEM) *www.thegateway.org*
- International Telementor Program *www.telementor.org*
- Learn the Net *www.learnthenet.com*
- Mathematics Archives *archives.math.utk.edu*
- National Archives and Records Administration *www.Archives.gov*
- National Center for Educational Statistics *nces.ed.gov*
- National Geographic Map Machine *www.nationalgeographic.com*
- NBPTS standards *www.nbpts.org*
- NetDay *www.netday.org*
- No Child Left Behind Act *www.ed.gov/legislation/esea02*
- Online field trips *www.thinkport.org*
- PDA use *www.scilib.ucsd.edu/bml/pda/intro.htm*
- PowerPoint use *www.electricteacher.com/tutorial3.htm*; *staff.philau.edu/bells/ppt.html*; *www.bitbetter.com/powertips.htm*
- Software Information & Industry Association *www.siia.net*
- Spreadsheet tutorials *www.teachers.teach-nology.com/themes/comp/spreadsheets*
- State education resource organizations directory *www.ed.gov/Programs/bastmp/SEA.htm*
- Teacher's Network *www.teachnet.org*
- Tech Corps *techcorps.org*
- U.S. Department of Education, Office of Technology *www.ed.gov/Technology/index.html*
- Word Processing Tutorials *www.tutorialfind.com/tutorials/computerbasics/wordprocessing*

FOR FURTHER READING

Bomar, L. (2006). iPods as reading tools. *Principal*, *85*(5), 52–53.

Coiro, J. (2005). Making sense of online text. *Educational Leadership*, *63*(2), 30–35.

Eagleton, M. B., & Dobler, E. (2007). *Reading the Web: strategies for Internet inquiry*. New York: Guilford.

Fay, K., & Whaley, S. (2005). The gift of attention. *Educational Leadership*, *62*(4), 76–79.

Guarino, C. M., Hamilton, L. S., Lockwood, J. R., & Rathbun, A. H. (2006). *Teacher qualifications, instructional practices, and reading and mathematics gains of kindergartners*. Washington, DC: National Center for Education Statistics.

Lee, J. P. (2005). The classroom of popular culture: What video games can teach us about making students want to learn. *Harvard Education Letter*, *21*(6), 8, 6–7.

New, J. (2006). Use digital storytelling in your classroom. *Edutopia*, *1*(9), 23.

Rodgers, C. (2002). Defining reflection: Another look at John Dewey and reflective thinking. *Teachers College Record*, *104*, 842–866.

Shaffer, D. W. (2007). The educational value of computer games. *Principal*, *86*(4), 66–67.

Standen, A. (2005). Grounded. *Edutopia*, *1*(7), 50–53.

Stronge, J. H. (2007). *Qualities of Effective Teachers*. Second edition. Alexandria, VA: Association for Supervision and Curriculum Development.

Sussman, G. L. (2006). The violence you don't see. *Educational Leadership*, *63*, 1–7. In *Helping All Students Succeed*, ASCD online journal at www.ascd.org:80/portal/site/ascd

Tomlinson, C. A., & Doubet, K. (2005). Reach them to teach them. *Educational Leadership*, *62*(7), 8–15.

Weinthal, E. (2005). Using photographs as teaching tools. *Principal*, *85*(1), 60–61.

Young, D., & Behounek, L. M. (2006). Kindergartners use PowerPoint to lead their own parent-teacher conferences. *Young Children*, *61*(2), 24–26.

Zirkel, P. A. (2005). Permission forms. *Principal*, *84*(3), 8–9.

Chapter 3

Developing Thinking and Questioning Skills

INTASC Principles	PRAXIS III Domains	NBPTS Standards
• The teacher understands the central concepts, tools of inquiry, and structures of the discipline(s) he or she teaches and can create learning experiences that make these aspects of subject matter meaningful to students. (Principle 1)	• Organizing content Knowledge for Student Learning (Domain A)	• Knowledge of Content and Curriculum

The key to meaningful learning is thinking. The skills of thinking can be taught and learned. Those same skills can and should be modeled by the teacher. The key to thinking effectively is, as was introduced in the preceding chapter, the strategy of questioning. In this chapter we will focus your attention on skills for teaching thinking and for using questioning.

In many ways, this chapter and the final chapter of this book are complementary, especially because of their combined focus on thinking, intelligent behavior, and integrated learning.

ANTICIPATED OUTCOMES

After completing this chapter, you should be able to do the following:

1. Describe no less than 10 characteristics of intelligent behavior.
2. Describe ways teachers can help children learn to think and behave intelligently.
3. Identify skills used in thinking, and identify specifically how to facilitate students' development of each skill.
4. For a grade level of your choice, write a sample question for each of the types of questions discussed in this chapter.
5. Explain the need for different types and levels of questions.
6. For use in a grade of your choice, write a series of appropriately sequenced questions for the development of an identified idea.
7. Describe and demonstrate ways to help students develop their metacognitive skills.
8. Describe the value of students' questions and how to use their questions.
9. Describe when and how a teacher should and should not respond to questions asked by students.
10. Compare and contrast ways of thinking with the levels of questions.
11. Demonstrate your ability to use questions by teaching a lesson to a group of children or a peer group. The microteaching demonstration should include framing and stating questions, pacing and sequencing questions, and acknowledging learner responses.

Asking questions is a natural way to learn and to satisfy one's curiosity. When young children first become aware of their surroundings and develop the ability to speak, they ask questions relentlessly. It is a process that goes on throughout life, albeit often with diminishing frequency. In fact, as you have undoubtedly heard before, when you stop asking questions, you stop learning.

Learning to think is perhaps education's highest-priority goal. To help children develop the intellectual skills associated with reflective thought, you will need to model and encourage questions that trigger their use of such skills. To this end, in this chapter we focus your attention on so-called *higher-level questions*—those that require respondents to apply knowledge and to analyze, synthesize, interpret, and evaluate information. In this context, so-called *lower-level questions*—those requiring only recall or reproduction of information—would not be appropriate. The idea of "levels" of questions comes from extensive use of Bloom's taxonomy for the

In teaching for thinking, we are interested not only in what children know, but also in how children behave when they do not know. Gathering evidence of the performance and growth of intelligent behavior requires watching children: observing students as they try to solve the day-to-day academic and real-life problems they encounter.

Scott Cunningham/Merrill

cognitive domain (see Chapter 5). Although the taxonomy was designed as a way of arranging educational objectives, we can use it as well to classify and study questions and the teaching of thinking (Hunkins, 1995). We begin this chapter with a discussion of direct teaching for thinking.

TEACHING THINKING

Pulling together what has been learned about learning and brain functioning, we encourage you to integrate explicit thinking instruction into daily lessons. In other words, help students develop their thinking skills to the point where the skills have become their disposition. In teaching for thinking, we are interested not only in what children know but also in how children behave when they don't know. Costa (1991, p. 19) states it as follows:

> Gathering evidence of the performance and growth of intelligent behavior requires "kid-watching": observing students as they try to solve the day-to-day academic and real-life problems they encounter. . . . By collecting anecdotes and examples of written, oral, and visual expressions, we can see students' increasingly voluntary and spontaneous performance of these intelligent behaviors.

We next consider the characteristics of intelligent behavior, the behaviors you will help children strive for.

Characteristics of Intelligent Behavior

Characteristics of intelligent behavior that you should model, teach for, and observe developing in your students, as identified by Costa and Kallick (2000), are described in the following paragraphs. (*Note:* See also Armstrong's (1998) 12 qualities of genius—curiosity, playfulness, imagination, creativity, wonderment, wisdom, inventiveness, vitality, sensitivity, flexibility, humor, and joy.)

Drawing on Knowledge and Applying It to New Situations
A major goal of formal education is for students to apply school-learned knowledge to real-life situations. To develop skills in drawing on past knowledge and applying that knowledge to new situations, students must be given opportunities to practice doing that very thing. Problem recognition, problem solving, and project-based learning are significantly important ways of providing that opportunity to students.

Finding Humor
The positive effects of humor on the body's physiological functions are well established (see Chapter 2). Humor liberates creativity and provides high-level thinking skills, such as anticipation, finding novel relationships, and visual imagery. The acquisition of a sense of humor follows a developmental sequence similar to that described by Piaget (1972) and Kohlberg (1981). Initially, young children and immature adolescents (and some immature adults) may find humor in all the wrong things—human frailty, ethnic humor, sacrilegious riddles, and ribald profanities. Later, creative young adolescents thrive on finding incongruity and will demonstrate a whimsical frame of mind during problem solving.

Creating, Imagining, Innovating
All students must be encouraged to do and discouraged from saying "I can't." Students must be taught in a way that encourages intrinsic motivation rather than reliance on extrinsic sources. Teachers must be able to offer criticism so that the student understands the criticism is not a criticism of self. In exemplary educational programs, students learn the value of feedback. They learn the value of their own intuition, of guessing—they learn "I can."

Listening with Understanding and Empathy
Some psychologists believe that the ability to listen to others, to empathize with and to understand their point of view, is one of the highest forms of intelligent behavior. Empathic behavior, nearly the exact opposite of egoism, is an important skill for conflict resolution. In class and advisory meetings, brainstorming sessions, think tanks, town meetings, advisory councils, board meetings, and legislative bodies, people from various walks of life convene to share their thinking, to explore their ideas, and to broaden their perspectives by listening to the ideas and reactions of others.

Children should be given many opportunities to present and discuss their learning with peers. The ability to listen to others, to empathize with and understand their point of view, is perhaps one of the highest forms of intelligent behavior.

Maria B. Vonada/Merrill

Managing Impulsivity   When learners develop impulse control they think before acting. Impulsive behavior can worsen conflict and inhibit effective problem solving (Goos & Galbraith, 1996). Students can be taught to think before shouting out an answer, to wait their turn, to raise their hand to be called on before answering, to think before beginning a project or task, and to think before arriving at conclusions with insufficient data. One of several reasons that teachers should routinely expect a show of student hands before selecting a student to respond or question is to help students develop control over the impulsive behavior of shouting out in class (Brandt, 2000; Harrington-Lueker, 1997). Indeed, research clearly indicates that the quality of one's emotional intelligence—that is, to exercise self-control, to empathize with others, to work collaboratively and cooperatively—is a much more significant predictor of success in the workplace than is any analytical measure of intelligence (Goleman, Boyatzis, & McKee, 2002).

Persisting   Persistence is staying with a task until it is completed. People with an internal locus of control (discussed in Chapter 2) tend to show more persistence. Consider the examples shown in Figure 3.1.

Remaining Open to Continuous Learning   Intelligent people are in a continuous learning mode, always eager to learn and find new ways to do things.

- *Rachel Carson.* Refusing to be intimidated by powerful external forces, Carson was persistent in her pursuit to educate society about the ill effects of pesticides. Her book, *Silent Spring,* published in 1963, was the seed for the beginning of the development of a more responsible ecological attitude.

- *Lewis H. Latimer.* Born in 1848 the son of slaves, Latimer served in the U.S. Navy during the Civil War. After the war he studied drafting, eventually becoming chief draftsman for both General Electric and Westinghouse. Among his career achievements were his patent drawings for Alexander Graham Bell's first telephone, his invention of a method to make a carbon filament for a lightbulb that was made by one of Thomas Edison's competitors, and supervision of the installation of the first electric lights in New York City, Philadelphia, Montreal, and London. Later, in 1884, he went to work for Edison.

- *Gordon Parks.* Born in 1912, last of 15 children of a poor farming family in a segregated town in Kansas, who after the death of his mother and by the age of 15, was living on the streets of St. Paul, hanging out in pool halls, playing piano in a brothel, working in a whites-only club, was despite his meager beginnings bound and determined to enter a world previously unavailable to African Americans. Using his photographic skills that were self-developed with a camera he bought from a pawnshop, he worked as a freelance photographer and eventually became the first black person to work at *Vogue* and *Life* magazines, published books on photography, and later was the first to write, direct, and score a Hollywood film that was financed by a major Hollywood studio, *The Learning Tree* (1969). He also was the director of the 1971 hit movie *Shaft* and a number of other significant films. At the time of his death in 2006, at the age of 93, he had just published a memoir and a book of poetry, both published by Simon & Schuster, and was composing a sonata for famed cellist Yo-Yo Ma.

- *Wilma Rudolf.* As the result of childhood diseases, Rudolf, at the age of 10, could walk only with the aid of leg braces. Just 10 years later, at the age of 20, she was declared to be the fastest-running woman in the world, having won three gold medals in the 1960 World Olympics.

FIGURE 3.1
Examples of persistence

Responding with Wonderment and Awe   Young children express wonderment, an expression that should never be stifled. Your students can be helped to recapture that sense of wonderment as you guide them into a sense of "I can" and an expression of the feeling of "I enjoy."

Striving for Accuracy   Growth in this behavior is demonstrated when students take time to check their work, review the procedures, and hesitate to draw conclusions when they possess only limited data.

Taking Responsible Risks: Venture Forth and Explore Ideas Beyond the Usual Zone of Comfort   Such exploration, of course, must be done with thoughtfulness; it must not be done in ways that could put the student at risk

---

1. The burglar was about 30 years old, white, 5' 10", with wavy hair weighing about 150 pounds.

2. The family lawyer will read the will tomorrow at the residence of Mr. Carlson, who died June 19 to accommodate his relatives.

3. Mrs. Maureen Doolittle, who went deer hunting with her husband, is very proud that she was able to shoot a fine buck as well as her husband.

4. Organ donations from the living reached a record high last year, outnumbering donors who are dead for the first time.

5. The dog was hungry and made the mistake of nipping a 2-year-old that was trying to force feed it in his ear.

6. We spent most of our time sitting on the back porch watching the cows playing Scrabble and reading.

7. Hunting can also be dangerous, as in the case of pygmies hunting elephants armed only with spears.

FIGURE 3.2
Sample sentences that lack clarity and precision

psychologically or physically. Using the analogy of a turtle going nowhere until it sticks its neck out, teachers should model this behavior and provide opportunities for students to develop this intelligent behavior by using techniques such as brainstorming strategies, divergent-thinking questioning, think-pair-share, cooperative learning, inquiry, and project-based learning.

Thinking and Communicating with Clarity and Precision   Strive for clarity and accurate communication in both written and oral form. Shown in Figure 3.2 are humorous sample sentences (taken from newspapers) that lack clarity and precision in written expression. A useful academic exercise is to have students, perhaps in dyads, read and then rewrite sentences such as these and then share and compare their rewrites.

Thinking About Thinking (Metacognition)   Learning to plan, monitor, assess, and reflect on one's own thinking is another characteristic of intelligent behavior. Small-group learning, journals, student-led portfolio conferences, self-assessment, and thinking aloud in dyads are strategies that can be used to help students develop this intelligent behavior (Stright & Supplee, 2002). Your own thinking aloud is good modeling for your students, helping them to develop their cognitive skills of thinking, learning, and reasoning (Astington, 1998).

Thinking Flexibly   Sometimes referred to as *lateral thinking* (De Bono, 1970), flexibility in thinking is the ability to approach a problem from "the side," or from a new angle, using a novel approach. With modeling by the teacher, students can develop this behavior as they learn to consider alternative points of view and to deal with several sources of information simultaneously.

Thinking Interdependently Real-world problem solving has become so complex that seldom can any person go it alone. As stated by Elias (2001, p. 2), "We live in an interdependent world; there is no such thing, in any practical sense, as independence and autonomy. We live lives of synergy and linkage." Not all children come to school knowing how to work effectively in groups. They may exhibit competitiveness, narrow-mindedness, egocentrism, ethnocentrism, or criticism of others' values, emotions, and beliefs. Listening, consensus seeking, giving up an idea to work on someone else's, empathy, compassion, group leadership, cooperative learning, knowing how to support group efforts, and altruism—these are behaviors indicative of intelligent human beings, and they can be learned by children at school and in the classroom.

Using All the Senses

As emphasized throughout this book, to best learn, children should be encouraged to use and develop all their sensory input channels (i.e., verbal, visual, tactile, and kinesthetic) as often as is feasible.

Questioning and Posing Problems

Children are usually full of questions, and unless discouraged, they do ask them. As educators, we want students to be alert to, and recognize, discrepancies and phenomena in their environment and to freely inquire about their causes. In exemplary educational programs, students are encouraged to ask questions and then from those questions to develop a problem-solving strategy to investigate their questions.

We should strive to help our own students develop these characteristics of intelligent behavior. In Chapter 2 you learned of specific teacher behaviors that facilitate this development. Now, let's review additional research findings that offer important considerations in the facilitation of student learning and intelligent behaving.

Direct Teaching for Thinking and Intelligent Behavior

The curriculum of any school includes developing the skills used in thinking. Because students' academic achievement increases when they are taught thinking directly, many researchers and educators concur that all students should receive direct instruction on how to think and behave intelligently (Costa, 1991).

Four research perspectives have influenced the direct teaching of thinking. The *cognitive view of intelligence* asserts that intellectual ability is not fixed but can be developed. The *constructivist approach to learning* maintains that learners actively and independently construct knowledge by creating and coordinating relationships in their mental repertoire. The *social psychology view of classroom experience* focuses on learners as individuals who are members of various peer groups and of a society. The *perspective of information processing* deals with the mechanics of acquiring, elaborating on, and managing information.

Direct Teaching of Skills Used in Thinking

Rather than assuming that students have developed thinking skills (such as *classifying, comparing, concluding, generalizing,* and *inferring*), you should devote classroom time to teaching them directly. When a thinking skill is taught directly, the subject content becomes the vehicle for thinking. For example, a social studies lesson can teach children how to distinguish fact and opinion, a language arts lesson instructs students how to compare and analyze, and a science lesson can teach them how to set up a problem for inquiry.

DEVELOPING SKILL IN USING QUESTIONS

Classifying questions in terms of a skill hierarchy has been useful in the effort to get teachers to focus more on questions that promote various kinds of thinking.

The terms *higher-level* and *lower-level questions* have nothing to do with how worthwhile the questions themselves are. Whether a question is good or bad depends on its purpose, how it is stated, and its suitability for the students to whom it is directed. So-called lower-level questions are not only good to use but are also absolutely essential in assessing certain aspects of your instructional program. For example, how else could you check students' reading comprehension other than to ask specific factual questions based on the passage read? Therefore, let us dispose of any notion that there is something inherently good about higher-level questions and something inherently bad about lower-level questions and think instead in terms of the educational purposes you serve by using each type of question.

There can be no doubt that, in general, teachers tend to overuse lower-level questions. These questions have to do with recalling and reproducing information—using such verbs as *name, locate, describe, list, identify*; they are also called "who, what, where, and when" questions. They are easy to formulate because you base them directly on the subject matter studied. If basing them on a passage students have read, you might instruct them to "put your finger on the sentence that answers the question," a practice that is fairly widespread in checking comprehension. The problem with such procedures is that they tend to exaggerate the importance of the content of the question. Your purpose may be simply to check the accuracy of students' reading, but they may be left with the idea that you are calling attention to an important piece of information.

Higher-level questions call for students to process information and to apply it in new situations. Students usually cannot answer higher-level questions directly from an information source such as the textbook or encyclopedia but must infer, surmise, or conclude from putting together pieces of information. One cannot answer a question of this type by pointing to a passage in a book. You often frame these questions evaluatively, such as by asking, "Why? How do you know? If that is true, then . . . ? What is likely to happen next? Can you summarize . . . ?" They require imaginative, creative responses linking together related bits of information into a thoughtful, logical conclusion. They are more difficult to frame, which probably is one reason teachers do not use them with greater frequency. Their purpose is mainly to give students experience in using reflective thinking processes.

There is a place for both lower- and higher-level questions in instruction. You need skill in using both types and must be sensitive to the need to balance the kinds of questions used. The questions themselves, when asked orally in class or when they appear in written form on examinations, indicate powerfully to students what you consider important for them to learn. They send out signals as surely as does anything else you do or say.

Three subskills are a part of skillful questioning: framing and stating questions, sequencing questions, and pacing questions. We discuss these subskills in the sections that follow.

Framing and Stating Questions

The first requirement for framing and stating classroom questions is that they be appropriate for the subject matter and the purpose for which you are asking them. But even if satisfactory on those counts, questions may be faulty for technical reasons. The following guidelines will help you prevent such problems.

1. The question should be grammatically correct and the syntax easy to follow. Keep the question brief and the vocabulary simple.
2. Express the question clearly enough that children understand what you want in the way of a response.
3. Avoid embedding giveaway clues in the question.
4. If you begin the question by asking, "What do you think . . . ?" or with some similar stem that calls for the expression of an *opinion*, be prepared to accept *any* response from your students.
5. State questions in an encouraging tone of voice.
6. State questions in a way that stimulates children's thinking. Try not to lead them to an expected answer.

To avoid difficulties, during your preactive phase of instruction, write into your lesson plan the key questions that you plan to ask during the lessons themselves. Many beginning teachers find it helpful to make and listen to a recording of their teaching or to assess their questions by asking them first to a friend.

Sequencing Questions

If you are to *develop* ideas in the course of a lesson, you must ask questions in a way that leads to a logical conclusion. Idea development means that the lesson has direction, that your questions lead somewhere. You cannot ask a series of random questions and expect ideas to build cumulatively. In the following sequence, based on a story of a young man's visit to an abandoned house, notice how each question builds on the one that precedes it.

1. Can you give an overall description of the house Charlie visited?
2. What was there about the house that made Charlie uneasy?

3. When was it that Charlie first discovered that something was out of the ordinary?
4. Why do you suppose Charlie did not leave at that time?
5. At what point was Charlie absolutely certain that someone else was in the house?
6. What, exactly, was it that happened that made Charlie know he was not alone?
7. Why could Charlie not go for help then?
8. What is there to be learned from Charlie's experience about going into strange or unfamiliar surroundings?

Even if you are not familiar with the story, you may infer essential elements of the story line from this sequence of questions. The same questions asked in a random order would not produce this desired effect.

Perhaps the easiest way to develop skill in asking questions sequentially is to teach a process that has a fixed sequence, such as following a product through its manufacturing process or discussing how an item gets from where it is produced to where it is used. Science experiments that necessitate a specific sequence lend themselves well to learning how to sequence questions, as do some operations in mathematics. This aspect of questioning is much like building a sequence for a computer program. Indeed, as a classroom teacher, you *are* the programmer much of the time. Accordingly, if learning is to proceed efficiently, you should provide questions that will deal with small increments of learning in a progressively more complex sequence.

Pacing the Questioning

Pacing refers to the frequency with which you ask questions. Two problems are commonly associated with pacing the questioning. One is asking questions too rapidly one after another, with students allowed little or no time for thinking or for developing ideas associated with one question before being asked another. Such rapid-fire questioning encourages if not demands short, low-level thinking responses. The second problem has to do with the amount of thinking time (also called *wait time*) allowed. Too often, teachers seem to feel that unless children respond immediately, the teacher then needs to restate or clarify their question or give learners cues to the answer. Actually, when given sufficient time to think, children *will* respond and usually with thoughtful responses.

Our position is that you should maintain a rather slow pace when questioning, and do not be hasty in providing cues, nor too quick to restate and clarify questions. The atmosphere should encourage reflection rather than quickness of response. Your questions should provoke thinking, and thinking requires time—more time for some children than for others and certainly more time for a group of 20 or so than when a one-on-one situation.

With older children you may get more thoughtful responses by having them write out their answers before responding orally. This will slow the pace and also has the advantage of involving all members of the class in thinking about the questions and in writing, both of which are important for critical thinking. When you do want to

Activity 3.1: Create a Story

Using the questions in the text about Charlie's visit to the old house, a primary grades teacher asks the children to create a story. With children in grades 4 through 6, a teacher might then have them try their hand at developing a set of questions that could be the basis of another story. Then show students a picture and have them frame questions and arrange them in sequential order to tell a story about it.

1. What skills are being used in this exercise?
2. How could you use this experience to enhance students' questioning skills?

use this strategy of thinking and writing before any oral response, be persistent in application of the expected procedure, as at first some students will balk at the seemingly unusual expectation. But your persistence will pay academic dividends.

THE TEACHER'S RESPONSES TO STUDENTS

It is important to know that your reply to a child's response to your question may be as important as the question itself. As a general guideline, your comments following children's responses should leave them with the perception that you both hear and accept them and feeling that they would like to respond again to another question. Let us examine some of the ways you can deal with student responses.

Passive (Nonjudgmental) Acceptance Response

There are a half dozen or so common expressions that teachers often use to acknowledge student responses, including "all right," "uh-huh," "yes," and "okay." These are noncommittal, nonevaluative (nonjudgmental), passive acceptance responses that simply recognize that a response has occurred. (Of course, these might be accompanied by nonverbal clues that carry powerful evaluative messages, such as an approving or disapproving facial expression, tone of voice, or body movement.) Passive acceptance responses are effective when you want to encourage discussion of the question. When you recognize a response in such a noncommittal way, students know that the matter is still open, and others may contribute their ideas to the discussion.

When listening to recordings of their class discussions, some teachers are surprised by how often they use the same expression, such as "okay" in acknowledging student responses. Some teachers use "okay" a hundred times a day and are not even aware of it. Rather than repeating the same verbal response, try to develop variety in your acknowledgment of students' contributions.

Evaluative (Judgmental) Response

Some teachers seem to think that they must evaluate every response with "Yes, that's right" or "No, that's not right." Of course, you need to evaluate children's work and should not ignore incorrect responses. But there is much wrong with a

Activity 3.2: How Would You Say It?

With each of the following questions, identify what is wrong with how it is stated and then rewrite it to improve its wording.

1. Indian people lived how on the plains before the coming of the Europeans?
2. At what point in a musical selection does the "finale" come?
3. Can you list the steps in doing the experiment from start to finish, beginning with the last step first?
4. I don't think it was a very good idea to use those colors for the picture, do you?
5. What would happen if—but, of course, you would never want to do anything like this—you were hiking alone, and you suddenly stepped on a rock, twisted your ankle, and couldn't walk any farther, and you had to get help but there was no one around?
6. If you saw a hot-air balloon one day as you were playing with your beach ball, what do you think would make it stay in the air?
7. Can you add ideas to the list of suggestions offered by Jason's friend that would help his situation?

procedure that necessitates such active acceptance (or nonacceptance) responses from you every time children answer a question or make a comment in class. First, you do not always *know* whether a response is right or wrong. Moreover, many responses cannot be categorized as totally correct or incorrect. Also, over time you will tend to fall into the habit of asking only questions that elicit answers you can evaluate in this way, which typically represent lower-order thinking (Becker, 2000; Wimer, Ridenour, Thomas, & Place, 2001). Some children will not participate in questioning of this type because they do not want their teacher to evaluate their responses negatively in front of their peers. Rather than risking such a contingency, they simply will not participate, and if called on, they will say that they do not know. Finally, evaluative statements tend to bring matters to closure. For example, if you respond to a student's answer with, "You're absolutely correct," you wouldn't seem to be leaving much of anything else for the class to discuss.

Restating and Clarifying

You will not need to restate and clarify every student response to every question, but this is good practice from time to time. It is especially appropriate when a student has responded so softly that the entire group could not hear. Also, you may know that further clarification will help to either promote continued thinking about the question or provide more precision to the response. For example, in a science lesson, you may ask, "If I have a gallon of water and I pour in a quart of oil, what happens to the oil?" A child responds by saying, "It goes to the top." You may restate and clarify, "You say it goes to the top. Do you mean that the oil will float on top of the water?" The child continues, "Yes, it separates. The oil floats on top of the water." Here, by asking another question, you are clarifying to verify that you have listened to and understood the child's response. (See also "Clarifying Whenever Necessary" in Chapter 2.)

Probing

Sometimes a student's response only partially answers your question, and you want to encourage a more complete answer. You can probe for additional information with statements such as these:

1. "Can you say a little bit more about that?"
2. "But why do you suppose he turned back?"
3. "Can you explain why it happened?"
4. "You said 'yes'; now tell why you think so."
5. "That is correct, but there is another important point you haven't mentioned."
6. "Can you give an example?"

Sometimes you can elicit a more elaborate response by simply repeating the last word or words of the child's response, inflected in a questioning tone: "freezes?" "tree frogs?" "disease?" "four trips?" However, when probing for a more complete response, avoid pressing children so hard that they become too anxious and nervous to respond at all. Such anxiety-producing probing is counterproductive to desired learning.

Cueing

It may be that your question draws a blank—a sea of empty faces, something that happens to every teacher at one time or another. It may mean that you stated the question poorly, or it may mean that the children simply did not know what you were asking. When this happens, you can give students a few leads, cues that will guide their thinking along the lines you intend. This involves more than simply repeating or rephrasing the question. In cueing, you provide small amounts of additional information, as in the following example:

Teacher:	What caused the candle to go out when we placed a jar over it?
Student:	It doesn't get any air.
Teacher:	(Probing.) Yes, but what is it in the air that the candle needs to keep burning?
Student:	(No response.)
Teacher:	(Cueing.) Do you remember when we learned about rust . . . ?
Student:	(Picking up on the cue.) Oxygen! The candle needs oxygen to burn. It goes out when there is no longer any oxygen.

Notice in the example that the teacher did not give the answer. The teacher simply provided a small hint that pointed the learner's thinking in the appropriate direction. In this case, the child was able to respond even before the teacher completed the cueing sentence.

SOCRATIC QUESTIONING

In the fifth century BCE, Socrates, the famous Athenian teacher, used the art of questioning so successfully that to this day we still hear of the Socratic method (Elder & Paul, 1998; Phillips, 2000; Schneider, 2000). What, exactly, is the Socratic method? Socrates' strategy was to ask his students a series of leading questions that gradually snarled them up to the point where they had to look carefully at their own ideas and think rigorously for themselves. Today that strategy is referred to as the Socratic approach or method.

Socratic discussions were informal dialogues taking place in a natural, pleasant environment. Although Socrates sometimes had to go to considerable lengths to ignite his students' intrinsic interest, their response was natural and spontaneous. In his dialogues, Socrates tried to aid students in developing ideas. He did not impose his own notions on the students. Rather, he encouraged them to develop their own conclusions and draw their own inferences. Of course, Socrates may have had preconceived notions about what the final learning should be and carefully aimed his questions so that the students would arrive at the desired conclusions. Still, his questions were open-ended, causing divergent rather than convergent thinking. The students were free to go mentally wherever the facts and their thinking led them.

Throughout history, teachers have tried to adapt that which they believe to be the methods of Socrates to the classroom. In some situations, they have been quite successful and are a major mode of instruction. However, it's important to understand that Socrates used this method in the context of a one-to-one relationship between the student and himself. Some teachers have adapted it for whole-class, direct instruction by asking questions first of one student and then of another, moving slowly about the class. This technique may work, but it is difficult because the essence of the Socratic technique is to build question on question in a logical fashion so that each question leads the student a step further toward the understanding sought. When you distribute the questions around the classroom, you may find it difficult to build up the desired sequence and to keep all the students involved in the discussion. Sometimes you may be able to use the Socratic method by directing all the questions at one student—at least for several minutes—while the other students look on and listen in. That is how Socrates did it. When the topic is interesting enough, this technique can be quite successful and even exciting, but in the long run, the Socratic method works best when the teacher is working in one-on-one coaching situations or with small groups of students, rather than in whole-class, direct instruction.

In using Socratic questioning, the focus is on the questions, not answers, and thinking is valued as the quintessential activity (Brogan & Brogan, 1995). In essence, to conduct Socratic questioning with the student or class, identify a problem (either student- or teacher-posed) and then ask the students a series of probing questions designed to cause them to examine critically the problem and potential solutions to it. The main thrust of the questioning and the key questions must be planned in advance so that the questioning will proceed logically. To think of quality probing questions on the spur of the moment is too difficult.

QUESTIONS THAT FOCUS ON SPECIFIC PURPOSES

You must be able to select appropriate questions in terms of purposes, or the results are likely to be disappointing. For example, teachers sometimes report their inability to involve children in discussions. An examination of the kinds of questions they ask often provides clues to why they are having this problem. If they ask only low-level questions, requiring only simple yes or no answers or specific recall, there is little to discuss. The level of your questions clue children to the level of thinking and involvement expected. Questions that repeatedly require little to no thinking will elicit little to no substantive involvement.

In the following subsections we discuss questions that you may ask to achieve specific educational purposes. Before we proceed, consider the following general rules, which you should apply to all your classroom questioning.

> *Practice calling on all students.* Related to Rule 4 in the box, "Guidelines for Practicing Equity When Questioning," you must call on not just the bright or the slow, not just boys or girls, not only on those in the front or middle of the room, but on all students. This takes concentrated effort on your part, but it is important. To help ensure calling on students equally, try this: Attach a laminated copy of the seating chart to a bright neon-colored clipboard (gives children a visual focus), and with a water-soluble marker, make a tally mark next to children's names each time you call on them. Erase the marks at the end of each day.

Guidelines for Practicing Equity When Questioning

To practice equity when using questioning, follow these four rules: (1) Avoid going to a boy to bail out a girl who fails to answer a question, and (2) avoid going to a boy to improve on a girl's answer. For the first, without seeming to badger, try to give the student clues until she can answer with success. For the second, hold and demonstrate high expectations for all students. For both, try to gauge carefully who you go to next in any questioning sequence. (3) Allow equal wait time regardless of student gender or any other personal characteristic. (4) Call on children with equal frequency, regardless of their ethnicity, gender, or any other personal differences.

> *Give the same minimum amount of wait time (think time) to all students.* This, too, will require concentrated effort on your part, but also is important. If you wait for less time when calling on certain students, such as students of one gender or of some other personal characteristic, you show prejudice toward or lack of confidence in these students, both of which are detrimental when you are striving to establish for all students a positive, equal, and safe environment for classroom learning. Show confidence in all children, and

never discriminate by expecting less or more from some than from others. Although some children may take longer to respond, it is not necessarily because they are not thinking or have less ability. For example, there may be cultural differences, in that some cultures simply allow more wait time than others do. It is important that you personalize, to allow children who need more time to have it. Do not vary wait time to single out students or to lead to lower expectations, but rather to allow for higher expectations.

Require students to raise their hands and be called on. This is true for teachers of kindergarten and for all teachers thereafter. When you ask questions, instead of allowing students to randomly shout out their answers, require them to raise their hands and to be called on before they respond. Establish this procedure and stick with it. This does not mean that you call only on children who have their hands raised; you can call on whomever you want. It does mean that children who want to make a contribution or ask a question must raise their hand and be acknowledged by you first. This helps to ensure that you call on all students equally, fairly distributing your interactions, and not interacting less with girls because boys tend to be more obstreperous. Even in college classrooms, male students tend to be more vociferous than female students and, when the instructor allows, tend to outtalk and to interrupt their female peers. Whether teaching kindergarten or adults or students in between, every teacher has the responsibility to guarantee a nonbiased classroom and an equal distribution of interaction time. This is impossible to achieve when the teacher allows students to speak and disrespectfully interrupt others at will.

Another important reason for this advice is to aid students in learning to control their impulsiveness, to help them develop self-control. As pointed out at the beginning of this chapter, controlling one's impulsiveness is a characteristic of intelligent behavior. It is, in our opinion, one of your many instructional responsibilities to help students develop this skill.

Actively involve as many children as possible in questioning–answering discussion sessions. The traditional method of the teacher asking a question and then calling on a student to respond is essentially a one-on-one interaction. Some children, those not called on, are likely to view it as their opportunity to disengage in the lesson at hand. When calling on one child you do not likely want others to mentally disengage. There are many effective ways to keep all children engaged. Consider the following suggestions: To keep all children mentally engaged, call on students who are sitting quietly and have not raised their hands as well as on those who have, but avoid badgering or humiliating an unwilling participant. When students have no response, you might suggest they think about it, and you will come back to them to make sure they eventually understand or can answer the original question. By dividing a single question into several parts, you can increase the number of students involved. For example, "What are the characteristics of animals known as insects? Who can give one characteristic?"

followed by, "Who can give another?" Or, you can involve several students in answering a single question. For example, ask one student for an answer such as to the question, "What was a characteristic given in the text for animals known as insects?" Then, have a second student read the text aloud to verify the first student's answer, and perhaps ask a third to explore the reason or thinking that makes it an accepted answer.

Procedural Questions

As teacher, you are likely to ask your students many questions that have to do with classroom procedures, the clarification of directions, transitional inquiries, or rhetorical queries. Some of these questions are a necessary part of teaching, of course, but often they amount to little more than time fillers while you gather your thoughts. They may even take the form of a threat (e.g., "Do you want me to move you to another seat?"). Frequently, students will not respond; indeed, you will not expect them to. Often, teachers are usually not even fully aware of the extent of their use of questions of this type; *most of which should not even be asked.* Consider the following examples.

EXAMPLES OF PROCEDURAL QUESTIONS WITH SUGGESTIONS FOR IMPROVEMENT

1. "Are there any questions?" Seldom will you get the answer you want when asking this question. Sometimes you will get answers you would just as soon not have gotten. When you want to check for comprehension it is usually better to randomly check several children by asking content questions and perhaps also to search for quizzical facial expressions.
2. "Will someone review for us what we planned to do during our music period today?" This isn't the right question. A better one would be, "By a show of hands, who can review for us what we planned to do during our music period today?" To help children develop their questioning skills, you must model the same, in this instance by properly wording the question.
3. "Jaime, would you please turn off the lights?" This is not likely to cause problems unless, of course, you ask a student who might say "No." It is better, generally, to give a statement or ask for a volunteer.
4. "Do you think we can figure out a better way to return the bats and balls to the storeroom?" You probably would not want a simple "No" answer to this question. However, as worded, you must be prepared to deal with such a succinct response. Instead, think about the answer that you want, and then word your question accordingly. In this instance try, "Who can make a suggestion about how we might better return the bats and balls to the storeroom?"
5. "Is there anyone in the group who has so little to do that he or she wants me to assign additional work?" Do you suppose the teacher who asked this question really expected an answer? Such a question is really intended to be a declarative threat because the teacher is losing control. Do not confuse students by sending confusing messages. You are not employed to confuse children. Say what you intend to say, as succinctly as you can.

6. "Why don't the five of you work at the table near the window?" Again, the teacher here is giving an instruction or order, not really intending to ask a question. It is best to ask questions only when you want responses.

Questions That Check Literal Comprehension

In subject-matter fields it is necessary for the teacher to know whether children are extracting the essential information presented in the required reading material. Questions used to check such literal comprehension should encourage good study habits; they should focus on important concepts and ideas rather than on inconsequential detail. For example, if you include too many low-level recall questions, children may assume that facts are all that are important in the material. It often is better to include a variety of questions—some asking students to identify important facts and ideas, others requiring understanding, and still others that make them apply, analyze, synthesize, and evaluate new knowledge. Construct your questions to help children identify the most relevant information presented in the material.

EXAMPLES OF QUESTIONS THAT HELP CHILDREN IDENTIFY RELEVANT INFORMATION

1. What costs are included in the price you pay for shoes?
2. After reading the passage in your science book, make a list of all the pollutants mentioned. Which ones are natural pollutants? Which are *people-made or people-caused* pollutants?
3. Draw a diagram to show that you understand the number relationships in a problem of indirect measurement. Can you state two basic ideas that explain indirect measurement?
4. Which statement in each paragraph identifies the cause-and-effect relationships between the items?
5. What characteristics of the countries of the Middle East would justify grouping them together as a region?
6. Exactly what happened at each of the four stages of the experiment?
7. Can you recall five fire-danger spots in a home that were mentioned in the text?

Reflective or "Thought" Questions

Reflective questions are open-ended and require higher-level thought processes. Their purpose is to stimulate learners' creative imaginations and thinking abilities. A reflective question may not have a right answer, in the sense that one and only one response is acceptable. Reflective questions are often tied to critical thinking and decision making, thereby requiring students to consider alternatives and the consequences of each. Reflective thinking requires such mental processes as application, analysis, synthesis, and evaluation.

For generations teachers have admonished their students to "think." Even today it is fairly common to hear teachers say, "Now think, boys and girls. Think real hard!" Simply telling children to think is not a satisfactory way to develop thinking abilities. You need to use activities, situations, and questions that require them to apply such intellectual skills as comparing and contrasting, noting cause and effect, considering alternatives, and drawing conclusions based on information.

EXAMPLES OF QUESTIONS ENCOURAGING REFLECTIVE THINKING

1. In the early years of our country, many people had comfortable homes and a good life in the 13 states along the Atlantic coast. Why do you suppose some chose to leave all that behind and go west, which promised a hard and often dangerous life?
2. Scientists think some chemicals are so dangerous to human health that they should not be used for insect and disease control. Can you think of conditions where they might be used, even though they are dangerous? Can you think of other examples where chemicals are dangerous but still used? What criteria do people use to determine when and when not to use a dangerous chemical?
3. What businesses and what kinds of work would be in greater demand were the workweek 4 days long rather than 5 or more?
4. How might the story have ended if the family had visited Aunt Sophie and Uncle Charlie one day sooner?
5. For what reason or reasons are some medicines sold only when prescribed by a medical doctor?
6. Do you think it would be wise to protect only those animals that are useful to human beings? Explain why or why not.
7. For what reason would authorities want to introduce wolves from Alberta, Canada, into Yellowstone National Park and central Idaho? Are there any groups that would be opposed to such action, and if so, why do they oppose it?

QUESTIONS FROM STUDENTS

The kinds of questions that students ask reveal a great deal about the effectiveness of your classroom management procedures and about your conduct of instruction. For example, a preponderance of student questions that call for your reassurance and approval ("Am I doing this right?" "Is this what you want us to do?" "Is it all right if I make my picture sideways?") indicates a general feeling of insecurity, that the children feel considerable risk in doing things that may displease you. It could mean, too, that there is a high level of student dependence on you. It might also mean that your directions are not clear and that children do not understand precisely what you expect of them.

Sometimes you may become annoyed when children ask endless procedural and permission questions ("May I sharpen my pencil?" "Please, may I get a book?" "May I take this book home?" "Can I get a drink?"). Yet, you should recognize that you might be contributing to the problem. If you do not provide children opportunities to develop self-direction and to assume responsibility for a certain amount of decision making, you may predict that they will turn to you for the authority to engage in routine procedures.

Children are likely to model their question-asking behavior on yours. As said before, from your questions children sense the level of thinking and participation you believe to be important. Thus, if you tend to ask provocative questions that enhance higher-level thinking, children in your classroom are likely to follow that example.

The Question-Driven Classroom

You can and should use student questions as springboards for further questioning, discussions, and investigations. Indeed, in a constructivist learning environment, student questions often drive content. [See, for example, Barrow (2002) in the end-of-chapter readings for how one teacher built instruction around the students' personal questions about insects.] Encourage students to ask questions that challenge the textbook, the process, or other persons' statements, and encourage them to seek the supporting evidence behind a statement. [See, for example, Beck & McKeown (2002) in the end-of-chapter readings].

Activity 3.3: And Then *You* Said. . . .

Imagine that you are the teacher in the following four situations. In each, you ask a question and a student responds. The response, however, is in some way inadequate. Supply what you would say next to move the instructional sequence along.

Situation 1

Teacher: You enjoyed the poem so much yesterday that I thought we could share another one today. What was it that you liked most about the poem we read yesterday?

Student: Rhymes.

And *you* said: _____

Situation 2

Teacher: Now you notice that this line on our graph [pointing to a line showing the amount of food produced] goes up, but this other line [pointing to a line showing number of people living on farms] goes down. What does this tell us about how farming has changed?

Student: It tells us that people moved away. They got other jobs.

And *you* said: _____

Situation 3

Teacher: An electric generator produces electricity by the rotation of a coil in a magnetic field. It needs some source of energy or power to rotate the coil. Thus, we see that an electric motor uses electrical energy to produce mechanical energy. A generator, however, uses mechanical energy to produce electrical energy. What forms of mechanical energy do we use to produce electrical energy?

Student: [No response. Dead silence.]

And *you* said: _____

Situation 4

Teacher: In our social studies, we have been learning how people get the things they need to live in our community. You remember that we learned two new—and big—words. [Children respond enthusiastically, "Consumer" and "Producer."] Yes, you remembered well. Now, who can tell us something about these words?

Student: All consumers are producers.

And *you* said: _____

Activity 3.4: And Elliot Eisner Said. . . .

The kind of school we need would be staffed by teachers who are as interested in the questions students ask after a unit of study as they are in the answers students give. On the whole, schools are highly answer-oriented. Teachers have the questions, and students are to have the answers. Even with a problem-solving approach, the focus of attention is on the student's ability to solve a problem that someone else has posed. Yet the most intellectually demanding tasks lie not so much in solving problems as in posing questions.

1. Do you agree with Mr. Eisner? Why or why not?
2. What does this say to you as a classroom teacher?
3. Return to this statement and read your answers to questions 1 and 2 after you have completed your study of this book. Do you want to make any changes to your responses to the two questions? If so, describe.

Source: E. W. Eisner, "The Kind of Schools We Need," *Phi Delta Kappan* 83(8): 579 (2002).

Questioning: The Cornerstone of Critical Thinking, Real-World Problem Solving, and Meaningful Learning

Real-world problem solving usually has no absolute right answers. Rather than "correct" answers, some simply are better than others. The person with a problem needs to learn how to (a) recognize the problem, (b) formulate a question about that problem (e.g., Should I tell Mom or not? Should I take this drug? Should the river be dammed?), (c) collect data, and (d) arrive at a temporarily acceptable answer, realizing that at some later time new data may dictate a review of this conclusion. For example, if an astronomer believes she has discovered a new planetary system, there is no textbook or teacher or any other outside authoritative source to which she may refer to inquire if she is correct. Rather, on the basis of her self-confidence in problem identification, asking questions, collecting enough data, and arriving at a tentative conclusion based on those data, she assumes that for now her conclusion is safe.

Encourage Students to Ask Questions About Content and Process

Question asking often indicates that the inquirer is curious, puzzled, and uncertain; it is a sign of being engaged in thinking about a topic (Fischer, 2002). And, yet, in too many classrooms, too few students ask questions (U.S. Department of Education, 1997). We cannot overstate this: Encourage your students to ask questions. From children, there is no such thing as a "dumb" question. Sometimes children, like everyone else, ask questions they could just as easily have looked up or that are irrelevant or that show lack of thought or sensitivity. Those questions can consume precious class time. For a teacher, they can be frustrating. Your initial reaction may be to quickly and mistakenly brush off this type of question with sarcasm, while assuming that the student is too lazy to look up an answer. In such instances, we advise you to think before responding and to respond kindly and professionally, although in your busy life as a classroom teacher that may not always be so easy to remember to do. However, be assured, there is a reason for every student's question, even if it is only signaling a need for recognition or

Activity 3.5: Think Time and the Art of Questioning

Role-play Simulation

From your class ask for four volunteers. One volunteer will read the lines of Marcella, a second will read the one "student" line, the third reads the narrative lines about the setting (such as the one at 9:01), while the fourth volunteer uses a stopwatch to direct Marcella and the student to speak their lines at the designated times. The rest of your class will pretend to be students in Marcella's fourthgrade language arts lesson.

9:00: *Marcella:* "Think of a man whom you admire, perhaps a father figure, and write a three-sentence paragraph describing that person." Students begin their writing.

9:00:05: *Marcella:* "Only three sentences about someone you look up to. It might be your father, uncle, anyone."

9:00:07: *Student:* "Does it have to be about a man?" *Marcella:* "No, it can be a man or a woman, but someone you truly admire."

9:01: Marcella is walking the room, seeing that all children are on task.

9:01:10 *Marcella:* "Three sentences are all you need to write."

9:01:15: *Marcella:* "Think of someone you really look up to, and write three sentences in a paragraph that describes that person."

9:01:30: *Marcella:* "Someone you would like to be like."

9:02: Marcella continues walking around the room, helping children who are having difficulty. All children are on task.

9:04: *Marcella:* "Now I want you to exchange papers with your reading partner, read that person's description of the person they admire, and describe a setting that you see that person in. Write a paragraph that describes that setting."

9:04–9:05: Students exchange papers; Marcella walks around seeing that everyone has received their partner's paper and is on task.

9:05: *Marcella:* "Where do you see that person being? Below the paragraph I want you to write a new paragraph describing where you see this person, perhaps in an easy chair watching a ball game, or on a porch, in a car, in the kitchen cooking."

9:05:10: *Marcella:* "Describe a scene you see this person in."

9:05:15: *Marcella:* "After you read the description I want you to create a setting for the person described."

9:05:18: Children seem confused either about what they are reading (e.g., asking the writer what a word is or means) or what they are supposed to do.

9:05:19: *Marcella:* "Anything is fine. Use your imagination to describe the setting."

9:05:22: *Marcella:* "Describe a setting for this person."

9:09: *Marcella:* "Now I want you to exchange papers with yet someone else, and after reading the two paragraphs the two other students wrote, write a third paragraph describing a problem you think this admired person has."

Class Discussion

Following the role playing, hold a whole-class discussion or small-group discussions using the following as a springboard:

a. Describe the apparent strength or depth of Marcella's preactive phase of instruction.

b. Describe what you believe are the good points and weak points of this portion of Marcella's language arts lesson and her implementation of it.

c. Describe the apparent strength or quality of Marcella's classroom management.

d. What would you predict will happen during the next few minutes of the lesson, say from 9:10 to 9:12? Why?

simply demanding attention. When a child makes an effort to interact with you, that can be a positive sign, so without judging the quality of the child's effort, gauge carefully your responses to those efforts. If a student's question is really off track, off the wall, out of order, and out of context with the content of the lesson, consider the following as a possible response: "That is an interesting question (or comment) and I would very much like to talk with you more about it. Could we meet at lunch or at some other time that is mutually convenient?"

Avoid Bluffing with a Question You Cannot Answer   Nothing will cause you to lose credibility with students faster than faking an answer. There is nothing wrong with admitting that you do not know. It helps children realize that you are human. It helps them maintain an adequate self-esteem, realizing that they are okay. What *is* important is that you know *where* and *how* to find possible answers and that you help students develop that same knowledge and those same process skills.

SUMMARY

Being able to ask questions may be more important than having right answers. Knowledge is derived from asking questions. Being able to recognize problems and knowing how to formulate questions are skills and keys to problem solving, critical-thinking skill development, and intelligent behavior. You have a responsibility to encourage students to formulate questions and to help them word their questions in such a way that they find tentative answers. This process is necessary for students to build a base of knowledge they can draw on whenever necessary to link, interpret, and explain new information in new situations. As the cornerstone to meaningful learning, thinking, communication, and real-world problem solving, you will continue to develop your skill in the art of questioning throughout your teaching career.

STUDY QUESTIONS AND ADDITIONAL ACTIVITIES

1. Is there ever a time that it is okay for a teacher to bluff an answer to a student's question? Explain your response.
2. Explain why it is important to wait after asking students a content question. For a specific grade level, tell how long a teacher should wait. What should you do if there is no student response after a certain amount of time?
3. To what extent should (or can) a classroom teacher allow student queries to determine content studied? To what extent should students' initial interest, or lack of interest, in a topic determine whether the topic gets taught?
4. Explain the meaning of the following statement: Rather than looking for what students can reiterate, we should look for what they can demonstrate and produce. Explain why you agree or disagree.
5. How many teachers can members of your class find during a designated period of time who actually plan and write the questions they ask children during a lesson? Discuss the results of your investigation.
6. For a subject area and grade level of your choice, write three to five questions that would be appropriate for each of the following modes of teaching: expository

(see Chapter 5), inquiry (see Chapter 9), and demonstration (see Chapter 9). Which ones were easiest to write? Why was this so? (You may wish to revisit your responses to this question following your completion of the study of this book.)

7. Describe the distinguishing characteristics that are associated with *higher-level* and *lower-level* questions. Using the same subject matter for each, create a higher-level and a lower-level question for a grade of your choice.

8. Were a principal to ask you to explain the meaning of the concept "wait time," what would be your reply?

9. It is claimed that questions stimulate certain kinds of thought responses. What mental operations must students engage in to answer this question: What is the most important reason that the desert has a small population? (That is, what would the child have to know and in what sequence would they have to process the information to answer this question?)

10. Explain why you believe it is or is not a good idea to assign reflective questions (i.e., open-ended, "thought" questions) for homework. What research evidence can you find to support or refute your opinion?

WEB SITES RELATED TO CONTENT OF THIS CHAPTER

- Creative Teaching Associates *www.mastercta.com/*
- Critical thinking about what is found on the Web *www.ithaca.edu/library/training/think.html*
- Teacher Created Materials *myconsumerguide.com/teacher_created_materials.htm*
- The Critical Thinking Co. *www.criticalthinking.com*

FOR FURTHER READING

Armone, M. P. (2003). *Using instructional design strategies to foster curiosity*. ED479842. Syracuse, NY: ERIC Clearinghouse on Information & Technology.

Aukerman, M. (2006). Who's afraid of the big "bad answer"? *Educational Leadership, 64*(2), 37–41.

Barrow, L. H. (2002). What do elementary students know about insects? *Journal of Elementary Science Education, 14*(2), 53–60.

Beck, I. L., & McKeown, M. G. (2002). Questioning the author: Making sense of social studies. *Educational Leadership, 60*(3), 44–47.

Chin, C., Brown, D. E., & Bruce, B. C. (2002). Student-generated questions: A meaningful aspect of learning in science. *International Journal of Science Education, 24*, 521–549.

Ciardiello, A. V. (2007). *Puzzle them first! Motivating adolescent readers with question-finding*. Newark, DE: International Reading Association.

Copeland, M. (2005). *Socratic circles*. Portland, ME: Stenhouse.

Denton, P. (2007). *The power of our words*. Turner Falls, MA: Northeast Foundation for Children.

Hawkins, J. (2006). Think before you write. *Educational Leadership, 64*(2), 63–66.

Kohn, A. (2004). Challenging students—and how to have more of them. *Phi Delta Kappan, 86*, 184–194.

Martinez, M. E. (2006). What is metacognition? *Phi Delta Kappan, 87*, 696–699.

Morocco, C. C., Walker, A., & Lewis, L. R. (2003). Access to a schoolwide thinking curriculum.

Journal of Special Education Leadership, 16(1), 5–14.

Ray, K. W. (2006). What are you thinking? *Educational Leadership, 64*(2), 59–62.

Reeves, C. A., & Reeves, R. (2003). Encouraging students to think about how they think! *Mathematics Teaching in the Middle School, 8,* 374–378.

Schielack, J. F., Chancellor, D., & Childs, K. M. (2000). Designing questions to encourage children's mathematical thinking. *Teaching Children Mathematics, 6,* 398–402.

Tower, C. (2000). Questions that matter: Preparing elementary students for the inquiry process. *The Reading Teacher, 53,* 550–557.

Vavilis, B., & Vavilis, S. L. (2004). Why are we learning this? What is this stuff good for, anyway? *Phi Delta Kappan, 86,* 282–287.

Walsh, J. A., & Sattes, B. D. (2005). *Quality questioning.* Thousand Oaks, CA: Corwin Press.

Whitehead, D. (2002). "The story means more to me now": Teaching thinking through guided reading. *Reading: Literacy and Language, 36*(1), 33–37.

Chapter 4

Planning and Managing the Classroom Learning Environment

INTASC Principles	PRAXIS III Domains	NBPTS Standards
• The teacher uses an understanding of individual and group motivation and behavior to create a learning environment that encourages positive social interaction, active engagement in learning, and self-motivation (Principle 5) • The teacher uses knowledge of effective verbal, nonverbal, and media communication techniques to foster active inquiry, collaboration, and supportive interaction in the classroom (Principle 6)	• Creating an Environment for Student Learning (Domain B)	• Learning Environment

Imagine yourself as the parent of a child who is about to enter elementary school. Your child will be placed in the care of an adult—your child's teacher—for approximately 5 hours each day for about 180 days each year for the next 7 or 8 years. As a parent, will you be concerned about how those teachers manage the affairs of the classrooms to which your child has been assigned? The question, of course, answers itself. You would be deeply concerned because you know that how those teachers manage their classrooms has a great deal to do with how well your child will succeed in school.

But if you are a thoughtful, caring parent, your concern will go far beyond the academic success of your child. The classrooms will doubtless have rules. If your child violates one or more of those rules, what will be the consequences? Will the teachers punish your child? How heavily will those teachers rely on punishment as a deterrent to rule infractions? Will teachers reward "good" behavior? What do those teachers perceive as "good" behavior? What system of rewards will teachers use? Do you want your child to grow up learning that one should behave properly to avoid punishment, or to get some kind of reward for good behavior? Or do you want your child to learn that one conducts oneself appropriately and responsibly because "it's the proper thing to do"? As an elementary-school teacher, you can be sure that the parents and guardians of the children in your classroom will be asking themselves many of these same questions.

Managing the classroom learning environment involves much more than establishing and maintaining orderly student behavior. The classroom is really a laboratory where young human beings are shaped and socialized in accordance with the established values and mores of the community and the larger society. What happens in those elementary-school classrooms for the 6 or 7 or more years that children spend in them has a great deal to do with how they will feel about themselves for years to come. A person's concept of self plays a major role in the success of that person in all aspects of life. In other words, from the dynamics of classroom living and learning, children receive many messages, both overt and covert, that help them form images of themselves, which in turn relate directly to their school success, their social competence, and their becoming responsible, caring, problem-solving and decision-making adults. It is our purpose in this chapter to help you begin deciding how you will manage your classroom learning environment.

Children come to school needing to know that

- I am accepted and acceptable here just as I am.
- I am safe here—physically, emotionally, and intellectually.
- People here care about me.
- People here listen to me.
- People know how I'm doing, and it matters to them that I do well.
- People acknowledge my interests and perspectives and act upon them.

—Carol Ann Tomlinson (2002, p. 8)

ANTICIPATED OUTCOMES

After completing this chapter, you should be able to do the following:

1. Describe the meaning of a *values-based management plan.*
2. Describe the contributions of leading experts regarding classroom management.
3. Describe the characteristics of a well-managed classroom learning environment.
4. Differentiate with examples between classroom procedures that are flexible and those that are inflexible.
5. Distinguish among classroom *control,* classroom *discipline,* and classroom *management.*
6. Describe characteristics of a safe, supportive, and effective classroom learning environment.
7. Describe characteristics of a classroom that is supportive and psychologically safe for children.
8. Describe the advantages and disadvantages of studying children's school records to discover which children have a history of causing trouble.
9. Distinguish between the concepts of "consequences" and "punishment" and between "rules" and "procedures" as related to classroom management.
10. Describe specific things you can do to help your students to develop their self-control.
11. Describe a teacher's reasonable first reaction in the classroom to each of the following students: one who is aggressively violent, one who habitually lies, one who is defiant, one who tosses paper at the wastebasket, and one who is sitting and doing nothing.
12. Describe steps you should take in dealing with conflict situations between children.
13. Describe specific steps you should take in preparing for the first few days of school.
14. Describe the meaning of and give an example of *sequenced consequences* as used for inappropriate student behavior.
15. Explain the value of using a classroom daily schedule.
16. Describe with examples how the physical arrangements of a classroom can affect learning.
17. Describe the characteristics of effective lesson and activity transitions.
18. Prepare an initial draft of your classroom management system.

A VALUES-BASED MANAGEMENT PLAN

It should be clear from this chapter's introduction that because we live in a democratic society, the foundation for your classroom management system must be a set of values consistent with such a society. There may be variation because of local community norms, but fundamentally, we are talking about a management plan based on such values as *accepting responsibility, sense of fair play, honesty,* and *respect for the rights, opinions, and possessions of others.*

As a teacher, your management system is the source of much of what children learn in school through the covert curriculum. If there are constant conflicts between children, if a general atmosphere of hostility prevails, if class morale is low, you need then to analyze the values that give direction to the management system. You also need to understand the sources of students' behavior and to reflect on your own behavior in the classroom. More often than not children inadvertently model the behaviors of the significant adults in their lives. Among the most significant adults in the life of any child are that child's parents or guardians and older family members and the child's schoolteacher.

A CLARIFICATION OF TERMS

The term *control* implies restraint, regulation, regimentation, and the direct use of power. "You have good control" is usually regarded as a compliment to a beginning teacher. One is never sure whether the meaning is intended in the broad sense (covering the larger umbrella of classroom management) or in the literal sense (meaning student behavior is so restrained that the classroom is teacher dominated). Used literally, the term *control* can easily be given unwarranted importance, becoming an end in itself rather than a means of enhancing the quality of living and learning in the classroom.

Control should not be thought of as a goal of teaching—nor should management, for that matter. You should perceive these as processes that are prerequisite for an environment conducive to teaching and learning. A negative example is a third-grade teacher who has "perfect control" of a class: the class is quiet, individuals are immobile, no one speaks out of turn, and so on. To achieve this calm, the teacher has children doing relatively meaningless busywork at their seats while she attends to other matters. These other matters may have to do with preparing lessons and materials, teaching small groups or individuals, or taking care of business relating to student accounting, reporting, or the lunch program. To achieve this level of restraint, the teacher does indeed need to control most of the physical and intellectual activities in the classroom. One must, of course, ask whether these kinds of training procedures, common to prisons and army boot training, are appropriate for the 21st-century elementary-school classroom and life in a democratic society.

An objectionable aspect of the control concept is the implication that teachers are wholly responsible for maintaining orderly classrooms. This runs counter to the idea that children need to learn responsible habits of self-direction. Some of the specific strategies developed to strengthen classroom control and discipline have stressed the importance of *reducing* the reliance on power and controls imposed externally and have, instead, focused on student responsibility and student involvement. Children need to learn to control their own behavior, not to please you, the teacher, but because, in so doing, they develop greater maturity and independence. Of course, children cannot manage to do this alone. Left unguided, they are likely to become unruly and mischievous. Learning to take care of oneself should be an important outcome of the school experience. It is not likely to be achieved if you constantly control your learners' behavior. In the words of Good and Brophy (2003, p. 107),

> Teachers who approach classroom management as a process of establishing and maintaining effective learning environments tend to be more successful than teachers who place more emphasis on their roles as authority figures or disciplinarians. Teachers *are* authority figures and need to require their students to conform to certain rules and procedures. However, these rules and procedures are not ends in themselves but are means for organizing the classroom to support teaching and learning. Thus, classroom management should be designed to support instruction and to help students to gain in capacity for self-control.

The term *discipline*, like *control*, may be used to mean various aspects of the larger umbrella of classroom management. "She has good discipline" usually means that the teacher maintains an orderly classroom. Discipline also connotes punishment. "Strong discipline" is used to describe teacher behavior that is rigid, firm, and unbending. There is an adversary quality to this meaning of *discipline*. When teachers say, "Anyone who gets out of their seat without permission will be disciplined," they mean that offenders will be punished. In this sense, discipline means both punishment and corrective treatment.

The modern concept of discipline is as an *intelligent behavior,* that is, in this instance, as an imposition of control on oneself to develop character, efficient work habits, proper conduct, consideration for others, orderly living, or control of one's impulses and emotions. The establishment of student *self-control* is the ultimate objective. But to develop self-control, learners must be given some independence, and the process of experimenting with such independence requires the teacher's guidance. Neither highly structured, teacher-dominated environments nor those that are completely permissive facilitate developing self-control.

As shown in Table 4.1 various specific approaches have been developed to help teachers understand and deal with managing student behavior and the classroom learning environment. Using the descriptors associated with them, among the best-known approaches are *assertive discipline, behavior modification, control theory, logical consequences,* and *self-discipline.* Other than the brief discussion that follows, in-depth analysis of the merits and limitations of each approach is beyond the scope of this book; sources are available to those who wish to learn more about them. As a part of your professional preparation, you may even be required to take a course that deals specifically with classroom management.

Used interchangeably, the terms *classroom climate, classroom environment,* and *classroom atmosphere* refer to the emotional tone and quality of the interpersonal relations that prevail. Classroom climate results from a composite of the interactions and transactions that take place in the classroom and may be described variously as relaxed, pleasant, flexible, rigid, autocratic, democratic, repressive, supportive, and so forth. Consequently, the nature of the climate of a particular classroom is cognate to the teacher's management system.

TABLE 4.1
Comparing Approaches to Classroom Management

Authority	To Know What Is Going On	To Provide Smooth Transitions
Canter/Jones	Realize that the student has the right to choose how to behave in your class with the understanding of the consequences that will follow his or her choice.	Insist on decent, responsible behavior.
Dreikurs/Nelsen/Albert	Realize that the student wants status, recognition, and a feeling of belonging. Misbehavior is associated with mistaken goals of getting attention, seeking power, getting revenge, and wanting to be left alone.	Identify mistaken student goals; act in ways that do not reinforce these goals.
Ginott/Kohn	Communicate with the student to find out his or her feelings about a situation and about that student in general.	Invite student cooperation.
Glasser/Gordon/ Rogers/Gathercoal/ Freiberg/Marshall/ Sprick	Realize that the student is a rational being who can control his or her own behavior.	Help the student make good choices; good choices produce good behavior, and bad choices produce bad behavior.
Kounin	Develop *withitness,* a skill enabling you to see what is happening in all parts of the classroom at all times.	Avoid jerkiness, which consists of thrusts (giving directions before your group is ready), dangles (leaving one activity dangling in the verbal air, starting another one, and then returning to the first activity), and flip-flops (terminating one activity, beginning another one, and then returning to the first activity you terminated).
Skinner	Realize value of nonverbal interaction (i.e., smiles, pats, and handshakes) to communicate to students that you know what is going on.	Realize that smooth transitions may be part of your procedures for awarding reinforcers (i.e., points and tokens) to reward appropriate behavior.

(Continued)

TABLE 4.1
(Continued)

To Maintain Group Alertness	To Involve Students	To Attend to Misbehavior
Set clear limits and consequences; follow through consistently; state what you expect; state the consequences and why the limits are needed.	Use firm tone of voice; keep eye contact; use nonverbal gestures and verbal statements; use hints, questions, and direct messages in requesting student behavior; give and receive compliments.	Follow through with your promises and the resonable, previously stated consequences that have been established in your class.
Provide firm guidance and leadership.	Allow students to have a say in establishing rules and consequences in your class.	Make it clear that unpleasant consequences will follow inappropriate behavior.
Model the behavior you expect to see in your students.	Build students' self-esteem.	Give a message that addresses the situation and does not attack the students' character.
Understand that class rules are essential.	Realize that classroom meetings are effective means for attending to rules, behavior, and discipline.	Accept no excuses for inappropriate behavior; see that reasonable consequences always follow.
Avoid slowdowns (delays and time wasting) that can be caused by overdwelling (too much time spent on explanations) and by fragmentation (breaking down an activity into several unnecessary steps). Develop a group focus (active participation by all students in the group) through accountability (holding all students accountable for the concept of the lesson) and by attention (seeing all the students and using unison and individual responses).	Avoid boredom by providing a feeling of progress for the students, offering challenges, varying class activities, changing the level of intellectual challenge, varying lesson presentations, and using many different learning materials and aids.	Understand that teacher correction influences behavior of other nearby students (the ripple effect).
Set rules, rewards, and consequences; emphasize that responsibility for good behavior rests with each student.	Involve students in "token economies," in contracts, and in charting behavior performance.	Provide tangibles to students who follow the class rules; represent tangibles as "points" for the whole class to use to "purchase" a special activity.

Children must be willing to cooperate with their teacher or else the teacher's management system will fail. Without their willing cooperation, an adversarial relationship develops between children and teacher. When this happens, the classroom climate becomes so tense that even the smallest issue can, and often does, become the cause of a major confrontation. If such relationships continue, the teacher becomes increasingly ineffective and will probably be forced to leave.

A teacher's procedures for *classroom control* reflect that teacher's philosophy about how children learn and the teacher's interpretation and commitment to the school's stated mission. In sum, those procedures represent the teacher's concept of *classroom management*. Although often eclectic in their approaches, today's teachers share a concern for selecting management techniques that enhance student self-esteem and that help children learn how to assume control of their behavior and ownership of their learning.

Effective classroom management is not a goal to achieve but a plan you have carefully thought out and skillfully implemented. That plan consists of a system of procedures and conditions that enable you and your students to attain valid educational goals and objectives. It has to do with the atmosphere of the classroom, daily procedures and routines, the deployment of students, the setting of standards of conduct, and the system of rewards and punishments that prevails. Good managers are not always good teachers, but inability to manage a classroom learning environment in ways that facilitate learning is usually a "fatal flaw" to your success as a teacher. Thus, our discussion of classroom management focuses your attention on that cluster of skills needed to plan, organize, and implement an appropriate program of instruction.

There can be little doubt that your skill in classroom management will be a major factor contributing to your teaching success. In student-teaching supervisory conferences more time is spent on classroom management than on anything else. Classroom management is the one aspect of a teacher's credentials that principals are most interested in. After all, most school administrators are probably aware that an analysis of a half century of research studies concluded that classroom management is the single most important factor to influence student learning (Want, Haertel, & Walberg, 1994). It is the one facet of a teacher's behavior that parents and guardians are most concerned about. When a teacher is in difficulty on the job, the chances are that the problem can be traced to either (a) poor decisions the teacher made relating to classroom management, (b) inadequate attention to the preactive phase of instruction, or (c) both. Both are related to planning. In other words, poor planning of either classroom management or of instruction, or both, is a precursor to ineffective teaching and eventual dismissal from that teaching position.

It is clear that management and instruction are two sides of the same coin we call teaching. Successful teaching cannot take place without both of these elements. The interaction of these two components of teaching means also that they affect each other. Skillful management facilitates the conduct of instruction. Inspired and interesting instruction reduces the likelihood of management problems.

Classroom Management: Contributions of Leading Experts

You are probably familiar with the term *behavior modification*, which describes several high-control techniques for changing behavior in an observable and predictable way; with **B. F. Skinner's** (Skinner, 1968, 1971) ideas about how students learn and how behavior can be modified by using reinforcers (rewards); and with how his principles of behavior shaping have been extended by others.

Behavior modification begins with four steps: (1) identify the behavior to be modified, (2) record how often and under what conditions that behavior occurs, (3) cause a change by reinforcing a desired behavior with a positive reinforcer, and (4) choose the type of positive reinforcers to award—*activity or privilege reinforcers*, such as choice of playing a game, decorating the classroom, choice at a classroom learning center, freed without penalty from doing an assignment or test, running an errand for the teacher; *social reinforcers*, such as verbal attention or private praise, and nonverbal such as proximity of teacher to student, and facial expression of approval, such as a wink or smile, or bodily expression of approval, such as a thumbs up or high five; *graphic reinforcers*, such as numerals and symbols; *tangible reinforcers*, such as edibles, badges, certificates, stickers, or books; and *token reinforcers*, such as points, stars, or script that can be accumulated and cashed in later for a tangible reinforcer, or tickets that can be used for something like a school athletic or musical event.

Using an approach that emphasizes both reinforcement for appropriate behaviors and punishment or consequences for inappropriate behaviors, **Lee Canter** and **Marlene Canter** developed their *assertive discipline* model that emphasizes four major points (Canter & Canter, 1992). First, as a teacher, you have professional rights in your classroom and should expect appropriate student behavior. Second, your students have rights to choose how to behave in your classroom, and you should plan limits for inappropriate behavior. Third, an assertive discipline approach means you clearly state your expectations in a firm voice and explain the boundaries for behavior. And fourth, you should plan a system of positive consequences (e.g., positive messages home, awards and rewards, special privileges) for appropriate behavior and establish consequences (e.g., time-out, withdrawal of privileges, parent/guardian conference) for inappropriate student misbehavior, and you follow through in a consistent way.

In his *logical consequences* approach, **Rudolf Dreikurs** emphasized six points (Dreikurs & Cassel, 1972; Dreikurs, Grunwald, & Pepper, 1982). First, be fair, firm, and friendly, and involve students in developing and implementing class rules. Second, students need to clearly understand the rules and the logical consequences for misbehavior. For example, a logical consequence for a student who has written graffiti on a school wall would be to either clean the wall or pay for a school custodian to do it. Third, allow the students to be responsible not only for their own actions but also for influencing others to maintain appropriate behavior in your classroom. Fourth, encourage students to show respect for themselves and for others, and provide each student with a sense of belonging to the classroom. Fifth, recognize and encourage student goals of belonging, gaining status, and gaining recognition. And sixth, recognize but do not reinforce correlated student goals of getting attention, seeking power, and taking revenge.

TPW Video Classroom

Series: Classroom Management

Module 2: Fostering Student Accountability

Video 1: Modeling Mutual Respect, Routines, and Transitions

Continuing the work of Dreikurs, **Linda Albert** (1989, rev. 1996) developed a *cooperative discipline* model. The cooperative discipline model makes use of Dreikurs' fundamental concepts, with emphasis added on the "three Cs": capable, connect, and contribute. Also building on the work of Dreikurs, **Jane Nelsen** (Nelsen, 1987; Nelsen, Lott, & Glenn, 1993) provides guidelines for helping children develop positive feelings of self. Key points made by Nelsen and that are reflected throughout this book include: (a) use natural and logical consequences as a means to inspire a positive classroom atmosphere, (b) understand that children have goals that drive them toward misbehavior (attention, power, revenge, and assumed adequacy), (c) use kindness (student retains dignity) and firmness when administering consequences for a student's misbehavior, (d) establish a climate of mutual respect, (e) use class meetings to give students ownership in problem solving, and (f) offer encouragement as a means of inspiring self-evaluation and focusing on the students' behaviors.

William Glasser (1965, 1969, 1986, 1990, 1993) developed his concept of *reality therapy* (i.e., the condition of the present, rather than of the past, contributes to inappropriate behavior) for the classroom. Glasser emphasizes that students have a responsibility to learn at school and to maintain appropriate behavior while there. He emphasizes that with the teacher's help, students can make appropriate choices about their behavior in school—can, in fact, learn self-control. Finally, he suggests holding classroom meetings that are devoted to establishing rules and identifying standards for student behavior, matters of misbehavior, and the consequences of misbehavior. Since the publication of his first book in 1965, Glasser has expanded his message to include the student needs of belonging and love, control, freedom, and fun, asserting that if these needs are ignored and unattended at school, students are bound to fail (Glasser, 1997).

Today's commitment to *quality education* is largely derived from the recent work of Glasser and the corresponding concept of the *personal-centered classrooms*, as advanced by **Carl Rogers** and **H. Jerome Freiberg** in their book, *Freedom to Learn* (Columbus, OH: Merrill, 1994). In schools committed to quality education and the person-centered classroom, students feel a sense of belonging, enjoy some degree of power of self-discipline, have fun learning, and experience a sense of freedom in the process (Freiberg, 1997, 1999).

Paul Gathercoal built his *judicious discipline* model on a synthesis of professional ethics, good-quality educational practice, and democratic principles and students' constitutional rights as outlined especially in the 1st, 4th, and 14th Amendments to the U.S. Constitution (Gathercoal, 1997). By allowing students the opportunity to experience individual freedoms and encouraging them to learn and practice the responsibilities emanating from their individual rights, students learn how to govern themselves. A number of schools report success in reducing student hostile behaviors by using a combination of judicious discipline and class meetings (Freiberg, 1999; McEwan & Gathercoal, 2000).

Haim G. Ginott emphasized ways for teacher and students to communicate in his communication model. He advised that a teacher send a clear message (or messages) about situations rather than about the child. And he emphasized that teachers must model the behavior they expect from their students. Ginott's suggested messages are those that express feelings appropriately, acknowledge students' feelings, give appropriate direction, and invite cooperation (Ginott, 1971; Manning & Bucher, 2001).

Thomas Gordon (1989) emphasizes influence over control and decries use of reinforcement (i.e., rewards and punishment) as an ineffective tool for achieving a positive influence over a child's behavior. Rather than using reinforcements for appropriate behavior and punishment for inappropriate behaviors, Gordon advocates encouragement and development of student self-control and self-regulated behavior. To have a positive influence and to encourage self-control, the teacher (and school) should provide a rich and positive learning environment with rich and stimulating learning activities. Specific teacher behaviors include active listening (exemplified, for example, by maintaining eye contact, rephrasing what the student has said, and asking relevant questions), sending I-messages (rather than you-messages), shifting from I-messages to listening when there is student resistance to an I-message, clearly identifying ownership of problems to the student when such is the case (i.e., not assuming ownership if it is a student's problem), and encouraging collaborative problem solving.

Fredric Jones (1987) also promotes the idea of helping students support their own self-control, essentially, however, by way of a negative reinforcement method—rewards follow wanted behavior. Preferred activity time (PAT), for example, is an invention derived from the Jones model. The Jones model makes four recommendations. First, you should properly structure your classroom so students understand the rules (the expectation standards for classroom behavior) and procedures (the means for accomplishing routine tasks). Second, you maintain control by selecting appropriate instructional strategies. Third, you build patterns of cooperative work. Finally, you develop appropriate backup methods for dealing with inappropriate student behavior.

Jacob Kounin (1970) is well known for his identification of the *ripple effect* (i.e., the effect of a teacher's response to one student's misbehavior on students whose behavior was appropriate) and of *withitness* and *overlapping* ability (both of which are discussed in Chapter 2).

CHARACTERISTICS OF AN EFFECTIVELY MANAGED CLASSROOM

Let us make this point perfectly clear: Thoughtful and thorough planning of your procedures for managing your classroom learning environment is as important a part of your preactive phase of instruction (discussed in Chapter 2) as is the preparation of units and lessons (discussed in Chapter 6). Through planning, you can anticipate and prevent problems. Let us now identify and discuss six characteristics of effective management. Effective management of the classroom learning environment.

1. Enhances children's mental and social development.
2. Facilitates the achievement of instructional goals that suit children's developmental levels.
3. Provides intellectual and physical freedom within specified and reasonable limits.
4. Establishes and maintains procedures and consequences.
5. Allows children to develop skills of self-direction and independence.
6. Establishes a firm, warm, and productive working relationship between teacher and students.

Enhancing Mental and Social Development

Establishing "control" of a class, in the sense of the teacher's ability to wield power over children, should not be much of a problem for you as an adult. You can create a situation in which you have absolute control over everything that takes place in the room. You may do this by using threats of low grades and failure, ridicule, punishment, and rigid rules and by keeping student activity controlled to the point where children cannot move or talk without permission. This may be justified on the grounds that it is the only way you can maintain order and therefore conduct instruction. But these repressive tactics can be detrimental to the mental and social development of children. Children may conform to classroom rules, but if they have not had the rationale for the rules explained, or if they do not understand the rationale for the rules, they will resent having to obey them.

It is well known that a positive self-concept is not only important to learning but also vital to an individual's total development (see, for example, Combs, 1962). In the type of distrustful setting just described, children are not likely to develop positive self-images. Moreover, the pressures that build up in some children as the result of a repressive authoritarian atmosphere in school erupt, either in or outside school, in various forms of aggression, tears, withdrawal, bedwetting, nail biting, or other more serious forms of maladaptive behavior. One cannot build a positive sense of self in an atmosphere of constant negativity.

The elementary school should be a laboratory for the social growth of children. Here, children learn to give and take, to share with others, to interact with peers, and to develop a degree of responsible independence. Children learn social skills partly through instruction but mainly by having opportunities to participate with others in social situations. Programs that have children working continually on an individual basis do not provide adequately for the social dimension of their learning. One can learn social skills only in social settings.

Good management reflects itself in a classroom where children are comfortable intellectually, emotionally, and socially. Your students will recognize and respect you as an authority figure but will not fear you or perceive you as a constant threat to their self-confidence. Your classroom is a confidence-building place where children grow in their competence as human beings.

> *By teaching students to raise their voices through writing on social issues that concern*
> *them, we teach them to participate actively in a democracy.*
>
> —Randy Bomer (2004)

Facilitating the Achievement of Instructional Goals

Mr. Campbell is working with a group of eight third-graders on phonetic skills in a reading lesson. Meanwhile, the remaining 20 children are moving about the room, talking loudly; occasionally, there is an altercation that necessitates Mr. Campbell's intervention. The noise level is high. The children in the reading group often ask to have things repeated because they cannot hear or are not paying attention to what is being said.

This is a serious matter because the student behavior resulting from Mr. Campbell's poor management is interfering with his instructional program. Phonetic analysis depends on fine sound discrimination; children therefore must be able to hear those sounds. This is difficult, perhaps even impossible, in the situation described. Moreover, Mr. Campbell himself cannot attend properly to the lesson because of the commotion in the room. Also, the children not in the reading group are reinforcing behavior patterns that contribute neither to good study habits nor to social skills.

Scott Cunningham/Merrill

The joy of teaching is never more real than when children express enthusiasm and exuberance in wanting to participate in the work of the class. A well-planned and interesting instructional program is the teacher's first line of defense against student disruptive behavior and other classroom management problems.

To establish conditions that make it possible to conduct instruction, you must develop a systematic method of organizing classroom activities. You need to steer a course somewhere between Mr. Campbell's lack of organization and the other end of the continuum, characterized by rigidity and teacher domination. For most classrooms, you will need a schedule of daily events. These will probably not vary much from day to day. Children like this. They like to know when each of their classes is to take place. They know when there is to be quiet time and when there is activity time. This type of flexible but planned organization of the day makes it possible for you to do your job and for the children to do theirs, so that instructional goals can be achieved.

Developmental differences in children require that you select age-appropriate learning goals and presentation modes. Young children need considerably more personal teacher interaction than do older ones. Learning objectives for younger children need to be quite explicit, and you must closely monitor their work so that you can adjust it for level of difficulty.

Providing Boundaries of Intellectual and Physical Freedom

If children grew up knowing the subject matter and skills of the curriculum and were completely socialized, well mannered, and well behaved, there would be no point in sending them to school. The object of school is precisely to teach children such subject matter and skills. For children to learn them, however, they need to be in a secure environment where they can be free to try to do new things. Not only that, they should also feel encouraged to do so without having to fear or be embarrassed by making mistakes.

Although children should be as free as possible to explore intellectually and should enjoy a great deal of physical freedom as well, they need also to learn that no one is totally free. There are rules, regulations, procedures, and consequences that apply in every classroom, no matter what your personal philosophy. For example, you cannot and must not allow children to do things that injure others, that are inhumane, that are disrespectful of others, or that destroy the property of others. Such behavior is simply not permitted.

When teachers have no classroom rules or fail to make them explicit, one can predict that they will have a stormy time of it. When there are no rules, no one knows what is expected. Children may run wild and in the process may injure themselves or each other. Even with explicit rules, children will test their outer edges. They seem to need to search out the limits of freedom, within which they then know they must function. When you make your procedures known, this testing will be more focused. Where rules and expected procedures are unknown, testing takes the form of trial and error—to find out your level of tolerance.

You must teach procedures and behavior expectations on a continuing basis. From time to time children need to be reminded of *why* room procedures were established in the first place. Encourage them to contribute their own ideas about how the classroom management system is working and how it might be improved.

They need to be involved in classroom management to some extent to have some sense of investment in what goes on.

Thinking in Terms of Procedures Rather Than Rules; Consequences Rather Than Punishment

To encourage a constructive and supportive classroom environment, you may wish to think and speak in terms of "procedures" (or "standards and guidelines") rather than of "rules," and of "consequences" rather than "punishment." The reason is this: When working with a cohort of children, some rules are of course necessary, but to many people, the term *rules* has a more negative connotation than does the term *procedures* (Queen, Blackwelder, & Mallen, 1997). For example, a classroom rule might be, "When one person is talking we do not interrupt until that person is finished." When that rule is broken, rather than reminding children of the "rule," you may change the emphasis to a "procedure" simply by reminding students by asking, "What is our procedure (or expectation) when someone is talking?"

It is the contention of some educators that thinking in terms of and talking about "procedures" and "consequences" are more likely to contribute to a positive classroom atmosphere than referring to "rules" and "punishment." Of course, some argue that you might as well tell it like it is. Especially if your group of students is linguistically and culturally mixed, you will need to be as direct and clear as possible to avoid sending confusing or mixed signals. But remember this: As a credentialed classroom teacher you are a professional, which means that, as always, after considering what experienced others have to say, the final decision is only one of many that you must make, and that it will be influenced by your own thinking and unique situation.

Developing Skills of Self-Direction and Responsible Involvement

It is a curious fact that some teachers expect children to develop self-direction and independence without permitting them to practice the necessary skills. That is rather like teaching them the alphabet without ever letting them put letters together to form words. Children are not likely to gain self-direction and independence in classrooms that are almost wholly teacher directed and teacher dependent. What is needed is a good balance: Provide sufficient guidance and direction on the one hand, and allow children to experiment with independence and self-direction on the other. The tendency is to be either too highly teacher directed or overly permissive. Neither provides an appropriate setting for learning.

Children should be active participants in some aspects of classroom management, thereby gaining practical experience in contributing to policy and decision making. Such involvement *empowers* children, giving them a sense of invested ownership of the classroom. Insofar as possible, you should encourage students to feel that it is not only your room but their room as well. However, as the most mature person in the classroom and the person with the legal responsibility, you are accountable for providing the leadership and guidance to make the operation safe and effectively functional.

Working Toward Warm Human Relations

Sometimes beginning teachers believe they can develop a close "buddy" relationship between the children and themselves. They encourage informality by allowing students to call them by their first name or a nickname. Teachers who attempt to assume somewhat of a peer relationship with children remove social distance. This rarely works well; it usually means that teaching authority is compromised in the process.

At the other extreme are teachers who feel they must not "get too close," who talk in a stilted way, and who cannot relax because they feel that if they did, children might take advantage of them. Remaining rather cold and distant, they are careful not to reveal much of the informal aspects of their personality.

Good teachers extend their warmth and "humanness" to children. They work with children in ways that show they enjoy young people. At the same time, they maintain the basic firmness that children need, expect, and indeed, want from respected adults in their lives.

SERIOUSNESS OF PROBLEMS

Described next in order of increasing seriousness are categories of student misbehavior that teachers sometimes must contend with. *Now* is the time in your career for you to begin thinking about how you will deal with such problems when they arise. Note that we didn't say "if they arise," but rather "when they arise." For no teacher, no matter how good or experienced, is exempt from these possibilities.

TPW Video Classroom

Series: General Methods

Module 4: Classroom Management

Video 1: Low Profile Classroom Management

Goofing Off

This category of least serious includes student behaviors such as fooling around, not doing assigned tasks, daydreaming, and just generally being off task. Fortunately, in most instances, this type of behavior is momentary, and sometimes it might even be best to pretend you are unaware of it; if it persists, all it may take to get a student back on task is an unobtrusive (silent and private) redirection. Unobtrusive teacher behaviors include eye contact and mobility and proximity control, such as moving and standing next to children who are off task. If this doesn't work, then go to the second intervention level by rather quietly calling the students by name and reminding them of the correct procedure or of what they are supposed to be doing.

Avoid asking an off-task child *any* question, such as a content question, knowing full well that the student has not been paying attention, or asking the question, "Serena, why are you doing that?" Avoid also making a threat such as "Serena, if you don't turn around and get to work I will send you to Ms. Johnson's room for a time-out." It is important you not make "mountains out of molehills," or you could cause more problems than you would resolve. Maintain Serena's focus on the lesson, that is, on the desired behavior, rather than on her off-task behavior.

Examples of trivial "misbehaviors" that you need not be concerned about unless they become disruptive, or are occurring with increasing frequency, are brief whispering during a lesson and short periods of inattentiveness, perhaps accompanied by visual wandering or daydreaming. Your responses to student behavior and enforcement of procedures such as raising hands and being recognized before speaking will naturally vary depending on a number of factors, such as the particular learning activity and students' age levels (see "Guidelines for Practicing Gender Equity When Questioning" in Chapter 3).

In addition, there is sometimes a tendency among teachers when they have a problem with students goofing off and being disruptive to assume, or to act like they believe, that the entire group is being unruly, when more often it is only one, two, or three students. You must avoid giving children any impression that you believe they all are being unruly. You may treat the group as if they all are "guilty" in an attempt to get group peer pressure to work in your favor; in fact, however, it is more likely to alienate the majority of children who are behaving properly.

Disruptions to Learning

This category includes incessant talking out of turn, frequent getting out of seat without permission, clowning, and tossing objects, behaviors that are more serious because they disrupt others' learning. In handling these common disruptive misbehaviors, it is important that you have explained their consequences to students, and then, following your stated procedures, promptly and consistently deal with violations. Usually a simple nonverbal reminder to disruptive children to return to the educational task at hand will suffice. Too many beginning teachers tend to ignore these class disruptions seemingly in hopes that they will stop if they don't acknowledge them. You must not ignore minor infractions of this type, for if you do, they most likely will escalate beyond your worst expectations. In other words, maintain your control of classroom events, rather than becoming controlled by them.

Defiance, Cheating, Lying, and Stealing

When a student refuses, perhaps with hostility, to follow your instructions, such defiance might be worthy of temporary or permanent removal from the class. Depending on how serious you judge the situation to be, you may simply give the student a time-out, such as by sending the child to a nearby classroom (be sure to prearrange such moves with the teacher involved), or you may suspend the student from class until

Activity 4.1: Shouldn't Punishment Fit the Crime?

During a physical education lesson, several of the 22 fifth graders who made up the class were goofing around by chasing each other, punching in jest, playing leapfrog, and generally ignoring the physical education teacher, who was trying to teach a lesson in basketball. Giving up trying to obtain their attention, the teacher sent for the school principal to come and assist in regaining control of the group. The principal came out to the play area and immediately ordered all 22 children into a classroom. There, as punishment, all 22 children were assigned pages to hand copy from an encyclopedia.

1. What were your initial thoughts after reading this case?

2. In your opinion, should the physical education teacher have done something different? If so, what?
3. Do you believe the principal should have done something different? If so, what?
4. In your opinion, is there ever a time when an entire class of children should be punished for the misbehavior of some of the children? Explain.
5. How would you react if you were the parent or guardian of one of the children who was not goofing off but who nevertheless was punished along with the others?
6. Is assigning writing ever an appropriate form of punishment? Explain why or why not.

you can hold a conference about the situation, perhaps involving you, the student, the student's parent or guardian, and a school official.

Any cheating, lying, or stealing may be an isolated act, and the child may only need a one-on-one talk to find out what precipitated the incident and what might be done to prevent it ever happening again. A student who *habitually* exhibits any of these behaviors may need to be referred to a specialist. Whenever you have reason to suspect such behavior, you should follow school policy, and you should discuss your concerns with appropriate colleagues or a school counselor or psychologist.

Bullying and Violence

As emphasized in Chapter 1, more and more often today, even in kindergarten, teachers are confronted with major problems of misbehavior that have ramifications beyond the classroom or that begin elsewhere and spill over into the classroom. If you experience any acts of written, verbal, or overt bullying or violence, please do not hesitate to ask for help. As a teacher, you must stay alert.

CONFLICT RESOLUTION

Jason is waiting in line at the drinking fountain when Eric approaches and tries to nudge his way ahead of him. Jason tries to close the gap with his body; Eric pushes him out of the way. Jason pushes back; Eric strikes him—and the altercation escalates into a full-blown fight. A teacher is called. The boys are separated, perhaps led off to the principal's office, and some attempt is made to resolve the matter. It may be that the issue is settled at that point or that the conflict continues, perhaps resulting in an afterschool fight on the way home.

Incidents involving two children or groups of children are fairly common in schools and are usually unpleasant for all concerned. Because dominance relationships are so widespread throughout nature, including among human beings, there is really no way to avoid conflict entirely. There is rarely a social relationship in which conflict is wholly absent. This applies whether we consider national and international issues or examine social relationships on a face-to-face basis within families, in neighborhoods, or on the school playground.

You can be prepared to deal with conflict situations in the following ways: (a) establish classroom conditions that minimize the possibility of conflict and that encourage harmonious social relations; (b) resolve interpersonal conflicts immediately, but plan for longer-range solutions to problems; and (c) include instruction on conflict and conflict resolution. We discuss each briefly in the following sections.

Minimizing Conflict and Encouraging Harmonious Social Relations

Why are some classrooms characterized by a higher degree of hostility and aggression than others? To answer this question, we must examine the conditions within classrooms that give rise to such behavior.

Perhaps the most powerful force affecting classroom climate is the nature of the words used and statements made by the teacher. A preponderance of negative and directive teacher statements will elevate the levels of tension and hostility in a classroom. This result is predictable, having been demonstrated over and over in human-relations laboratories. One of the most effective ways for you to reduce hostility and aggression in groups is to increase the number of positive, constructive statements you make and to eliminate those that are negative, directive, and critical.

Hostility and aggression also escalate when children are under great pressure to work rapidly or when they are required to do more than they are able to in the time provided. We may generalize: *Any procedure that continually frustrates children is likely to reflect itself in aggression and conflict.* Those who cannot perform satisfactorily under tension-producing conditions are likely to turn on others to vent their hostilities. A conflict on the playground may be the result of frustrations built up in the classroom. A more comfortable and relaxed instructional pace, coupled with realistically achievable requirements, can go a long way toward reducing the possibility of interpersonal conflicts.

Your classroom atmosphere can be more conducive to improved human relations if competitive situations are kept in proper perspective. Competition can be wholesome to the productive output of a group, provided it does not get out of hand. Children need to engage in fair competition and to learn the appropriate behavior associated with winning and losing. When children engage in competitive sports and games, the meaning of good sportsmanship is one of the important lessons they should learn. Good sportsmanship is part of the American tradition. The classroom, of course, is not a sports arena, but it can be a place where competitiveness is handled with an attitude of fairness and goodwill. When classroom competition becomes intense, with some students rudely flaunting their superiority, there is likely to be hostility leading to conflict. Cooperative group efforts by the class can do much to reduce the ill effects of competition and can teach children the values associated with consideration for others.

Resolving Conflicts Immediately, with a Plan for Longer-Range Solutions

You must intervene immediately when conflicts occur between individual children or between groups of children. Intervention may take care of a problem for the moment, but you also should undertake some type of longer-range corrective measures. A teacher who stops a fight in the lunchroom may be treating the symptoms rather than the causes of conflict. Very often, the intervening teacher begins by asking who is responsible. Of course, the children blame each other ("She hit me first," says one; "But she started it by swiping the ball," says the other). After some discussion, the children apologize to each other and shake hands, and the matter seems to be settled. When there have been hurt feelings, however, this is not a satisfactory settlement of the issue. It does little good to force an apology from a youngster or to have children shake hands unless you do something about the conditions that brought about the conflict in the first place. Exploring the conflict will often show that both children are contending for something of value, whether it is approval by classmates, peer leadership roles, positions on athletic teams, or the favor of a high-status classmate.

TPW Video Classroom

Series: Classroom Management

Module 5: Maintaining Appropriate Student Behavior

Video 1: Empowering Students to Resolve Conflicts

Providing Instruction on Conflict and Conflict Resolution

Traditionally, much of the work with conflict in the elementary school might be described as little more than moral injunctions against conflict. "Good" children do not fight, quarrel, or bully others. They show proper respect and consideration for others. They are kind to each other. They are admonished to "turn the other cheek" rather than to strike back at someone who has offended them. Although there may be some need for this kind of instruction at early levels, overall these approaches have not proved to be effective strategies for dealing with conflict. Some children and adults continue to fight, quarrel, and bully each other; they do not show respect and consideration for others—despite valiant efforts by the home, church, and school. We still read about ill-tempered persons who hurt or even kill others as a result of conflicts over trivial matters. The hours each week that American children spend watching television undoubtedly add little to their desire or ability to resolve conflicts rationally.

The "law of the gun" associated with life on the frontier of the Old West seemingly has become the method of choice to resolve conflicts in modern America. Dueling was outlawed as a way of settling disputes many years ago, but people in this country continue to shoot each other at an alarming rate. A frightening fact is the young age of many of the victims and perpetrators of violent acts.

One would have to conclude that powerful forces in society are causing monumental frustrations, hostility, and anger among people. Doubtless, much of this is poverty and drug related. We are not likely to see many positive changes until the societal conditions that cause the problems are adequately addressed. The physical safety of your students must be one of your priorities, as the safety of all in the school must be a schoolwide priority. Some Internet resources about maintaining school safety are listed at the end of this chapter.

The Model for Instruction in Conflict Resolution   Instruction in conflict resolution involves three important elements. The first is identifying all the facts of the case: Who did what to whom, when, how many times, with what consequences? The second is identifying the issues involved: Why is there a problem? What is the source of the conflict? How and why are the facts perceived and interpreted differently? The third is defining all *possible decisions* that can be made regarding a resolution of the situation, along with the ensuing consequences of each decision. By using this model to study cases of conflict, children will learn that usually one party is not wholly wrong and the other wholly right; issues often involve value choices among options, more than one of which may be acceptable. Applying this model to the study of conflict resolution, you may devise cases, relying on children's real-life conflict experiences. Simulation games and role-playing are particularly well suited to instruction in conflict resolution.

ORGANIZATIONAL ASPECTS OF CLASSROOM MANAGEMENT

The way you organize your classroom will not, of course, eliminate management problems. But your choices can move you a long way down the road toward preventing problems and resolving them when they arise. In this regard, two principles are so important that they must precede all else said on this subject:

- The first few days of the school year are critical in setting the standard of behavior in a classroom.
- Preventing problems from arising is always easier than is correcting them once they have occurred.

Starting the School Term Well

The first few days of school are a time when children are most aggressive in testing the teacher's management capability. If you are lax in establishing standards of conduct during these first few critical days, it will be almost impossible to do so later in the year. Experienced teachers know that it is easy to become more permissive as the school year progresses without compromising standards of conduct, but that it is enormously difficult to become more strict once a permissive pattern becomes the norm. Because beginning teachers want children to like them, they are sometimes reluctant to take a firm stand on student conduct for fear they will offend children. This form of indulgence is almost always a mistake. The time for firm, strict, formal (but always, of course, fair) teacher action is during the first few days of the school year. Your students will immediately respect you if you are firm but fair. Over time they may even learn to like you.

There are three important keys to getting your school term off to a good beginning. First, be *prepared* and be *fair*. Your preparation for the first day of school should include determining your classroom procedures and your basic expectations for students' behavior while they are under your supervision. Your procedures and expectations must be consistent with school policy and must seem reasonable to your students, and in enforcing them you must be a fair and consistent professional. However, being coldly consistent is not the same as being fair and professional. As a teacher, you are a professional who deals in matters of human relations and who must exercise professional judgment. You are not a robot, nor are any of your students. Human beings differ from one another, and seemingly similar situations can vary substantially because the people involved are different. Consequently, your response, or lack of response, to each of two separate but quite similar situations may differ. To be most effective, learning must be enjoyable for students; they cannot enjoy it when their teacher consistently acts like a drill sergeant. If a student breaks a rule, rather than assuming why, or seeming to not care why, or overreacting to the infraction, *find out why* before deciding your response.

Second, in preparing your classroom management system, remember that too many rules and detailed procedures at the beginning can be a source of trouble. To avoid trouble, it is best at first to present only those procedural expectations necessary for an orderly start to the school term, and then add perhaps a new one each day and reteach and reinforce each one every day.

Third, your consequences for not following established procedures must be reasonable, clearly understood, and fairly applied. In addition, apply consequences privately if at all possible, that is, without embarrassing the recipient. But remember this: Children are individuals with different needs, who behave and react differently, and each needs to be treated differently. A consequence that is fair for one child may not necessarily be fair for another. Procedures should be quite specific so that students know exactly what you do and do not expect and what the consequences are when they violate procedures. For example, "If you make a mess, you

First Offense—Results in a direct but reasonably unobtrusive (nonverbal) reminder to the student. You may, for example, establish eye contact and frown.

Second Offense—Results in a private but direct verbal warning. You may, for example, lean over and whisper to the child to attend to the instructional task.

Third Offense—Results in the student being given a time-out in an isolation area (one with adult supervision) followed, perhaps, by a private teacher–student conference and a phone call home.

Fourth Offense—Results in suspension from class until you can hold a student–parent/guardian–teacher conference.

Fifth Offense—Results in the student being referred to the principal or counselor's office (depending on school policy), sometimes followed by suspension or even expulsion from school.

FIGURE 4.1
Sample five-step model of consequences for inappropriate behaviors

clean it up"; "If you want my attention, you must raise your hand and wait for me to acknowledge you."

Most teachers who are effective managers of their classroom learning environment make routine their procedures for handling inappropriate behavior and ensure that children understand the consequences for not following procedures. It is often desirable to post procedures and consequences in the classroom. Consequences will vary considerably depending on whether you are teaching kindergarten, eighth grade, or a grade level in between. Consequences might resemble the five-step model shown in Figure 4.1 (although perhaps in a more abbreviated form).

Whether offenses subsequent to the first are those that occur on the same day or within a designated period of time, such as 1 week, is one of the many decisions that you, members of a teaching team, or the entire faculty must make.

In a way, the firmness being suggested as appropriate at the beginning of the school year is a prevention strategy. An interesting, stimulating, instructional program, combined with appropriate rewards for expected behavior, is a much more effective deterrent to disruptive student behavior than is punishment or the threat of punishment. When children know clearly what is expected and when teachers follow through on learner expectations and do not permit gradual erosion of standards of conduct, children's behavior can usually be kept within manageable limits. Of course, no classroom is totally free of behavior problems. Thus, you *should not* wait until an incident of student misbehavior has occurred to think about a management strategy to deal with it. Use Activity 4.2 to begin developing your own management plan, a process that will continue throughout your career.

Activity 4.2. My Emerging Plan for Classroom Management

Grade level (or range) _____

My name _____

Plans Before the First Day

1. Describe your classroom with respect to the physical room arrangement and organization and the positive and caring classroom community that you aim to create.
2. Describe communication you will initiate with your students and their families prior to the first day of school.
3. Describe characteristics of your classroom that will signal to the children that it is a friendly and safe place to be.
4. Describe how you will get to know the children and what you will do to help the children get to know you and each other.

The First Day

5. Describe how you will greet the children when they arrive for the first day.
6. Describe the rules or procedural expectations that you will have already in place and how they will be presented to the children.
7. Describe how you will have children contribute to these rules expectations.
8. Describe your classroom procedures for
   - absences; making up missed work and instruction
   - assigning helpers for classroom jobs such as taking care of pets, plants, the calendar, bathroom monitor, and so forth
   - being in the classroom before and after school, and at recess and lunch time
   - bringing toys, plants, and pets into the classroom
   - collecting notes, money, and forms
   - distributing and collecting papers and materials
   - eating and drinking in the classroom
   - going to the bathroom
   - late arrival and early dismissal
   - movement in the halls
   - storing personal belongings
   - taking attendance
   - using the classroom sink, if there is one
   - using the pencil sharpener
   - using the teacher's desk
   - using the water fountain
   - using other materials and equipment
   - wearing hats and other articles of clothing in the classroom
   - what to do in an emergency situation
   - when a visitor comes into the classroom
9. Describe the class or morning opening; the class or day's closure.

Managing the Curriculum

10. Describe how you will help the children with their organization and assignments.
11. Describe your homework expectations. Will there be homework? How much and how often? Will parents and guardians be informed? If so, how? What is their involvement to be? Is there a school homework hotline?
12. Describe your procedure for incomplete, unacceptable, or incorrect student work. Is there a recovery option?
13. Do you plan to provide comments, feedback, or corrections on student work?
14. Will you use marks of some sort—grades, value words, figures, and so forth?
15. Will students be rewarded for their group work? How will you assess group learning? How will you assess individual learning from group work?
16. Describe the student portfolio expectation. Where will the portfolios be stored? When will students work on their portfolios?
17. Describe your plan for communication with parents/guardians.

Maintaining Classroom Relations and Personal Behavior

18. Describe how you will bring an off-task child back on task.
19. Describe how students will know what is and what is not an appropriate level of classroom noise.
20. Describe how you will signal a need for hands and when, if ever, it is okay to call out without using hands.
21. Describe how you will indicate your support for appropriate student behavior.
22. Describe how you will discourage inappropriate student behavior.
23. Describe your order of indirect and direct behavior intervention strategies.
24. Describe how you will signal your need for attention from the class and from a distracted student.
25. Describe how you will respond when two errant behaviors are happening simultaneously but at opposing locations in the classroom.

When the Going Gets Tough

26. Describe your pattern of escalating consequences.
27. Describe how you will deal with disrespectful, inappropriate comments from students.
28. Describe how you will respond to remarks that are sexist or racist or that stereotype people in inappropriate and cruel ways.
29. Describe how you will respond to serious and dangerous student behaviors.
30. Identify one person you can go to for support.

Source: Adapted from an unpublished form. Adapted by permission of Linda Current.

Schedule and Routines

Children respond best to established routines. This includes an established daily schedule of classroom events. Although the inflexibility created by clinging slavishly to a minute-by-minute schedule can hardly be condoned, this is not the same as saying there should be no schedule. By not planning and observing a daily schedule of events, you can create all sorts of management problems for yourself.

Because of the ordinary requirements imposed on teachers to attend to various areas of the curriculum, it will be possible for you to block out large periods of time to be devoted to reading, social studies, science, mathematics, language arts, expressive arts, health and physical education, and so on. Your schedule can be tentative, and you may change it from time to time during the year, if necessary. Perceive your schedule as reasonably flexible. If on some days you need a few more minutes to complete an important task, take the time. If, however, you find every lesson exceeds your budgeted time or does not require the amount of time allotted, this is evidence of weak planning, poor lesson pacing, inaccurate estimating of the time needed, or all these things.

If you make a schedule and observe it reasonably closely, you will ensure that all children and all areas of the curriculum receive the attention each deserves. When you are careless about scheduling classroom events, days may go by without finding the time for some subjects. What usually happens is that your favorite subject areas get the lion's share of time; those you are less fond of, or in which you are not particularly strong, get shortchanged. Also, if you work with subgroups within the class, some groups may not get an adequate amount of your time. If this happens once in a while, it is not a serious matter, but if it occurs regularly, it cannot help but be detrimental to a well-balanced instructional program and will therefore contribute to management problems.

Closely related to schedule setting is establishing routines that regularize your day-to-day classroom activities, including entering and leaving the classroom, taking roll, moving from one grouping configuration to another, using the classroom learning centers, going to the restroom, getting books and supplies, coming to order after recess, checking out athletic equipment, and so on. Routines prevent the altercations, bickering, and conflicts that are inevitable when such activities are handled ad hoc. (Note: What we refer to as a classroom learning center is not to be confused with what in some schools is a place on the campus, sometimes referred to as a Modified Learning Center, that is staffed usually by a paraprofessional, sometimes a social worker, where students may be sent from the regular classroom for a variety of reasons, such as to complete an assignment, as a place to calm down, because of inappropriate classroom behavior, for conflict resolution and problem solving, and as an on-campus suspension.)

When your routines are reasonable and you implement them sensibly, children do not find them objectionable. As a matter of fact, they receive security from knowing what to do and how to do it.

Activity 4.3: Ms. Badger's Effort to Empower Children

Long before the opening of school, Ms. Badger had decided what behavior standards she wanted in her classroom and had constructed a set of procedures concerning student conduct. She now feels uneasy about this, however, because she remembers what one of her professors had said about children being more willing to respect and accept rules if they have a hand in formulating them. Ms. Badger resolves her dilemma in the following way.

On the first day of school, she explains to her students that she is sure that all of them want to do their best work. For this to happen, there need to be behavioral standards and procedures. If everyone does anything they please at any time, without consideration for others, no one will get anything done, and the room will not be a very pleasant place. The children, of course, understand and expect this. She goes on to explain that because standards of behavior affect everyone, the class should help her establish them. This, too, receives a favorable reaction. It

is agreed that the children will suggest procedures, and when the group accepts them, Ms. Badger will write them on the writing board.

As children make suggestions, Ms. Badger involves the class in discussing each one. She is careful not to reject any suggestion, but when one surfaces that she has already decided she wants, she says something like, "Now, that's a good idea!" By the time the period ends, the standards and procedures adopted by the class are those Ms. Badger had decided on three weeks before the opening of school, and the children seem pleased with "their" standards and procedures.

1. Do you find anything objectionable about Ms. Badger's strategy?
2. What would you predict to be the lasting effect of standards and procedures generated in this way?
3. Would you establish your procedures differently? If so, how?

Clarity of Directions and Goals

It is important that you give children clear directions. When you give directions carelessly or ambiguously, children do not know what they are to do and will consequently ask to have you clarify or repeat yourself, sometimes several times. Some teachers respond with annoyance and may then establish a rule that they will give directions once only. This is generally a bad idea because it is patently unfair. There will be times when, for obvious reasons, directions need to be repeated. Such a teacher is then placed in the position of having to violate one of the classroom rules. If you are careful about your preactive planning, about obtaining the attention of all children before you give directions, and to skillfully give directions clearly and completely, it is not likely that children will misunderstand you.

In addition to giving clear instructions, activities flow best when children understand their purpose. Like most of us, children are annoyed when you ask them to do things without telling them your reasons for doing them. Children in school are often assigned specific tasks without the least idea of how the task fits into the larger, long-range framework. Time you take to discuss and explain what everyone will be doing and where the activities will lead is usually time well spent.

Physical Arrangements

There is much in the arrangement of an elementary-school classroom that can either contribute to or alleviate management problems. There is no one "best way"

In conducting instruction, whether to the whole group, small subgroups, or while working with individuals, you should consistently position yourself so you can easily monitor children's behavior.

Lori Whitley/Merrill

to arrange students in a classroom. Most professionals agree that the arrangement should be kept flexible and that students should be deployed in the ways most suitable for accomplishing specific tasks.

The guideline is simple. Just as is true with adults, when children are seated side by side, it is perfectly natural for them to talk to each other. Therefore, if your purpose is to encourage social interaction, seat children close together; if you would rather they work independently, separate them. It is unreasonable to place children in situations that encourage maximum interaction and then to admonish or berate them for whispering and talking.

You will not (or should not) be seated much of the time during the day; therefore, it matters little where your desk is located except that it is out of the way. You will move about the room, supervising, clarifying, answering questions, and providing individual instruction. In conducting instruction in small subgroups, working with individuals, or supervising seatwork, you should habitually position yourself so you can monitor children's behavior; the children should be aware of your presence.

TPW Video Classroom

Series: Classroom Management

Module 1: Organizing Your Classroom and Supplies

Video 1: Arranging Furniture and Materials

Activity 4.4: First Day of Spring—What Would You Have Done?

Today is the first really warm, spring day that Middleton has had this year. In fact, it is downright hot. And the children love it! After a long cold winter and a damp and rainy spring, it seems as though summer has arrived with one big burst of sunshine, and energy that was pent up during the many dreary months has released itself like a mountain of water flowing through a broken dam! During the noon hour, the children play hard, run and yell, and have a great time in the welcomed sunshine. Now the "first" bell rings, and several hundred very reluctant children find their way into the building and to their respective classrooms, still talking loudly, perspiring profusely, and with flushed faces.

Mr. Gardner had scheduled math immediately following lunch. Today, the children are hardly ready for the concentration needed for a math lesson. Mr. Gardner sees the hopelessness of the situation confronting him and immediately decides to alter his schedule.

1. Do you think Mr. Gardner's decision was wise?
2. Can Mr. Gardner forget about math each time they have a beautiful day?
3. If this is a persistent problem, what long-term solution might Mr. Gardner find?

TEACHER PREP

MERRILL
PRENTICE HALL

TPW Video Classroom

Series: Classroom Management

Module 2: Fostering Student Accountability

Video 1: Modeling Mutual Respect, Routines, and Transitions

Transitions

As long as children are at their assigned desks or work stations in the classroom, busily at work on a learning activity that is meaningful to them, there is usually little problem with disruptive behavior, although, to not disturb the learning going on in neighboring classrooms, you may need to remind the children to be "using their 6-inch voices."

But classrooms do not and cannot operate that way all the time. Children must move about from time to time; different materials are used for different subjects and skills; group configuration changes in accordance with teaching and curriculum requirements. These breaks in the classroom work, when children move from one set of tasks to another, are referred to as *transitions*. There are many such transitions during the school day, and in the least efficient classroom management too much classroom time is wasted while shifting from one activity to another.

Transitions are a most troublesome time for many beginning teachers. Transitions are less trouble when you plan them carefully during your preactive phase of instruction and write them into your lesson plan. In other words, the way to prevent management problems and loss of valuable instructional time during transitions (or, for that matter, during any other time) is to think through the process in advance and structure the situation in such a way that the change can occur smoothly, efficiently, and with the least disruption. We suggest the following procedures:

1. Avoid delays of any kind, where children sit or stand with nothing to do.

2. Have the learning materials needed for the next task available, in sufficient quantity, and easily accessible to students.

3. Use student helpers to disseminate materials. Give children responsibilities, not only for assisting in transitions but in all aspects of the daily classroom activities.

4. At the close of one activity and before another is to begin, obtain students' undivided attention, and then give clear directions regarding the next task. Avoid giving the directions before you have students' complete attention.

5. Establish reasonable time limits within which to complete the transition. If you allow too little time, children are apt to rush around excitedly and bump into furniture or one another, which contributes to unnecessary commotion and potential accidents. Moves should be made expeditiously but not in a hurried or stressful way.

6. Insofar as is possible, make transitions in the same way each day. Establish a routine that becomes familiar to all children.

7. Avoid saying or doing things that raise children's excitement level. When children begin to raise their voices, are speaking rapidly, or rushing about the room, you should know the steps to take to calm the group. A short quiet-time break or a silent activity will usually reduce the stimulation. A recess break at

Activity 4.5: What's Wrong Here?

Ms. Fox knows that if she is to succeed as a beginning teacher she must have good "control" in her classroom. She is determined, therefore, not to allow the slightest infraction of room conduct to go unnoticed. When children enter the room, she is usually seen standing at the door, where she can monitor children's behavior in the hallway and in the classroom at the same time. She likes to think of herself as a "no-nonsense" teacher who will not put up with any "foolishness" from her fifth graders. Many of her comments to the children during the day run along this line:

"Stop running in the hall, boys."

"Now settle down quickly, boys and girls."

"Karen, what are you doing over there? Please take your seat."

"I want it quiet in here. What are you two talking about over there? Is that Billy's book you have, Cindy? Give it back to him, and get on with your own work."

"Everyone listen carefully to the directions, because I will give them only once."

"Clear everything from the top of your desks except the book we will be using. [Pause.] Mark, put that ruler away. Sally—put the pencil inside your desk! Jim, the waste paper goes in the basket."

Although the children have nicknamed her "Hawk-eye," they really do not dislike Ms. Fox. But they often talk about the good times they had with Ms. James the year before, and this bothers Ms. Fox.

The classroom gives the outward appearance of orderliness, yet one senses an unnatural tenseness about the room. There is more carping and petty bickering among the children than one would expect. They comply with Ms. Fox's expectations, but there is little evidence of cooperation among them or between them and Ms. Fox. When the principal visits her classroom, she advises Ms. Fox to try to develop a more positive approach to room management but does not provide examples of what this entails.

1. If you were Ms. Fox, what would you do to implement the principal's recommendation?

2. What behavior can one expect if teacher talk is mainly directive, negative in content, and perhaps hostile in tone?

3. Do you think Ms. Fox will still be a teacher 2 years from now? Explain your answer.

such a time may exacerbate the problem because the freedom will additionally excite the children.

8. It is sometimes a good idea to make transitions by small groups rather than
having the entire class move at one time.

9. As soon as children are engaged in the new activity, make sure that you are
available to provide assistance to those children who seem to be having a
problem getting on task.

SUMMARY

No doubt, individual differences make it easier for some teachers and more difficult for others to develop professional competencies. However, most can succeed
at it. Professional competence can be strengthened through sound scholarship and
by thorough preparation, planning, and reflection.

The teacher is the most influential and powerful personality in the classroom.
The teacher's behavior will determine the quality of the interactions in the group.
If the teacher is warm and caring, the chances are that children will model these
traits. Conversely, if the teacher is domineering, arbitrary, carping, and critical,
children are likely to reflect these behaviors.

You must appreciate the powerful influence of the unspoken cues teachers provide when communicating with children. Sometimes overt but more often quite
subtle, these nonverbal cues may range from a gesture to a facial expression to
simply the expression of a mood. As examples, a restless child may be calmed by
your reassuring smile. You may place a hand on the shoulder of a child who seems
to need emotional support. Or you will show sincere enthusiasm in your eyes as a
child is relating an exciting experience. Or, while talking to the class you detect a
student starting to show restlessness and casually move over next to the student
(using proximity control), perhaps gently placing a hand on the student's shoulder
to avert misbehavior. Some authors have referred to this system of communication
as the "silent language" or "body language."

It may be that teachers communicate more profoundly through such nonverbal
cues than in any other way. We always manipulate words to come out the way we
think most appropriate. But true feelings and attitudes are laid bare by those unspoken messages that flow between human beings, messages that children, in their
innocence, are so skillful in decoding. It is these signals that tell children whether
a teacher is, indeed, a concerned and caring adult. These unspoken messages will
have much to do with your management of the classroom and will, in the long run,
be the deciding factor in whether your classroom is to be a fertile seedbed for the
growth of an enlightened and sensitive humanity.

It is well known that before you can teach you must have, and then you must
maintain, your learners' attention. With your written plan for accomplishing that
now underway, in Chapters 5 and 6 we focus your attention on the topics of first
what content to teach and then how to plan to teach it.

STUDY QUESTIONS AND ADDITIONAL ACTIVITIES

1. Flexibility seems to be an essential quality of elementary-school classrooms. For a specified grade level, generate a list of five or six rules or procedures that you would wish to establish in your classroom. Indicate which ones you could flexibly enforce and which ones you could not. How do you determine which is which?

2. Ms. Jacobs, a third-grade teacher, required surgery to repair a displaced bone and a torn ligament caused when Bryan, a 10-year-old, erupted in a tantrum in the classroom. The school principal allowed Bryan to remain in Ms. Jacob's class but later moved Bryan to another teacher's classroom after Bryan tried to throw a classmate down a flight of stairs. What are your initial thoughts having read this brief scenario? Share then with those of your classmates.

3. Interview two experienced teachers. Ask what procedures they use at the beginning of the school year to establish a setting for responsible student conduct. Discuss with these teachers the specific strategies they use to obtain students' cooperation and the degree of success they believe they are having so far.

4. Sometimes, teachers encourage disruptive student behavior or even misbehavior by what they do or don't do or by what they say. Teachers may not even be aware that students find their behavior irritating and that it "gets on their nerves." As you observe teachers (even college teachers will suffice), take notice of any teacher behaviors or idiosyncrasies that seem to encourage student hostility. Share what you discover with your colleagues and discuss your findings and how they relate to your own development as a teacher.

5. It has been said that good classroom managers are not necessarily good teachers. Do you agree or disagree? Why? Is the reverse true, that is, are good teachers necessarily good classroom managers? Explain why or why not.

6. A teacher punished children for tardiness by assigning them 20 additional math problems as homework. What effect, if any, do you think such an experience might have on the children's attitude toward mathematics? Toward school? Toward that teacher? Does it matter whether punishment is logically related to the misbehavior? Discuss, and provide real experience examples to illustrate your points.

7. Do you believe there is anything a teacher should or should not do when hearing children using the "n-word?" Explain your initial response. Does it matter if the word is used without malice in the classroom, with malice in the classroom, outside the classroom but on the school campus? Share your thoughts with your classmates.

8. One student hit a pregnant teacher, another exposed himself, and another stabbed a classmate with a pencil. All were suspended from school for up to 2 weeks during the 2002–03 school year. All were kindergartners. Some experts believe that the youngest schoolchildren are being suspended from school with greater frequency than ever. At schools in your geographic area, investigate and share with others in your class what you can find about the use of home suspension versus on-campus suspension. Describe what you can find about the advantages and disadvantages of each.

9. Experts say that "learning is easier and more pleasant when we are shown what *to* do rather than told what *not to* do" (Good & Brophy, 2003, p. 126). What does that statement say regarding how to present classroom rules and procedures? About a teacher's language and demeanor in general?

10. A historical review of disciplinary practices used in U.S. classrooms shows that corporal punishment has been a consistent and conspicuous part of schooling since the beginning. Many educators are concerned about the increased violence in schools, represented by possession of weapons, bullying, intimidation, gang or cult activity, arson, and the continued corporal punishment of students. They argue that schools are responsible for turning children's behavior into opportunities to teach character and self-control. When self-disciplined adults create a problem, they apologize, accept the consequences, make restitution, and learn from their mistakes. We have a responsibility for teaching children to do the same. An important characteristic of exemplary schooling is that of maintaining respect for children's dignity even when responding to their inappropriate behavior. Saturday School may be an acceptable alternative to more harmful disciplinary practices, as well as a step toward developing more internal rather than external student control methods. Are there any such programs in your geographic area? What is your opinion about using corporal punishment at any level of schooling? Hold a class debate on the issue.

WEB SITES RELATED TO CONTENT OF THIS CHAPTER

- Bell activity *www.dailybite.com*
- Bullying
  Bullying.org www.bullying.org
  Bullyfreeme www.bullyfreeme.com
  Bullying Prevention program www.clemson.edu/olweus
  Bullyproof www.wcwonline.org
  Second Step www.cfchildren.org/cc/ssf/ssindex
- California Home Visiting Center *www.scusd.edu/cahvcenter*
- Center for the Study and Prevention of Violence *www.colorado.edu/cspv*
- Marshall's raising responsibility at *www.MarvinMarshall.com*
- National Alliance for Safe Schools *www.safeschools.org*
- PeaceBuilders *www.peacebuilders.com*
- Peace Games *www.peacegames.org*
- Randy Sprick's *Safe and Civil Schools www.safeandcivilschools.com*
- Sound amplification systems
  Audio Enhancement www.audioenhancement.com
  Califone International www.califone.com
  Phonic Ear www.phonicear.com
- The Safetyzone *www.safetyzone.org*
- Voice Academy *www.voiceacademy.org*

FOR FURTHER READING

Clark, R. (2003). *The essential 55.* New York: Hyperion.

Denton, P. (2007). *The power of our words.* Turner Falls, MA: Northeast Foundation for Children.

DeVries, R., & Zan, B. (2003). When children make rules. *Educational Leadership, 61*(1), 64–67.

Dougherty, J. W. (2004). *Torts and liability: An educator's short guide.* Fastback 527. Bloomington, IN: Phi Delta Kappa Educational Foundation.

Fisher, R. S., Henry, E., & Porter, D. (2006). *Morning meeting messages, K-6.* Northeast Foundation for Children: Turners Falls, MA.

Flook, L., Repetti, R. L., & Ullman, J. B. (2005). Classroom social experiences as predictors of academic performance. *Developmental Psychology, 41,* 319–327.

Franklin, J. (2004). A safer place for learning: How some schools are banishing bullying. *Education Update, 46*(2), 4–5.

Hehir, T. (2005). The changing role of intervention for children with disabilities. *Principal, 85*(2), 22–25.

Intrator, S. M. (2004). The engaged classroom. *Educational Leadership, 62*(1), 20–24.

Smith, R. (2005). *Conscious classroom management.* Thousand Oaks, CA: Corwin Press.

Stone, R. (2005). *Best classroom management practices for reaching all learners.* Thousand Oaks, CA: Corwin Press.

Sussman, G. L. (2006). The violence you don't see. *Educational Leadership, 63,* 1–7. In *Helping All Students Succeed,* ASCD online journal at www.ascd.org:80/portal/site/ascd.

Wright, J. (2005). Intervention ideas that really work. *Principal, 85*(2), 12–16.

Chapter 5

Planning the Curriculum

INTASC Principles	PRAXIS III Domains	NBPTS Standards
• The teacher plans instruction based upon knowledge of subject matter, students, community, and curriculum goals. (Principle 7)	• Organizing Content Knowledge for Student Learning (Domain A)	• Multiple Paths to Knowledge

Schools are expected to serve the purposes that society has established for them. These purposes are generally represented in the school's self-prescribed mission statement, which from school to school will vary in length and detail. As reflected in the sample mission statements shown in Figure 5.1, schools in the United States have traditionally been expected to develop *literacy,* to provide *citizenship education,* to contribute to children's *personal development,* and to provide *quality education* for every child. Over the years, these purposes have found expression through *educational goals* that contain statements of the desired outcomes of schooling. Such statements as "to develop literacy in oral and written English," "to develop an understanding and appreciation of our cultural heritage," and "to develop a healthy self-concept" are examples of educational goals that reflect the traditional purposes of schooling. Each of these statements identifies an expected outcome of public education. Effective accomplishment of the goals, that is, effective teaching, does not just happen; it is produced through the thoughtful planning of each phase of the learning process. Most effective teachers begin their planning months before meeting their students for the first time. Daily lessons form parts of a larger scheme, which is designed to accomplish the teacher's long-range curriculum goals for the semester or year and to mesh with the school's mission statement and academic goals standards (addressed later in this chapter).

- **Branciforte Elementary School** (Santa Cruz, CA) is committed to maximizing the potential of all students to show continuous improvement towards mastery of academic standards. We believe in providing a positive and safe climate for learning in which all students become compassionate, responsible, and contributing members of our diverse community. This mission is accomplished through excellence in teaching and through partnership with parents and our community.

- The mission of **Jeffery Elementary School** (Kenosha, WI) is to provide a child-centered environment where all students are offered the opportunity to become responsible citizens and productive life-long learners.

- The mission of **Longwood Elementary School** (Shalimar, FL) is to provide a quality academic environment for students to become responsible self-directed life-long learners.

- **Timothy Edwards Middle School** (South Windsor, CT) is a place where children are inspired to grow and learn in an atmosphere of respect, love, and caring. We believe that our charge as educators is (a) to offer intellectual challenge in order to promote academic development, (b) to address the needs of each student as an individual, (c) to foster in each child a sense of belonging and appreciation for self and others, and (d) to help students to become contributing citizens of the world. We . . . are committed to these goals—the keys to a healthy, interesting, and prosperous environment where a child's positive self-concept is cultivated through academic, physical, and social/emotional growth.

FIGURE 5.1
Sample school mission statements (Used by permission)

If learning is defined only as the accumulation of bits and pieces of information, then we already know everything about how to teach and how students learn. However, the accumulation of pieces of information is at the lowest end of a spectrum of types of learning. Discoveries are still being made about the processes involved in higher forms of learning—that is, for meaningful understanding and the reflective use of that understanding. The results of recent research support the use of instructional strategies that help students make connections as they learn (Findley, 2002). These strategies include discovery learning, inquiry, collaborative and cooperative learning, interdisciplinary thematic instruction, and project-based learning, with a total curriculum that is integrated and connected to students' life experiences.

As said in Chapter 2, the methodology uses what is referred to as *hands-on* and *minds-on* learning—that is, the learner is learning by doing and is thinking about what she or he is learning and doing. When thoughtfully coupled, these approaches help construct, and often reconstruct, the learner's perceptions. Hands-on learning engages the learner's mind, causing questioning, turning a learner's mind on. Hands-on/minds-on learning encourages students to question and then, with the teacher's guidance, devise ways of investigating satisfactory, although sometimes only tentative, answers to their questions.

As a classroom teacher, your instructional task then is twofold: (1) to plan hands-on experiences, providing the materials and the supportive environment necessary for students' meaningful exploration and discovery, and (2) to facilitate the most meaningful and longest-lasting learning possible once the learner's mind has been engaged by the hands-on learning, including although not necessarily limited to student learning of any curriculum that may be mandated by your state and local school district. To accomplish this requires your knowledge about curriculum and competence in the use of varied and developmentally appropriate methods of instruction. To assist you in the acquisition of that knowledge and competence is the primary purpose of this book. But it is just the beginning; a more detailed presentation will come in your subsequent teacher preparation coursework, particularly those courses that deal individually with methods of teaching in the various subjects of the elementary school curriculum such as mathematics, science, reading/language arts, and social studies.

Competent elementary school teaching is a kaleidoscopic, multifaceted, eclectic process. When preparing and writing a book to prepare one to teach, by necessity its authors must separate that kaleidoscopic process into separate topics, which is not always possible to do in a way that makes equal sense to all users of the book. So, here is the plan and our advice for you. This chapter and the next address the instructional planning aspect, first the necessary planning of the curriculum and then, following in Chapter 6, is the detailed instructional planning necessary to bring the planned curriculum to fruition. As you proceed through these chapters and begin the development of your instructional plans, from time to time you will want to refer to particular topics in Chapters 7, 8, and 9. The rationale for careful planning and the components of that planning are topics pursued now in this chapter.

ANTICIPATED OUTCOMES

Specifically, upon completion of this chapter you should be able to:

1. Anticipate controversial topics and issues that may arise while teaching, and what you might do if and when they do arise.
2. Demonstrate ability to select and plan the sequence of content for instruction in a particular subject that is typically taught at a particular grade level, K–8.
3. Demonstrate an understanding of the rationale for planning for instruction, the levels of planning, and the components of a total instructional plan.
4. Demonstrate knowledge of the value of various types of documents that can be resources for planning curriculum and instruction.
5. Demonstrate understanding of how to help students to develop meaningful understandings while still scoring well on standardized achievement tests.
6. Demonstrate understanding of the concept of integrated curriculum and its relevance to curriculum and instruction.
7. Demonstrate an understanding of the distinction between curriculum content that is *essential* and that which is *supplemental*.
8. Demonstrate an understanding of the value and limitations of a syllabus, textbook, and other print resources for student learning.
9. Describe the relationship of instructional planning to the preactive and reflective thought-processing phases of instruction.
10. Differentiate among diagnostic assessment, formative assessment, and summative assessment and explain the place and use of each in instructional planning.
11. Explain both the value and the limitations afforded by using instructional objectives.
12. Explain the difference and the relationship between hands-on and minds-on learning.
13. Explain the connection among curriculum standards, instructional objectives, and assessment of student learning.
14. Explain the value of students being empowered with some decision making about curriculum planning.
15. Prepare learning objectives for each of the three domains of learning and at various levels within each domain.

HELPING CHILDREN MAKE SUCCESSFUL TRANSITIONS

Within the framework of school organization lie several components that form a comprehensive, albeit ever-changing, program. Central to the school's purpose and its organizational structure is the concerted effort to see that all students make successful transitions from one level to the next, from one grade to the next, from one school to the next, and ultimately from high school to work and/or postsecondary education. Every aspect of the school program is, in some way, designed to guide students in their making successful transitions. Combining to form the program that students experience are two terms you will frequently encounter, *curriculum* and *instruction*. Let us next clarify those terms as they are used in this book.

CURRICULUM AND INSTRUCTION: CLARIFICATION OF TERMS

Originally derived from a Latin term referring to a racecourse for the Roman chariots, among educators the term *curriculum* still has no singularly accepted definition. Some define it as the planned subject matter content and skills to be presented to students. Others say that the curriculum is only what students actually learn. Still others hold the broad definition that the curriculum is all experiences students encounter, whether planned or unplanned, learned or unlearned.

Four programs are identified that contribute in different ways to student learning, that do, in fact, comprise the broadest definition of curriculum:

a. the program of studies (subjects studied; courses offered)
b. the program of student activities (e.g., sports, clubs, and organizations)
c. the program of services (e.g., transportation, meals, counseling, nurse station)
d. the hidden (or covert, informal) curriculum (i.e., the unplanned and subtle message systems within schools, such as the school climate, the feelings projected from the teacher and other adults to students and from the students to one another).

This working definition considers curriculum as the *entire school program*, that is, all that is intentionally designed to accomplish the school's mission.

Activity 5.1: What Really Is Being Learned?

Although it is almost never assessed, children do learn through the covert curriculum. What hidden message is being sent to the children by each of the following teachers? Discuss your response with your classmates.

• Ms. Wong is a first-year teacher. After visiting her fifth-grade classroom, the principal suggested that she brighten the classroom and decorate the walls with a display of student work. When the principal returned to the classroom 2 weeks later, Ms. Wong had put up a display—a chart of the homework and test records of students.

Hidden message being sent: _____

• Mr. Lever, a second-grade teacher, has decorated one wall of his classroom with pictures and stories of famous scientists, all of whom are men.

Hidden message being sent: _____

• While Ms. Gushé is talking to her fourth-grade students, the school principal walks into the room. Ms. Gushé stops her talk and walks over to greet the principal and find out what the principal wants.

Hidden message being sent: _____

• Mr. Latte is nearly always late in arriving to his classroom after lunch, seldom beginning class until at least 5 minutes past the scheduled start time.

Hidden message being sent: _____

• During sustained silent reading in Mrs. Silencia's sixth-grade reading class, Mrs. Silencia asks for everyone's attention, verbally reprimands two students for horsing around, and then writes out a referral for each of the two students.

Hidden message being sent: _____

Instruction, too, has several definitions, some of which are not clearly distinguishable from curriculum. Whereas curriculum is usually associated with the content of the learning, instruction is associated with *methods* or *strategies*—that is, with ways of presenting content, conveying information, and facilitating student learning. Obviously, curriculum and instruction must be in tandem to affect student learning.

Curriculum Components

What we refer to as "curriculum" can be divided into three components—the core curriculum, exploratories, and cocurricular student activities. A brief review of each of these three areas follows.

Core Curriculum   Core subjects of the curriculum as defined by the *No Child Left Behind* (NCLB) *Act of 2001* are English, reading or language arts, mathematics, science, foreign languages, civics and government, economics, arts, history, and geography. It is within these subjects, individually or in some combination, that *interdisciplinary thematic units* (ITUs) are taught (discussed later in this chapter and in detail in Chapter 6). The purpose of teaching subject matter on a central theme is to avoid communicating a wrong message to students—that learning is piecemeal and separate from one experience to another. To the contrary, the core curriculum facilitates the integration of subjects of the thematic units taught in tandem by a single teacher or by a teaching team.

Curriculum Content: Essential versus Supplemental   Content that is specified by mandated state curriculum standards is that which is required, that *must* be covered by instruction—it is *essential*. On the other hand, *supplemental content* is *not* mandated by the state standards, but rather is curriculum that is arbitrary and dependent on the discretion of the local district, the teacher, or the teaching team.

Exploratory Opportunities   Usually, by grade 5 exploratory opportunities are a substantial part of the school curriculum, perhaps, however, and in our opinion unfortunately so, somewhat diminished of recent as a result of responses to the NCLB legislation. Where they still do exist in some fashion or another, the purpose of exploratory opportunities is to provide a variety of experiences to assist students in their discovery of areas of interest for future pursuit that will perhaps develop into a lifelong passion. Allowing students opportunities to discover and explore unusual and novel topics can spawn or rekindle interests in life and school. Exposing them to a range of academic, vocational, and recreational subjects for career options, community service, enrichment, and enjoyment, exploratories build on the inherent curiosity of young adolescents. For example, emphasizing the early encouragement impact that elementary school experiences have on children, recent research has shown that young adolescents who expected to have a career in science were, in fact, more likely to graduate from college with a degree in science (Tai, Liu, Maltese, & Fan, 2006).

Cocurricular versus Extracurricular   Traditionally, student activities involving clubs and athletics, have been commonly referred to as "extracurricular." That is because they are considered separate from the academic learning of the regular school day. However, in exemplary schools many activities are significant components of the total educational program and are "cocurricular," rather than extracurricular. *Cocurricular* means that regardless of whether they occur before, during, or after school, or in some combination, the activities are vital to the total curriculum. They are integral to the total school experience and to the needs of the students, not simply add-ons or extras. Example cocurricular program components are intramurals, study skills, and advisory (discussed next).

The sports program in the exemplary elementary schools in particular emphasizes intramural participation rather than interscholastic competition. Some middle-level schools try to offer both, but most experts agree that emphasis on an intramural program is better suited to the needs of all children (McEwin, Jenkins, & Dickinson, 1996). Intramural sports programs are developed to promote participation by all children. The emphasis is on fun, teamwork, socialization, and peer relationships in an unthreatening and relaxed environment. Assessment is based on a student's willingness to cooperate with others and to participate, rather than on the student's skill or performance. Through intramurals, all students can recognize and feel that they are members of a cohesive group, that they are of value as individuals, and that more important than skilled performance is regular, physical exercise.

The physical education component of the elementary school curriculum contributes to children's development by providing an organized program of experiences that (1) focuses on bodily movement, (2) emphasizes physical fitness, (3) teaches teamwork skills and attitudes, and (4) enriches children's lives by teaching them socially relevant games and sports.

Major Morris/PH College

Advisory Program   The advisory (also called "homebase") program is usually a separate class, ideally of 8 to 12 students (although, in reality, closer to 15 to 25) that meets daily for no less than 20 minutes, without interruptions, often at the beginning of the school day. The primary function of the advisory is to ensure adult advocacy for each student, that each student is known well by at least one adult who can give positive and constructive individual attention to that student. In fact, in some schools the homebase teacher remains with the same students throughout several to all their years at that school.

Regardless of its housing and its label, the advisory program should promote a student's feeling of belonging to a group and is not intended to be used for mechanical tasks (although, in reality, it is sometimes a time for announcements and other maintenance tasks). The program is for purposeful, individual and small-group activities that deal with students' social relationships, transitioning, health education, and emotional/psychological development and well-being. The program should be a vehicle for dealing with students' affective needs; for teaching skills in organization and studying, thinking, problem solving, decision making, violence prevention; and for ensuring meaningful contacts with parents and guardians. In short, for the student, the advisory program, with its planned adult advocacy for each student, can be a very significant aspect of the total school curriculum.

PLANNING FOR INSTRUCTION: THREE LEVELS

For a classroom teacher, planning for instruction is a major professional responsibility. You will be responsible for planning at three levels—the school year, the units, and the lessons—with critical decisions to be made along the way and at each level.

You need not do all your instructional planning from scratch, and you need not do all your planning alone. As a matter of fact, much of the time you *should not* do all your planning alone. In many schools, teams of teachers develop the curricula. Teams of teachers collectively plan special programs for their specific cohorts of students. Team members either plan together or split the responsibilities and then share their individual plans. A final plan is then developed collaboratively.

Some elementary schools subscribe to packaged curriculum programs, especially in reading and mathematics, which are preplanned and sometimes highly scripted for teacher use. The teacher's manual for the program includes an actual script and specifies the time to spend on a particular activity. The writers of published scripted curriculum programs wrote for students of a particular developmental level in general; they did not know your students specifically. As a teacher using a scripted program, you still should tweak the program to address the needs of your particular group of students, making decisions about the content, instructional objectives, materials, teaching strategies, your responses to student behaviors, and assessments of the learning experiences. Without making such adjustments for a particular group of students, it would be impossible for any teacher to differentiate the instruction to adequately attend to the personal needs and differences of individual students.

> The most effective education of children is the result of the combined efforts of competent teachers using the best tools, not the result of tools alone.

In summary, regardless of whether planning is done alone and from scratch, or in collaboration with others, or from a commercially published, scripted program, the heart of productive planning is good decision making. To some degree or another, for every plan and at each of the three levels, you and your team must make decisions about educational standards to be addressed, goals and learning objectives to be set, the subject to be introduced, materials and equipment to be used, methods to be adopted, assessments to be made, and the tools to be used for those assessments. This decision-making process is complicated because so many options are available at each level. Decisions made at all three levels result in a total plan.

> It is, at least in our opinion, this decision-making obligation and privilege that defines the teacher as an artist and classroom teaching as a profession.

Although the planning process continues year after year, the task becomes somewhat easier after the first year as you learn to recycle plans. The process is also made easier via research and communication—by reviewing documents and sharing ideas and plans with your colleagues.

Teacher–Student Collaborative Planning

Even with the current emphasis on standardized achievement testing, exemplary classrooms tend to be more project-oriented and student- and group-centered than the common teacher- and subject-centered classroom of the past, in which the teacher served as the primary provider of information. Although most assuredly the teacher today is no less a determiner of what is ultimately learned by the students, today's students more actively participate in their learning in collaboration with the teacher or teaching team (Weasmer & Woods, 2000). The teacher and teaching team provide some structure and assistance, but the *collaborative approach* requires that students inquire and interact, generate ideas, seriously listen and talk with one another, and recognize that their thoughts and experiences are valuable and essential to learning that is most meaningful and longest lasting.

Many teachers and teaching teams encourage their students to participate in the planning of some phase of their learning. Such participation tends to give students a proprietary interest in the activities, to satisfy the developmental need to explore knowledge, and a sense of ownership to their learning, thereby increasing their motivation for learning. What students have contributed to the plan often seems more meaningful to them than what others have planned for them. And students like to see their own plans succeed. Thus, teacher–student collaboration in planning is usually a very effective motivational tool.

Reasons for Planning

Planning is done for a number of important reasons, perhaps foremost of which is to ensure curriculum coherence, that is, to ensure that what is supposed to be learned is, in fact, learned. Periodic lesson plans are an integral component of a larger plan, represented by school- and districtwide mission statements and target standards and by grade level and course goals and objectives. Students' learning experiences are thoughtfully planned in sequence and then orchestrated by teachers who understand the rationale for their respective positions in the curriculum. Such plans do not preclude, of course, an occasional diversion from predetermined activities.

Another reason for planning is to ensure that the curriculum is developmentally appropriate for the intended students, that is, to give consideration to students' experiential backgrounds, developmental needs, learning capacities and styles, reading abilities, and exceptionalities. Without careful planning it would be impossible for any teacher to individualize the instruction and adequately attend to students' needs and differences.

Planning is necessary to ensure efficient and effective teaching with a minimum of classroom-control problems. After deciding what to teach, you face the important task of deciding how to teach it. To efficiently use precious instructional time,

Careful planning is done to ensure that to the fullest extent possible students are actively involved in their learning—that is, they are both physically active (hands-on learning) and mentally active (minds-on learning).

Scott Cunningham/Merrill

planning should be accomplished with two goals in mind: to not waste anyone's time during the time allotted for instruction and to select strategies that most effectively promote the anticipated student learning. As emphasized throughout this book, a large portion of the instruction will be via student-centered, indirect instruction, although not exclusive of direct instruction. (See, for example, the discussion, "Degrees of Directness," in Chapter 6.)

Planning helps ensure program continuation. The program must continue even if you are absent and a substitute teacher is needed. Planning provides a criterion for reflective practice and self-assessment. After a learning activity and at the end of a school term, you can reflect on and assess what was done and how it affected student learning. Your plans represent a criterion recognized and evaluated by supervisors and administrators.

Not only does good planning provide a boost to your own feelings of confidence and self-assuredness but also from the preceding you realize there are many other reasons a teacher must plan carefully. With those experienced in such matters, it is clear that inadequate planning is usually a precursor to incompetent teaching. Put simply, failing to plan is planning to fail.

COMPONENTS OF AN INSTRUCTIONAL PLAN

A total instructional plan has several major components, described as follows.

Rationale component. This is a statement about why the content of the plan is important and about how students will learn it. The statement should be consistent with the school's mission statement and with the school district's benchmark curriculum standards.

Goals and objectives (standards) component. The goals and objectives represent the learning targets, that is, the specific knowledge, skills, and attitudes to be gained from the study. The plan's learning targets should be consistent with the rationale statement. This topic is discussed in the section that follows, titled "Curriculum Standards."

Articulation component. The articulation component shows the plan's relationship to the learning that preceded and the learning and experiences that will follow. This is referred to as *vertical articulation*. The plan should also indicate its *horizontal articulation*, which is its connectedness with other learning and activities occurring simultaneously across the grade level. Writing, literacy, and thinking skills development are examples. Vertical and horizontal articulation representations are usually illustrated in curriculum documents and programs by scope and sequence charting.

Learning activities component. This is the presentation of organized and sequential units and lessons appropriate for the subject and for the age and diversity of the learners.

Resources component. This is a listing of resources needed, such as print and electronic resources, artifacts (or realia), and community resource ideas, such as guest speakers or presenters, service learning projects, and field trip locations.

Assessment component. This is the appraisal of student learning and occurs as three parts: (a) before instruction begins, a *preassessment* (or diagnostic assessment) of what students already know or think they know about the topic; (b) during the instruction (*formative assessment*) to uncover whether students are learning that which is intended; and (c) at the end of the instruction (*summative assessment*) to determine the extent the students actually did learn.

Special considerations component. This is a place to make notes to remind yourself to consider special populations of students in your classroom, such as gifted learners, challenged learners (students with exceptionalities), and English-language learners.

CURRICULUM CONTENT SELECTION: DOCUMENTS THAT PROVIDE GUIDANCE

Whether for a semester, a school year, or some other interval of time, when planning the content of the curriculum you should decide what specifically is to be accomplished in that time interval. To help in setting goals, you will examine school and other resource documents for mandates and guidelines, communicate with colleagues to learn of common expectations, and probe, analyze, and translate your own convictions, knowledge, and skills into behaviors that foster the intellectual and psychological, and in some instances, the physical development of your students.

A Continuing Dilemma for the Classroom Teacher

Breadth versus Depth of Content Coverage

Many more things are worth teaching than we have time to teach in school, so breadth of topic coverage must be balanced against depth of development of each topic. This is an enduring dilemma that can only be managed in sensible ways, not a problem that can be solved once and for all. School curricula have drifted into addressing far too many topics and including too many trite or pointless details. Analyses in all of the subject areas suggest the need for teacher decision making about how to reduce breadth of coverage, structure the content around powerful ideas, and develop these ideas in depth.

Source: Good & Brophy (2003, p. 410)

With the guidance provided by the activities that follow, you will examine major documents that assist you in selecting the content of your curriculum. These are national and state curriculum standards, school or district benchmark standards, curriculum frameworks and courses of study, and school-adopted materials. Sources for your examination of these documents include the Internet (see Web site listings at end of this chapter), your college or university library, and personnel at local schools.

Curriculum Standards

What are curriculum standards? *Curriculum standards* are a definition of what students should know (content) and be able to do (process and performance). At the national level, curriculum standards did not exist until those developed and released for mathematics education by the National Council of Teachers of Mathematics in 1989 (revised in 2000). Shortly after the release of the mathematics standards, support for national goals in education was endorsed by the National Governors Association, and the National Council on Education Standards and Testing recommended that in addition to those for mathematics, national standards for subject matter content in K–12 education be developed for the arts, civics/social studies, English/language arts/reading, geography, history, and science. The U.S. Department of Education provided initial funding for the development of national standards. In 1994, the U.S. Congress passed the *Goals 2000: Educate America Act*, which was amended in 1996 with an Appropriations Act that encouraged states to set curriculum standards. Long before, however, as was done for mathematics, national organizations devoted to various disciplines were already defining standards.

What are the national standards? The national standards represent the best thinking by expert panels, including teachers from the field, about what are the essential elements of a basic core of subject knowledge that all K–12 students should acquire. They serve not as national mandates but rather as voluntary guidelines to encourage curriculum development to promote higher student achievement.

National Curriculum Standards by Content Area   The following paragraphs describe current national curriculum standards and the related professional organizations for teachers specifically relevant to the elementary grades. Relevant Web sites are listed at the end of this chapter.

Arts (Visual and Performing)   The National Standards for Arts Education were developed jointly by the American Alliance for Health, Physical Education, Recreation, and Dance (AAHPERD), the National Art Education Association (NAEA), the National Dance Association, and the Music Educators National Conference.

English Language Arts   Standards for English education were developed jointly by the International Reading Association (IRA), the National Council of Teachers of English (NCTE), and the University of Illinois Center for the Study of Reading.

Foreign Languages   *Standards for Foreign Language Learning: Preparing for the 21st Century* was developed by the American Council on the Teaching of Foreign Languages (ACTFL).

Geography   Standards for geography education were developed jointly by the Association of American Geographers, the National Council for Geographic Education (NCGE), and the National Geographic Society.

Health   *National Health Education Standards: Achieving Health Literacy* was developed by the Joint Committee for National School Health.

History/Civics & Government/Social Studies   The Center for Civic Education and the National Center for Social Studies developed standards for civics and government, the National Center for History in the Schools developed the standards for history, and standards for social studies were developed by a Task Force of the National Council for Social Studies (NCSS).

Mathematics   *Principles and Standards for School Mathematics* was developed by the National Council of Teachers of Mathematics (NCTM).

Physical Education   *Moving into the Future: National Standards for Physical Education*, 2nd edition in 2004, was published by the National Association of Sport and Physical Education (NASPE).

Science   With input from the American Association for the Advancement of Science (AAAS) and the National Science Teachers Association (NSTA), the National Research Council's (NRC) National Committee on Science Education Standards and Assessment published the standards for science education.

Technology   With initial funding from the National Science Foundation (NSF) and the National Aeronautics and Space Administration (NASA), and in collaboration with the International Technology Education Association, National Educational Technology Standards were developed.

Supplements to the national standards are available from the Bureau of Indian Affairs (BIA) for the arts (dance, music, theater, and visual), civics and government, geography, health, language arts, mathematics, science, and social studies. *The American Indian Supplements* may be used by Indian nations as guides in their preparation of tribally specific local standards. They are also useful to school districts serving American Indian children in adapting state standards to be more culturally relevant to their communities.

State Curriculum Standards   Strongly influenced by the national standards, nearly all states have completed or are implementing at least some of their own standards for the various disciplines. For example:

- For the state of Florida, standards are available for the arts (dance, music, theater, and visual), foreign languages, health, language arts, mathematics, physical education, science, and social studies.
- For the state of Illinois, standards are available for English/language arts, mathematics, science, social science, physical development and health, fine arts, and foreign languages.
- For the state of Montana, standards are available for art, communication arts (reading, literature, media literacy, speaking and listening, and writing), health,

library media, mathematics, science, social studies, technology, workplace competencies, and world languages.

- And, for the state of Texas, the Texas Essential Knowledge and Skills (TEKS) are in the foundation areas of English-language arts and reading, mathematics, science, social studies, languages other than English, health education, physical education, fine arts, economics, agricultural science & technology, marketing, trade & industrial education, technology applications, career orientation, and Spanish language arts and English as a second language.

Curriculum Standards and High-Stakes Testing

Both national and state standards, accessible on the Internet (see listings at end of this chapter), provide guidance to the developers of the standardized tests that are used in what is referred to today as high-stakes testing, that is, the tests being given to determine student achievement, promotion, rewards to schools and even to individual teachers, and, in many states, as a requirement for graduation from high school.

The adoption of tougher learning standards throughout the United States coupled with an emphasis on increased high-stakes testing to assess how schools and teachers are doing with respect to helping their students meet those standards has, as we said in Chapter 1, provoked considerable debate, actions, and reactions among educators, parents, politicians, and from the world of business. Some argue that this renewed emphasis on testing means too much "teaching to the test" at the expense of more meaningful learning, that it ignores the leverage that home, community, and larger societal influences have over the education of children and young people today.

Nevertheless, responding to the call for increased accountability, especially although not exclusively when state and federal funding may be withheld and/or jobs are on the line for schools, teachers, and administrators where students do not score well, teachers in some schools put aside the regular curriculum for several weeks in advance of the testing date and concentrate on the direct preparation of their students for the test.

Although interest has been rekindled in recent years, this oft-called "drill and kill" practice is certainly not new. For example, one of the authors can recall as a high school student in Ohio in the early 1950s being given the *Every Pupil Test*, twice a year, one version in December, another in April. For several weeks, twice each year, before the scheduled test, each teacher would set aside the regular curriculum to prepare the students directly for those tests by distributing and reviewing with them older versions of the tests. Today's interest in annual statewide testing caused us to consider how it compares with past practices.

When comparing standardized testing of today with that of about a half century ago, it is probably safe to conclude that (a) the purpose for statewide standardized testing remains unchanged—it is to determine how well children are learning, at least to the extent determined by the particular test instrument; (b) test design is accomplished today with much greater precision and accuracy; but (c) today's focus on testing is taking precious time away from the most creative aspects of teaching and learning; and (d) the manner in which test results are being used today, and the long-term results of that use, may have ramifications considerably more serious than at any time before.

In schools with the required technology that subscribe to software programs such as *eduTest.com* and *Homeroom.com*, and that have the appropriate number of computers necessary to provide access time to individual students, students can practice and prepare for the state-mandated tests online. Proponents of such on-line preparation argue that a major advantage is the immediate scoring of practice testing with feedback about each student's areas of weakness, thereby providing the teacher with information necessary for immediate remediation. If the arguments are accurate, then it would seem axiomatic that children of such technology-rich schools would clearly be at an advantage over children in schools where this technology is not available. (Note: The disparity between those who have computer access and those who do not is sometimes referred to as *digital inequality* or the *digital divide*.) It would only follow that district and government agencies that mandate the standards and specific assessment practices should provide avenues and tools to ensure equity and success for all children toward reaching the expected learning outcomes within the designated learning time. Is in fact this so-called digital divide closing? According to recent studies, "there is no doubt that more American children of all incomes and backgrounds are using computers and the Internet than ever before. But it is also clear that some groups of young people—primarily low income and minority youth—have poorer access to technology than others" (Henry J. Kaiser Family Foundation, 2004, p. 1).

Student Textbooks

For several reasons—recognition of the diversity of learning styles, capacities, and modalities of students; changing concepts about literacy and habits of thought; enhanced graphics capabilities; economic pressures in the publishing industry; and

---

Activity 5.2: Examining Curriculum Documents and Standards

Using Internet addresses provided at end of chapter, review the national and state standards that interest you. Use the following questions as a guideline for small-group discussions. Following the small-group discussion, share the big ideas about the standards and perceptions of your group with the rest of your class.

Subject area _____

- Name of the standards documents reviewed, year of publication, and development agency for each document.
- Major educational goals as specified by the standards.
- Are the standards specific as to subject matter content for each level of schooling, K–12? Explain.

- Do the standards offer specific strategies for instruction? Describe.
- Do the standards offer suggestions for teaching students who are culturally different, for students with special needs, and for students who are intellectually gifted and talented? Describe.
- Do the standards offer suggestions or guidelines for dealing with controversial topics and issues? Describe.
- Do the standards documents or their accompanying materials offer suggestions for specific resources? Describe.
- Do the standards refer to assessment? Describe.

the availability of electronic and other nonprinted materials—textbook appearance, content, and use have changed considerably in recent years and in all likelihood will continue to change.

> As schools grow more diverse, so to must our understanding of what it means to be lite1rate.
>
> *Source:* Dana G. Thames & Kathleen C. York (2003, p. 609)

Within the span of your teaching career, you will likely witness and even be a contributor to a revolution in the continuing redesign of school textbooks. Already some schools allow teachers in certain disciplines the option of choosing between traditional printed textbooks, textbook-loaded laptop computers, interactive computer programs, or some combination of these (Gordon, 2002).

With the continuing developments in electronics and microcomputer chip technology, textbooks may take on a whole new appearance. With that will come dramatic changes in the importance and use of texts as well as new problems for the teacher, some that are predictable, and others we can't even imagine. On the positive side, it is probable that the classroom teacher will have available a variety of "textbooks" to better address the reading levels, interests, abilities, and perhaps even the primary language of individual students. With these changes, the distribution and maintenance of reading materials could create a greater demand on the teacher's time. Regardless, dramatic and exciting events have begun to affect the teaching tool that had not changed much throughout the 20th century. The textbook of the not-so-distant future may become a handheld, multimedia, interactive, and personal tool that encompasses digitized text, sound, and video and allows for global communications.

Still, today, printed textbooks regulate a large percentage of the learning activity in K–8 classrooms. School districts periodically adopt new textbooks (usually every 5 to 8 years). If you are a student teacher or a first-year teacher, this will most likely mean that someone will tell you, "Here are the books you will be using."

Benefit of Textbooks to Student Learning It is unlikely that anyone could rationally argue that textbooks are of no benefit to student learning. Textbooks can provide: (a) an organization of basic or important content for the students that includes and is built around state curriculum standards, (b) a basis for deciding content emphasis, (c) previously tested activities and suggestions for learning, (d) information about other readings and resources to enhance student learning, and (e) a foundation for building higher-order thinking activities (e.g., inquiry discussions and student research) that help develop critical thinking skills. The textbook, however, should not be the "be-all and end-all" of the instructional experiences.

Problems With Reliance on a Single Textbook   The student textbook is only one of many teaching tools, and not the ultimate word. Of the many ways in which you may use textbooks for student learning, the *least* acceptable is to show a complete dependence on a single book and require students simply to memorize material from it. This is the lowest level of textbook use and learning; furthermore, it implies that you are unaware of other significant resources and have nothing more to contribute to student learning.

Another potential problem brought about by reliance on a single textbook is that because textbook publishers prepare books for use in a larger market—that is, for national or statewide use—a state- and district-adopted book may not adequately address issues of special interest and importance to the community in which you teach. That is one reason why some teachers and schools provide supplementary printed and electronic resources.

Still another problem brought about by reliance on a single source is that the adopted textbook may not be at the appropriate reading level for many students. In today's heterogeneous classrooms, the level of student reading can easily vary by as much as two thirds of the chronological age of the students. This means that if the chronological age is 12 years (typical for seventh graders), then the reading-level range would be eight years—that is, the class may have some students reading at only the preschool level, if at all, whereas others have college-level reading ability. Think about that for a moment!

Guidelines for Using Textbooks   Generally speaking, students benefit by having their own copies of a textbook in the current edition. However, because of budget constraints, this may not always be possible. The book may be outdated, and quantities may be limited. When the latter is the case, students may not be allowed to take the books home or perhaps may only occasionally do so. In some high-poverty area schools, students are not allowed to take textbooks from the classroom. In other classrooms, because of inadequate or misappropriated funding, there may be no textbook at all.

Encourage students to respect books by covering and protecting them and not marking in them. In many schools this is a rule; at the end of the term, students who have damaged or lost their books are charged a fee. As a matter of fact, this is why, as said in the previous paragraph, that in some high-poverty area schools books are not issued at all. If their students lose or damage their books and are charged a fee, the fee goes unpaid because neither the students nor their parents/guardians can afford to pay it.

Yet, in classrooms of some school districts, there are two sets of the textbook, one set that remains for use in the classroom and another set that is assigned to students to use for studying at home. With that arrangement, students don't have to carry around in their backpacks the heavy books used for many subjects taught in today's elementary schools. The paragraphs that follow offer general guidelines for using the textbook as a learning tool.

Progressing through a textbook from the front cover to the back in one school term is not necessarily an indicator of good teaching. The textbook is one resource; to enhance their learning, students should be encouraged to use a variety of

Activity 5.3: Examining Student Textbooks and Teacher's Editions

It is useful for you to become familiar with textbooks that you may be using in your teaching. Student textbooks are usually accompanied by a teacher's edition or guide that contains specific objectives, strategies, activities, assessments, and suggested resources. Your university library, local schools, and cooperating teachers are sources for locating and borrowing these enhanced materials. For a subject field and/or grade level of interest, select a textbook that is accompanied by a teacher's edition/guide and examine the contents of both using the format that follows. After completion of the analysis, share the book and your analysis of it with your colleagues.

Title of book:
Author:
Date of publication:
Publisher:
Grade level(s):

1. My analysis of the teacher's edition/guide. (Answer each with a yes or no, followed by any comment you wish to make.)
   a. Are its goals consistent with those of local and state documents?
   b. Are there specific objectives for each lesson?
   c. Are scope and sequence charts provided for teacher reference?
   d. Are units and lessons sequentially developed?
   e. Are there suggested time allotments for each lesson?

   f. Are there provision for individual differences?

      for reading levels?
      for students with special needs?
      for students who may be gifted/talented?
      for students who have limited proficiency in English language?
      other?

   g. Are there recommended strategies/techniques?
   h. Are there listings of suggested aids, materials, and resources?
   i. Are there suggested extension activities?
   j. Are there specific guidelines for assessment of student learning?
2. My analysis of the student textbook.
   a. Does the book treat content with adequate depth?
   b. Does it treat ethnic minorities fairly?
   c. Does it treat genders with equality?
   d. Is the format attractive?
   e. Is the format useful and easy to follow?
   f. Does the book have quality binding with suitable print size?
   g. Are illustrations and other visuals attractive and useful?
   h. Is the reading clear and understandable for the intended user?
   i. Is the content current and accurate?
3. Would you like to use the book in your teaching? Explain your response.

resources. Encourage students to search additional sources to update the content of the textbook. This is especially important in certain disciplines such as the sciences and social sciences, where the amount of new information is growing rapidly, and students may have textbooks that are several years old. The library and sources on the Internet should be researched by students for the latest information on certain subjects, always keeping in mind, however, that just because something is found in print or on the Net doesn't mean that the information is accurate or even true. Maintain supplementary reading materials for student use in the classroom. School and community librarians and resource specialists usually are delighted to cooperate with teachers in the selection and provision of such resources.

Individualize the learning for students of various reading abilities. Consider differentiated reading and workbook assignments in the textbook and several supplementary sources (see "Multitext and Multireadings Approach," a topic that follows). Except to make life simpler for the teacher, there is no advantage in all students working out of the same book and exercises. Some students benefit from the drill, practice, and reinforcement afforded by workbooks or software programs that accompany textbooks, but this is not true for all students, nor do all students benefit from the same activity. In fact, the traditional printed workbook may eventually become extinct, as it is replaced by the modern technology afforded by electronic software. Computers and other interactive media provide students with a psychologically safer learning environment, where they have greater control over the pace of the instruction, can repeat instruction if necessary, and can ask for clarification without the fear of having to do so publicly.

Creative teachers continue to invent methods to help students develop their higher-level thinking skills and their comprehension of expository material. Some of these methods are shown in Figure 5.2.

- KQHL: Students ask what they want to know (K) about a topic, ask what questions (Q) do we need/want answered, ask how (H) might we find answers, and then later identify what they have learned (L) (Long, Drake & Halychyn, 2004).
- KWL: Students recall what they already know (K) about a topic, determine what they want to learn (W), and later assess what they have learned (L) (Ogle, 1986).
- KWLQ: Students record what they already know about a topic (K), formulate questions about what they want to learn about the topic (W), search for answers to their questions (L), and ask questions for further study (Q) (source unknown).
- KWHLS: Students identify what they already know about the topic of study (K), what they want to learn (W), how they plan to learn it (H), then what they learned (L), and finally how they will share that new knowledge with others (S) (source unknown).
- POSSE: *Predict* ideas, *organize* ideas, *search* for structure, *summarize* main ideas, and *evaluate* understanding (Englert & Mariage, 1991).
- PQRST: *Preview, question, read, state* the main idea, and *test* yourself by answering the questions you posed earlier (Kelly, 1994).
- QAR: Helping children understand *question-and-answer relationships* (Mesmer & Hutchins, 2002).
- RAP: *Read* paragraphs, *ask* questions about what was read, and *put* in your own words (Schumaker, Denton, & Deshler, 1984).
- Reciprocal teaching: Students are taught and practice the reading skills of summarizing, questioning, clarifying, and predicting (Palincsar & Brown, 1984).
- SQ3R: *Survey* the chapter, ask *questions* about what was read, *read*, *recite*, and *review* (Robinson, 1961).
- SQ4R: *Survey* the chapter, ask *questions* about what was read, *read* to answer the questions, *recite* the answers, *record* important items from the chapter into their notebooks, then *review* it all (source unknown).
- SRQ2R: *Survey, read, question, recite*, and *review* (Walker, 1995).

FIGURE 5.2
Methods for helping students develop their higher-level thinking skills and their comprehension of expository material

> Just because it is found in print or on the Internet or on broadcast news doesn't mean it's accurate or even true.

Encourage students to be alert for errors in the textbook, both in content and printing—perhaps offering some sort of credit reward when they bring an error to your attention. This can help students develop the skills of critical reading, critical thinking, and healthy skepticism.

Multitext and Multireadings Approach   Rather than a single textbook approach, consider using a strategy that incorporates many readings that vary in difficulty, detail, and vocabulary but have a common focus. Whatever the unit, teachers can include a wide range of materials: informational picture and chapter books; biographies and photographic essays; and Internet, newspaper, and magazine articles. Giving students a choice in what they read, the multiple reading source strategy helps all students become a part of the same community of readers (Robb, 2002). Especially useful for interdisciplinary thematic instruction, the strategy also allows for differences in reading ability and interest level and stimulates a sharing of what is read and being learned.

BEGINNING TO THINK ABOUT THE SEQUENCING OF CONTENT

As you have reviewed the rationale and components of instructional planning, examined curriculum standards, curriculum documents, and student reading materials, you have undoubtedly reflected on your own opinion regarding content that should be included in a subject at a particular grade level. Now it is time to obtain some practical experience in long-range planning.

Although some authors believe that after selecting the content the first step in preparing to teach is to prepare the objectives, others believe that a more logical starting point is to prepare a sequential topic outline—the next step in this chapter—from which you can then prepare the major target objectives (benchmark standards). With today's pressure on teachers to work from established and mandated benchmark standards it may well be that many teachers today do, in fact, begin their curriculum development from those objectives.

Regardless of the approach used, the curriculum plan should satisfy three organizational requirements:

1. The plan should be organized around important ideas, concepts, and questions, all of which should correlate with mandated content standards.
2. The plan should reflect the interests and concerns of the recipient students.
3. The plan should be oriented toward the assessments and tasks that will be used for students in demonstrating what they have learned.

The curriculum plans, topic outlines, and instructional objectives may be presented to most beginning teachers with the expectation that they will teach from

Activity 5.4: Preparing A Full-Semester Content Outline

With *three levels of headings* (see example that follows), prepare a sequential topic outline for a subject and grade level you intend to teach (K–8). Identify the subject by title, and clearly state the grade level. The outline is to be of topic content only and does *not* need to include subject activities associated with the learning of that content (i.e., do not include experiments, assignments, or assessments).

For example, for the study of earth science, three levels of headings might include

    I. The Earth's surface
       A. Violent changes in the Earth's surface
          1. Earthquakes
          2. Volcanoes
       B. Earth's land surface
          1. Rocks
      etc.

If the study of earth science was but one unit for a grade level's study of the broader areas of science, then three levels of headings for that study might include

    I. Earth science
       A. The Earth's surface
          1. Violent changes in the Earth's surface
      etc.

Share your completed outline to obtain feedback from your colleagues and course instructor. Because content outlines are never to be "carved into stone," make adjustments to your outline when and as appropriate.

Content Outline Assessment Checklist

For the development of your own outline, and for assessment of outlines by others, here is an assessment checklist that you may copy and attach to your outline:

✓ Does the outline follow a logical sequence, with each topic logically leading to the next?
   Yes ___ No ___ Comment:

✓ Does the content assume prerequisite knowledge or skills that the students are likely to have?
   Yes ___ No ___ Comment:

✓ Is the content inclusive and to an appropriate depth?
   Yes ___ No ___ Comment:

✓ Does the content consider individual student differences?
   Yes ___ No ___ Comment:

✓ Does the content allow for interdisciplinary (integrated) studies?
   Yes ___ No ___ Comment:

✓ Is the outline complete, without serious content omissions?
   Yes ___ No ___ Comment:

✓ Is there content that is of questionable value for this level of instruction?
   Yes ___ No ___ Comment:

Save your outline and completed assessment checklist(s) for later when you are working on Activities 6.2 and 6.3 of Chapter 6.

them. For you this may be the case, but someone had to have written those outlines and objectives and that someone was one or more present or former classroom teachers. As a new teacher, you must know how this is done, for someday it will be your task. To experience preparing a full semester content outline for a subject and grade level that you intend to teach, we suggest you do Activity 5.4 now.

PREPARING FOR AND DEALING WITH CONTROVERSY

Controversial content and issues abound in teaching in most disciplines. For example:

- Continuing debate over sex education and to what extent, if at all, it should be approached in public schools

- In English/reading/language arts, over certain books (*Note:* Although efforts to censor books used in schools is nothing new, challenges seem to be escalating [Franklin, 2002])
- In science, over creationist theory (Joiner, 2003, Terry, 2004)
- In social studies, over use of the Pledge of Allegiance

As a general rule, if you have concern that a particular topic or activity might create controversy, it probably will. During your teaching career, you undoubtedly will have to make decisions about how you will handle such matters. When selecting content that might be controversial, consider the paragraphs that follow as guidelines.

Maintain a perspective with respect to your own goal, which is at the moment to obtain your teaching credential, and then a teaching job, and then tenure. Student teaching, in particular, is not a good time to become embroiled in controversy. If you communicate closely with your cooperating teacher and your college or university supervisor, you should be able to prevent major problems dealing with controversial issues.

Sometimes, during normal discussion in the classroom, a controversial subject will, however, emerge spontaneously, catching the teacher off guard. If this happens, think before saying anything. You may wish to postpone further discussion until you have a chance to talk over the issue with members of your teaching team or your supervisors. Controversial topics can seem to arise from nowhere for any teacher, and this is perfectly normal. Your students are in process of developing their moral and value systems, and they need and want to know how adults feel about issues that are important to them, particularly those adults they hold in esteem—their teachers. Our youth need to discuss issues that are important to society, and there is absolutely nothing wrong with dealing with those issues as long as certain guidelines are followed.

First, students should learn about all sides of an issue. Controversial issues are open-ended and should be treated as such. They do not have "right" answers or "correct" solutions. If they did, there would be no controversy. (*Note:* As used in this discussion, an "issue" differs from a "problem" in that a problem generally has a solution, whereas an issue has many opinions and several alternative solutions.) Therefore, the focus should be on process as well as on content. A major goal is to show students how to deal with controversy and to mediate wise decisions on the basis of carefully considered information. Another goal is to help students learn how to disagree without being disagreeable—how to resolve conflict. To that end, students need to learn the difference between conflicts that are destructive and those that can be constructive, in other words, to see that conflict (disagreement) can be healthy, and that it can have value. A third goal, of course, is to help students learn about the content of an issue so, when necessary, they can make decisions based on knowledge, not on ignorance.

Second, as with all lesson plans, one dealing with a topic that could lead to controversy should be well thought out ahead of time. Potential problem areas and resources must be carefully considered and prepared for in advance.

Problems for the teacher are most likely to occur when the plan has not been well conceived.

Third, at some point all persons directly involved in an issue have a right to input: students, parents and guardians, community representatives, and other faculty. This does not mean, for example, that people outside the school necessarily have the right to censor a teacher's plan, but it does mean that parents or guardians and students should have the right *sans penalty* to not participate and to select an alternate activity. Most school districts have written policies that deal with challenges to instructional materials. As a beginning teacher, you should become aware of policies of your school district. In addition, professional associations such as the NCTE, NCSS, NBTA, and NSTA publish guidelines for dealing with controversial topics, materials, and issues.

Fourth, there is nothing wrong with students knowing a teacher's opinion about an issue as long as it is clear that the students may disagree without reprisal or penalty of any sort. However, it is probably best for a teacher to wait and give her or his opinion only after the students have had full opportunity to study and report on facts and opinions from other sources. Sometimes it is helpful to assist students in separating facts from opinions on a particular issue being studied by setting up on the overhead or writing board a fact–opinion table, with the issue stated at the top and then two parallel columns, one for facts, the other for related opinions, as shown here.

Issue: _____

Facts	Opinions

A characteristic that makes this nation so great is the freedom for all its citizens to speak out on issues. We agree with others in that this freedom proffered by the First Amendment of the Bill of Rights of the U.S. Constitution should not be excluded from public school classrooms (Haynes, Chaltain, Ferguson, Hudson, & Thomas, 2003). Teachers and students should be encouraged to express their opinions about the great issues of today, to study the issues, to learn how to suspend judgment while collecting data, and then to form and accept each other's reasoned opinions. We must understand the difference between teaching truth, values, and morals and teaching about truth, values, and morals.

As a teacher of children in a public school there are limits to your academic freedom, much greater than are the limits, for example, on a university professor working with college students. You must understand this fact. The primary difference is that the students with whom you will be working are not yet adults; because they are juveniles, they must be protected from dogma and provided the freedom to learn and to develop their values and opinions, free of coercion from those who have power and control over their learning.

AIMS, GOALS, AND OBJECTIVES: THE ANTICIPATED LEARNING OUTCOMES

Now that you have examined content typical of the curriculum, have experienced preparing a tentative content outline for a subject that you intend to teach, and understand some important guidelines for dealing with controversial topics, you are ready to write instructional objectives for that content learning.

Instructional objectives are statements describing what the student will be able to do on completion of the planned learning experience. Whereas some authors distinguish between *instructional objectives* (hence referring to objectives that are not behavior specific) and *behavioral* or *performance objectives* (objectives that *are* behavior specific), the terms are used here as if they are synonymous to emphasize the importance of writing instructional objectives in terms that are measurable.

As a teacher, you frequently will encounter the compound structure that reads "goals and objectives," as you likely found in the curriculum documents that you reviewed earlier in this chapter. A distinction needs to be understood. The easiest way to understand the difference between the two words, *goals* and *objectives*, is to look at your *intent*.

Goals are ideals that you intend to reach, that is, ideals that you would like to have accomplished. Goals may be stated as teacher goals, as student goals, or, collaboratively, as team goals. Ideally, in all three, the goal is the same. If, for example, the goal is to improve students' reading skills, it could be stated as follows:

"To help students develop
their reading skills"   *Teacher or course goal*

                or

"To improve my reading skills"   *Student goal*

The bottom line in education is not the amount of time spent on instruction, nor the amount of dollars expended on it, nor the certification requirements of teachers. What counts in the end are the results: what children have learned, how well they have learned it, and the difference that the learning has made in their lives.

Anthony Magnacca/Merrill

Educational goals are general statements of intent and are prepared early in course planning. (*Note*: Some writers use the phrase "general goals and objectives," but that is incorrect usage. Goals *are* general; objectives are specific.) Goals are useful when planned cooperatively with students and/or when shared with students as advance mental organizers to establish a mind-set. The students then know what to expect and will begin to prepare mentally to learn it. From the goals, objectives are prepared. Objectives are *not* intentions. They are actual behaviors that students are expected to display. In short, objectives are what students *do*.

The most general educational objectives are often called *aims;* the objectives of schools, curricula, and courses are called *goals*; the objectives of units and lessons are called *instructional* or *target objectives*. Aims are more general than goals, and goals are more general than objectives. Instructional objectives are quite specific. Aims, goals, and objectives represent the targets, from general to specific statements of learning expectations, to which curriculum is designed and instruction is aimed.

Instructional Objectives and Their Relationship to Aligned Curriculum and Authentic Assessment

As implied in the preceding paragraphs, goals guide the instructional methods; objectives drive student performance. Assessment of student achievement in learning should be an assessment of that performance. When the assessment procedure matches the instructional objectives, that is sometimes referred to as assessment that is *aligned* or *authentic*. (*Note:* If the term *authentic assessment* sounds rather silly to you, we concur. After all, if the objectives and assessment don't match, then that particular assessment should be discarded or modified until it does match. In other words, assessment that is not authentic is "poor assessment" and should not be used.) When objectives, instruction, and assessment match the stated goals, we have what is referred to as an *aligned curriculum*. (Again, a curriculum that does not align is nonsensical and should be either corrected or discarded. You can even find in some literature the terms authentic instruction and authentic teaching. The rule still applies, and that is, instruction or teaching that is not authentic. . . . Need we say more?)

Goals are general statements, usually not even complete sentences, often beginning with the infinitive "to," which identify what the teacher intends the students to learn. Objectives, stated in performance terms, are specific actions and should be written as complete sentences that include the verb "will" *to indicate what each student is expected to be able to do as a result of the instructional experience.* The last portion of the previous sentence is emphasized because when writing instructional objectives for their unit and lesson plans, one of the most common errors made by teachers is to state what *they*, the teachers, intend to do rather than what the anticipated student performance is. The value of stating learning objectives in terms of student performance is well documented by research (Baker & Martin, 1998; Good & Brophy, 2003).

Although instructional goals may not always be quantifiable (i.e., readily measurable), instructional objectives should be measurable. Furthermore, those objectives then become the essence of what is measured for in instruments designed to assess student learning; they are the learning targets. Consider the following examples.

Goals

1. To acquire knowledge about the physical geography of North America.
2. To develop reading skills.

Objectives

1. When given a map of North America, the student will identify specific rivers.
2. When given a passage to read in class the student will read it with no errors.

Learning Targets and Goal Indicators: Meaning of "Quality Learning"

One purpose for writing objectives in performance terms is to be able to assess with precision whether the instruction has resulted in the desired behavior. In many schools the educational goals are established as *learning targets*, competencies that the students are expected to achieve and that were derived from the district and state curriculum standards. These learning targets are then divided into performance objectives, sometimes referred to as goal indicators. Instruction is designed to teach toward those objectives. When students perform the competencies called for by these objectives, their education is considered successful. This is known variously as *criterion-referenced, competency-based, performance-based, results-driven,* or *outcome-based education.* When the objectives are aligned with specific curriculum standards, as they usually are or should be, then it can also be referred to as *standards-based education.* Expecting students to achieve one set of competencies before moving on to the next set is called *mastery* (or *quality*) *learning* (discussed further in Chapter 8). The success of the student achievement, teacher performance, and the school may each be assessed according to these criteria.

Overt and Covert Performance Outcomes

Assessment is not difficult to accomplish when the desired performance outcome is overt behavior, which can be observed directly. Each of the sample objectives of the preceding section is an example of an overt objective. Assessment is more difficult to accomplish when the desired behavior is covert, that is, when it is not directly observable. Although certainly no less important, behaviors that call for "appreciation," "discovery," or "understanding," for example, are not directly observable because they occur within a person and so are covert behaviors. Because covert behavior cannot be observed directly, the only way to tell whether the objective has been achieved is to observe behavior that may be indicative of that achievement. The objective, then, is written in overt language, and evaluators can only assume or trust that the observed behavior is, in fact, reasonably close to being indicative of the expected learning outcome.

Furthermore, when assessing whether an objective has been achieved—that learning has occurred—the assessment device must be consistent with the desired learning outcome. Otherwise, the assessment is not aligned; it is invalid. When the measuring device and the learning objective are compatible, we say that the assessment is authentic. For example, a person's competency to teach specific skills in mathematics to seventh graders is best (i.e., with highest reliability) measured by directly observing that person *doing* that very thing—teaching specific skills in mathematics to seventh graders. Using a standardized paper-and-pencil test of multiple-choice items to determine a person's ability to teach specific math skills to seventh-grade students is not authentic assessment. Although the particular multiple-choice item assessment device might be valid, it is *not* authentic.

Balance of Behaviorism and Constructivism

Although behaviorists (behaviorism) assume a definition of learning that deals only with changes in overt behavior, constructivists hold that learning entails the construction or reshaping of mental schemata and that mental processes mediate learning. Thus, people who adhere to constructivism or cognitivism or constructionism are concerned with both overt and covert behaviors (DeLay, 1996; *Educational Leadership*, 1999; Geelan, 1997). Does this mean that you must be one or the other, a behaviorist or a constructivist? Probably not. For now, the point is that when writing instructional objectives, you should write most or all of your basic expectations (minimal competency expectations) in overt terms (the topic of the next section). On the other hand, you cannot be expected to foresee all learning that occurs nor to translate all that is learned into performance terms—most certainly not before it occurs.

TEACHING TOWARD MULTIPLE OBJECTIVES, UNDERSTANDINGS, AND APPRECIATIONS: THE REALITY OF MODERN CLASSROOM INSTRUCTION

Any effort to write all learning objectives in performance terms is, in effect, to neglect the individual learner for whom it purports to be concerned; such an approach does not allow for diversity among learners. Learning that is most meaningful to students is not so neatly or easily predicted or isolated. Rather than teaching one objective at a time, much of the time you should direct your teaching toward the simultaneous learning of multiple objectives, understandings, and appreciations. However, when you assess for learning, assessment is cleaner when objectives are assessed one at a time. More on this matter of objectives and their use in teaching and learning follows later in this chapter. Let's now consider how objectives are prepared.

PREPARING INSTRUCTIONAL OBJECTIVES

When preparing instructional objectives, you must ask yourself, "How is the student to demonstrate that the objective has been reached?" The objective must include an action that demonstrates that the objective has been achieved. Inherited from behaviorism, this portion of the objective is sometimes called the *anticipated measurable performance*.

Components of a Complete Objective

When completely written in performance terms, an instructional objective has four components, although in practice you are unlikely to use all four. To aid your understanding and as a mnemonic for remembering, you can refer to these components as the ABCDs of writing objectives.

One component is the *audience*. The *A* of the ABCDs refers to the student for whom the objective is intended. To address this, sometimes teachers begin their objectives with the phrase, "The student will be able to . . . ," or, to personalize the objective, "You will be able to . . . ," (*Note*: To conserve space and to eliminate useless language, in examples that follow we delete the "be able to," and write simply "The student will . . ." As a matter of fact we prefer use of "will" over "be able to." For brevity, writers of objectives sometimes use the abbreviation "TSWBAT . . ." for "The student will be able to . . ." or more simply "TSW . . ." for "The student will . . .")

The second component is the expected *behavior*, the *B* of the ABCDs. It is this second component that represents the learning target. The expected behavior (or performance) should be written with verbs that are measurable—that is, with action verbs—so that it is directly observable that the objective, or target, has been reached. As discussed in the preceding section, some verbs are too vague, ambiguous, and not clearly measurable. When writing overt objectives, you should avoid verbs that are not clearly measurable, covert verbs such as "appreciate," "comprehend," and "understand" (see Figure 5.3). For the two example objectives given earlier, the behaviors (action or overt verbs) are "will *identify*" and "will *read*."

Most of the time, when writing objectives for your unit and lesson plans, you will not bother yourself with including the next two components. However, as you will learn, they are important considerations for assessment.

appreciate	enjoy	indicate	like
believe	familiarize	know	realize
comprehend	grasp	learn	understand

FIGURE 5.3
Verbs to avoid when writing overt objectives

Activity 5.5: Recognizing Verbs That Are Acceptable for Overt Objectives

Instructions: The purpose of this activity is to check your recognition of verbs that are suitable for use in overt objectives. From the list of verbs below, circle those that *should not* be used in overt objectives—that is, those verbs that describe covert behaviors not directly observable and measurable. Check your answers against the answer key that follows. Discuss any problems with your classmates and instructor.

1. apply	11. design	21. know
2. appreciate	12. diagram	22. learn
3. believe	13. enjoy	23. name
4. combine	14. explain	24. outline
5. comprehend	15. familiarize	25. predict
6. compute	16. grasp*	26. realize
7. create	17. identify	27. select
8. define	18. illustrate	28. solve
9. demonstrate	19. indicate	29. state
10. describe	20. infer	30. understand

Answer Key: The following verbs should be circled: 2, 3, 5, 13, 15, 16, 21, 22, 26, and 30. If you missed more than a couple, then you need to read the previous sections again and discuss your errors with your classmates and instructor. * Note: Words in English often have more than one meaning. For example, "grasp," as listed here could mean "to take hold," or it could mean "to comprehend." For the former it would be an acceptable verb for use in overt objectives; for the latter it would not.

The third component is the *conditions*, the *C* of the ABCDs—the setting in which the behavior will be demonstrated by the student and observed by the teacher. Conditions are forever changing; although the learning target should be clearly recognizable long before the actual instruction occurs, the conditions may not. Thus, in curriculum documents in particular, conditions are not often included in the objectives. However, when preparing to assess student learning toward specific objectives, you must consider the conditions within which the performance will be displayed. For the first sample objective, the conditions are: "on a map." For the second sample objective, for "the student will read . . . ," the conditions are: "when given a passage to read in class."

The fourth component, again, that is not always included in objectives found in curriculum documents, is the *degree (or level) of expected performance*—the *D* of the ABCDs. This is the ingredient that allows for the assessment of student learning. When mastery learning is expected, the level of expected performance is usually omitted (because it is understood). In teaching for mastery learning, the performance-level expectation is 100%. In reality, however, the performance level will most likely be 85 to 95%, particularly when working with a group of students, rather than with an individual student. The 5 to 15% difference allows for human error, as can occur when using written and oral communication. As with conditions, the level of performance will vary depending on the situation and purpose and thus is not normally included in the unit and lessons that teachers prepare.

Activity 5.6: Recognizing the Parts of Criterion-Referenced Instructional Objectives

Instructions: The purpose of this activity is to practice your skill in recognizing the four components of an instructional objective. In the following two objectives, identify the parts of the objectives by underlining once the *audience*, twice the *performance (behavior)*, three times the *conditions*, and four times the *performance level* (i.e., the degree or standard of performance).

Check your answers against the answer key that follows, and discuss any problems with this activity with your classmates and instructor.

1. Given a metropolitan transit bus schedule, at the end of the lesson the student will be able to read the schedule well enough to determine at what times buses are scheduled to leave randomly selected locations, with at least 90% accuracy.

2. Given five rectangular figures, you will correctly compute the area in square centimeters of at least four, by measuring the length and width with a ruler and computing the product using an appropriate calculation method.

Answer Key:

	Objective 1	*Objective 2*
Audience (underlined once)	The student	You
Behavior (underlined twice)	will be able to read the schedule	will compute
Conditions (underlined three times)	given a metropolitan transit bus schedule	given five rectangular figures
Performance level (underlined four times)	well enough to determine (and) with at least 90% accuracy	correctly compute the area in square centimeters of at least four

Performance level is used to assess student achievement, and sometimes it is used to evaluate the effectiveness of the teaching. Student grades might be based on performance levels; evaluation of teacher effectiveness might be based on the level of student performance. Indeed, with today's use of state-mandated, standardized testing, schools, administrators, and teachers are evaluated on the basis of student performance on those tests.

Classifying Instructional Objectives

When planning instructional objectives, it is useful to consider the three domains of learning objectives:

cognitive domain—involves intellectual operations from the lowest level of simple recall of information to complex, high-level thinking processes;

affective domain—involves feelings, emotions, attitudes, and values, and ranges from the lower levels of acquisition to the highest level of internalization and action;

psychomotor domain—ranges from the simple manipulation of materials to the communication of ideas, and finally to the highest level of creative performance.

Activity 5.7: Recognizing Objectives that are Measurable

Instructions: The purpose of this activity is to assess your ability to recognize objectives that are measurable. Place an *X* before each of the following that is an overt, student-centered instructional objective, that is, a learning objective that is clearly measurable. Although "audience," "conditions," or "performance levels" may be absent, ask yourself, "As stated, is this a student-centered and measurable objective?" If it is, place an *X* in the blank. A self-checking answer key follows. After checking your answers, discuss any problems with the activity with your classmates and instructor.

_____ 1. To develop an appreciation for literature.

_____ 2. To identify those celestial bodies that are known planets.

_____ 3. To provide meaningful experiences for the students.

_____ 4. To recognize antonym pairs.

_____ 5. To convert Celsius temperatures to Fahrenheit.

_____ 6. To analyze and compare patterns of data on specific quartile maps.

_____ 7. To develop skills in inquiry.

_____ 8. To identify which of the four causes is most relevant to the major events leading up to the Civil War.

_____ 9. To use maps and graphs to identify the major areas of world petroleum production and consumption.

_____10. To know explanations for the changing concentration of atmospheric ozone.

Answer Key: You should have marked items 2, 4, 5, 6, 7, 8, and 9. Items 1, 3, 7, and 10 are inadequate because of their ambiguity. Item 3 is not even a student learning objective; it is a teacher goal. "To develop" and "to know" can have too many interpretations. Although the conditions are not given, items 2, 4, 5, 6, 8, and 9 are clearly measurable. The teacher would have no difficulty recognizing when a learner had reached those objectives.

The Domains of Learning and the Developmental Characteristics of Children

Educators attempt to design learning experiences to coincide with the five areas of developmental characteristics and needs of children: intellectual, physical, emotional/psychological, social, and moral/ethical. As an elementary-school teacher, you must include objectives that address learning within each of these categories. Although the intellectual needs are primarily within the cognitive domain and the physical are within the psychomotor, the other three categories mostly are within the affective domain.

Too frequently, teachers focus on the cognitive domain while only assuming that the psychomotor and affective will take care of themselves. If the current nationwide focus on standardized achievement testing sustains, this may become even more so. Many experts argue, however, that teachers should do just the opposite; that when the affective is directly attended to, the psychomotor and cognitive naturally develop. They argue that unless the social and emotional needs of students are adequately addressed, little happens cognitively (Hopping, 2000). Whether the domains are attended to separately or simultaneously, you should plan your teaching so your students are guided from the lowest to highest levels of operation within each domain.

The three developmental hierarchies are discussed next to guide your understanding of each of the five areas of needs. Notice the illustrative verbs within each hierarchy. These verbs help you fashion objectives when you are developing unit plans and lesson plans. (To see how goals and objectives are fit into one lesson plan, see Figure 6.10 in Chapter 6, Multiple-Day, Project-Centered, Interdisciplinary and Transcultural Lesson Using World-Wide Communication via the Internet.) However, caution is urged, for there can be considerable overlap among the levels at which some action verbs may appropriately be used. For example, action verb "will identify" is appropriate in each of the following objectives at different levels (identified in parentheses) within the cognitive domain.

The student will identify the correct definition of the term "magnetism." (knowledge)

The student will identify examples of natural and artificial magnetism. (comprehension)

The student will identify the effect when iron filings are sprinkled on a sheet of paper placed on a bar magnet. (application)

The student will identify the effect on iron filings when two magnetic north poles are brought close together. (analysis)

Cognitive Domain Hierarchy

In a widely accepted taxonomy of objectives, Bloom and his associates (Bloom, 1984) arranged cognitive objectives into classifications according to the complexity of the skills and abilities they embodied. The result was a ladder ranging from the simplest to the most complex intellectual processes. Within each domain, prerequisite to a student's ability to function at one particular level of the hierarchy is the ability to function at the preceding level or levels. In other words, when a student is functioning at the third level of the cognitive domain, that student is automatically also functioning at the first and second levels. Rather than an orderly progression from simple to complex mental operations, as illustrated by Bloom's taxonomy, other researchers prefer an organization of cognitive abilities that ranges from simple information storage and retrieval, through a higher level of discrimination and concept attainment, to the highest cognitive ability to recognize and solve problems (Gagné, Briggs, & Wager, 1994).

The six major categories (or levels) in Bloom's taxonomy of cognitive objectives are (a) knowledge—recognizing and recalling information, (b) comprehension—understanding the meaning of information, (c) application—using information, (d) analysis—dissecting information into its component parts to comprehend their relationships, (e) synthesis—putting components together to generate new ideas, and (f) evaluation—judging the worth of an idea, notion, theory, thesis, proposition, information, or opinion. In this taxonomy, the top four categories or levels—application, analysis, synthesis, and evaluation—represent what are called higher-order cognitive thinking skills. (Note: Compare Bloom's higher-order cognitive thinking skills with R. H. Ennis's "A Taxonomy of Critical Thinking Dispositions and

Abilities" and Qellmalz's "Developing Reasoning Skills," both in Barron and Sternberg [1987], and with Marzano's "Complex Thinking Strategies" [Marzano, 1992].)

Although space limitation prohibits elaboration here, Bloom's taxonomy includes various subcategories within each of these six major categories. It is probably less important that an objective be absolutely classified than it is to be cognizant of hierarchies of thinking and doing and to understand the importance of attending to student intellectual behavior from lower to higher levels of operation in all three domains. Discussion of each of Bloom's six categories follows.

Knowledge   The basic element in Bloom's taxonomy concerns the acquisition of knowledge—that is, the ability to recognize and recall information. Although this is the lowest of the six categories, the information to be learned may not itself be of a low level. In fact, it may be of an extremely high level. Bloom includes here knowledge of principles, generalizations, theories, structures, and methodology, as well as knowledge of facts and ways of dealing with facts.

Action verbs appropriate for this category include *choose, complete, cite, define, describe, identify, indicate, label, list, locate, match, name, outline, recall, recognize, select*, and *state*.

The following are examples of objectives at the knowledge level. Note especially the verb (in italics) used in each example:

- From memory, the student *will recall* the letters in the English alphabet that are vowels.
- The student *will list* the organelles found in animal cell cytoplasm.

The remaining five categories of Bloom's taxonomy of the cognitive domain deal with the *use* of knowledge. They encompass the educational objectives aimed at developing cognitive skills and abilities, including comprehension, application, analysis, synthesis, and evaluation of knowledge. As said previously, the last four—application, analysis, synthesis, and evaluation—are referred to as *higher-order thinking skills*, as are the higher categories of the affective and psychomotor domains.

Comprehension   Comprehension includes the ability to translate, explain, or interpret knowledge and to extrapolate from it to address new situations. Action verbs appropriate for this category include *change, classify, convert, defend, describe, discuss, distinguish, estimate, expand, explain, generalize, give example, infer, interpret, paraphrase, predict, recognize, retell, summarize,* and *translate*. Examples of objectives in this category are

- From a sentence, the student *will recognize* the letters that are vowels in the English alphabet.
- The student *will describe* each of the organelles found in animal cell cytoplasm.

Application   Once learners understand information, they should be able to apply it. Action verbs in this category of operation include *apply, calculate, compute,* *demonstrate, develop, discover, exhibit, manipulate, modify, operate, participate, perform, plan, predict, relate, show, simulate, solve,* and *use.* Examples of objectives in this category are

- The student *will use* in a sentence a word that contains at least two vowels.
- The student *will predict* the organelles found in plant cell cytoplasm.

Analysis This category includes objectives that require learners to use the skills of analysis. Action verbs appropriate for this category include *analyze, arrange, break down, categorize, classify, compare, contrast, debate, deduce, diagram, differentiate, discover, discriminate, group, identify, illustrate, infer, inquire, organize, outline, relate, separate,* and *subdivide.* Examples of objectives in this category are

- From a list of words, the student *will differentiate* those that contain vowels from those that do not.
- Using the microscope, the student *will identify* the organelles found in animal cell cytoplasm.

Synthesis This category includes objectives that involve such skills as designing a plan, proposing a set of operations, and deriving a series of abstract relations. Action verbs appropriate for this category include *arrange, assemble, categorize, classify, combine, compile, compose, constitute, create, design, develop, devise, document, explain, formulate, generate, hypothesize, imagine, invent, modify, organize, originate, plan, predict, produce, rearrange, reconstruct, revise, rewrite, summarize, synthesize, tell, transmit,* and *write.* Examples of objectives in this category are

- From a list of words, the student *will rearrange* them into several lists according to the vowels contained in each.
- The student *will devise* a classification scheme of the organelles found in animal cell and plant cell cytoplasm according to their functions.

Evaluation This, the highest category of Bloom's cognitive taxonomy, includes offering opinions and making value judgments. Action verbs appropriate for this category include *appraise, argue, assess, choose, compare, conclude, consider, contrast, criticize, decide, describe, discriminate, estimate, evaluate, explain, interpret, judge, justify, predict, rank, rate, recommend, relate, revise, standardize, summarize, support,* and *validate.* Examples of objectives in this category are

- The student *will listen to and evaluate* other students' identifications of vowels from sentences written on the board.
- While observing living cytoplasm under the microscope, the student *will justify* his or her interpretation that certain structures are specific organelles of a plant or an animal cell.

Affective Domain Hierarchy

Krathwohl, Bloom, and Masia (1964) developed a useful taxonomy of the affective domain. The following are their major levels (or categories), from least internalized to most internalized: (a) *receiving*—being aware of the affective stimulus and beginning to have favorable feelings toward it; (b) *responding*—taking an interest in the stimulus and viewing it favorably; (c) *valuing*—showing a tentative belief in the value of the affective stimulus and becoming committed to it; (d) *organizing*—placing values into a system of dominant and supporting values; and (e) *internalizing*—demonstrating consistent beliefs and behavior that have become a way of life. Although there is considerable overlap from one category to another within the affective domain, these categories do give a basis by which to judge the quality of objectives and the nature of learning within this area. A discussion of each of the five categories follows.

Receiving   At this level, which is the least internalized, the learner exhibits willingness to give attention to particular phenomena or stimuli, and the teacher is able to arouse, sustain, and direct that attention. Action verbs appropriate for this category include *ask, choose, describe, differentiate, distinguish, give, hold, identify, locate, name, point to, recall, recognize, reply, select,* and *use.* Examples of objectives in this category are

- The student *listens attentively* to the instructions for the project assignment.
- The student *demonstrates sensitivity* to the property, beliefs, and concerns of others.

Responding   At this level, learners respond to the stimulus they have received. They may do so because of some external pressure, because they find the stimulus interesting, or because responding gives them satisfaction. Action verbs appropriate for this category include *answer, applaud, approve, assist, command, comply, discuss, greet, help, label, perform, play, practice, present, read, recite, report, select, spend (leisure time in), tell,* and *write.* Examples of objectives at this level are

- The student *completes* the project assignment.
- The student *cooperates* with others during group learning activities.

Valuing   Objectives at the valuing level deal with a learner's beliefs, attitudes, and appreciations. The simplest objectives concern the acceptance of beliefs and values; the higher ones involve learning to prefer certain values and finally becoming committed to them. Action verbs appropriate for this level include *argue, assist, complete, describe, differentiate, explain, follow, form, initiate, invite, join, justify, propose, protest, read, report, select, share, study, support,* and *work.* Examples of objectives in this category are

- The student *protests* against discrimination of any sort.
- The student *argues* a position against or for animal cloning.

Organizing   This fourth level in the affective domain concerns the building of a personal value system. Here the learner is conceptualizing and arranging values into a system that recognizes their relative importance. Action verbs appropriate for this level include *adhere, alter, arrange, balance, combine, compare, defend, define, discuss, explain, form, generalize, identify, integrate, modify, order, organize, prepare, relate,* and *synthesize.* Examples of objectives in this category are

- The student *recognizes* the value of serendipity when problem solving.
- The student *defends* the values of a particular subculture.

Internalizing   This is the last and highest category within the affective domain, at which the learner's behaviors have become consistent with his or her beliefs. Action verbs appropriate for this level include *act, complete, discriminate, display, influence, listen, modify, perform, practice, propose, qualify, question, revise, serve, solve,* and *verify.* Examples of objectives in this category are

- The student's behavior *displays* self-assurance in working alone.
- The student *practices* cooperative behaviors in group activities.

Psychomotor Domain Hierarchy

Whereas identification and classification within the cognitive and affective domains are generally agreed on, there is less agreement on the classification within the psychomotor domain. Originally, the goal of this domain was simply to develop and categorize proficiency in skills, particularly those dealing with gross and fine muscle control. The classification of the domain presented here follows this lead, but includes at its highest level the most creative and inventive behaviors, thus coordinating skills and knowledge from all three domains. Consequently, the objectives are in a hierarchy ranging from simple gross locomotor control to the most creative and complex, requiring originality and fine locomotor control—for example, from simply turning on a computer to designing a software program. The following taxonomy of the psychomotor domain is from Harrow: (a) *moving,* (b) *manipulating,* (c) *communicating,* and (d) *creating* (Harrow, 1977). (Note: A similar taxonomy is that of Simpson [1972].)

Moving   This level involves gross motor coordination. Action verbs appropriate for this level include *adjust, carry, clean, grasp, jump, locate, obtain,* and *walk.* Sample objectives for this category are

- The student *will jump* a rope 10 times without missing.
- The student *will correctly grasp* the pencil.

Manipulating   This level involves fine motor coordination. Action verbs appropriate for this level include *assemble, build, calibrate, connect, play, thread,* and *turn.* Sample objectives for this category are

- The student *will assemble* the lettered blocks in alphabetical order.
- The student *will connect* the dots.

Activity 5.8: Assessing Recognition of Objectives According to Domain

Instructions: The purpose of this activity is to assess your ability to identify objectives correctly according to their domain. For each of the following instructional objectives, identify by the appropriate letter the domain involved: (C) cognitive, (A) affective, or (P) psychomotor. Check your answers, and discuss the results with your classmates and instructor.

_____ 1. The student will shoot free throws until he or she can complete 80% of the attempts.

_____ 2. The student will identify on a map the mountain ranges of the eastern United States.

_____ 3. The student will summarize the historical development of the Democratic Party in the United States.

_____ 4. The student will demonstrate a continuing desire to learn more about using the classroom computer for word processing by volunteering to work at it during free time.

_____ 5. The student will volunteer to tidy up the storage room.

_____ 6. After listening to several recordings, the student will identify their respective composers.

_____ 7. The student will translate a favorite Cambodian poem into English.

_____ 8. The student will calculate the length of the hypotenuse.

_____ 9. The student will indicate an interest in the subject by voluntarily reading additional library books about earthquakes.

_____ 10. The student will successfully stack five blocks.

Answer Key: 2, 3, 6, 7, 8, = C; 1, 10 = P; 4, 5, 9, = A

Communicating This level involves the communication of ideas and feelings. Action verbs appropriate for this level include *analyze, ask, describe, draw, explain,* and *write*. Sample objectives for this category are

- The student *will draw* what he or she observes on a slide through the microscope.
- The student *will describe* his or her feelings about animal cloning.

Creating Creating is the highest level of this domain, and of all domains, and represents the student's coordination of thinking, learning, and behaving in all three domains. Action verbs appropriate for this level include *create, design,* and *invent*. Sample objectives for this category are

- The student *will design* a mural.
- The student *will design* and build a kite pattern.

USING THE TAXONOMIES

Theoretically, the taxonomies are constructed so that students achieve each lower level before being ready to move to the higher levels. However, because categories and behaviors overlap, as they should, this theory does not always hold in practice. Furthermore, as explained by others (Caine & Caine, 1997), feelings and thoughts

Activity 5.9: Preparing Instructional Objectives
for Use in My Teaching

For a subject and grade level of your choice (K–8), prepare 10 specific behavioral objectives. (Refer to Activities 6.2A and 6.3.) It is not necessary to include audience, conditions, and performance level unless required by your course instructor. When done, exchange your objectives with those of your classmates; discuss and make changes where necessary.

Subject: *Grade level:*

1. Cognitive knowledge:

2. Cognitive comprehension:

3. Cognitive application:

4. Cognitive analysis:

5. Cognitive synthesis:

6. Cognitive evaluation:

7. Psychomotor (low level):

8. Psychomotor (high level):

9. Affective (low level):

10. Affective (highest level):

are inextricably interconnected; they cannot be neatly separated as might be applied by the taxonomies.

The taxonomies are important in that they emphasize the various levels to which instruction and learning must aspire. For learning to be worthwhile, you must formulate and teach to objectives from the higher levels of the taxonomies as well as from the lower ones. Student thinking and behaving must be moved from the lowest to the highest levels of thinking and behavior. When all is said and done, it is, perhaps, the highest level of the psychomotor domain (creating) to which we aspire.

In using the taxonomies, remember that the point is to formulate the best objectives for the job to be done. In today's schools, using results-driven education models, those models describe levels of mastery standards (*rubrics*) for each outcome. The taxonomies provide the mechanism for ensuring that you do not spend a disproportionate amount of time on facts and other low-level learning and can be of tremendous help where teachers are expected to correlate learning activities to one of the school or district's target outcome standards (see Figure 5.4).

Preparing objectives is essential to the preparation of good items for the assessment of student learning. Clearly communicating your performance expectations to students and then specifically assessing student learning against those expectations makes the teaching most efficient and effective, and it makes the assessment of the learning closer to being authentic. This does not mean to imply that you will write performance objectives for everything taught, nor will you always be able to accurately measure what students have learned. As said earlier, learning that is

Results-driven education helps produce people who are lifelong learners, effective communicators, have high self-esteem, and:

PROBLEM SOLVERS

- are able to solve problems in their academic and personal lives
- demonstrate higher-level analytical thinking skills when they evaluate or make decisions
- are able to set personal and career goals
- can use knowledge, not just display it
- are innovative thinkers

SELF-DIRECTED LEARNERS

- are independent workers
- can read, comprehend, and interact with text
- have self-respect with an accurate view of themselves and their abilities

QUALITY PRODUCERS

- can communicate effectively in a variety of situations (oral, aesthetic/artistic, nonverbal)
- are able to use their knowledge to create intelligent, artistic products that reflect originality
- have high standards

COLLABORATIVE WORKERS

- are able to work interdependently
- show respect for others and their points of view
- have their own values and moral conduct
- have an appreciation of cultural diversity

COMMUNITY CONTRIBUTORS

- have an awareness of civic, individual, national, and international responsibilities
- have an understanding of basic health issues
- have an appreciation of diversity

FIGURE 5.4
Sample learning outcome standards

meaningful to students is not as easily compartmentalized as the taxonomies of educational objectives would seem to imply.

Observing for Connected (Meaningful) Learning: Logs, Portfolios, and Journals

In learning that is most important and that has the most meaning to students, the domains are inextricably interconnected. Consequently, when assessing for student learning, both during instruction (formative assessment) and at the conclusion of the instruction (summative assessment), you must look for those connections.

Ways of looking for connected learning include

- Maintain a teacher's (or team's) log with daily or nearly daily entries about the progress of each student.
- Have students maintain personal learning journals in which they reflect on and respond to their learning.
- Have students assemble personal learning portfolios that document students' thinking, work, and learning experiences.

Dated and chronologically organized items that students place in their portfolios can include notes and communications; awards; brainstorming records; photos of bulletin board contributions and of charts; drawings, posters, displays, and models made by the student; records of peer coaching; visual maps; learning contract; record of debate contributions and demonstrations or presentations; mnemonics created by the student; peer evaluations; reading record; other contributions made to the class or to the team; record of service work; and test and grade records.

The use of portfolios and student journals is discussed further in Chapters 7 and 8, respectively.

Character Education and the Domains of Learning

Related especially to the affective domain, although not exclusive of the cognitive and psychomotor domains, is an interest in the development of students' values, especially those of honesty, kindness, respect, and responsibility, an interest in what is sometimes called *character education* (see the discussion that follows). For example, Wynne and Ryan (1997, p. 1) state that "transmitting character, academics, and discipline—essentially, 'traditional' moral values—to pupils is a vital educational responsibility." Thus, if one agrees with that interpretation, then the teaching of moral values is the transmission of character, academics, and discipline and clearly implies learning that transcends the three domains of learning presented in this chapter.

In what seems a cycle, arising in the 1930s, again in the late 1960s, and in the 1990s and continuing today, interest is high in the development of students' values, especially those of honesty, kindness, respect, and responsibility. Today, this interest is frequently referred to as *character education*. Whether defined as ethics, citizenship, moral values, or personal development, character education has long been a component of public education in this country (Otten, 2000). Stimulated by a perceived need to act to reduce students' antisocial behaviors and produce more respectful and responsible citizens, many schools and districts recently have or are developing curricula in character education with the ultimate goal of "developing mature adults capable of responsible citizenship and moral action" (Burrett & Rusnak, 1993, p. 15).

You can teach toward positive character development in two general ways: by providing a conducive classroom atmosphere where children actively and positively share in the decision making, and by serving as a model students can proudly emulate. Acquiring knowledge and developing understanding can enhance the learning of attitudes.

Nevertheless, changing an attitude is often a long and tedious process, requiring the commitment of the teacher and the school; cooperation and assistance from parents, guardians, and the community; and the provision of numerous experiences that will guide students to new convictions. Here are some specific practices, most of which are discussed in various places in this book (see the subject index).

- Build a sense of community in the school and in the classroom, with shared goals, optimism, cooperative efforts, and clearly identified and practiced procedures for reaching those goals.
- Collaboratively plan with students action- and community-oriented projects that relate to curriculum themes; solicit student family and community members to assist in projects.
- Make student service projects visible in the school and community.
- Promote higher-order thinking about value issues through the development of students' skills in questioning.
- Sensitize students to issues and teach skills of conflict resolution through debate, role play, simulations, and creative drama.
- Share and highlight examples of class and individual cooperation in serving the classroom, school, and community.
- Teach students to negotiate; practice and develop skills in conflict resolution and skills such as empathy, problem solving, impulse control, and anger management.

LEARNING THAT IS NOT IMMEDIATELY OBSERVABLE

Unlike behaviorists, constructivists do not limit the definition of learning to that which is observable behavior, nor should you. Bits and pieces of new information are stored in short-term memory, where the new information is "rehearsed" until ready to be stored in long-term memory. If the information is not rehearsed, it eventually fades from short-term memory. If it is rehearsed and made meaningful through connections with other stored knowledge, then this new knowledge is transferred to and stored in long-term memory, either by building existing schemata or by forming new schemata. As a teacher, your responsibility is to provide learning experiences that will result in the creation of new schemata as well as the modification of existing schemata.

To be an effective teacher of young people, the challenge is to use performance-based criteria, but simultaneously with a teaching style that encourages the development of intrinsic sources of student motivation and that allows, provides, and encourages coincidental learning—learning that goes beyond what might be considered predictable, immediately measurable, and representative of minimal expectations.

It has become increasingly clear to many teachers that to be most effective in helping children to develop meaningful understandings, much of the learning in each discipline can be made more effective and longer lasting when that learning is integrated with the whole curriculum and made meaningful to the lives of the students, rather than when simply taught as an unrelated and separate discipline at the same time each day.

As noted at the start of this chapter, if learning is defined only as the accumulation of bits and pieces of information, then we already know how that is learned and how to teach it. However, the accumulation of pieces of information is at the lowest end of a spectrum of types of learning. For higher levels of thinking and for learning that is most meaningful and longest lasting, the results of research support using (a) a curriculum where disciplines are integrated and (b) instructional techniques that involve the children in social, interactive learning, such as project-centered learning, cooperative learning, peer tutoring, and cross-age teaching.

> When compared with traditional instruction, one characteristic of exemplary instruction today is the teacher's encouragement of purposeful dialogue among children in the classroom, to debate, discuss, and explore their own ideas.

INTEGRATED CURRICULUM

When learning about *integrated curriculum* (IC), it is easy to be confused by the plethora of terms that are used, such as *integrated studies, thematic instruction, multidisciplinary teaching, integrated curriculum, interdisciplinary curriculum,* and *interdisciplinary thematic instruction*. In essence, regardless of which of these terms is being used, the reference is to the same thing.

Because the demarcation between the term *curriculum* and the term *instruction* is not always clear, let's assume for the sake of better understanding the meaning of *integrated curriculum*, there is no difference between the two terms, that is, between what is curriculum and what is instruction. In other words, for this discussion, *integrated curriculum* and *integrated instruction* will refer to the same thing.

The term *integrated curriculum* (or any of its synonyms mentioned at the start of this section) refers to both a way of teaching and a way of planning and organizing the instructional program so the discrete disciplines of subject matter are related to one another in a design that (a) matches the developmental needs of the learners and (b) helps to connect their learning in ways that are meaningful to their current and past experiences. In that respect, integrated curriculum is the antithesis of traditional, disparate, subject matter–oriented teaching and curriculum designations.

The reason for the various terminology is, in part, because the concept of an integrated curriculum is not new. In fact, it has had a roller coaster ride throughout the history of education in this country. Over time those efforts to integrate student learning have had varying labels.

People talk about how difficult it is to implement an integrated curriculum, which is taking the standard subject areas and combining them. That is ridiculous. The *world* is integrated! What is difficult is what schools do every day: unravel the world and all its vast knowledge and put it into boxes called subjects and separate things that are not separate in the real world.

Source: Dennis Littky (2004, p. 29)

Today's interest in curriculum integration has arisen from several inextricably connected sources:

1. The success at curriculum integration enjoyed by middle-level schools since the 1960s.
2. The literature-based, whole-language movement in reading and language arts that began in the 1980s. (*Note:* Various movements and approaches have been used over the years to try to find the most successful approach to teaching English and the language arts—movements with names such as *whole language, integrated language arts, communication arts and skills, literature-based,* and so forth. Whatever the cognomen, certain common elements and goals prevail: student choice in materials to be read, student reading and writing across the curriculum, time for independent and sustained silent reading in the classroom, use of integrated language arts skills across the curriculum, and use of nonprint materials)
3. The diversity of learners in the regular classroom coupled with growing acceptance of the philosophy that a certain percentage of school students will drop out is not a viable assumption.
4. Recent research in cognitive science and neuroscience demonstrating the necessity of helping students establish bridges between school and life, knowing and doing, content and context, with a parallel rekindled interest in constructivism as opposed to a strictly behaviorist philosophical approach to teaching and learning.

An integrated curriculum approach may not necessarily be the best approach for every school, nor the best for all learning for every student, nor is it necessarily the manner by which every teacher should or must always plan and teach. As evidenced by practice, the truth of this statement becomes obvious. And, as you should be well aware now, it is our belief that a teacher's best choice as an approach to instruction—and to classroom management—is one that is eclectic.

Because there are various interpretations to curriculum integration, each teacher must make his or her own decisions about its use.

Least Integrated Level 1	Level 2	Level 3	Level 4	Most Integrated Level 5
Subject-specific topic outline	Subject-specific	Multidisciplinary	Interdisciplinary thematic	Integrated thematic
No student collaboration in planning	Minimal student input	Some student input	Considerable student input in selecting themes and in planning	Maximum student and teacher collaboration
Teacher solo	Solo or teams	Solo or teams	Solo or teams	Solo or teams
Student input into decision making is low.		Student input into decision making is high.		Student input into decision making is very high.

FIGURE 5.5
Levels of curriculum integration

In attempts to connect students' learning with their experiences, efforts fall at various places on a spectrum or continuum, from the least integrated instruction (level 1) to the most integrated (level 5), as illustrated in Figure 5.5. It is not our intent that this illustration be interpreted as going from "worst-case scenario" (far left) to "best-case scenario" (far right), although some people may interpret it in exactly that way. Figure 5.5 is meant solely to show how efforts to integrate fall on a continuum of sophistication and complexity. The following is a description of each level of the continuum.

Level 1 Curriculum Integration

Level 1 curriculum integration is the traditional organization of curriculum and classroom instruction, where teachers plan and arrange the subject-specific scope and sequence in the format of topic outlines, much as you did for Activity 5.4. If there is an attempt to help students connect their experiences and their learning, then it is up to individual classroom teachers to do it. A student in a school and classroom that has subject-specific instruction at varying times of the day (e.g., language arts at 8:00, mathematics at 9:00, social studies at 10:30, and so on) from one or more teachers is likely learning at a Level 1 instructional environment, especially when what is being learned in one subject has little or no connection with content being learned in another. The same applies for a student, as found in many junior high schools, who moves during the school day from classroom to classroom, teacher to teacher, subject to subject, from one topic to another. A topic in science, for example, might be "earthquakes." A related topic in social studies might be "the social consequences of natural disasters." These two topics may or may not be studied by a student at the same time.

Level 2 Curriculum Integration

If the same students are learning English/language arts, social studies/history, mathematics, or science using a thematic approach rather than a topic outline, then they are learning at Level 2. At this level, themes for one discipline are not necessarily planned and coordinated to correspond or integrate with themes of another or to be taught simultaneously. At Level 2, the students may have some input into the decision making involved in planning themes and content from various disciplines. Before going further in this presentation of the levels of curriculum integration, let's stop and consider what is a topic and what is a theme.

Integrated Thematic Unit: Topic versus Theme

The difference between what is a topic and what is a theme is not always clear. For example, whereas "earthquakes" and "social consequences of natural disasters" are topics, "a survival guide to local natural disasters" could be the theme or umbrella under which these two topics could fall. In addition, themes are likely to be problem-based statements or questions; they often result in a product and are longer in duration than are topics. A theme is the point, the message, or the idea that underlies a study. When compared to a topic, a theme is more dynamic; the theme explains the significance of the study. It communicates to the student what the experience means. Although organized around one theme, many topics make up an ITU. Often the theme of a study becomes clearer to students when an overall guiding question is presented and discussed, such as, "What could we do to improve our living environment?" or "What happens in our community after natural disasters?"

Some educators predict the integrated curriculum of the future will be based on broad, unchanging, and unifying concepts (i.e., on conceptual themes). If so, it would be the recycling of an approach of the 1960s, as supported by the writings of Jerome Bruner (1960) and implemented in some of the National Science Foundation–sponsored curriculum projects of that era. In fact, there is already action in that direction. For example, forming the basis for the national curriculum standards (discussed earlier in this chapter) for social studies are 10 thematic strands, including "people, places, and environments," and "power, authority, and governance." The national standards for science education are centered on unifying conceptual schemes, such as "systems, order, and organization" and "form and function." Many of the state curriculum documents are now centered on major concepts and central themes rather than on isolated facts.

Level 3 Curriculum Integration

When the same students are learning two or more of their core subjects around a common theme, such as the theme natural disasters, from one or more teachers, they are then learning at Level 3 integration. At this level, teachers agree on a common theme, then they separately deal with that theme in their individual subject areas, usually at the same time during the school year. So what the student is learning from a teacher in one class is related to and coordinated with what the student is concurrently learning in another or several others. At Level 3, students may have some input into the decision making involved in selecting and planning themes and content. Some authors may refer to levels 2 or 3 as *coordinated* or *parallel curriculum*.

Level 4 Curriculum Integration

When teachers and students collaborate on a common theme and its content, and when discipline boundaries begin to disappear as teachers teach about this common theme, either solo or as an interdisciplinary teaching team, Level 4 integration is achieved.

Level 5 Curriculum Integration

When teachers and their students have collaborated on a common theme and its content, discipline boundaries are truly blurred during instruction, and teachers of several grade levels and of various subjects teach toward student understanding of aspects of the common theme, then this is Level 5, an *integrated thematic approach* (Note: For detailed accounts of teaching at this level of integration, see Stevenson and Carr [1993].)

Guidelines for integrating topics and for planning and developing an interdisciplinary thematic unit are presented in Chapter 6.

Integrated Curriculum in a Standards-Based Environment

Although it is still too early to obtain reliable data on how students in integrated curriculum programs fare on mandatory, statewide standardized proficiency tests, it should be reassuring to today's classroom teacher to know that students in any type of interdisciplinary or integrative curriculum do as well as, or often many times even better than, students in a conventional departmentalized program. Furthermore, this seems to hold true whether the program is taught by one teacher in a self-contained or block-time class or by an interdisciplinary teaching team (Vars & Beane, 2000).

PLANNING FOR INSTRUCTION: A THREE-LEVEL AND SEVEN-STEP PROCESS

Earlier in the chapter it was noted that complete planning for instruction occurs at three levels: the year, the units, and the lessons. There are seven steps in the process. They are as follows.

1. *Course, grade level, and school goals.* Consider and understand your curriculum goals and their relationship to the mission and goals of the school. Your course is not isolated on the planet Jupiter, but is an integral component of the total school curriculum.

2. *Expectations.* Consider topics, knowledge, and skills that you are expected to teach, such as those found in the districtwide standards and the course of study.
3. *Academic year, semester, trimester, or quarter plan.* Think about the goals you want the students to reach months from now. Working from your tentative content outline, and with the school calendar in hand, you begin by deciding the amount of time (e.g., the number of days) to be devoted to each topic (or unit), penciling those times into the outline. (Unless you are doing your planning at a computer, you may wish to use a pencil because the times are likely to be modified frequently.)

> Important advice: Have on hand your school's academic year calendar, as you may need to work around mandatory, standardized achievement testing dates in such a way that the testing does not interrupt the flow of student learning.

4. *Course schedule.* This schedule becomes an element in the course syllabus that is presented to parents, guardians, and students at the beginning (discussed in the next section) of the term. However, the schedule must remain flexible to allow for the unexpected, such as the cancellation or interruption of a class meeting, a serendipitous discovery and inquiry by the students, or an extended study of a particular topic.
5. *Plans for each class meeting.* Working from the calendar plan or the course schedule, you are ready to prepare plans for each class meeting, keeping in mind the abilities and interests of your students while making decisions about appropriate strategies and learning experiences. The preparation of daily plans takes considerable time and continues throughout the year as you arrange and prepare instructional notes, demonstrations, discussion topics and questions, classroom exercises, learning centers, guest speakers, materials and equipment, field trips, and tools for the assessment of student learning.

> Because the content of each class meeting is often determined by the accomplishments of and your reflections on the preceding one, lessons are never "set in concrete" but need your continual revisiting, reflection, adjustments, and assessment.

6. *Instructional objectives.* Once you have the finalized schedule, and as you prepare the daily plans, you will complete your preparation of the instructional objectives. Those objectives are critical for proper development of the next and final step.

7. *Assessment.* The final step is that of deciding how to assess for student achievement. Included in this component are your decisions about how you will accomplish diagnostic or preassessment (i.e., the assessment of what students know or think they know at the start of a new unit or a new topic), formative assessment (the ongoing assessment on what the students are learning that takes place almost daily during a unit of study), and summative assessment (the assessment of students' learning at the conclusion of a unit of study). Also included in the assessment component are your decisions about assignments (discussed in Chapter 8) and the grading procedures (discussed in Chapter 7).

In Chapter 6, you proceed through these steps as you develop your first instructional plan. However, before starting that, let's consider one more topic relevant to the overall planning of the course—the syllabus. There is often confusion about what is and what is not a syllabus.

THE SYLLABUS

A *syllabus* is a written statement of information about the workings of a particular class or course. As a student in postsecondary education, you have seen a variety of syllabi written by professors, each with their individual ideas and personal touches about what general and specific logistic information is most important for students to know about a course. Some instructors, however, err in thinking that a course outline constitutes a course syllabus; a course outline is only one component of a syllabus.

Not all elementary school teachers use a course syllabus, at least as is described here, but for reasons that are explored in this discussion, we believe at least teachers of grades 4 and up should. (Note: You might seek sample syllabi from teachers in schools where you are visiting or from your course instructor.) Related to that belief are several questions that are answered next: "Why should teachers use a syllabus?" "What value is it?" "What use can be made of it?" "What purpose does it fulfill?" "How do I develop one?" "Can students have input into its content and participate in its development?" "Where do I start?" "What information should be included?" "When should it be distributed?" "To whom should it be distributed?" and "How rigidly should it be followed?"

Use and Development of a Syllabus

The syllabus is printed information about the class or the course that is usually presented to the parents/guardians and to the students at the start of school or at the start of a course. The syllabus may be developed completely by you or in collaboration with members of your teaching team. As you shall learn, it also can be developed collaboratively with students. As always, the final decision about its development is yours to make. However it is developed, the syllabus should be designed so that it helps establish a rapport among students, parents or guardians, and the teacher; helps students feel more at ease by providing an understanding of what is expected of them; and helps them to organize, conceptualize, and synthesize their learning experiences.

The syllabus should provide a reference, helping eliminate misunderstandings and misconceptions about the nature of the class—its rules, expectations, procedures, requirements, and other policies. It should provide students with a sense of connectedness (often by allowing students to work collaboratively in groups and actually participate in fashioning their own course syllabus).

The syllabus should also serve as a plan to be followed by the teacher and the students, and it should serve as a resource for substitute teachers and (when relevant) members of a teaching team. Each team member should have a copy of every other member's syllabus. In essence, the syllabus stands as documentation for what is taking place in the classroom for those outside the classroom (i.e., parents or guardians, school board members, administrators, other teachers, and students). For access by parents and other interested persons, some teachers include at least portions of their course syllabus, such as homework assignment specifications and due dates, with the school's Web site on the Internet.

Usually, the teacher long before the first class meeting prepares the syllabus, or at least portions of it. If you maintain a syllabus template on your computer, then it is a simple task to customize it for each group of students you teach. You may find it is more useful if students participate in the development of the syllabus, thereby having an ownership of it and a commitment to its contents. By having input into the workings of a course and knowing that their opinions count, students usually will take more interest in what they are doing and learning. Some teachers give students a brief syllabus on the first day and then, collaboratively with the students and other members of the teaching team, develop a more detailed syllabus during the initial days of the start of school.

Content of a Syllabus

A syllabus should be concise, matter-of-fact, uncomplicated, and brief—perhaps no more than two pages—and, to be thorough and most informative, include the following information:

Descriptive information about the class or course. This includes the teacher's name, the course or class title, class period, days of class meetings, beginning and ending times, and room number.

Importance of the course. This information should describe the course, cite the ways students will profit from it, tell whether the course is a required course and from which program in the curriculum (e.g., a core course, an elective, exploratory, or some other arrangement).

Learning targets. This should include major goals, related curriculum standards, and a few objectives.

Materials required. Explain what materials are needed—such as a textbook, notebook, binder, calculator, supplementary readings, apron, safety goggles—and specify which are supplied by the school, which must be supplied by each student, and what materials must be available each day.

Types of assignments that will be given. These should be clearly explained in as much detail as possible this early in the school term. There should be a statement of your estimate of time required (if any) for homework each night. There should also be a statement about where daily assignments will be posted in the classroom (a regular place each day), the procedures for completing and turning in assignments, and (if relevant) for making corrections to assignments after they've been turned in and returned. Include your policy regarding late work. Also, parents/guardians may need to know your expectations of them regarding helping their child with assignments.

Attendance expectations. Explain how attendance is related to achievement grades and to promotion (if relevant) and the procedure for making up missed work. Typical school policy allows that with an excused absence, missed work can be completed without penalty if done within a reasonable period of time following the student's return to school.

Assessment and marking/grading procedures. Explain the assessment procedures and the procedures for determining grades. Will there be quizzes (announced or not?), tests, homework, projects, and group work? What will be their formats, coverage, and weights in the procedure for determining grades? For group work, how will the contributions and learning of individual students be evaluated?

Other information specific to the class or course. Field trips? Special privileges? Computer work? Parental/guardian expectations? Homework hotline? Classroom procedures and expectations should be included here.

If you are a beginning teacher or are new to the school, to affirm that your policies as indicated in the first draft of your syllabus are not counter to any existing school policies, you probably should share your first draft of the syllabus with members of your team, your mentor, or the department chairperson for their feedback.

SUMMARY

In your comparison and analysis of courses of study and teachers' editions of student textbooks, you have probably discovered that many are accompanied by sequentially designed resource units from which the teacher can select and build specific teaching units. A *resource unit* usually consists of an extensive list of objectives, a large number and variety of activities, suggested materials, and extensive bibliographies for teacher and students.

As you may have also found, some courses of study contain actual teaching units that have been prepared by teachers of the school district. Beginning teachers and student teachers often ask, "How closely must I follow the school's curriculum guide or course of study?" In this day of statewide achievement testing, the answer is likely to be "very close," but to obtain an accurate answer, you must talk with teachers and administrators of the school before you begin teaching.

In conclusion, your final decisions about what content to teach are guided in various degrees by (a) discussions with other teachers; (b) review of state curriculum documents, local courses of study, and articles in professional journals; (c) your personal convictions, knowledge, and skills; and (d) the unique characteristics of your students.

In this chapter you learned of the differences among the terms *aims*, *goals*, and *objectives*. Regardless of how these terms are defined, the important point is this: *Teachers must be clear about what it is they want their students to learn, about the kind of evidence needed to verify their learning, and to communicate those things to the students so they are clearly understood.*

Many teachers do not bother to write specific objectives for all the learning activities in their teaching plans. However, when teachers do prepare specific objectives (by writing them themselves or by borrowing them from textbooks and other curriculum documents), by teaching toward them and assessing students' progress against them, student learning is enhanced; this is called performance-based teaching and criterion-referenced measurement. It is also known as an aligned curriculum. In schools using results-driven education mastery learning models, those models describe levels of mastery standards or rubrics for each outcome or learning target. The taxonomies are of tremendous help in schools where teachers are expected to correlate learning activities to the school's outcome standards, and for today that includes most, if not all, schools.

As a teacher, you will be expected to (a) plan your lessons well, (b) convey specific expectations to your students, and (c) assess their learning against that specificity. However, because it tends toward high objectivity, there is the danger that such performance-based teaching could become too objective, which can have negative consequences. If students are treated as objects, then the relationship between teacher and student becomes impersonal and counterproductive to real learning. Highly specific and impersonal teaching can be discouraging to serendipity, creativity, and the excitement of discovery, to say nothing of its possibly negative impact on the development of students' self-esteem.

Performance-based instruction works well when teaching toward mastery of basic skills, but the concept of mastery learning is inclined to imply that there is some foreseeable end to learning, an assumption that is obviously erroneous. With performance-based instruction, the source of student motivation tends to be extrinsic. Teacher expectations, marks and grades, society, and peer pressures are examples of extrinsic sources that drive student performance. To be a most effective teacher, your very real challenge today is to use performance-based criteria together with a teaching style that encourages the development of intrinsic sources of student motivation and that allows for, provides for, and encourages coincidental learning—learning that goes beyond what might be considered as predictable, immediately measurable, and representative of minimal expectations. In other words, although you must have clear goals and objectives and a routine that students can rely on from day to day, the most effective teachers consider and build on the interests, experiences, and spontaneous nature of their students. Good teaching is *not* an inhuman experience.

With knowledge of the content of the school curriculum and the value of instructional objectives, you are now ready to prepare detailed instructional plans with sequenced lessons, the subject of the next chapter.

STUDY QUESTIONS AND ADDITIONAL ACTIVITIES

1. If you were asked during a teaching job interview, tell how you would differentiate between the terms *curriculum* and *instruction*.

2. Some schools recently have eliminated or cut back the number of recesses each day to have children spending more time on academic instruction. In elementary schools in your geographic area, what is the status of recesses for the various grade levels, K–8?

3. More frequently in recent years we hear both beginning and experienced elementary-school teachers complaining that there isn't enough time to teach all curriculum content they are supposed to teach, with less to no time to teach topics they prefer to teach. We hear that they have less and less freedom to decide what is important for children to learn and do and to create learning activities for that learning. That they are told they must spend more time on direct instruction and less on indirect instruction. That there is not enough time for student-initiated exploratory learning. That they have less time during the school year to teach because of the increased amount of time given to testing. That there is less time for students to reflect on what is being learned. That interdisciplinary thematic instruction takes too much time, time they do not have because they must teach the prescribed curriculum to prepare the students for the state proficiency exams given in the spring. And once the spring testing is done it is nearly impossible to refocus students on further learning—that once the testing is done, the students act as if the school year is over. Do any of these comments sound familiar to you? If so, what do you believe may be causing these concerns? Is there any danger to the profession if the act of teaching becomes so highly prescriptive? How will you plan to counter your own negative thinking as a teacher?

4. A teacher with three years of experience left teaching at age 25 to devote her time to her family. Now, at the age of 50, with three children grown, the former teacher wants to return to a grade 5 classroom. If this teacher were teaching in your subject field, what will this person find has changed most and what the least? Why? How will the person's teaching schedule today likely be different from that of 25 years ago?

5. With today's emphasis on curriculum standards and high-stakes proficiency testing, the challenge is to design standards and tests that are not so high that many students cannot reach them nor so low that they become meaningless and risk boring quicker-learning children. The reality is, for example, on any middle-grades campus there are students doing algebra and there are students

who cannot do simple multiplication, and they're the same age. The question is this: For a subject field (specify which), is one set of standards sufficient or should there be multiple standards, such as a set of minimal standards and another set that will challenge the most capable students? Share your thoughts about this with your classmates.

6. It is sometimes said that teaching less can be better. Think back to your own schooling. What do you really remember? Do you remember lectures and drill sheets, or do you remember projects, your presentations, the lengthy research you did and your extra effort for artwork to accompany your presentation? Maybe you remember a compliment by a teacher or a compliment by peers. Most likely you do not recall the massive amount of academic content that was covered. Write a no longer than one-page essay expressing and defending your agreement or disagreement with the first sentence of this paragraph. Share your essay with those of your classmates.

7. It has been said that affective learnings tend to be "caught" rather than "taught." How do you feel about the statement? Provide specific suggestions about what you as a teacher can do to facilitate affective learning. Some people object to the term *indoctrination* when applied to the process of instilling values and beliefs in others. Do you believe it is possible that the fear of indoctrination could mean that preferred values and beliefs are not taught at all? Are there, in fact, "preferred" values and beliefs in our society today? Where and how should children learn, for example, the basic value and acts of common courtesy?

8. Some people say that it is easier to write learning objectives after a lesson has been taught. What is the significance, if any, of that notion?

9. Describe characteristics of a classroom that enhance affective learning. Do you believe the enhancement of students' affective learning is an important responsibility to you as an elementary-school teacher? Explain why or why not.

10. It is stated that the collapse of history instruction in the first eight grades is a direct result of the pressure caused by NCLB (Rothman, 2005). Talk with experienced teachers of the subject field(s) of your interest and ask what effect, if any, NCLB legislation has had on their curriculum and instruction.

WEB SITES RELATED TO CONTENT OF THIS CHAPTER

National Curriculum Standards by Content Area with Professional Organizations

American Indian Supplements www.doi.gov/bureau-indian-affairs.html

Arts (visual and performing)
- AAHPERD www.aahperd.org
- MTNA www.mtna.org

English/language arts/reading.
- IRA www.reading.org/
- NCTE www.ncte.org/

Foreign languages, ACTFL www.actfl.org

Geography, NCGE www.ncge.org

Health, AAHPERD www.aahperd.org

History/social studies.
- National Center for History in the Schools www.sscnet.ucla.edu/nchs
- NCSS www.ncss.org/

Mathematics, NCTM www.nctm.org

Physical education, AAHPERD www.aahperd.org

Science, NSTA www.nsta.org

Technology, ISTE www.iste.org

Character education
- Character Counts! www.charactercounts.org
- Character Education Partnership www.character.org
- Giraffe Project www.giraffe.org

Miscellaneous
- Connected Mathematics Project www.math.msu.edu/cmp
- Excellence in Curriculum Integration through Teaching Epidemiology www.cdc.gov/excite
- First Amendment Schools http://www.firstamendmentschools.org
- Freedom Forum http://www.freedomforum.org
- National Commission on Service Learning www.servicelearningcommission.org
- Parents and Students for Academic Freedom (K–12) http://www.psaf.org
- Reading Rockets http://www.reading.rockets.org
- Smartpaper Networks http://www.smartpaper.net
- Standards state by state www.statestandards.com
- TouchSmart Publishing www.touchsmart.net

FOR FURTHER READING

Berkowitz, M. W., & Bier, M. C. (2005). Character education: Parents as partners. *Educational Leadership, 63*(1), 64–69.

Bogen, M. (2007). Getting advisory right. *Harvard Education Letter 23*(1), 4–6.

Chapko, M. A., & Buchko, M. (2004). Math instruction for inquiring minds. *Principal, 84*(2), 30–33.

Commeyras, M. (2007). Scripted reading instruction? What's a teacher educator to do? *Phi Delta Kappan, 88*, 404–407.

Connor, C. M., Morrison, F. J., Fishman, B. J., Schatschneider, C., & Underwood, P. (2007). Algorithm-guided individualized reading instruction. *Science, 26*, 464–465.

DeMitchell, T. A., & Carney, J. J. (2005). Harry Potter and the public school library. *Phi Delta Kappan, 87*, 159–165.

Dombchik, L. (2004). Storm busters: A science and technology integrated unit. *Middle Ground, 7*(3), 35–36.

Edwards, L., Nabors, M. L., Branscombe, N. A., & Janas, M. (2005). Science & social studies in a nutshell. *Science and Children, 42*(6), 26–29.

Fairbanks, E. K., Clark, M., & Barry, J. (2005). Developing a comprehensive homework policy. *Principal, 84*(3), 36–39.

Fang, Z. (2006). The language demands of science reading in middle school. *International Journal of Science Education, 28*, 491–500.

Kahn, S. (2005). Savvy consumers through science. *Science and Children, 42*(6), 30–34.

Kellough, R. D., Cangelosi, J. S., Collette, A. T., Chiappetta, E. L., Souviney, R. J., Trowbridge, L. W., & Bybee, R. W. (1996). *Integrating mathematics and science for intermediate and middle school students.* Englewood Cliffs, NJ: Merrill Prentice Hall.

Kellough, R. D., Jarolimek, J., Parker, W. C., Martorella, P. H., Tompkins, G. E., & Hoskisson, K. (1996). *Integrating language arts and social studies for intermediate and middle school students.* Englewood Cliffs, NJ: Merrill Prentice Hall.

Lessow-Hurley, J. (2003). *Meeting the needs of second language learners: An educator's guide.* Alexandria, VA: Association for Supervision and Curriculum Development.

Morris, R. V. (2005). The Clio Club: An extracurricular model for elementary social studies enrichment. *Gifted Child Today, 28*(1), 40–48.

Phillips, S. K., Duffrin, M. W., & Geist, E. A. (2004). Be a food scientist. *Science and Children, 41*(4), 24–29.

Reys, B. J., Reys, R. E., & Chavez, O. (2004). Why mathematics textbooks matter. *Educational Leadership, 61*(5), 61–66.

Richards, J. C. (2006). Question, connect, transform (QCT): A strategy to help middle school students engage critically with historical fiction. *Reading & Writing Quarterly, 22,* 193–198.

Roberts, P. L., & Kellough, R. D. (2008). *A guide for developing interdisciplinary thematic units* (4th ed.). Upper Saddle River, NJ: Merrill Prentice Hall.

Sorel, K. (2005). The integrated curriculum. *Science and Children, 42*(6), 21–25.

Victor, E., Kellough, R. D., & Tai, R. H. (2008). *Science K–8: An integrated approach* (11th ed.). Upper Saddle River, NJ: Pearson Merrill Prentice Hall.

Whitin, D. J., & Whitin, P. (2004). *New visions for linking literature and mathematics.* Reston, VA: National Council of Teachers of Mathematics and the National Council of Teachers of English.

Chapter 6

Planning the Instruction

INTASC Principles	PRAXIS III Domains	NBPTS Standards
• The teacher understands the central concepts, tools of inquiry, and structures of the discipline(s) he or she teaches and can create learning experiences that make these aspects of subject matter meaningful to students. (Principle 1) • The teacher understands how children learn and develop and can provide learning opportunities that support their intellectual, social, and personal development. (Principle 2)	• Organizing Content Knowledge for Student Learning (Domain A)	• Respect for Diversity • Meaningful Applications of Knowledge • Knowledge of Integrated Content and Curriculum

• The teacher understands how students differ in their approaches to learning and creates instructional opportunities that are adapted to diverse learners. (Principle 3)		

People preparing to become teachers are sometimes left with a feeling of unreality when their instructors work with them on developing plans for teaching. "Do teachers *really* take this much time writing out the details of their lesson plans?" they ask skeptically. This is a reasonable concern, and the truth is that most teachers do not spend the same time and energy on the written aspect of planning their lessons as they did during their student teaching days. Planning for teaching is really a way of thinking about what you need to do, and experienced teachers have exactly that—the advantage of experience. Teachers on the job can do much of their planning mentally because they know from experience how to identify appropriate objectives, what materials they will need to teach a specific lesson, where those materials are located, where to anticipate problems, and what to look for when assessing learning.

The teacher's edition of the student textbook and other resource materials may expedite your planning but should not substitute for it. You *must* understand how to create a good instructional plan. In this chapter, you will learn how it is done and then do it.

ANTICIPATED OUTCOMES

Specifically, upon completion of this chapter you should be able to:

1. Complete a unit of instruction with sequential lesson plans.
2. Demonstrate understanding of the significance of the planned unit of instruction and the concept of planning curriculum and instruction as an organic process.
3. Differentiate between two types of instructional units—the standard unit and the integrated thematic unit.
4. Demonstrate understanding of the place and role of each of the four decision-making and thought-processing phases in unit planning and implementation.
5. Demonstrate understanding of self-reflection as a common thread important to the reciprocal process of teaching and learning.
6. Demonstrate an understanding of the differences between direct and indirect instruction and the advantages and limitations of each.
7. For a discipline and specific group of young learners, give examples of learning experiences from each of these categories, and when and why you would use each one: verbal, visual, vicarious, simulated, and direct; and examples of how, why, and when they could be combined.

8. Demonstrate your growing understanding of the meaning of *developmentally appropriate practice.*
9. Demonstrate growing awareness of various styles of teaching and learning and their implications for instructional design.
10. Demonstrate an understanding of the significance of the concepts of learning modalities and learning capacities and their implications for appropriate educational practice.
11. Demonstrate your growing understanding of the cyclical nature of instruction.

THE INSTRUCTIONAL UNIT

The instructional unit is a major subdivision of a course of study (for one course of study there are from several to many units of instruction) and is comprised of learning activities that are planned around a central theme, topic, issue, or problem. Organizing the content of the semester or year into units makes the teaching process more manageable than when the teacher has no plan or makes only random choices.

The instructional unit is not unlike a chapter in a book, an act or scene in a play, or a phase of work when undertaking a project such as building a house. Breaking down information or actions into component parts and then grouping the related parts makes sense of learning and doing. The unit brings a sense of cohesiveness and structure to student learning and avoids the piecemeal approach that might otherwise unfold. You can learn to articulate lessons within, between, and among unit plans and focus on important elements while not ignoring tangentially important information. Students remember "chunks" of information, especially when those chunks are related to specific units.

Although the steps for developing any type of instructional unit are basically the same, units can be organized in a number of ways. For the purposes of this book, let's consider two basic types of units—the standard unit and the integrated thematic unit (ITU), both of which you are likely to use as an elementary-school teacher.

A *standard unit* (known also as a *conventional* or *traditional unit*) consists of a series of lessons centered on a topic, theme, major concept, or block of subject matter. Each lesson builds on the previous lesson by contributing additional subject matter, providing further illustrations, and supplying more practice or other added instruction, all of which are aimed at bringing about mastery of the knowledge and skills on which the unit is centered.

When a standard unit is centered on a central theme, the unit may be referred to as a *thematic unit*. When, by design, the thematic unit integrates disciplines, such as combining the learning of science and mathematics, or combining social studies and English/language arts, or combining any number of disciplines, then it is called an *integrated* (or *interdisciplinary*) *thematic unit* (ITU), or simply, an integrated unit.

Planning and Developing Any Unit of Instruction

Whether for a standard unit or an integrated thematic unit, steps in planning and developing the unit are the same and are described in the following paragraphs.

1. *Select a suitable theme, topic, issue, or problem.* These may be already laid out in your course of study or textbook or already agreed to by members of the teaching team.
2. *Select the goals of the unit and prepare the overview.* The goals are written as an overview or rationale, covering what the unit is about and what the students are to learn. In planning the goals, you should (a) become as familiar as possible with the topic and materials used; (b) consult curriculum documents, as listed in Chapter 5, for ideas; (c) decide the content and procedures (i.e., what the students should learn about the topic and how); (d) write the rationale or overview, where you summarize what you expect the students will learn about the topic; and (e) be sure your goals are congruent with the goals and standards of the course or grade level program.
3. *Select instructional objectives.* In doing this, you should (a) include understandings, skills, attitudes, appreciations, and ideals; (b) be specific by avoiding vagueness and generalizations; (c) write the objectives in performance terms; and (d) be as certain as possible that the objectives will contribute to the major learning described in the overview.
4. *Detail the instructional procedures.* These procedures include the subject content and the learning activities, established as a series of lessons. Proceed with the following steps in your initial planning of the instructional procedures.
   a. By referring to curriculum documents, resource units, and colleagues as resources, gather ideas for learning activities that might be suitable for the unit.
   b. Check the learning activities to make sure they will actually contribute to the learning designated in your objectives, discarding ideas that do not contribute.
   c. Make sure the learning activities are feasible. Can you afford the time, effort, or expense? Do you have the necessary materials and equipment? If not, can they be obtained? Are the activities suited to the intellectual and maturity levels of your students?
   d. Check resources available to be certain they support the content and learning activities.
   e. Decide how to introduce the unit. Provide *introductory activities* to arouse student interest; inform students of what the unit is about; help you learn about your students—their interests, their abilities, and experiences and present knowledge of the topic; provide transitions that bridge this topic with what students have already learned; and involve the students in the planning.
   f. Plan *developmental activities* to sustain student interest, provide for individual student differences, promote the learning as cited in the specific objectives, and promote a project.

g. Plan *culminating activities* to summarize what has been learned, bring together loose ends, apply what has been learned to new situations, provide students with the opportunity to demonstrate their learning, and provide transfer to the unit that follows.

5. *Plan for preassessment and assessment of student learning.* Preassess what students already know or think they know. Assessment of student progress in achievement of the learning objectives should permeate the entire unit (i.e., as often as possible, assessment should be a daily component of lessons; that is, formative assessment, both formal and informal, is embedded in your daily teaching. (Assessment is the topic of the next chapter.) Plan to gather information in several ways, including informal observations, checklist observations of student performance and their portfolios, and paper-and-pencil tests. Remember, assessment must be congruent with the instructional objectives.

6. *Provide for the materials and tools needed to support the instruction.* The unit cannot function without materials. Therefore, you must plan long before the unit begins for media equipment and materials, references, reading materials, reproduced materials, and community resources. When given ample time to do so, librarians and media center personnel are usually more than willing to assist in finding appropriate materials to support your planned unit of instruction.

Unit Format, Inclusive Elements, and Time Duration

Follow those six steps to develop any type of unit. In addition, two general points should be made. First, although there is no single best format for a teaching unit, there are minimum inclusions. Particular formats may be best for specific disciplines, topics, and types of activities. If you are in student teaching, your program for teacher preparation and/or your cooperating teacher(s) may provide the format you will be expected to follow. Regardless of the format, in any unit plan the following seven elements should be evident: (a) identification factors, including, for example, grade level, subject, topic, and time duration of the unit; (b) statement of rationale and general goals for the unit; (c) objectives of the unit; (d) materials and resources needed; (e) lesson plans; (f) assessment strategies; and (g) identification of how the unit will address student differences, such as variations in students' reading levels, experiential backgrounds, and special needs.

Second, there is no set time duration for a unit plan, although, for specific units, curriculum guides will recommend certain time spans. Units may extend for a minimum of several days or, as in the case of some interdisciplinary thematic units, for several weeks, an entire semester, or even longer. However, be aware that when standard units last more than 2 or 3 weeks, they tend to lose the character of clearly identifiable units. Sometimes, in the case of extended duration, units may even overlap. For any unit of instruction, the exact time duration will be dictated by several factors, including the topic, problem or theme, the interests and maturity of the students, intensity of the study, and the scope of the learning activities.

THEORETICAL CONSIDERATIONS FOR THE SELECTION OF INSTRUCTIONAL STRATEGIES

As you prepare to detail your instructional plan, you will be narrowing in on selecting and planning the instructional activities. In Chapter 2, you learned about specific teacher behaviors that must be in place for students to learn. In the paragraphs that follow, you will learn more, not only about how to implement some of those fundamental behaviors, but also about the large repertoire of other strategies (see Figure 6.1), aids, media, and resources available to you. You will learn about how to select and implement from this repertoire.

Decision Making and Strategy Selection

You must make myriad decisions to select and effectively implement a particular teaching strategy. The selection of a strategy depends partially on your decision of whether to deliver information directly (direct, expository, or didactic instruction) or to provide students with access to information (indirect, or facilitative, instruction). Direct instruction tends to be teacher centered, whereas indirect instruction is more student centered.

Autotutorial	Homework	Questioning
Brainstorming	Individualized instruction	Reading partner
Coaching	Inquiry	Review & practice
Collaborative learning	Interactive media	Role-play
Cooperative learning	Investigation	Self-instructional module
Debate	Journal writing	Script writing
Demonstration	Laboratory investigation	Silent reading
Diorama	Laser videodisk or CD	Simulation
Discovery	Learning center	Study guide
Drama	Lecture	Symposium
Drill	Library/resource center	Telecommunication
Dyad learning	Metacognition	Term paper
Expository	Mock-up	Textbook
Field trip	Multimedia	Tutorial
Game	Panel discussion	
Guest presenter	Project	

FIGURE 6.1
A list of instructional strategies

Direct and Indirect Instruction: A Clarification of Terms   By now you are probably well aware that professional education is rampant with its own special jargon, which can be confusing to the neophyte. The use of the term *direct instruction* (or its synonym, *direct teaching*), and its antonym, *direct experiences*, are examples of how confusing the jargon can be. The term *direct instruction* (or *direct teaching, expository teaching*, or *teacher-centered instruction*) can also have a variety of definitions, depending on who is doing the defining. For now, you should keep this distinction in mind—do not confuse the term *direct instruction* with the term *direct experience*. The two terms indicate two separate (though not incompatible) instructional modes. The dichotomy of pedagogical opposites shown in Figure 6.2 provides a useful visual distinction of the opposites. Although the terms in one column are similar, if not synonymous, they are near or exact opposites of those in the other column.

TPW Video Classroom

Series: General Methods

Module 6: Teaching Strategies for Concepts

Video 1: The Indirect Instruction Model

Degrees of Directness   Rather than thinking and behaving in terms of opposites, as may be suggested by Figure 6.2, more likely your teaching will be distinguished by "degrees of directness" or "degrees of indirectness." For example, for a unit of instruction, directions for a culminating project may be given by the teacher in a direct or expository minilecture, followed by a student-designed inquiry that leads to the final project.

Rather than focus your attention on the selection of a particular model of teaching, we emphasize the importance of an eclectic model—selecting the best from various models or approaches. As indicated by the example of the preceding

Delivery mode of instruction	versus	Access mode of instruction
Didactic instruction	versus	Facilitative teaching
Direct instruction	versus	Indirect instruction
Direct teaching	versus	Direct experiencing
Expository teaching	versus	Discovery learning
Teacher-centered instruction	versus	Student-centered instruction

FIGURE 6.2
Pedagogical opposites

paragraph, sometimes you will want to use a direct, teacher-centered approach, perhaps by a minilecture or a demonstration. Many more times you will want to use an indirect, student-centered, or social-interactive approach, such as the use of cooperative learning and investigative projects. Perhaps there will be even more times when you will be doing both at the same time, such as working with a teacher-centered approach with one small group of students, giving them direct instruction, while another group or several groups of students in other areas of the classroom are working on their project studies (a student-centered approach). The information that follows and specific descriptions in Chapters 8 and 9 will help you make decisions about when each approach is most appropriate and provide guidelines for their use. But first, to assist in your selection of strategies, it is important that you understand the terms and basic principles of learning summarized as follows.

Principles of Classroom Instruction and Learning: A Synopsis

A student does not learn to write by learning to recognize grammatical constructions of sentences. Neither does a person learn to play soccer solely by listening to a lecture about soccer. Learning is superficial unless the instructional methods and learning activities are developmentally and intellectually appropriate—that is, are (a) developmentally appropriate for the learners and (b) intellectually appropriate for the understanding, skills, and attitudes desired. Memorizing, for instance, is not the same as understanding. Yet far too often, memorization seems all that is expected of children in many classrooms. The result is low-level learning, a mere verbalism or mouthing of poorly understood words and sentences. The orchestration of short-term memory exercises is not intellectually appropriate, and it is not teaching. A mental model of learning that assumes a brain is capable of doing only one thing at a time is invidiously incorrect (Baker & Martin, 1998; Jensen, 1998).

When selecting the mode of instruction, you should bear in mind basic principles of classroom instruction and learning, as shown in Figure 6.3.

Conceptual and Procedural Knowledge

Conceptual knowledge (also called *declarative knowledge*) refers to the understanding of relationships and abstractions, whereas *procedural knowledge* entails recording in memory the meanings of symbols and rules and procedures needed to accomplish tasks. (Motor skills, habits, and perceptual skills are examples of procedural knowledge.) Unless it is connected in meaningful ways for the formation of conceptual knowledge, the accumulation of memorized, procedural knowledge is fragmented, is ill fated, and will be maintained in the brain for only a brief time.

To help children establish conceptual knowledge, the learning for it must be meaningful. To help make learning meaningful for your students, you should use direct and real experiences as often as is practical and possible. Vicarious

- Although children differ in their styles of learning and in their learning capacities, each can learn.
- Learning is most meaningful and longest lasting when it is connected to real-life experiences.
- No matter what else you are prepared to teach, you are primarily a teacher of literacy and of thinking, social, and learning skills.
- Physical activity enhances learning. It is advisable that every lesson includes, to some degree, an activity involving the kinesthetic learning modality.
- Students must be actively involved in their own learning and in the assessment of their learning.
- Students need constant, understandable, positive, and reliable feedback about their learning.
- Students should be engaged in both independent study and cooperative learning and give and receive tutorial instruction.
- To a great degree, the mode of instruction determines what is learned and how well it is learned.
- The teacher must hold high expectations for the learning of each child (but not necessarily identical expectations for every child) and not waver from those expectations.

FIGURE 6.3
Basic principles of instruction and learning

experiences are sometimes necessary to provide students with otherwise unattainable knowledge; however, direct experiences that engage all the students' senses and all learning modalities are more powerful. Students learn to write by writing and by receiving coaching and feedback about their progress in writing. They learn to play soccer by playing soccer and by receiving coaching and feedback about their developing skills and knowledge in playing the game. They learn these things best when they are actively (hands-on) and mentally (minds-on) engaged in doing them. This is real learning, learning that is meaningful; it

TEACHING IN PRACTICE Students Restless During Direct Instruction

Pat, a social studies teacher, has a class of 28 eighth graders who, during lectures, teacher-led discussions, and recitation lessons, are restless and inattentive, creating a problem for Pat in classroom management. At Pat's invitation, the school psychologist tests the students for learning modality and finds that of the 28 students, 24 are predominately kinesthetic learners.

Questions for Class Discussion
1. What value dos this information provide to Pat?
2. Describe what, if anything, Pat should try as a result of this information.

Learning that involves children in direct experiencing, that engages all or most of their senses, is the kind of learning that is the most meaningful and longest lasting.

Scott Cunningham/Merrill

is *authentic learning*. It is the learning that is most developmentally appropriate for elementary-school children.

Direct versus Indirect Instructional Modes: Strengths and Weaknesses of Each

When selecting an instructional strategy, there are two distinct choices (modes) from which you must make a decision: Should you deliver information to students directly, or should you provide students with access to information? (Refer to Figure 6.2.)

The *delivery mode* (known also as the *didactic, expository,* or *traditional style*) is to deliver information. Knowledge is passed on from those who know (the teachers, with the aid of textbooks) to those who do not (the students). Within the delivery mode, traditional and time-honored strategies are textbook reading, the lecture (formal teacher talk), questioning, and teacher-centered or teacher-planned discussions.

With the *access mode,* instead of direct delivery of information and direct control over what is learned, you provide students with access to information by working *with* the students. In collaboration with the students, experiences are designed that facilitate the building of their existing schemata and their obtaining new knowledge and skills. Within the access mode, important instructional strategies include cooperative learning, inquiry, and investigative, student-centered project learning, each of which most certainly will use questioning (although the questions more frequently will come from the students than from you or the textbook or some other source extrinsic to the student). Discussions and lectures on particular topics also may be involved. However, when used in the access mode, discussions and lectures occur during or after (rather than preceding) direct, hands-on learning by the students. In other words, rather than preceding student inquiry, discussions and lectures *result from* student inquiry and then may be followed by further student investigation.

You are probably more experienced with the delivery mode. To be most effective as an elementary-school teacher, however, you must become knowledgeable and skillful in using access strategies. You should appropriately select and effectively use strategies from both modes, but with a strong favor toward access strategies. Strategies within the access mode clearly facilitate students' positive learning and acquisition of conceptual knowledge and help build their self-esteem. Thus, from your study of Chapters 8 and 9, you will become knowledgeable about specific techniques so you can make intelligent decisions for choosing the best strategy for particular goals and objectives for your own discipline and the interests, needs, and maturity level of your own unique group of students.

Figures 6.4 and 6.5 provide an overview of the specific strengths and weaknesses of each mode. By comparing those figures, you can see that the strengths and weaknesses of one mode are nearly mirror opposites of the other. As noted

Delivery Mode	*Access Mode*
Strengths	*Strengths*
• Much content can be covered within a short span of time, usually by formal teacher talk, which then may be followed by an experiential activity.	• Students learn content in more depth.
• The teacher is in control of what content is covered.	• The sources of student motivation are more likely intrinsic.
• The teacher is in control of time allotted to specific content coverage.	• Students make important decisions about their own learning.
• Strategies within the delivery mode are consistent with competency-based instruction.	• Students have more control over the pacing of their learning.
• Student achievement of specific content is predictable and manageable.	• Students develop a sense of personal self-worth.
Potential Weaknesses	*Potential Weaknesses*
• The sources of student motivation are mostly extrinsic.	• Breadth of content coverage may be more limited.
• Students have little control over the pacing of their learning.	• Strategies are time consuming.
• Students make few important decisions about their learning.	• The teacher has less control over content and time.
• There may be little opportunity for divergent or creative thinking.	• The specific results of students learning are less predictable.
• Student self-esteem may be inadequately served.	• The teacher may have less control over class procedures.

FIGURE 6.4
Delivery mode: Its strengths and weaknesses

FIGURE 6.5
Access mode: Its strengths and weaknesses

earlier, although as a teacher you should be skillful in the use of strategies from both modes, for the most developmentally appropriate teaching you should concentrate more on using strategies from the access mode. Strategies within that mode are more student centered, hands on, and concrete; students interact with one another and are actually or closer to doing what they are learning to do—that is, the learning is likely more authentic. Learning that occurs from the use of that mode is longer lasting (fixes into long-term memory). And, as the students interact with one another and with their learning, they develop a sense of "can-do," which enhances their self-esteem.

SELECTING LEARNING ACTIVITIES THAT ARE DEVELOPMENTALLY APPROPRIATE

Returning to our soccer example, can you imagine a soccer coach teaching 5- to 14-year-olds the skills and knowledge needed to play soccer without ever letting them experience playing the game? Can you imagine a science teacher instructing students on how to read a thermometer without ever letting them actually read a real thermometer? Can you imagine a geography teacher teaching students how to read a map without ever letting them put their eyes and hands on a real map? Can you imagine a piano teacher teaching a student to play piano without ever allowing the student to touch a real keyboard? Unfortunately, still today, too many teachers do almost those exact things—they try to teach students to do something without letting the students practice doing it.

In planning and selecting developmentally appropriate learning activities, an important rule to remember is to select activities that are as close to the real thing as possible. That is *learning through direct experiencing*. When students are involved in *direct experiences*, they are using more of their sensory input channels, their learning modalities (i.e., auditory, visual, tactile, kinesthetic). And when all the senses are engaged, learning is more integrated and is most effective, meaningful, and longest lasting. This learning by doing is *authentic learning*—or, as referred to earlier, *hands-on/minds-on learning*.

STYLES OF LEARNING AND IMPLICATIONS FOR INSTRUCTIONAL PLANNING

Elementary-school teachers who are most effective are those who adapt their teaching styles and methods to their students, using approaches that interest the children, that are neither too easy nor too difficult, match the students' learning styles and learning capacities, and are relevant to the students' lives. This adaptation process is further complicated because each student is different from every other one. All do not have the same interests, abilities, backgrounds, or learning styles and capacities. As a matter of fact, not only do students differ from one

Instructional strategies occurring within the access mode are more student-centered, hands on, and concrete. A child learns to paint by painting. Learning that occurs from the use of the access mode is longer lasting, and from that learning a child develops a sense of "can-do," which in turn contributes to the enhancement of the child's self-esteem.

Krista Greco/Merrill

another, but also each student's learning style can change to some extent from one day to the next (Harrison, Andrews, & Saklofske, 2003). What appeals to a child today may not have the same appeal tomorrow. Therefore, you need to consider both the nature of your students in general and each student in particular. Because you probably have already completed a course in the psychology of learning, what follows is only a brief synopsis of knowledge about learning.

Learning Modality

Learning modality refers to the *sensory portal* (or input channel) by which a student prefers to receive sensory reception (modality preference), or the actual way a student learns best (modality adeptness). Some young people prefer learning by seeing, a *visual modality*; others prefer learning through instruction from others (through talk), an *auditory modality*; whereas many others prefer learning by doing and being physically involved, the *kinesthetic modality*, and by touching objects, the *tactile modality*. A student's modality preference is not always that student's modality strength.

Although primary modality strength can be determined by observing children, it can also be mixed and can change as the result of experience and intellectual maturity. As one might suspect, modality integration (i.e., engaging more of the sensory input channels, using several modalities at once or staggering them) has been found to contribute to better achievement in student learning.

Because many children neither have a preference or strength for auditory reception, elementary-school teachers should severely limit their use of the lecture method of instruction, that is, of too much reliance on formal teacher talk.

Furthermore, instructions using a singular approach, such as auditory (e.g., talking to the students), cheat students who learn better another way. This difference can affect student achievement. A teacher, for example, who only talks to the students or uses discussions day after day is shortchanging the education of children who learn better another way—who are, for example, kinesthetic and visual learners.

As a general rule, most children in grades K–8 prefer and learn best by touching objects, by feeling shapes and textures, by interacting with each other, and by moving things around. In contrast, learning by sitting and listening are difficult for many of them.

Some learning style traits significantly discriminate between students who are at risk of dropping out of school and students who perform well. Students who are underachieving and at risk need (a) frequent opportunities for mobility; (b) options and choices; (c) a variety of instructional resources, environments, and sociological groupings, rather than routines and patterns; (d) to learn during late morning, afternoon, or evening hours, rather than in the early morning; (e) informal seating, rather than wooden, steel, or plastic chairs; (f) low illumination, because bright light contributes to hyperactivity; and (g) tactile/visual introductory resources reinforced by kinesthetic (i.e., direct experiencing and whole-body activities)/visual resources or introductory kinesthetic/visual resources reinforced by tactile/visual resources (Brand, Dunn, & Greb, 2002; Dunn, 1995; Rayneri, Gerber, & Wiley, 2003).

Regardless of the grade level and subject(s) you teach, an effective approach is to use strategies that integrate the modalities. When well designed, thematic units and project-based learning incorporate modality integration. In conclusion, then, when teaching any group of children of mixed learning abilities, modality strengths, language proficiency, and cultural backgrounds, integrating learning modalities are a must for the most successful teaching.

Learning Style

A related concept to learning modality is *learning style*, which can be defined as independent forms of knowing and processing information. Although some children may be comfortable with beginning their learning of a new idea in the abstract (e.g., visual or verbal symbolization), most need to begin with the concrete (e.g., learning by actually doing it). Many children prosper while working in groups, whereas others prefer working alone. Some are quick in their studies, whereas others are slow, methodical, cautious, and meticulous. Some can sustain attention on a single topic for a long time, becoming more absorbed in their study as time passes. Others are slower starters and more casual in their pursuits but are capable of shifting with ease from subject to subject. Some can study in the midst of music, noise, or movement, whereas others need quiet, solitude, and a desk or table. The point is this: Your students will vary not only in their skills and preferences in the way knowledge is received, but also in how they mentally process information once it has been received. This latter is a person's style of learning.

Classifications of Learning Styles   It is important to note that learning style is *not* an indicator of intelligence, but rather an indicator of how a person learns. Although there are probably as many types of learning styles as there are individuals, David Kolb (1984) described two major differences in how people learn: how they perceive situations and how they process information. On the basis of perceiving and processing and earlier work by Carl Jung on psychological types (Jung, 1923), Bernice McCarthy (1997) described four major learning styles, which are presented in the following paragraphs.

The *imaginative learner* perceives information concretely and processes it reflectively. Imaginative learners learn well by listening and sharing with others, integrating the ideas of others with their own experiences. Imaginative learners often have difficulty adjusting to traditional teaching, which depends less on classroom interactions and students' sharing and connecting of their prior experiences. In a traditional (teacher-centered) classroom, the imaginative learner is likely an at-risk student.

The *analytic learner* perceives information abstractly and processes it reflectively. Analytic learners prefer sequential thinking, need details, and value what their teachers have to offer. Analytic learners do well in traditional classrooms.

The commonsense learner perceives information abstractly and processes it actively. The *commonsense learner* is pragmatic and enjoys hands-on learning. Commonsense learners sometimes find school frustrating unless they can see immediate use for what is being learned. By the middle grades, and in the traditional classroom, the commonsense learner is likely a learner who is at risk of not completing school, of dropping out.

The *dynamic learner* perceives information concretely and processes it actively. The dynamic learner also prefers hands-on learning and is excited by anything new. Dynamic learners are risk takers and by middle grades are frequently frustrated if they perceive learning as tedious and sequential. In a traditional classroom the dynamic learner is likely an at-risk student.

The Three-Phase Learning Cycle

To understand conceptual development and change, researchers in the 1960s developed a Piaget-based theory of learning in which students are guided from concrete, hands-on learning experiences to the abstract formulations of concepts and their formal applications. This theory became known as the *three-phase learning cycle* (Karplus, 1974). Long a popular strategy for teaching science, the learning cycle is useful in other disciplines as well, such as art, language arts, mathematics, and social studies (Barojas & Dehesa, 2001; Bevevino, Dengel, & Adams, 1999; Sowell, 1993). The three phases are (a) the *exploratory hands-on phase*, where students can explore ideas and experience assimilation and disequilibrium that lead to their own questions and tentative answers; (b) the *invention* or *concept development phase*, where, under the guidance of the teacher, students invent concepts and principles that help them answer their questions and reorganize their ideas (i.e., the students revise their thinking to allow the new information to fit), and (c) *the expansion* or *concept application phase*, another hands-on phase in which students try out their new ideas by applying them to situations that are relevant and meaningful to them. (*Note:* The three phases of the learning cycle are comparable to the three levels of thinking, the three levels of questioning (Chapter 3), and are described variously by others. For example, in Eisner (1979) the levels are referred to as descriptive, interpretive, and evaluative.) During application of a concept, the learner may discover new information that causes a change in the learner's understanding of the concept being applied. Thus, the process of learning is cyclical.

Variations on the Theme Recent interpretations or modifications of the three-phase cycle include McCarthy's 4MAT. With the 4MAT system, teachers employ a learning cycle of instructional strategies to try to reach each student's learning style. In the cycle, in the words of McCarthy, learners "sense and feel, they experience, then they watch, they reflect, then they think, they develop theories, then they try out theories, they experiment. Finally, they evaluate and synthesize what they have learned so to apply it to their next similar experience. They get smarter. They apply experience to experiences" (McCarthy, 1990, p. 33). In this process, they are likely using all four learning modalities.

The *constructivist learning theory* suggests that learning is a process involving the active engagement of learners who adapt the educative event to fit and expand their individual worldview (as opposed to the behaviorist pedagogical assumption that learning is something done to learners) and accentuates the importance of student self-assessment (DeLay, 1996). In support of that theory, some variations of the learning cycle include a separate phase of assessment. However, because we believe assessment of what students know or think they know should be a continual process, permeating all three phases of the learning cycle, we reject any treatment of assessment as a self-standing phase.

Learning Capacities: The Theory of Multiple Intelligences

In contrast to learning styles, Gardner (1996) introduced what he calls learning capacities exhibited by individuals in differing ways. Originally and sometimes still referred to as multiple intelligences, or ways of knowing, capacities thus far identified are

- *Bodily/kinesthetic:* Ability to use the body skillfully and to handle objects skillfully
- *Existentialist:* Ability to understand and pursue the ultimate philosophical questions, meanings, and mysteries of life
- *Interpersonal:* Ability to understand people and relationships
- *Intrapersonal:* Ability to assess one's emotional life as a means to understand oneself and others
- *Logical/mathematical:* Ability to handle chains of reasoning and recognize patterns and orders
- *Musical/rhythmic:* Sensitivity to pitch, melody, rhythm, and tone

- *Naturalist:* Ability to draw on materials and features of the natural environment to solve problems or fashion products
- *Verbal/linguistic:* Sensitivity to the meaning and order of words
- *Visual/spatial:* Ability to perceive the world accurately and to manipulate the nature of space, such as through architecture, mime, or sculpture

Many educators believe, as is implied in the presentation of McCarthy's four types of learners, that many of the students who are at risk are those who may be dominant in a cognitive learning style not in synch with traditional teaching methods. Traditional methods of instruction are largely of McCarthy's analytic style: Information is presented in a logical, linear, and sequential fashion. Traditional methods also reflect three of the Gardner types: verbal/linguistic, logical/mathematical, and intrapersonal. Consequently, to better synchronize methods of instruction with learning styles, some teachers and schools (see the Classroom Vignette, "Using the Theory of Learning Capacities") have restructured the curriculum and instruction around Gardner's learning capacities (Bolak, Bialach, & Dunphy, 2005; Campbell & Campbell, 1999) or around Sternberg's Triarchic Theory (English, 1998; Sternberg, 1998). Sternberg identified seven metaphors for the mind and intelligence (geographic, computational, biological, epistemological, anthropological, sociological, and systems) and proposed a theory of intelligence consisting of three elements: analytical, practical, and creative (Sternberg, 1998; Sternberg, Grigorenko, & Jarvin, 2001).

From the preceding information about learning, you must realize at least two important facts:

1. *Intelligence is not a fixed or static reality, but can be learned, taught, and developed.* This concept is important for students to understand, too. When students understand that intelligence is incremental, that it is developed through use over time, they tend to be more motivated to work at learning than when they believe intelligence is a fixed entity (Brandt, 2000).

CLASSROOM VIGNETTE Using the Theory of Learning Capacities (Multiple Intelligences) and Multilevel Instruction

In one fifth-grade classroom, during 1 week of a 6-week thematic unit on weather, students were concentrating on learning about the water cycle. For this study of the water cycle, with the students' help, the teacher divided the class into several groups of three to five students per group. While working on six projects simultaneously to learn about the water cycle: (a) one group of students designed, conducted, and repeated an experiment to discover the number of drops of water that can be held on one side of a new one-cent coin versus the number that can be held on the side of a worn one-cent coin; (b) working in part with the first group, a second group designed and prepared graphs to illustrate the results of the experiments of the first group; (c) a third group of students created and composed the words and music of a song about the water cycle; (d) a fourth group incorporated their combined interests in mathematics and art to design, collect the necessary materials, and create a colorful and interactive bulletin board about the water cycle; (e) a fifth group read about the water cycle in materials they researched from the Internet and various libraries; and (f) a sixth group created a puppet show about the water cycle. On Friday, after each group had finished, the groups shared their projects with the whole class.

TEACHING SCENARIO Joan Makes Significant Changes
in Her Classroom Atmosphere

Joan is a fifth-grade teacher of a self-contained classroom. Her classroom consists of one wall in particular that is mostly windows. Until recently she kept the window curtains closed to keep students from being distracted by the outdoors. She heard teachers talking of reports of preliminary studies indicating that children learn mathematics in particular better with a background of soft classical music, and in natural lighting rather than in artificial lighting, so now she plays a background of soft classical music when children are learning mathematics and keeps the curtains open and the ceiling lights turned off as often as possible. She also heard that some children learn certain subjects better at particular times of the day, so now rather than teaching each subject at the same time every day, she has established a new weekly schedule that varies the schedule from day to day. Although it is too early to say that student learning in any subject has significantly improved as a result of these changes, Joan has noticed a marked improvement in student behavior and motivation for learning.

Questions for Class Discussion

1. What were your thoughts on reading about Joan and her teaching?
2. Can you find research evidence relevant to any of the changes made by Joan?
3. Have you ever heard of the Hawthorne effect? Do you suppose that might be a factor explaining the changes in student behavior noticed by Joan?
4. Has this case given you any ideas for use in your own teaching?

2. *Not all students learn and respond to learning situations in the same way.* A student may learn differently according to the situation or according to the student's ethnicity, cultural background, or socioeconomic status. A teacher who, for all students, uses only one style of teaching or who teaches to only one or a few styles of learning day after day is shortchanging those students who learn better another way.

THE LEARNING EXPERIENCES LADDER

The Learning Experiences Ladder (Figure 6.6) is a visual depiction of a range of kinds of learning experiences from which a teacher may select. Hands-on/minds-on learning is at the bottom of the ladder. At the top are abstract experiences, where the learner is exposed only to symbolization (i.e., letters and numbers) and uses only one or two senses (auditory or visual). The teacher lectures while the students sit and watch and hear. Visual and verbal symbolic experiences, although impossible to avoid when teaching, are less effective in ensuring that planned and meaningful learning occurs. This is especially so with learners who have special needs, learners with ethnic and cultural differences, and English language learning (ELL) students. Thus, when planning learning experiences and selecting instructional materials, you are advised to select activities that engage the students in the most direct experiences possible and that are developmentally and intellectually appropriate for your specific group of students.

Verbal Experiences

Teacher talk, written words; engaging only one sense; using the most abstract symbolization; students physically inactive. *Examples:* (1) Listening to the teacher talk about tide pools. (2) Listening to a student report about the Grand Canyon. (3) Listening to a guest speaker talk about how the state legislature functions.

Visual Experiences

Still pictures, diagrams, charts; engaging only one sense; typically symbolic; students physically inactive. *Examples:* (1) Viewing slide photographs of tide pool. (2) Viewing drawings and photographs of the Grand Canyon. (3) Listening to a guest speaker talk about the state legislature and show slides of it in action.

Vicarious Experiences

Laser videodisc programs, computer programs, video programs; engaging more than one sense; learner indirectly "doing"; may be some limited physical activity. *Examples:* (1) Interacting with a computer program about wave action and life in tide pools, (2) Viewing and listening to a video program about the Grand Canyon. (3) Taking a field trip to observe the state legislature in action.

Simulated Experiences

Role-playing; experimenting, simulations, mock-up, working models; all or nearly all senses engaged; activity often integrating disciplines; closest to the real thing. *Examples:* (1) Building a classroom working model of a tide pool. (2) Building a classroom working model of the Grand Canyon. (3) Designing a classroom role-play simulation patterned after the operating procedure of the state legislature.

Direct Experiences

Learner actually doing what is being learned, true inquiry: all senses engaged; usually integrates disciplines; the real thing. *Examples:* (1) Visiting and experiencing a tide pool. (2) Visiting and experiencing the Grand Canyon. (3) Designing an elected representative body to oversee the operation of the school-within-the-school program and patterned after the state legislative assembly.

A B S T R A C T ↑

↓ C O N C R E T E

FIGURE 6.6

The Learning Experiences Ladder

Sources: Earlier versions of this concept were Charles F. Hoban, Sr., et al., *Visualizing the Curriculum* (New York: Dryden, 1937), p. 39; Jerome S. Bruner, *Toward a Theory of Instruction* (Cambridge, MA: Harvard University Press, 1966), p. 49; Edgar Date, *Audio-Visual Methods in Teaching* (New York: Holt, Rinehart & Winston, 1969), p. 108; and Eugene C. Kim and Richard D. Kellough, *A Resource Guide for Secondary School Teaching,* 2nd. ed (Englewood Cliffs, NJ: Merrill/Prentice Hall, 1978), p. 136.

The most effective and longest-lasting learning is that which engages most or all of the learner's senses.

Anthony Magnacca/Merrill

As can be inferred from the Learning Experiences Ladder, when teaching about tide pools (the first example for each step), the most effective mode is to take the students to a tide pool (direct experience), where students can see, hear, touch, smell, and perhaps even taste (if not polluted with toxins) the tide pool. The least-effective mode is for the teacher to merely talk about the tide pool (verbal experience, the most abstract and symbolic experience), engaging only one sense—auditory.

Of course, for various reasons—such as time, matters of safety, lack of resources, and/or geographic location of your school—you may not be able to take your students to a tide pool. You cannot always use the most direct experience, so sometimes you must select an experience higher on the ladder. Self-discovery teaching is not always appropriate. Sometimes it is more appropriate to build on what others have discovered and learned. Although learners do not need to reinvent the wheel, for elementary-school-age learners in particular the most effective and longest-lasting learning is the one that engages most or all of their senses. On the Learning Experiences Ladder, those are the experiences that fall within the bottom three categories—direct, simulated, and vicarious.

Direct, Simulated, and Vicarious Experiences Help Connect Student Learning

Another value of direct, simulated, and vicarious experiences is they tend to be interdisciplinary; that is, they blur or bridge subject-content boundaries. That makes those experiences especially useful for teachers who want to help students connect the learning of one discipline with that of others and to bridge what is being learned with their own life experiences. Direct, simulated, and vicarious experiences are more like real life. That means the learning resulting from those experiences is authentic.

PLANNING AND DEVELOPING AN INTERDISCIPLINARY THEMATIC UNIT

The steps outlined earlier in this chapter are essential for planning any type of teaching unit, including the interdisciplinary thematic unit (ITU), which may consist of smaller subject-specific conventional units developed according to the immediately foregoing guidelines.

The primary responsibility for the development of ITUs can depend on a single teacher or on the cooperation of several teachers. A teaching team may develop from one to several interdisciplinary thematic units a year. Over time, then, a team will have several units that are available for implementation. However, the most effective units are often those that are the most current or the most meaningful to students. This means that ever-changing global, national, and local topics provide a veritable smorgasbord from which to choose, and teaching teams must constantly update old units and develop new and exciting ones.

Be careful to see that one teaching team's unit does not conflict with others at the same or another grade level. If a school has two or more teams at the same grade level, for example, the teams may want to develop units on different themes and share their products. And as another example, a seventh-grade team must guard against developing a unit quite similar to one that the students had or will have at another grade level. Clear and open communication within, between, and among teams and schools within a school district are critical to the success of interdisciplinary thematic teaching.

Specific Guidelines for Developing an ITU

Specific guidelines to guide you in developing an ITU are presented in the following paragraphs.

Agree on the Nature or Source of the Unit Team members should view the interdisciplinary approach as a collaborative effort in which all members can participate if appropriate. Write what you want the students to receive from interdisciplinary instruction. Troubleshoot potential stumbling blocks.

Discuss Subject-Specific Standards, Goals, and Objectives, Curriculum Guidelines, Textbooks and Supplemental Materials, and Units Already in Place for the School Year Focus on what you are obligated or mandated to teach, and explain the scope and sequence of the teaching so all team members understand the constraints and limitations.

Choose a Theme Topic and Develop a Time Line From the information provided by each subject-specialist teacher in the preceding guideline, start listing possible theme topics that can be drawn from within the existing course outlines. Give-and-take is essential here, as some topics will fit certain subjects better than others. The chief goal is to find a topic that can be adapted to each subject without detracting from the educational plan already in place. This may require choosing and merging content from two or more other units previously planned. The theme is then drawn from the topic.

Sometimes themes are selected by the teacher or by a teaching team before meeting the students for the first time. Other times teachers in collaboration with students select them. Even when the theme is preselected, with guidance from the teacher, students still should be given major responsibility for deciding the final theme title (name), topics within the theme, and corresponding learning activities. Integrated thematic instruction works best when students have ownership in the study, that is, when they have been empowered with major decision-making responsibility.

The basis for theme selection should satisfy two criteria. The theme should (a) fit within the expected scope and sequence of mandated content and (b) be of interest to the students. Regarding the first criterion, many teachers have said that when they and their students embarked on an interdisciplinary thematic study, they did so without truly knowing where the study would go or what the learning outcomes would be—and they were somewhat frightened by that realization. But when the unit was completed, their students had learned everything (or nearly everything) that the teacher would have expected them to learn were the teacher to use a more traditional approach. And, it was more fun because the students were more intrinsically motivated! See Figure 6.7 for important questions to ask when selecting a theme.

- Is the theme within the realm of understanding and experience of the teachers involved?
- Will the theme interest all members of the teaching team?
- Do we have sufficient materials and resources to supply information we might need?
- Does the theme lend itself to active learning experiences?
- Can this theme lead to a unit of the proper duration, that is, not too short and not too long?
- Is the theme helpful, worthwhile, and pertinent to the instructional objectives?
- Will the theme be of interest to students, and will it motivate them to do their best?
- Is the theme one with which teachers are not already so familiar that they cannot share in the excitement of the learning?
- Will this theme be of interest to students, and will it motivate them to do their best?

FIGURE 6.7
Questions to ask when selecting a theme

The second criterion is easy to satisfy, as it will most assuredly be when students are truly empowered with decision-making responsibility for what they learn and how they learn it. So, once a general theme is selected (one that satisfies the first criterion), its final title, subtopics, and corresponding procedural activities should be finalized in collaboration with the students.

Establish Two Time Lines The first is for the team only and is to ensure that each member meets deadlines for specific work required in developing the unit. The second time line is for both students and teachers and shows the intended length of the unit, when it will start, and (if relevant) in which classrooms or classes it will be taught.

Develop the Scope and Sequence for Content and Instruction To develop the unit, follow the six steps for planning and developing a unit of instruction outlined earlier in this chapter. This should be done by each team member as well as by the group during common planning time so members can coordinate dates and activities in logical sequence and depth. This is an organic process and will generate both ideas and anxiety. Under the guidance of the team leader, members should strive to keep this anxiety at a level conducive to learning, experimenting, and arriving at group consensus.

Share Goals and Objectives Each team member should have a copy of the goals and target objectives of every other team member. This helps to refine the unit and lesson plans and to prevent unnecessary overlap and confusion.

Give the Unit a Name The unit has been fashioned and is held together by the theme that is chosen. Giving the theme a name and using that name communicates to the students that this unit of study is integrated, important, and meaningful to school and to life. Sample names of actual ITUs, their number of lessons and discipline connections are shown in Figure 6.8.

Changes: Spring as a Time of Growth, Beauty, and Transformation.
Written for primary but adaptable for early middle grades. Art, science, language arts, and mathematics. Five lessons.

Early Civilizations: Dawn of a New Age in Ancient Greece.
Prepared for grade 6. Literature, geography, mathematics, physical education, science, and social studies. Eleven lessons.

Migrations: Early Newcomers in North America.
For grades 4 and up. English/language arts, history/social studies, and geography. Ten lessons.

FIGURE 6.8
Sample ITU titles showing their discipline connections and number of lesson plans (These ITUs are available in their entirety in Roberts and Kellough, listed in the suggested readings at the end of this chapter.)

Share Subject-Specific Units, Lesson Plans, and Printed and Nonprinted Materials   Exchange the finalized unit to obtain one another's comments and suggestions. Keep a copy of each teacher's unit(s) as a resource, and see if you could present a lesson using it as your basis (some modification may be necessary). Lesson planning is the topic that follows.

Field-Test the Unit   Beginning at the scheduled time and date, present the lessons. Team members may trade classes from time to time. Team teaching may take place.

Reflect, Assess, and Perhaps Adjust and Revise the Unit   During planning time, team members should share and discuss their successes and failures and determine what needs to be changed and how and when that should be done to make the unit successful. Adjustments can be made along the way, and revisions for future use can be made after completion of the unit.

The preceding are not absolutes and should be viewed only as guidelines. Differing teaching teams and levels of teacher experience and knowledge make the strict adherence to any plan less productive than would be the use of group-generated plans. In practice, the process that works well—one that results in meaningful learning for the students and in their positive feelings about themselves, about learning, and about school—is the appropriate process. For example, some teaching teams use what is sometimes called a *backward design* for their curriculum planning (Wiggins & McTighe, 1998). The procedure is generally as follows: (a) the involved teachers first study the state and district standards; (b) from the standards they select and establish target goals and objectives for their students; (c) they think of projects that will provide opportunities for their students to demonstrate that they have acquired the expected learning; and (d) they finalize their plan with supportive instructional activities.

Developing the Learning Activities: The Heart and Spirit of the ITU

Activities that engage the students in meaningful learning constitute the heart and spirit of the ITU and are of three types.

- Activities that start a unit into motion, that initiate the unit—the *initiating activities*
- Activities that comprise the heart of the unit—the *ongoing developmental activities*
- Activities that bring the unit to a close—the *culminating activities*

The Common Thread

Central to the selection and development of all learning activities for interdisciplinary thematic instruction is a common thread of four tightly interwoven components: (a) the instruction is centered around a big and meaningful idea (theme)

CLASSROOM VIGNETTE Learning from Dinosaurs

Once a theme is determined, instruction is planned around a sequence of activities that focus on that theme. Common to many elementary school teachers and to some middle school teachers as well is a theme that centers on the topic of dinosaurs. Whatever its selected title might be in a given situation, a thematic unit on dinosaurs can encompass any number of multidisciplinary activities related to the topic. For example,

- *History.* Students develop a graphic time line showing the long period of time that dinosaurs were dominant on this earth; they visit a museum that features dinosaur exhibits.
- *Mathematics.* Students categorize the types of dinosaurs and create graphs illustrating the variety and proportional size of dinosaurs.
- *Reading, writing, and art.* Students create and write illustrated stories about a favorite dinosaur.
- *Science.* Students speculate on both why the dinosaurs were so successful and on the events that led to their rather quick disappearance.

In her self-contained second-grade classroom, Kristie guided her students in a thematic unit on dinosaurs. Learning activities integrated science and math, drawing and crafts, music and reading, and publishing original books to support the study. Connecting reading to music, the students listened to a song about each dinosaur being studied. Students read sentence strips with the words of the song. They added sound effects, sang the song several times, and added a rhythmic beat with their own dinosaur-shape of books, wrote original pages, and created illustrations. To survey favorite dinosaurs, graphing was introduced. The students built their own graph in the classroom by drawing a favorite dinosaur and contributing it to a large graph. Students used individual copies of the graph to record what was added to the large graph and marked Xs with their pencils in the appropriate places. When the class graph was finished, the students read it and talked about the information they had gathered, guided by the teacher.

The culminating event took place at the school's spring Open House. Each student's assignment for Open House was to bring an adult and to explain to that person what he or she had been learning at school. Confidently, the students told their visitors about dinosaurs and proudly displayed their dinosaur books, dinosaur mobiles, dinosaur body shapes made from felt, and dinosaur clay models.

rather than on factitious subject areas; (b) the students and the teacher share in the decision making and responsibility for learning; (c) the learning activities are selected so all students are actively engaged in their learning—that is, they are both physically active (hands-on learning) and mentally active (minds-on learning); and (d) there is steady reflection on and frequent sharing of what is being done and what is being learned.

Initiating Activities

An ITU can be initiated by a limitless variety of ways. You must decide which ways are appropriate for your educational goals and objectives, intended time duration, and your own unique group of students, considering the extent and diversity of their interests, abilities, and skills. You might start with a current event, a community problem, an artifact, a book, a media presentation, or something interesting found on the Internet. See Figure 6.9's description of *Katy and the Big Snow* to see

KATY AND THE BIG SNOW, AN INTERDISCIPLINARY THEMATIC UNIT FOR KINDERGARTEN

Rationale: This unit is designed to teach children about maps. Over a unit duration of 10 days, a variety of disciplines and topics are addressed, such as reading, art, graphing, counting, writing, concept of community, science, music, and learning together. The unit is centered on the book *Katy and the Big Snow*, by Virginia Lee (Houghton Mifflin, 1976). Children compare and contrast the locations of people, places, and environments through studying the maps and being able to find a variety of places. By studying several maps and a world globe, the students learn to distinguish between land and water and locate general areas referenced in historically based legends and stories. Students learn how to use map symbols and legend references to land, water, roads, and cities. Students will become able to use maps to determine the relative location of objects using near/far, left/right, and behind/in front. The students will construct maps of their neighborhood community.

Goals and objectives: The goal of this unit is for children to develop an understanding of the concept of maps, how to use maps, and to be able to create their own simple map. Specifically, the children will be able to [Framework Standard identified in parentheses but not included here]:

- Identify land versus water places on a map.
- Identify and name continents and oceans on a map.
- Demonstrate understanding that maps are drawings of places.
- Demonstrate understanding that a globe is a map of the world.
- Identity north, south, east, and west on a map.
- Identify the North and South Poles on a world map.
- Demonstrate understanding that countries are portions of larger continents.
- From a map or globe, Identify each continent of the world.
- Demonstrate an understanding of how to read a map.
- Construct a map.
- Create a story map for *Katy and the Big Snow.*
- Grow crystals, and compare and contrast the crystals with snow.

Materials: [not included here]
Vocabulary: [not included here]
Content outline for unit: [not included here]

LESSON 1

- Display the local neighborhood/community map. Ask the children to name buildings and places that are in their community and show children where these places are on the map.
- Discuss briefly with the children what a community is.
- Ask for a volunteer to help you cover the map with the snow. This is the initiatory activity designed to help children connect with the coming story.
- Ask children to describe the qualities of snow.
- Ask children what would happen to a town if it is covered with a hard snowfall. How would they get around if the town is covered with snow?
- Explain to the children that they are going to hear a story that takes place in a town like theirs, that the story takes place where it is very cold and snowy.
- Display the book *Katy and the Big Snow*. Discuss the cover, title page, author, and illustrator. Discuss with the children what Katy is and what Katy might do. Instruct the children to listen to find out what Katy does when the big snowstorm hits town.
- Read the story and discuss it as you go along.
- End this lesson by teaching the children a winter song.

LESSONS 2–10 [NOT INCLUDED HERE]

ASSESSMENT

Formative assessment will be through observation of the children during discussions and activities and oral quizzing on their understanding of specifics about maps and mapping. [Checklists and rubrics are not included here.]
Materials and resources: [not included here]

FIGURE 6.9
Sample partial ITU for kindergarten
Source: Courtesy of Tara Richardson.

how a kindergarten teacher helps students connect learning about mapping with the story they are about to hear the teacher read.

Developmental Activities

Once the ITU has been initiated, students become occupied with a variety of ongoing (developmental) activities. In working with students to select and plan the developmental activities, you will want to keep in mind the concept represented by the Learning Experiences Ladder (Figure 6.4) as well as the preselected goals and target objectives.

Culminating Activity

Just as with other types of unit plans, an ITU is brought to close with a culminating activity. Such an activity often includes an exhibition or sharing of the product of the students' study. You could accept the students' suggestions for a culminating activity if it engages them in summarizing what they have learned with others. A culminating activity that brings closure to a unit can give the students an opportunity for synthesis (by assembling, constructing, creating, inventing, producing, or incorporating something) and even an opportunity to present that synthesis to an audience, such as by sharing their product on an existing school Web site.

Culminating activities serve two purposes. First, they are opportunities for students to proudly demonstrate and share their learning and creativity in different and individual ways. Second, it is from the culminating activity that you, the teacher, can do the summative assessment to determine how well target objectives were met. Examples of actual culminating activities and products of an ITU are endless. For example, the culminating activity of the kindergarten unit *Katy and the Big Snow* (see Figure 6.9) is a treasure hunt (the children are each given a treasure map of the classroom, and in pairs, they use their map to find "hidden" treasures), the culmination from the study by the students of West Salem Middle School (see the school vignette: "Interdisciplinary Thematic Instruction at West Salem Middle School") was the design and development of a community nature preserve.

Students at King Middle School (Portland, ME) studied the shore life of Maine's Casco Bay for a year. The culminating activity of their study was the writing and publishing of a book that includes their original illustrations and scientific descriptions of the flora and fauna found along the seashore. The book is now in the city's libraries, where it can be borrowed for use by anyone taking a walk along the seashore.

For additional ideas for culminating projects, see, "A Collection of Annotated Motivational Teaching Strategies with Ideas for Lessons, Interdisciplinary Teaching, Transcultural Studies, and Student Projects" in Chapter 8.

CLASSROOM VIGNETTE Interdisciplinary Thematic Instruction
at West Salem Middle School

What began as an isolated, single-grade, telecom-munications-dependent project for students at West Salem Middle School (Wisconsin) eventually developed into a longer-term, cross-grade interdisciplinary program of students and adults working together to design and develop a local nature preserve. Students began their adventure by interacting with explorer Will Steger as he led the International Arctic Project's first training expedition. Electronic online messages, via the Internet, allowed students to receive and send messages to Will and his team in real time. Students delved into the Arctic world, researching the physical environment and the intriguing wildlife, reading native stories and novels about survival, keeping their own imaginary expedition journals, learning about the impact of industrialized society on the Arctic, and conversing with students from around the world. But something very important was missing—a connection between the students' immediate environment and the faraway Arctic.

West Salem Middle School's focus became the local 700-acre Lake Neshonoc, an impoundment of the LaCrosse River, a tributary of the Mississippi. Although many students had enjoyed its recreational opportunities, they had never formally studied the lake. The Neshonoc Partners, a committee of parents, community leaders, teachers, students, and environmentalists, was established to assist in setting goals, brainstorming ideas, and developing the program for a year's study of the lake. Right from the start, students showed keen interest in active involvement in the project. A second committee, involving parents, students, and the classroom teacher, met during lunch time on a weekly basis to allow for more intensive discussions about the lake and the overall project.

The team of teachers brainstormed ideas to further develop an interdisciplinary approach to the study of Lake Neshonoc. Special activities, including an all-day "winter survival" adventure, gave students a sense of what the real explorers experience. Students learned about hypothermia, winter trekking by cross-country skiing, and building their own snow caves.

For several weeks, students learned about the ecosystem of Lake Neshonoc through field experiences led by local environmentalists and community leaders. Guest speakers told their stories about life on the lake and their observations about the lake's health. Student sketchbooks provided a place to document personal observations about the shoreline, water testing, animal and plant life, and the value of the lake. From these sketchbooks, the best student creations were compiled to create books to share electronically with students with similar interests in schools from Russia, Canada, Missouri, South Carolina, Nevada, Wisconsin, and Washington, D.C. The opportunity to share findings about their local watershed sparked discussions about how students can make a difference in their own community. Comparative studies gave students a chance to consider how humans and nature impact other watersheds.

West Salem students worked with the local County Parks and Recreation Department to assist in developing a sign marking the new County Park where the nature sanctuary will reside. Students brainstormed design ideas and then constructed a beautiful redwood sign with the help of a local technical educational teacher. Today the sign is a symbol of the partnership that has been established between the students and the community. It is a concrete reminder that together we can work for the common good of the community and the environment. Students celebrated the study of the lake with a closure. Will Steger, along with community leaders, parents, school board members, and staff, commended the students for what is sure to be the start of a long and enduring relationship—a partnership created out of common respect and appreciation for the value of our ecosystem.

Source: From "The Neshonoc Project: Profiles in Partnership," by J. Wee, Fall 1993, *World School for Adventure Learning Bulletin,* pp. 2–3, Adapted by permission.

PREPARING THE LESSON PLANS: RATIONALE AND ASSUMPTIONS

As described earlier, one of the steps of instructional planning is the preparation for class meetings. The process of designing a lesson is important in learning to provide the most efficient use of valuable and limited instructional time and the most effective learning for the students that meets the unit goals.

Notice that the title of this section does not refer to the "*daily* lesson plans," but rather, "*the* lesson plans." The focus is on how to prepare a lesson plan, one that may, in fact, be a daily plan, or it may not. In some instances, a lesson plan may extend for more than one class meeting, perhaps 2 or 3 days (e.g., the lesson plan shown later in Figure 6.13). In other instances, the lesson plan is, in fact, a daily plan and may run for an entire class meeting. In block scheduling, common to many middle-level schools, one lesson plan may run for part of or for an entire 2-hour block of time. See "The Problem of Time" discussion later in this section.

Effective teachers are always planning for their class meetings. For the long range, they plan the scope and sequence and develop content. Within this long-range planning, they develop units, and within units, they design the activities to be used and the assessments of learning to be done. They familiarize themselves with books, materials, media, and innovations in their fields of interest. Yet, despite all this planning activity, the lesson plan remains pivotal to the planning process.

Rationale for Preparing Written Plans

First, *carefully prepared and written lesson plans show everyone—first and foremost your students, then your mentor, colleagues, your administrator, and, if you are a student teacher or teaching intern, your supervisor—that you are a committed professional*. Sometimes, beginning teachers are concerned with being seen by their students using a written plan in class, thinking it may suggest that the teacher has not mastered the material. On the contrary, a lesson plan is tangible evidence that you are working at your job and demonstrates respect for the students, yourself, and the profession. A written lesson plan shows that preactive thinking and planning have taken place. There is absolutely no excuse for appearing before a classroom of children without evidence of being prepared.

Written and detailed lesson plans provide an important sense of security, which is especially useful to a beginning teacher. Like a rudder on a ship, it helps keep you on course. Without it, you are likely to drift aimlessly. Sometimes a disturbance in the classroom can distract from the lesson, causing the teacher to get off track or forget an important element of the lesson. A written and detailed lesson plan provides a road map to guide you and help keep you on track.

Written lesson plans help you to be or become a reflective decision maker. Without a written plan, it is difficult or impossible to analyze how something might have been planned or implemented differently after the lesson has been taught. Written lesson plans serve as resources for the next time you teach the same or a similar lesson and are useful for teacher self-evaluation and for the evaluation of student learning and of the curriculum.

Written lesson plans help you organize material and search for loopholes, loose ends, or incomplete content. Careful and thorough planning during the preactive phase of instruction includes anticipation of how the lesson activities will develop as the lesson is being taught. During this anticipation, you will actually visualize yourself in the classroom teaching your students. Use that visualization to anticipate possible problems.

Written plans help other members of the teaching team understand what you are doing and how you are doing it. This is especially important when implementing an interdisciplinary thematic unit. *Written lesson plans also provide substitute teachers with a guide to follow if you are absent.*

Those reasons just given clearly express the need to write detailed lesson plans. The list is not exhaustive, however, and you may discover additional reasons why written lesson plans are crucial to your teaching. In summary, two points must be made: (a) lesson planning is an important and ongoing process, and (b) teachers must take time to plan, reflect, write, test, evaluate, and rewrite their plans to reach optimal performance. In short, planning and preparing written lesson plans is important work.

Assumptions About Lesson Planning

Not all elementary-school teachers need elaborate written plans for every lesson. Sometimes effective and experienced teachers need only a sketchy outline. Sometimes they may not need written plans at all. Veteran teachers who have taught the topic many times in the past may need only the presence of a class of children to stimulate a pattern of presentation that has often been successful (though frequent use of old patterns may lead one into the rut of unimaginative and uninspiring teaching and most certainly does not take into full consideration the unique characteristics of the students in the present).

Considering the diversity among elementary-school teachers, their instructional styles, their students, and what research has shown, certain assumptions can be made about lesson planning.

- A plan is more likely to be carefully and thoughtfully plotted during the preactive phase of instruction when the plan is written out.
- Although not all teachers need elaborate written plans for all lessons, all effective teachers do have clearly defined goals and objectives in mind and a planned pattern of instruction for every lesson, whether that plan is written out or not.
- Beginning teachers need to prepare detailed, written lesson plans.
- The depth of knowledge a teacher has about a subject or topic influences the amount of planning necessary for the lessons.
- The diversity of children within today's classroom necessitates careful and thoughtful consideration about individualizing the instruction—these considerations are best implemented when they have been thoughtfully written into lesson plans.

- The skill a teacher has in remaining calm and in following a trend of thought in the presence of distraction will influence the amount of detail necessary when planning activities and writing the lesson plan.
- Today's emphasis on meeting grade-level curriculum standards places renewed importance on lesson planning.
- There is no particular pattern or format that all teachers need to follow when writing out plans—some teacher preparation programs have agreed on certain lesson plan formats for their teacher candidates; you need to know if this is the case for your program.

In summary, well-written lesson plans provide many advantages: They give a teacher an agenda or outline to follow in teaching a lesson; they give a substitute teacher a basis for presenting appropriate lessons to a class—thereby retaining lesson continuity in the regular teacher's absence; they are certainly very useful when a teacher is planning to use the same lesson again in the future; they provide the teacher with something to fall back on in case of a memory lapse, an interruption, or some distraction such as a call from the office or a fire drill; using a written plan demonstrates to students that you care and are working for them; and above all, they provide beginners security because, with a carefully prepared plan, a beginning teacher can walk into a classroom with confidence and professional pride gained from having developed a sensible framework for that day's instruction. Naturally, this will require a great deal of work for at least the first year or two, but the reward of knowing that you have prepared and presented effective lessons will compensate for that effort. You can expect a busy first year of teaching.

A Continual Process

Lesson planning is a continual process even for experienced teachers, for there is always a need to keep materials and plans current and relevant. Because no two classes of students are ever identical, today's lesson plan will need to be tailored to the peculiar needs of each classroom of students. Moreover, because the content of instruction and learning will change as each distinct group of students and their needs and interests give input, and as new thematic units are developed, new developments occur, or new theories are introduced, your objectives and the objectives of the students, school, and teaching faculty will change.

For these reasons, lesson plans should be in a constant state of revision—never set in concrete. Once the basic framework is developed, however, the task of updating and modifying becomes minimal. If your plans are maintained on a computer, making changes from time to time is even easier.

Making Adjustments as Needed

The lesson plan should provide a tentative outline of the time period given for the lesson but should always remain flexible. A carefully worked plan may have to be

Activity 6.1: Was This Lesson Set in Concrete?

In a multiage classroom at Centerville Joint Unified Intermediate School, Magdalena was teaching a humanities block, a course that integrates student learning in social studies, reading, and language arts. On this particular day during a teacher-directed whole-class lecture/discussion on the topic of "manifest destiny," one student raised his hand and, when Magdalena acknowledged him, asked, "Why aren't we [the United States] still adding states? [that is, adding still more territory to the United States]." Magdalena immediately replied, "There aren't any more states to add," and then hastily continued with her planned lesson.

1. By responding so quickly, did Magdalena miss a teachable moment, one of those too-rare moments when a teacher has her students right where she wants them: where the students are thinking and asking high-order questions?

2. Regarding Magdalena's response, consider: When was Hawaii added as a state? Why hasn't Puerto Rico become a state? Or Guam? Aren't those possibilities? Why aren't more states or territories being added? What are the political, economic, and social ramifications today and how do they differ from those of the 1800s?

3. How else might Magdalena have responded to the student's question? (Refer to Chapter 3 for in-depth discussion on using student questions as teachable moments.)

set aside because of the unpredictable, serendipitous effect of a teachable moment (see the vignette in Figure 6.1) or because of unforeseen circumstances, such as a delayed school bus, an impromptu school assembly program, an emergency drill, or the cancellation of school due to inclement weather conditions. Student teachers often are appalled at the frequency of interruptions during a school day and of disruptions to their lesson planning that occur. A daily lesson planned to cover six aspects of a given topic may end with only three of the points having been considered. Although far more frequent than necessary in too many schools, these occurrences are natural in a school setting, and the teacher and the plans must be flexible enough to accommodate this reality.

Implementation of Today's Lesson May Necessitate Changes in Tomorrow's Plan Although you may have your lesson plans completed for several consecutive lessons, as can be inferred by the vignette involving Magdalena and her students (Activity 6.1), what actually transpires during the implementation of today's lesson may necessitate last-minute adjustments to the lesson you had planned for tomorrow. More than just occasionally, teachers have discontinued the rest of the week's planned lessons because the feedback received on Tuesday indicated that students didn't comprehend Monday's lesson well enough to move on to the next planned lesson.

Consequently, during student teaching in particular, it is neither uncommon nor unwanted to have last-minute changes penciled in your lesson plan. If, however, penciled-in modifications are substantial and might be confusing to you during implementation of the lesson, then it's better to rewrite the lesson plan.

> The greatest pedagogical error of our time is a simplistic insistence on clarity. To spell out every act of education for students so that they are never forced to look deep into themselves and come face to face with the primal "Huh?" is to deny them access to one of the most important parts of their humanity: the right to shape their own destiny.
>
> *Source:* Andrew K. Davis (2001, p. 789)

The Problem of Time

A lesson plan should provide enough materials and activities to consume the entire class period or time allotted. As mentioned earlier, you must understand that in your planning for teaching, you need to plan for every minute of every class period. The lesson plan, then, is more than a plan for a lesson to be taught; it is a plan that accounts for the entire time that you and your students are together in the classroom. Because planning is a skill that takes years of experience to master, especially when teaching a block of time that may extend for 90 or more minutes and that involves more than one discipline and perhaps more than one teacher, as a beginning teacher, rather than run the risk of having too few activities to occupy the time the students are in your classroom, you should overplan. One way of ensuring that you overplan is to include "if time remains" activities in your lesson plan.

When a lesson plan does not provide sufficient activity to occupy the entire class period or time that the students are available for the lesson, that is when behavior problems mount. Thus, it is best to prepare more than you likely can accomplish in a given period of time. This is not to imply that you should involve the students in meaningless busywork. Students can be very perceptive when it comes to a teacher who has finished the plan and is attempting to bluff through the minutes that remain before dismissal. And, they are not usually favorably responsive to meaningless busywork.

If you ever do get caught short—as most teachers do at one time or another—one way to avoid embarrassment is to have students work on what we describe as an *anchor activity* (or *transitional activity*). This is an ongoing assignment, and students understand that whenever they have spare time in class, they should be working on it. One decision a teacher must make is whether or not students are going to be mobile during anchor activity work. Another is whether students work alone or can work in small groups. Those are decisions that each teacher must make depending on the circumstances for that teacher.

Anchor activities can include any number of activities, including, but not limited to,

- Journal writing
- Lab work, alone or in pairs
- Long-term project work, alone or in small groups

- Portfolio organization
- Review material that has been covered that day or in recent days, alone or in pairs
- Work at a learning center, alone or in pairs
- Work on homework for this or another teacher's class

Regardless of how you handle time remaining, it works best when you plan for it and write that aspect into your lesson plan. Make sure students understand the purpose and procedures for these anchor assignments.

The Pressure of Standards-Based and High-Stakes Testing and the Felt Need to "Cover" the Prescribed Curriculum

As we prepare this ninth edition of this book, we continue with our concern that because of today's heavy pressure on teachers to teach to the standards, to cover the curriculum, so that their students do well on the mandated proficiency tests, and because for any given grade level or subject, there is more content expected to be taught than there is time to teach it, fewer and fewer teachers will even recognize, let alone grasp and run with the already too-few precious teachable moments that occur for every teacher. Your challenge, of course, is to find your way of doing both—that is, to help students accomplish the required learning while not stifling the most meaningful and longest-lasting learning that often is entirely unpredictable. As we have said before, because it tends toward high objectivity, there is the possibility that such prescriptive teaching could become so objective that it produces negative consequences. The danger is when the relationship between teacher and student becomes so impersonal. Highly specific and impersonal teaching can be discouraging to serendipity, creativity, and the excitement of discovery, to say nothing of its possible negative impact on the development of students' self-esteem. Indeed, due to today's emphasis on standardized testing coupled with the fact that access mode strategies tend to consume more instructional time than do standard expository strategies, access strategies may indeed be too infrequently used in today's classroom (Jorgenson & Vanosdall, 2002).

Caution about "The Weekly Planning Book"

A distinction needs to be made between actual lesson plans and the book for planning that some schools require teachers to maintain and even submit to their supervisors a week in advance (see Figure 6.10). Items that a teacher writes into the boxes in a weekly planning book most assuredly are *not* lesson plans; rather, the pages are a layout by which the teacher writes into the boxes to show what lessons will be taught during the day, week, month, or term. Usually the book provides only a small lined box for time periods for each day of the week. These books are useful for outlining the topics, activities, and assignments projected for the week or term, and supervisors sometimes use them to check the adequacy of teachers' course plans, but they are not lesson plans. Teachers and their supervisors who

WEEKLY PLANNING BOOK				
Teacher_____ Lesson or unit _____				
Date	Content	Materials	Procedure	Assessment
Monday				
Tuesday				
Wednesday				
Thursday				
Friday				

FIGURE 6.10
Weekly planning book

believe that the notations in the weekly planning book are actual lesson plans are fooling themselves. Student teachers and teaching interns should not use these in lieu of authentic lesson plans.

LESSON PLAN CONSTRUCTION: FORMAT, ELEMENTS, AND SAMPLES

Although it is true that each teacher develops a personal system of lesson planning—the system that works best for that teacher in each unique situation—a beginning teacher needs a more substantial framework from which to work. For that, this section provides a "preferred" lesson plan format (see Figure 6.11). Nothing is hallowed about this format, however. Review the preferred format and samples, and unless your program of teacher preparation insists otherwise, use it with your own modifications until you find or develop a better model. All else being equal, you are encouraged, however, to begin your teaching by following as closely as possible this "preferred" format.

For Guidance, Reflection, and Reference

While student teaching and during your first few years as an employed teacher, your lesson plans should be printed from a computer, or, if that isn't possible, then written out in an intelligible style. Until you have considerable experience, you need to prepare and maintain detailed lesson plans for guidance, reflection, and reference. There is valid reason to suspect the effectiveness of teachers who say they have no need for a written plan because they have their lessons "in their heads." The hours and periods in a school day range from several to many, as do the number of students in each class. When multiplied by the number of school days in a week, a semester, or a school year, the task of keeping so many things in one's head becomes mind-boggling. Few persons could effectively do that. The

1. Descriptive Data

Teacher: _____ Class: _____ Date: _____ Grade level: _____

Room number: _____ Period: _____ Unit: _____ Lesson Number: _____ Topic: _____

Anticipated noise level (high, moderate, low)

2. Goals and Objectives

Instructional goals:

Specific objectives:

[Note: all three domains not always present in every lesson]

Cognitive:

Affective:

Psychomotor.

3. Rationale [Note rationale not always present in every lesson]

FIGURE 6.11

Preferred lesson plan format with seven components

4. Procedure [Procedure with modeling examples, planned transitions, etc.; should usually take up most of the space of lesson plan, often a full page]
Content:
___ minutes. Activity 1: Set (introduction)

___ minutes. Activity 2:

___ minutes. Activity 3: (the exact number of activities in the procedures will vary)

___ minutes. Final Activity (Lesson Conclusion or Closure):

If time remains:

5. Special Considerations, Notes, and Reminders to Myself

6. Materials and Equipment Needed
    Audiovisual:
    Media:
    Software:
    Other:

7. Assessment, Reflection, and Revision
    Assessment of student learning, how it will be done:

    Reflective thoughts about lesson after taught:

    Suggestions for revision if used again:

FIGURE 6.11
Continued

1. Descriptive Data

Teacher: _____   Class: <u>Kindergarten</u>   Date: _____

Lesson: <u>Journal write</u>   Time duration: <u>Final 20 minutes of school day</u>

2. Purpose

Daily, during the last 20 minutes of each school day, students share their thoughts on a question asked of them during the Theme portion of the day. This gives them an opportunity to express themselves verbally, receiving immediate validation. Additionally, class journal writing is an excellent way to review and expand on the various daily components that make up the weekly theme. This week's theme is Finding Friends. (Daily topics include: ___ is my friend. I like to share ___ with my friends. When I meet someone new, I ___. I feel left out when ___. I like when my friends ___._

3. Objectives

3.1. Through sharing individual responses during the whole-class activity, students will transfer their thought processes from nonverbal (that is the written, the anticipatory set) to oral. [cognitive]

3.2. By watching the teacher write their very own words on the big journal paper in front of the room, without making any changes (grammatical, syntactical, or otherwise), students will develop a sense of validation and authentic purpose in their writing. [affective]

3.3. Through observing the teacher write their complete sentences and reading them aloud with her, students will acquire knowledge of certain fundamental components of English language literacy (e.g., left to right and top to bottom orientations; sound-letter correlation, alphabetic principle; sight word recognition; recognition of repeating words). [cognitive]

4. Instructional procedure

Anticipatory set: Earlier in the class period, during Theme Time, the teacher will read various books focusing on friendship and how it feels to be excluded from certain friendships and activities (including *Franklin's Secret Club,* by Paulette Bourgeois, illustrated by Brenda Clark [New York: Scholastic, 1998], and *Who Will Be My Friends?* by Syd Hoff [New York: HarperCollins, 1985]).

The teacher will then model the complete sentence format by discussing times when she feels excluded and call on students to share times when they feel left out, how it makes them feel, and so on.

Students will then draw individual pictures of a time when they felt left out and dictate a sentence to the teacher who will write it and "touch and read" the sentence with the student—(I feel left out when ___).

During Workshop the teacher will also read through First Step Story #3 (New York: SRA, 1997).

5. Lesson Development (times approximate) **with Special Reminders**

(1–2 minutes) Wait (in silence) until students are completely seated in a semicircle formation.

(1 minute) Read today's date and time of day (journal) aloud <u>with class</u>. Point out color pattern chosen by calendar and counting helpers.

FIGURE 6.12

Lesson plan sample: Daily journal writing

Source: Courtesy of Erin L. McKeown.

(7 minutes) Call on quiet hands to share with class when they feel left out. (Reminder: be sure to watch to see if José raises his hand today and call on him if he does.) Write their responses (verbatim) on the journal paper with their names to their sentences. Alternate color of markers for a, b, a, b, etc. pattern. Point to words as I read sentences aloud. Ask students, "what color we would use next if we were to write another sentence?"

(6 minutes) Ask students if they notice any words that they see more than once. Have students come to the easel and circle recurring words. (Reminder: be sure to allow Elisa to come forward if she does raise her hand.)

(4 minutes) Wrap up the day by sharing any projects from Activity Time (if time allows) and dismissing students according to times when they feel left out (that is, the last group to be dismissed can be those who feel left out when they are the last ones to be able to collect their belongings and go home for the day!)

6. Materials Needed

Markers for writing; big journal paper on easel

7. Assessment, Reflection, and Revision

Assessment: A running record of who contributes to the class journal is added to every day after the students have left the classroom. The teacher can tune in to whom she should make a point of calling on tomorrow to contribute to the journal by reviewing the record. Also, a copy of the week's journal is copied and sent home with the students every Friday for parents/guardians to review with their children. Copies of the weekly journal kept by the teacher serve as a running record of the student's oral language and concepts about print development.

Reflections and Points for Revision or Change for Tomorrow:

FIGURE 6.12
Continued

guidelines in this book are written for those teachers who want to be effective and exemplary, not mediocre to ineffective.

Basic Elements of a Lesson Plan

The preferred lesson plan format of the authors of this book contains the following seven basic elements: (a) descriptive course data, (b) goals and objectives, (c) rationale, (d) procedure, (e) assignments and assignment reminders, (f) materials and equipment, and (g) a section for assessment of student learning, reflection on the lesson, and ideas for lesson revision. Compare those seven elements with those of whatever plan your program of teacher preparation expects you to use. These seven elements need not be present in every written lesson plan, nor must they be presented in any particular order. Nor are they inclusive or exclusive. You might choose to include additional components or subsections. Figure 6.12 displays a completed multiple-day lesson that includes the seven elements and also incorporates many of the developmentally appropriate learning activities discussed in this book.

Following next are descriptions of the seven major elements of the preferred format, with examples and explanations of why each is important.

Descriptive Data   A lesson plan's descriptive data is demographic and logistical information that identifies details about the class. Anyone reading this information should be able to identify when and where the class meets, who is teaching it, and what is being taught. Although as the teacher you know this information, someone else may not. Members of the teaching team, administrators, and substitute teachers (and, if you are the student teacher, your university supervisor and cooperating teacher) appreciate this information, especially when asked to fill in for you, even if only for a few minutes during a class session. Most teachers find out which items of descriptive data are most beneficial in their situation and then develop their own identifiers.

> The mark of a well-prepared, clearly written lesson plan is the ease with which someone else (such as another member of your teaching team or a substitute teacher) could implement it.

As shown in the sample plans of Figures 6.12 (writing), 6.13 (language arts/science/social studies), and 6.14 (physical science), the descriptive data include the following:

1. *Name of course or class.* These serve as headings for the plan and facilitate orderly filing of plans.
   Journal Write (in kindergarten class)
   Language Arts/Science/Social Studies (integrated block class)
   Physical Science

2. *Name of the unit.* Inclusion of this facilitates the orderly control of the hundreds of lesson plans a teacher constructs. For example:

Journal Write	*Unit: (n/a: a daily activity to close each meeting)*
Language Arts/Science/Soc Studies	*Unit: Investigative Research and Generative Writing*
Physical Science	*Unit: What's the Matter?*

3. *Topic to be considered within the unit.* This is also useful for control and identification. For example:

Journal Write	(N/A)	(N/A)
Language Arts/Science/ Social Studies	Unit: Investigative Research and Generative Writing	*Topic: Writing Response and Peer Assessment via the Internet*
Physical Science	Unit: What's the Matter?	*Topic: Density of Solids*

---

1. Descriptive Data

Teacher:_____ Class: Integrated Language Arts/Science/Social Studies Date: _____
Grade level: 5–8
Unit: Investigative Research and Generative Writing
Lesson Topic: Writing Response and Peer Assessment via Internet
Time duration: Several days

2. Goals and Objectives of Unit

Instructional Goals:

2.1. One goal for this lesson is for students to collaborate with and prepare response papers to peers from around the world who have shared the results of their own experimental research findings and research papers about ozone concentrations in the atmosphere.

2.2. The ultimate goal of this unit is for students around the world to prepare and publish for world-wide dissemination a final paper about global ozone levels in the atmosphere.

Objectives:

Cognitive:

a. Through cooperative group action, students will conduct experimental research to collect data about the ozone level of air in their environment. (application)

b. In cooperative groups, students will analyze the results of their experiments. (analyze)

c. Students will compile data and infer from their experimental data. (synthesis and evaluation)

d. Through collaborative writing groups, the students will prepare a final paper that summarizes their research study of local atmospheric ozone levels. (evaluation)

e. Through sharing via Internet, students will write response papers to their peers from other locations in the world. (evaluation)

f. From their own collaborative research and worldwide communication with their peers, the students will draw conclusions about global atmospheric ozone levels. (evaluation)

Affective:

a. Students will respond attentively to the response papers of their peers. (attending)

b. Students will willingly cooperate with others during the group activities. (responding)

c. The students will offer opinions about the atmospheric level of ozone. (valuing)

d. The students will form judgments about local, regional, and worldwide ozone levels. (organizing)

e. The students will communicate accurately their findings and attend diligently to the work of their worldwide peers. (internalizing)

Psychomotor:

a. The students will manipulate the computer so that their e-mail communications are transmitted accurately. (manipulating)

b. In a summary to the study, students will describe their feelings about atmospheric ozone concentrations. (communicating)

c. The students will ultimately create a proposal for worldwide dissemination. (creating)

FIGURE 6.13

Lesson plan sample: Multiple-day, project-centered, interdisciplinary, and transcultural lesson using worldwide communication via the Internet

3. Rationale

3.1 Important to improvement in one's writing and communication skills are the processes of selecting a topic, decision making, arranging, drafting, proofing, peer review, commenting, revising, editing, rewriting, and publishing the results—processes that are focused on in the writing aspect of this unit.

3.2 Student writers need many readers to respond to their work. Through worldwide communication with peers and dissemination of their final product, this need can be satisfied.

3.3 Students learn best when they are actively pursuing a topic of interest and meaning to them, Resulting from brainstorming potential problems and arriving at their own topic, this unit provides that experience.

3.4 Real-world problems are interdisciplinary and transcultural, involving writing (English), science, mathematics (data collecting, graphing, etc.), and intercultural communication. This unit is an interdisciplinary transcultural unit.

4. Procedure

Content:

At the start of this unit, collaborative groups were established via Intercultural E-mail Classroom Connections (IECC) with other classes from schools around the world. These groups of students from around the world conducted several scientific research experiments on the ozone level of their local atmospheric air. To obtain relative measurements of ozone concentrations in the air, students set up experiments that involved stretching rubber bands on a board, then observing the number of days until the bands broke. Students maintained daily journal logs of the temperature, barometric pressure, and wind speed/direction, and of the number of days that it took for bands to break. After compiling their data and preparing single-page summaries of their results, via the Internet, students exchanged data with other groups. From data collected worldwide, students wrote a one-page summary as to what conditions may account for the difference in levels of ozone. Following the exchange of students' written responses and their subsequent revisions based on feedback from the worldwide peers, students are now preparing a final summary report about the world's atmospheric ozone level. The intention is to disseminate this final report worldwide (to newspapers and via Internet).

Activity 1: Introduction (10 minutes)
Today, in think-share-pairs, you will prepare initial responses to the e-mail responses we have received from other groups from around the world. (Teacher shares the list of places from which e-mail has been received.) Any questions before we get started?

As we discussed earlier, here are the instructions: In your think-share-pairs (each pair is given one response received via e-mail), prepare written responses according to the following outline: (a) note points or information you would like to incorporate in the final paper to be forwarded via Internet: (b) comment on one aspect of the written response you like best: (c) provide questions to the sender to seek clarification or elaboration. I think you should be able to finish this in about 30 minutes, so let's try for that.

Activity 2: (30 minutes, if needed)
Preparation of dyad responses.

Activity 3: (open)
Let's now hear from each response pair.

Dyad responses are shared with whole class for discussion of inclusion in the response paper to be sent via Internet.

FIGURE 6.13
Continued

Activity 4: (open)
Discussion, conclusion, and preparation of final drafts to be sent to each e-mail corresponder to be done by cooperative groups (the number of groups needed to be decided by the number of e-mail corresponders at this time).

Activity 5: (open)
Later, as students receive e-mail responses from other groups the responses will be printed and reviewed. The class then responds to each using the same criteria as before and returns this response to the e-mail sender.

Closure:

The process continues until all groups (from around the world) have agreed upon and prepared the final report for dissemination.

5. Special Considerations, Notes, and Reminders

6. Materials and Equipment Needed

School computers with Internet access; printers
Copies of e-mail responses

7. Assessment, Reflection, and Revision

Assessment of student learning for this lesson is formative:
journals, daily checklist of student participation in groups, writing drafts

Reflective thoughts about lesson and suggestions for revision [to be filled in after lesson is completed]:

FIGURE 6.13
Continued

UNIT PLAN SAMPLE WITH A DAILY LESSON

Course   *Science*

Teacher _____   **Duration of Unit** *10 days*

Unit Title *What's the Matter?*   **Grade Level** *Grades 5–8*

Purpose of the Unit
This unit is designed to develop students' understanding of the concept of matter. At the completion of the unit, students should have a clearer understanding of matter and its properties, of the basic units of matter, and of the source of matter

Rationale of the Unit
This unit topic is important for building a foundation of knowledge for subsequent courses in science. This can increase students' chances of success in those courses, and thereby improve their self-confidence and self-esteem. A basis understanding of matter and its properties is important because of daily decisions that affect the manipulation of matter. It is more likely that students will make correct and safe decisions when they understand what matter is, how it changes form, and how its properties determine its use.

FIGURE 6.14
Sample of a unit plan with one daily lesson integrated
Source: Courtesy of Will Hightower.

Goals of the Unit

The goals of this unit are for students to

1. Understand that all matter is made of atoms.

2. Understand that matter stays constant and that it is neither created nor destroyed.

3. Develop certain basic physical science laboratory skills.

4. Develop a positive attitude about physical science.

5. Look forward to taking other science courses.

6. Understand how science is relevant to their daily lives.

Instructional Objectives of the Unit

Upon completion of this unit of study, students should be able to

1. List at least 10 examples of matter.

2. List the four states of matter, with one example of each.

3. Calculate the density of an object when given its mass and volume.

4. Describe the properties of solids, liquids, and gases.

5. Demonstrate an understanding that matter is made of elements and that elements are made of atoms.

6. Identify and explain one way the knowledge of matter is important to their daily lives.

7. Demonstrate increased self-confidence in pursuing laboratory investigations in physical science.

8. Demonstrate skill in communicating within the cooperative learning group.

9. Demonstrate skill in working with the triple-beam balance.

Unit Overview

Throughout this unit, students will be developing a visual learning map of matter. Information for the map will be derived from laboratory work, class discussions, lectures, student readings, and research. The overall instructional model is that of concept attainment. Important to this is an assessment of students' concepts about matter at the beginning of the unit. The preassessment and the continuing assessment of their concepts will center on the following:

1. What is matter and what are its properties? Students will develop the concept of matter by discovering the properties that all matter contains (that is, it has mass and takes up space).

2. Students will continue to build upon their understanding of the concept of matter by organizing matter into its four major states (that is, solid, liquid, gas, plasma). The concept development will be used to define the attributes of each state of matter, and students will gather information by participating in laboratory activities and class discussions.

3. What are some of the physical properties of matter that make certain kinds of matter unique? Students will experiment with properties of matter such as elasticity, brittleness, and density. Laboratory activities will allow students to contribute their observations and information to the further development of their concept of matter. Density activities enable students of practice their lab and math skills.

FIGURE 6.14

Continued

4. What are the basic units of matter, and where did matter come from? Students will continue to develop their concept of matter by working on this understanding of mixtures, compounds, elements, and atoms.

Assessment of Student Achievement
For this unit, assessment of student achievement will be both formative and summative. Formative evaluation will be done daily by checklists of student behavior, knowledge, and skills, Summative evaluation will be based on the following criteria:

1. Student participation as evidenced by completion of daily homework, classwork, laboratory activities, and class discussions, and by the information on the student behavior checklists.

2. Weekly quizzes on content.

3. Unit test.

Lesson Number _____   **Duration of Lesson** 1–2 *hours* _____

Unit Title *What's the Matter?* _____   **Teacher** _____

Lesson Title *Mission Impossible* _____   **Lesson Topic** *Density of Solids* _____

Objectives of the Lesson
Upon completion of this lesson, students should be able to

1. Determine the density of a solid cube.

2. Based on data gathered in class, develop their own definition of density.

3. Prepare and interpret graphs of data.

4. Communicate the results of their experiments to others in the class.

Materials Needed

1. Two large boxes of cereal and two snack-size boxes of the same cereal.

2. Four brownies (two whole and two cut in halves).

3. Four sandboxes (two large plastic boxes and two small boxes, each filled with sand).

4. Two triple-beam balances.

5. Several rulers.

6. Six hand-held calculators.

7. Eighteen colored pencils (six sets with three different colors per set).

8. Copies of lab instructions (one copy for each statement).

Instructional Procedure with Approximate Time Line

Set (10–15 Minutes)

Begin class by brainstorming to find what students already know about density. Place the word on the board or overhead, and ask students if they have heard of it. Write down their definitions and examples. Hold up a large box of cereal in one hand and the snack-size box in the other. Ask students which is more dense. Allow them time to explain their responses. Then tell them that by the end of this lesson they will know the answer to the question and that they will develop their own definition of density.

FIGURE 6.14
Continued

LABORATORY INVESTIGATION (30–60 MINUTES)

Students are divided into teams of four students of mixed abilities. Each member has a role:

1. *Measure master:* In charge of the group's ruler and ruler measurements.
2. *Mass master:* In charge of the group's weighings.
3. *Engineer:* In charge of the group's calculator and calculations.
4. *Graph master:* In charge of plotting the group's data on the graph paper.

Each team has 8 minutes before switching stations. Each team completes three stations and then meets to make their graphs and to discuss results.

***Station 1:* Cereal Box Density.** Students calculate the density of a large and a small box of cereal to determine if a larger and heavier object is more dense. The masses versus the volumes of the two boxes are plotted on graph paper using one of the pencil colors.

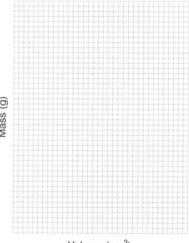

Volume (cm³)

Instructions

1. The density of any object is determined by dividing its mass by its volume. Density in grams is divided by volume in cubic centimeters. Example: $20\ g/10\ cm^3 \div 2\ g/cm^3$.

2. Measure the volume of the small cereal box (length × width × height), and use the balance to determine its mass in grams. The engineer can do the calculations on the calculator. The graph master should graph the results of each trial and connect two points with a straight line.

3. Repeat the procedure using the large box of cereal.

4. The engineer computes the density of both cereal boxes with the calculator and records the results on the proper blank below the graph.

   a. Density of large box of cereal _____

   b. Density of small box of cereal_____

   c. Density of large brownie _____

FIGURE 6.14
Continued

d. Density of small brownie _____

e. Density of large sandbox _____

f. Density of small sandbox _____

Station 2: **Brownie Density.** Students calculate the density of a full-size brownie and a half-size brownie. Results are plotted on the same graph as in Station 1, but with the second color.

Instructions

1. The density of any object is determined by dividing its mass by its volume. Density in grams is divided by volume in cubic centimeters. Example: $20 \text{ g}/10 \text{ cm}^3 \div 2 \text{ g/cm}^3$.

2. Measure the volume of a small brownie (length × width × height), and use the balance to deter-mine its mass in grams. The engineer can do the calculations on the calculator. The graph master should graph the results of each trial and connect two points with a straight line.

3. Repeat the procedure using the large brownie.

4. The engineer computes the density of both brownies and records the result on the proper blank.

Station 3: **Sandbox Density.** Students calculate the density of a large and a small box filled with sand. Results are plotted on the graph, but with the third color.

Instructions

1. The density of any object is determined by dividing its mass by its volume. Density in grams is divided by volume in cubic centimeters. Example: $20 \text{ g}/10 \text{ cm}^3 \div 2 \text{ g/cm}^3$.

2. Measure the volume of the small sandbox (length × width × height), and use the balance to deter-mine its mass in grams. The engineer can do the calculations on the calculator. The graph master should graph the results of each trial and connect two points with a straight line.

3. Repeat the procedure using the large sandbox.

4. The engineer computes the density of both boxes and records the result on the proper blank.

Lab Worksheet. Teams return to their seats to do the graphing, analyze the results, and answer the following questions from their lab sheets:

1. Is a larger, heavier object more dense than its smaller counterpart? Explain your evidence.

2. What is your definition of density?

3. Which is more dense, a pound of feathers or a pound of gold? Explain your answer.

LESSON CLOSURE (10 MINUTES OR MORE)
When all teams are finished, teams should display their graphs and share and discuss the results.

Concepts

1. Density is one of the properties of matter.

2. Mass and volume are related.

3. Density is determined by dividing mass by volume.

Extension Activities

1. Use a density graph to calculate the mass and volume of a smaller brownie.

2. Explore the story of Archimedes and the king's crown.

Evaluation, Reflection, and Revision of Lesson
Upon completion of this lesson and of the unit, revision in this lesson may be made on the basis of teacher observations and student achievement.

FIGURE 6.14
Continued

Although not included in the sample lesson plans in this book, the teacher might include in the descriptive data the category of "anticipated classroom noise level," such as "high," "moderate," and "low." Its inclusion, or at least considering the idea, is useful during the planning phase of instruction insofar as thinking about how active and noisy the students might become during the lesson, how you might prepare for that, and whether you should warn an administrator and teachers of neighboring classrooms.

Goals and Objectives   The instructional goals are general statements of intended accomplishments from that lesson. They usually are related to state- and/or district-mandated curriculum standards. This is where that information can be identified and shown.

Teachers and students need to know what the lesson is designed to accomplish. In clear, understandable language, the general goal statement provides that information. From the sample of Figure 6.13, the goals are

- To collaborate and prepare response papers to peers from around the world who have shared the results of their own experimental research findings and research papers about ozone concentrations in the atmosphere.
- For students worldwide to prepare and publish for worldwide dissemination a final paper about worldwide ozone levels in the atmosphere.

And, from the sample unit of Figure 6.14, goals are

- Understand that all matter is made of atoms.
- Develop a positive attitude about physical science.

Because the goals are also included in the unit plan, sometimes a teacher may include only the objectives in the daily lesson plan and not the goals. As a beginning teacher, it usually is a good idea to include both.

Setting the Learning Objectives

A crucial step in the development of any lesson plan is that of setting the objectives. It is at this point that many lessons go wrong and where many beginning teachers have problems.

A Common Error and How to Avoid It   Teachers sometimes confuse "learning activity" (*how* the students will learn it) with the "learning objective" (*what* the student will learn as a result of the learning activity). For example, teachers sometimes mistakenly list what they intend to do—such as "lecture on photosynthesis" or "lead a discussion on the causes of the Civil War." They fail to focus on just what the learning objectives in these activities truly are—that is, what the students will be able to do (performance) as a result of the instructional activity. Or, rather than specifying what the student will be able to do as a result of the learning activities, the teacher mistakenly writes what the students will do in class (the learning activity)—such as, "in pairs the students will do the 10 problems on page 72"—as if that were the learning objective. Although solving the problems correctly may well be the objective, "doing the 10 problems" is not. At the risk of sounding trite or belaboring the point, we emphasize the importance of the teacher being an accurate communicator. If the teacher's stated expectations are fuzzy, then the students may never get it.

When you approach this step in your lesson planning, to avoid error, ask yourself, "What should students be able to do as a result of the activities of this lesson?" Your answer to that question is your objective! Objectives of the lesson are included then as specific statements of performance expectations, detailing precisely what students will be able to do as a result of the instructional activities.

No Need to Include All Domains and Hierarchies in Every Lesson   We have known teachers to worry needlessly over trying to include objectives from all three domains (cognitive, affective, and psychomotor) in every lesson they write. Please understand that not all three domains are necessarily represented in every lesson plan. As a matter of fact, any given lesson plan may be directed to only one or two, or a few, specific objectives. Over the course of a unit of instruction, however, all domains, and most if not all levels within each, should be addressed.

From the lesson shown in Figure 6.13, sample objectives and the domain and level (in parentheses) within that domain are

- Through cooperative group action, students will conduct experimental research to collect data about the ozone level of air in their environment. (cognitive, application)
- Through the Internet, students will write and share response papers to their peers from other locations in the world. (cognitive, evaluation)
- Students will form judgments about local, regional, and world ozone levels. (affective, organizing)
- Students will create a proposal for worldwide dissemination. (psychomotor, creating)

And, from the lesson illustrated in Figure 6.14, sample objectives are

- Determine the density of a solid cube. (cognitive, application)
- Communicate the results of their experiments to others in the class. (psychomotor, communicating)

Rationale   The rationale is an explanation of why the lesson is important and why the instructional methods chosen will achieve the objectives. Parents, students, teachers, administrators, and others have the right to know why specific content is being taught and why the methods employed are being used. Prepare yourself well by setting a goal for yourself of always being prepared with intelligent answers to those two questions. This is a proper place to connect the lesson with the mandated benchmark standards.

Teachers become reflective decision makers when they challenge themselves to think about *what* (the content) students are learning, *how* (the learning activities) they are learning it, and *why* (the rationale) it must be learned. As illustrated in the sample unit of Figure 6.14, sometimes the rationale is included within the unit introduction and goals, but not in every lesson plan of the unit. Some lessons are carryovers or continuations of a lesson; we see no reason to repeat the rationale for a continuing lesson.

Procedure   The procedure consists of the instructional activities for a scheduled period of time. The substance of the lesson—the information to be presented, obtained, and learned—is the content. Appropriate information is selected to meet the learning objectives, the level of competence of the students, and the grade level or course requirements. To be sure your lesson actually covers what it should, you should write down exactly what minimum content you intend to cover. This material may be placed in a separate section or combined with the procedure section. The important thing is to be sure that your information is written so you can refer to it quickly and easily when you need to.

If, for instance, you intend to conduct the lesson using discussion, you should write the key discussion questions. Or, if you are going to introduce new material using a 10-minute lecture, then you need to outline the content of that lecture. The word *outline* is not used casually—you need not have pages of notes to sift through, nor should you ever read lengthy declarative statements to your students. You should be familiar enough with the content so that an outline (in as much detail as you believe necessary) will be sufficient to carry on the lesson, as in the following example of a content outline

Causes of Civil War
A. Primary causes
    1. Economics
    2. Abolitionist pressure
    3. Slavery
    4. etc.
B. Secondary causes
    1. North–South friction
    2. Southern economic dependence
    3. etc.

The procedure or procedures to be used, sometimes referred to as the *instructional components*, comprise the *procedure* element of the lesson plan. It is the section that outlines what you and your students will do during the lesson.

Appropriate instructional activities are chosen to meet the objectives, to match the students' learning styles and special needs, and to ensure that all students have an equal opportunity to learn. Ordinarily, you should plan this section of your lesson as an organized entity having a beginning (an introduction or *set*), a middle, and an end (called the *closure*) to be completed during the lesson. This structure is not always needed, because some lessons are simply parts of units or long-term plans and merely carry on activities spelled out in those long-term plans. Still, most lessons need to include in the procedure the following elements.

a. *Introduction*, the process used to prepare the students mentally for the lesson, sometimes referred to as the set (establishes a mind-set), or initiating activity (initiates the lesson)
b. *Lesson development*, the detailing of activities that occur between the beginning and the end of the lesson, including the transitions that connect activities
c. Plans for *practice*, sometimes referred to as the follow-up—that is, ways that you intend to have students interacting in the classroom (such as individual practice, in dyads, or small groups)—receiving guidance or coaching from each other and from you
d. *Lesson conclusion* (or closure), the planned process of bringing the lesson to an end, thereby providing students with a sense of completeness and, with effective teaching, accomplishment and comprehension by helping students to synthesize the information learned from the lesson
e. *Timetable* that serves simply as a planning and implementation guide
f. *Contingency plan* for what to do if you finish the lesson and time remains
g. *Assignments*, that is, what students are instructed to do as follow-up to the lesson, either as homework or as in-class work, providing students an opportunity to practice and enhance what is being learned.

Let's now consider some of those elements in detail.

Introduction to the Lesson Like any good performance, a lesson needs an effective beginning. In many respects, the introduction sets the tone for the rest of the lesson by alerting the students that the business of learning is to begin. The introduction should be an attention-getter. If it is exciting, interesting, or innovative, it can create a favorable mood for the lesson. In any case, a thoughtful introduction serves as a solid indicator that you are well prepared. Although it is difficult to develop an exciting introduction to every lesson taught each day, every day of the school week, a variety of options are always available by which to spice up the launching of a lesson. You might, for instance, begin the lesson by briefly reviewing the previous lesson, thereby helping students connect the learning. Another possibility is to review vocabulary words from previous lessons and to introduce new ones. Still another possibility is to use the key point of the day's lesson as an introduction and then again as the conclusion. Sometimes teachers begin a lesson by demonstrating a discrepant event (i.e., an event that is contrary to what one might expect), sometimes referred to as a hook. Yet another possibility is to begin the lesson with a writing activity on some controversial aspect of the ensuing lesson. Sample introductions are

For U.S. history, study of westward expansion:

- The teacher asks, "Who has lived somewhere other than (name of your state)?" After students show hands and answer, the teacher asks individuals why they moved to (name of your state). The teacher then asks students to recall why the first European settlers came to the United States and then moves into the next activity.

For science, study of the science process skill of predicting:

- The teacher takes a glass filled to the brim with colored water (colored so it is more visible) and asks students to discuss and predict (in dyads) how many pennies can be added to the glass before any water spills over the rim of the glass.

In short, you can use the introduction of the lesson to review past learning, tie the new lesson to the previous lesson, introduce new material, point out the objectives of the new lesson, help students connect their learning with other disciplines or with real life, or, by showing what will be learned and why the learning is important, inducing in students motivation and a mind-set favorable to the new lesson.

Lesson Development   The developmental activities that comprise the bulk of the plan are the specifics by which you intend to achieve the lesson objectives. They include activities that present information, demonstrate skills, provide reinforcement of previously learned material, and provide other opportunities to develop understanding and skill. Furthermore, by actions and words, during lesson development you should model the behaviors expected of the students. Students need such modeling. By effective modeling, you can exemplify the anticipated learning outcomes. Activities of this section of the lesson plan should be described in some detail so you will know exactly what it is you plan to do and during the intensity of the class meeting, you do not forget important details and content. It is for this reason that you should consider, for example, noting answers (if known) to questions you intend to ask and solutions (if known) to problems you intend to have students solve.

Lesson Conclusion   Having a concise closure to the lesson is as important as having a strong introduction. The concluding activity should summarize and bind together what has ensued in the developmental stage and should reinforce the principal points of the lesson. One way to accomplish these ends is to restate the key points of the lesson. Another is to briefly outline the major points. Still another is to review the major concept. Sometimes the closure is not only a review of what was learned but also the summarizing of a question left unanswered that signals a change in your plan of activities for the next day. In other words, it becomes a *transitional closure*.

Timetable   To estimate the time factors in any lesson can be very difficult, especially for the inexperienced teacher. A useful procedure is to gauge the amount of time needed for each learning activity and make a note of that alongside the activity and strategy in your plan, as shown in the preferred sample lesson plan format and in the sample lesson plan in Figure 6.14. Placing too much faith in your time estimate may be foolish—an estimate is more for your guidance during the preactive phase of instruction than for anything else. To avoid being embarrassed from running out of material, try to make sure you have planned enough meaningful work to consume the entire class period. If nothing else, this may include an anchor activity. Another important reason for including a time plan in your lesson is to give information to students about how much time they have for a particular activity, such as a group activity.

Assignments   When an assignment is to be given, it should be noted in your lesson plan. When to present an assignment to the students is optional, but it should never be yelled as an afterthought as the students are exiting the classroom at the end of the class period. Whether they are to be begun and completed during class time or done outside class, assignments should be written on the writing board, in a special place on the bulletin board, on the school's Web site, in each student's assignment log maintained in a binder, and/or on a handout. Take extra care to be sure that assignment specifications are clear to the students. Many teachers give assignments to their students on a weekly or other periodic basis. When given on a periodic basis, rather than daily, assignments should still show in your daily lesson plans so to remind yourself to remind students of them.

Once assignment specifications and due dates are given, it is a good idea *not* to make major modifications to them, and it is especially important not to change assignment specifications several days after an assignment has been given. Last-minute changes in assignment specifications can be very frustrating to students who have already begun or completed the assignment; it shows little respect to those students.

Understand the difference between assignments and procedures. An assignment tells students what is to be done, whereas procedures explain how to do it. Although an assignment may include procedures, spelling out procedures alone is not the same thing as giving an academic assignment. When students are given an assignment, they need to understand the reasons for doing it as well as have some notion of ways the assignment might be done.

Allowing time in class for students to begin work on homework assignments and long-term projects is highly recommended; it provides an opportunity for the teacher to provide individual attention to students. Being able to coach students is the reason for in-class time to begin assignments. The benefits of *coached practice* include being able to (a) monitor student work so a student doesn't go too far in a wrong direction, (b) help students to reflect on their thinking, (c) assess the progress of individual students, (d) provide for peer tutoring, and (e) discover or create a teachable moment. For the latter, for example, while observing and monitoring student practice, the teacher might discover a commonly shared student misconception. The teacher then stops and discusses that and attempts to clarify the misconception or, collaboratively with students, plans a subsequent lesson centered on focusing on the common misconception.

Special Considerations, Notes, and Reminders   We recommend that in your lesson plan format you have a regular place for special notes and reminders, perhaps in the same location as assignments as illustrated in the preferred format. In that special section that can be referred to quickly, you can place reminders concerning such things as announcements to be made, school programs, assignment due dates, and makeup work or special tasks for certain students. For example, for every student in your class who has an individualized education plan (IEP) you need to specifically describe what you plan to do to ensure the student's success. By consulting the guidelines provided in Chapter 8, you can describe what you will do to accommodate that student. (Note: As an example of reminders in a lesson plan, in the sample plan of Figure 6.12, the teacher put reminders in her plan to call on certain students during class who she felt needed some success recognition, José, a recent newcomer who is still struggling with learning English, and Elisa, who is severely mentally handicapped.)

The teacher must assure that proper resources and materials are available for lessons. That takes planning. Children can't use what they don't have.

Anne Vega/Merrill

Materials and Equipment to Be Used   Materials of instruction include books, media, handouts, and other supplies necessary to accomplish the lesson's learning objectives. You must be *certain* that the proper and necessary materials and equipment are available for the lesson; to be certain requires planning. Teachers who, for one reason or another, have to busy themselves during class time looking for materials or equipment that should have been readied before class began are likely to experience classroom control problems. Plus, if it happens very often, it demonstrates incompetency, and the teacher loses credibility with the students. Teachers want students to be prepared; students expect competent teachers to be prepared.

Assessment, Reflection, and Revision   Details of how you will assess how well students *are learning* (called *formative assessment*) and how well they have learned (called *summative assessment*) should be included in your lesson plan. This does not mean to imply that both types of assessment will be in every daily plan. Comprehension checks for formative assessment can be in the form of questions you ask and that the students ask during the lesson (in the procedural section), as well as various kinds of checklists.

For summative assessment, teachers typically use review questions at the end of a lesson (as a closure) or the beginning of the next lesson (as a review or transfer introduction), independent practice or summary activities at the completion of a lesson, and tests.

In most lesson plan formats, for the reflective phase of instruction there is a section reserved for the teacher to make notes or reflective comments about the lesson. Many student teachers seem to prefer to write their reflections at the end or on the reverse page of their lesson plans. As well as being useful to yourself, reflections about the lesson are useful for those who are supervising you if you are a student teacher or a teacher being mentored or considered for tenure. Sample reflective questions you might ask yourself are shown in Figure 2.1 (Chapter 2).

Writing and later reading your reflections can provide not only ideas that may be useful if you plan to use the lesson again at some later date, but also offer catharsis, easing the tension caused from teaching. To continue working effectively at a challenging task (i.e., to prevent intellectual downshifting, or reverting to earlier learned, lower cognitive level behaviors) requires significant amounts of reflection.

Activity 6.2A: Preparing a Lesson Plan

Instructions: Use the model lesson format or an alternative format that is approved by your instructor to prepare a _____-minute lesson plan (length to be decided in your class) for a grade-level and subject of your choice. After completing your lesson plan, use Activity 6.2b for the evaluation, before turning it in for your instructor's evaluation. This activity may be connected with Activity 6.3.

Activity 6.2B: Peer and Self-Assessment of My Lesson Plan

Instructions: You may duplicate blank copies of this form for evaluation of the lesson you developed for Activity 6.2a. Have your lesson plan evaluated by two of your peers and yourself. For each of the items below, evaluators should check either "yes" or "no," and write instructive comments. Compare the results of your self-evaluation with the other evaluations.

	No	Yes	Comments
1. Are descriptive data adequately provided?	____	____	_____
2. Are the goals clearly stated?	____	____	_____
3. Are the objectives specific and measurable?	____	____	_____
4. Are objectives correctly classified?	____	____	_____
5. Are objectives only low-order or is higher-order thinking expected?	____	____	_____
6. Is the rationale clear and justifiable?	____	____	_____
7. Is the plan's content appropriate?	____	____	_____
8. Is the content likely to contribute to achievement of the objectives?	____	____	_____
9. Given the time frame and other logistical considerations, is the plan workable?	____	____	_____
10. Will the opening (set) likely engage the students?	____	____	_____
11. Is there a preassessment strategy?	____	____	_____
12. Is there a proper mix of learning activities for the time frame of the lesson?	____	____	_____
13. Are the activities developmentally appropriate for the intended students?	____	____	_____
14. Are transitions planned?	____	____	_____
15. If relevant, are key questions written out and key ideas noted in the plan?	____	____	_____
16. Does the plan indicate how coached practice will be provided for each student?	____	____	_____
17. Is adequate closure provided in the plan?	____	____	_____
18. Are the materials and equipment needed identified, and are they appropriate?	____	____	_____
19. Is there a planned formative assessment, formal or informal?	____	____	_____
20. Is there a planned summative assessment?	____	____	_____
21. Is the lesson coordinated in any way with other aspects of the curriculum?	____	____	_____

22. Is the lesson likely to provide a sense of meaning for the students by helping bridge their learning?

____ ____ _____

23. Is an adequate amount of time allotted to address the information presented?

____ ____ _____

24. Is a thoughtfully prepared and relevant student assignment planned?

____ ____ _____

25. Could a substitute who is knowledgeable follow the plan?

____ ____ _____

Additional comments:

Activity 6.3: Bringing It All Together: Preparing An Instructional Unit

Instructions: The purpose of this activity is threefold: (a) to give you experience in preparing an instructional unit, (b) to assist you in preparing an instructional unit that you can use in your teaching, and (c) to start your collection of instructional units that you may be able to use later in your teaching. This assignment will take several hours to complete, and you will need to read ahead in this text. Our advice, therefore, is to start the assignment early, with a due date much later in the course. Your course instructor may have specific guidelines for your completion of this assignment; what follows is the essence of what you are to do.

First, with help from your instructor, divide your class into two teams, each with a different assignment pertaining to this activity. The units completed by these teams are to be shared with all members of the class for feedback and possible use later.

Team 1

Members of this team, individually or in dyads, will develop standard teaching units, perhaps with different grade levels, grades K–8, in mind. (You will need to review the content of Chapters 6–9.) Using a format that is practical, *each member or pair of this team* will develop a minimum 2-week (10-day) unit for a particular grade level, subject, and topic. Regardless of the format chosen, each unit plan should include the following elements:

1. Identification of (a) grade level, (b) subject, (c) topic, and (d) time duration.

2. Statement of rationale and general goals.
3. Separate listing of instructional objectives for each daily lesson. Wherever possible, the unit should include objectives from all three domains— cognitive, affective, and psychomotor.
4. List of materials and resources needed and where they can be obtained (if you have that information). These should also be listed for each daily lesson.
5. Ten consecutive daily lesson plans (see Activity 6.2A).
6. List of all items that will be used to assess student learning during and at completion of the unit of study.
7. Statement of how the unit will attend to the diversity of students one is likely to find, such as pertaining to students' reading levels, socioethnic backgrounds, and special needs.

Team 2

In collaboration, members of this team will develop interdisciplinary thematic units. Depending on the number of students in your class, Team 2 may actually comprise several teams, with each team developing an ITU. Each team should be comprised of no less than two members (e.g., a math specialist and a science specialist) and no more than four (e.g., history/social studies, English/language arts/reading, mathematics, and science).

SUMMARY

You have learned of the importance of learning modalities and instructional modes. You have learned about the importance of providing an accepting and supportive learning environment, as well as about teacher behaviors that are necessary to facilitate student learning beyond that of procedural knowledge.

With this chapter in particular, you continued building your knowledge base about why planning is important and how units with lessons are useful pedagogical tools. Developing units of instruction that integrate student learning and provide a sense of meaning for the students requires coordination throughout the curriculum. Hence, for students, learning is a process of discovering how information, knowledge, and ideas are interrelated so they can make sense out of self, school, and life. Preparing chunks of information into units and units into lessons helps students to process and understand knowledge. You have developed your first unit of instruction and are well on your way to becoming a competent planner of instruction.

In these first six chapters of this book, you have been guided through the preinstructional processes necessary to prepare yourself to teach in a classroom. Later, after you have studied Chapters 7 to 9 on assessment practices and specific instructional strategies, you may choose to revisit this chapter and to make revisions to your completed unit and lessons. Remember this always: Teaching plans, quite similar to this book, should never be set in concrete, but subject to constant assessment and revision.

STUDY QUESTIONS AND ADDITIONAL ACTIVITIES

1. Talk with experienced teachers and ask them what, if any, kinds of changes they have made to their lesson planning as a direct result of NCLB legislation and its aftermath.
2. Explain the importance of the notion that all elementary-school teachers are teachers of literacy and of thinking, social, and learning skills. Explain why you agree or disagree with that notion. Indicate one way specifically you would address each in your teaching.
3. Give several reasons why both a student teacher and a first-year teacher need to prepare detailed lesson plans. Describe when, if ever, the teacher can or should divert from the written lesson plan.
4. Divide your class into subject-area and/or grade-level interest groups. Have each group devise two separate lesson plans to teach the same topic to the same group of students (identified), but one plan uses direct instruction while the other uses indirect. Have groups share the experiences and outcomes of this activity with one another.
5. Explain why, when taught by access strategies, students learn less content but learn it more effectively? For a teacher using access strategies extensively, might this cause a problem? Explain.

6. Recall one vivid learning experience from your own early schooling and reflect on that experience with respect to its position on the Learning Experiences Ladder. In small groups, share your reflection with members of your class. After sharing, discuss what, if anything, can be concluded.

7. From the content outline that you prepared in Chapter 5, select a topic that is typically taught by the use of symbolization (at or near the top of the Learning Experiences Ladder); then devise a technique by which, with limited resources, that same content could be taught more directly (at or close to the bottom of the ladder). Share your proposal with your classmates for their feedback.

8. Explain the importance of organizing instruction into units. Is there ever a time when you might not do so? Share your response with your classmates for their critiques and thoughts.

9. You may want to brainstorm answers to this question in class in small groups. Identify a lesson typically taught somewhere in grades K–8, perhaps a lesson you recently have observed being taught. Taking the essence of that lesson, identify nine activities you would include in that lesson, one for each of the nine learning capacities (multiple intelligences) identified earlier in this chapter.

10. Explain why you agree or disagree with the notion that knowing your students well is critical to competent planning for instruction. If you agree with the notion, explain in detail three things you can do in your planning for the first week or two of school to better get to know the children you are assigned to teach.

WEB SITES RELATED TO CONTENT OF THIS CHAPTER

- Africa Access *www.africaaccessreview.org*
- Classroom Connect *www.classroomconnect.com*
- Council of the Great City Schools *www.cgcs.org*
- Education World *www.education-world.com*
- FedWorld *www.fedworld.gov*
- GLOBE (Global Learning and Observations to Benefit the Environment) Program *www.globe.gov*
- Intercultural E-mail Classroom Connections (IECC) *www.iecc.org*
- Lesson plans for various subjects at *artsedge.kennedy-center.org* and *www.pbs.org/teachersource*
- Lesson plans for mathematics at *coolmath.com* and at *mathworld.wolfram.com*
- Opening activity *www.dailybite.com*
- ReadWriteThink *www.readwritethink.org*
- The Global Schoolhouse *www.gsh.org*
- Verizon Literacy Network at *www.literacynetwork.verizon.org*

FOR FURTHER READING

Armstrong, T. (2003). *The multiple intelligences of reading and writing*. Alexandria, VA: Association for Supervision and Curriculum Development.

Bintz, W. P., Moore, S. D., Hayhurst, E., Jones, R., & Tuttle, S. (2006). Integrating literacy, math, and science to make learning come alive. *Middle School Journal, 37*(3), 30–37.

Carolan, J., & Guinn, A. (2007). Differentiation: Lessons from master teachers. *Educational Leadership, 64*(5), 44–47.

Dombchik, L. (2004). Storm busters: A science and technology integrated unit. *Middle Ground, 7*(3), 35–37.

Eisner, E. (2004). Multiple intelligences: Its tensions and possibilities. *Teachers College Record, 106*(1), 31–39.

Guarino, C. M., Hamilton, L. S., Lockwood, J. R., & Rathbun, A. H. (2006). *Teacher qualifications, instructional practices, and reading and mathematics gains of kindergartners*. Washington, DC: National Center for Education Statistics.

Kellough, R. D., Cangelosi, J. S., Collette, A. T., Chiappetta, E. L., Souviney, R. J., Trowbridge, L. W., & Bybee, R. W. (1996). *Integrating mathematics and science for intermediate and middle school students*. Englewood Cliffs, NJ: Merrill/Prentice Hall.

Kellough, R. D., Jarolimek, J., Parker, W. C., Martorella, P. H., Tompkins, G. E., & Hoskisson, K. (1996). *Integrating language arts and social studies for intermediate and middle school students*. Englewood Cliffs, NJ: Merrill/Prentice Hall.

McTighe, J., & O'Connor, K. (2005). Seven strategies for effective learning. *Educational Leadership, 63*(3), 10–17.

Mehigan, K. R. (2005). The strategy toolbox: A ladder to strategic teaching. *The Reading Teacher, 58*, 552–566.

Moran, S., Kornhaber, M., & Gardner, H. (2006). Orchestrating multiple intelligences. *Educational Leadership, 64*(1), 22–27.

Ownbey, M., & Thompson, M. (2003). Combining P.E. and music. *Principal, 82*(3), 30.

Potter, R. L. (2005). *Teaching K–8 literature with trade books*. Fastback 530. Bloomington, IN: Phi Delta Kappa Educational Foundation.

Rieben, L., Ntamakiliro, L., Gonthier, B., & Favol, M. (2005). Effects of various early writing practices on reading and spelling. *Scientific Studies of Reading, 9*, 145–166.

Roberts, P. L., & Kellough, R. D. (2008). *A guide for developing an interdisciplinary thematic unit* (4th ed.). Upper Saddle River, NJ: Prentice Hall.

Rog, L. J. (2007). *Marvelous minilessons for teaching beginning writing, K–3*. Newark, DE: International Reading Association.

Roush, B. E. (2005). Drama rhymes: An instructional strategy. *Reading Teacher, 58*, 584–587.

Whitin, D. J., & Whitin, P. (2004). *New visions for linking literature and mathematics*. Reston, VA: National Council of Teachers of Mathematics and the National Council of Teachers of English.

Chapter 7

Assessing and Evaluating Student Performance

INTASC Principles	PRAXIS III Domains	NBPTS Stadards
• The teacher understands and uses formal and informal assessment strategies to evaluate and ensure the continuous intellectual, social, and physical development of the learner. (Principle 8)	• Organizing Content Knowledge for Student Learning (Domain A)	• Assessment

How can we tell if children are performing at a satisfactory level of educational achievement? What standards of achievement should we expect of them? Can we provide for individual differences among learners and, at the same time, expect a minimal level of performance from all children? Should we promote children to the next grade if they do not attain the minimal standard of achievement for their current grade placement? What should the school do with those children who do not succeed in achieving these standards a second, third, or fourth time? Do we pass them anyway? How does the school achievement of U.S. children compare with that of other modern, industrialized nations? These questions deal with the topic of assessment of student learning; they are difficult questions that have bothered teachers, the public, and politicians for many years.

Assessment is an integral part and ongoing process in the educational arena. Curricula, buildings, materials, specific courses, teachers, supervisors, administrators, equipment—all must be periodically assessed in relation to student learning, the purpose of the school. When gaps between anticipated results and student achievement exist, those responsible try to eliminate those factors that seem to be limiting the educational output or find some other way to improve the situation. Thus, educational progress occurs. In this book we can only begin to scratch the surface of this huge and enormously important topic of assessment of student learning.

ANTICIPATED OUTCOMES

After completing this chapter, you should be able to do the following:

1. Demonstrate your understanding of the importance of assessment in teaching and learning.
2. Describe the relationship of assessment to goals and objectives.
3. Explain the concept of "authentic assessment."
4. Explain the value of and give an example of a performance assessment that you could use at a particular grade level or discipline.
5. Explain why criterion-referenced grading is preferable to norm-referenced grading.
6. Explain how teachers use rubrics, checklists, and portfolios in assessing student learning.
7. Differentiate among *diagnostic, summative,* and *formative assessment,* giving examples of when and how to use each with a particular grade level or discipline.
8. Describe the importance of self-assessment in teaching and learning.
9. Describe the importance of involving parents and guardians in their children's education, and identify at least three ways to involve them.
10. Complete the diagnostic, formative, and summative assessment tools of the unit plan that you began working on in Chapter 6.

TEACHING IN PRACTICE Teachers Caught Cheating: Trying to Gain an Advantage for Their Students (or Trying to Make Themselves Look Good)

- A teacher was placed on leave and more than a dozen eighth graders were retested after they allegedly were prepped with questions that showed up on their state social studies exam.
- In another state, students reported that adult tutors guided their pencils to the correct answers while they took the mandatory state math test.
- In yet another state, it was reported that some teachers read answers to students during the test, finished sentences for students in essays, allowed students to correct wrong answers, and photocopied secure tests to review in class.

Questions for Class Discussion

1. After reading this, what were your thoughts?
2. What do you suppose causes teachers to commit such behaviors? Have you as a student ever experienced similar behavior from a teacher?
3. What lessons are learned by the students of teachers who commit such acts as these?
4. How, as a teacher, will you handle pressures caused by mandatory achievement testing?

THE LANGUAGE OF ASSESSMENT

We first explain some of the terms and concepts associated with the process of determining whether children are achieving satisfactorily.

Evaluation, Assessment, and Measurement

Evaluation is a generic term having to do with determining the extent to which goals and objectives of teaching and learning have been attained. *Assessment* has much the same meaning, and some authors use the terms interchangeably. In the strictest sense, however, assessment has to do with gathering data used to make value judgments about student progress. Evaluation specifically refers only to the *judgment* part of this process. Some value of preference is associated with both evaluation and assessment because standards serve as the basis both for estimating and measuring performance (assessment) and then for judging its adequacy (evaluation).

Measurement has to do with using objective tests and procedures whose results can be converted into quantitative data. The data per se do not tell anything about the quality of the performance. For example, if a child obtained a score of 75 on a test, this score by itself does not indicate whether it is high or low, acceptable or unsatisfactory. If you knew that 500 children took the test, that the average score was 45, and that the second highest score was 63, you would then be inclined to say 75 was, indeed, a high score. However, if you were informed that the 500 children who took the test were all developmentally disabled (mild mental retardation), you might need to qualify your interpretation of 75 as a high score. This example illustrates how *measurement* provides data that can be useful in making an *evaluation*.

Authentic and Performance Assessment

Children's development encompasses growth in the cognitive, affective, and psychomotor domains. Traditional objective paper-and-pencil tests provide only a portion of the data needed to indicate student progress in these domains. Many experts today, as indeed they have in the past, question the traditional sources of data and encourage searching for, developing, and using alternative means to more authentically assess students' development of thinking and higher-level learning. Although many things are not yet clear, it is clear that you must employ various assessment techniques to determine how students work, what they are learning, and what they can produce as a result of that learning. As a teacher, you must develop a repertoire of ways to assess learner behavior and academic progress.

When assessing for student achievement, it is important that you use procedures that are compatible with the expected outcomes, that is, with your instructional objectives. This is referred to as *authentic assessment* (also called *accurate, active, aligned, alternative,* and *direct assessment*). Although some teachers call this *performance assessment,* performance assessment specifically refers to the type of student response being assessed, whereas authentic assessment refers to the assessment situation. Although not all performance assessments are authentic, assessments that *are* authentic are most assuredly performance assessments. For example, you would best measure (i.e., with the highest reliability) someone's competency to teach specific skills in physical education to second-grade students by directly observing the person doing exactly that—teaching specific skills in physical education to second graders. Using a standardized paper-and-pencil test of multiple-choice items to determine a person's ability to teach specific physical education skills to second-grade children is not authentic assessment.

Consider another example: "If students have been actively involved in classifying objects using multiple characteristics, it sends them a confusing message if they are then required to take a paper-and-pencil test that asks them to 'define classification' or recite a memorized list of characteristics of good classifications schemes" (Rakow, 1992, p. 3). An authentic assessment technique would be a performance item that actually involves students in classifying objects. In other words, to accurately assess students' learning, you would use a performance-based assessment procedure, that is, a procedure that requires them to produce rather than to select a response, such as in the following three examples:

1. Write a retelling of your favorite myth and create a diorama to accompany it.
2. As a culminating project (as a summative assessment tool) for a unit on sound, the teacher challenged groups of students to design and make their own musical instruments. The performance assessment instructions included the following:
   a. Play your instrument for the class.
   b. Show us the part of the instrument that makes the sound.
   c. Describe the function of other parts of your instrument.
   d. Demonstrate how you change the pitch of the sound.
   e. Share with us how you made your instrument.
3. Measure and calculate the area of our outdoor playing field to the nearest square meter.

1. Specify the performance objective (anticipated outcome).
2. Specify the test conditions.
3. Establish the standards (a scoring rubric) for judging student performance.
4. Prepare directions in writing, outlining the situation, with instructions students are to follow.
5. Share the procedure with a colleague for feedback before using it with students.

FIGURE 7.1
Steps for setting up a performance assessment situation

Advantages claimed for authentic assessment include (a) the *direct* (also called *performance-based, criterion-referenced,* or *outcome-based*) measurement of what students should know and can do and (b) emphasis on higher-order thinking. On the other hand, disadvantages of authentic assessment include (a) a higher cost and (b) problems with validity, reliability, and comparability.

Performance testing can be difficult and time consuming to administer to a group of children. An adequate supply of materials could be a problem. Scoring may tend to be subjective. It may be difficult to give makeup tests to students who were absent. To the extent possible in your own teaching, use your creativity to design and use performance tests, as they tend to measure well your most important objectives. To reduce subjectivity in scoring, prepare distinct scoring guidelines (rubrics). To set up a performance assessment situation, follow the steps shown in Figure 7.1.

TPW Video Classroom

Series General Methods
Module 10: Learner Assessment
Video 2: Performance Assessment

Formative and Summative Assessment

Teachers on the job are constantly observing children's work and behavior and making judgments about their quality. Perhaps they supplement these observations with short progress tests or quizzes that provide feedback about how well children are learning. In terms of these observations and tests, they will modify their instruction to be certain that it remains focused on the target. This type of ongoing assessment of children's learning is referred to as *formative evaluation*.

Formative evaluation contrasts with *summative evaluation* in that the latter occurs at or near the conclusion of a unit, at the end of a school term or semester, or at the end of the academic year. Summative evaluation is generally used to provide an accounting of learners' achievement status—individually or as a group—rather than to fine-tune the instructional process in progress.

Norm-Referenced and Criterion-Referenced Tests

In *norm-referenced tests*, the level of achievement against which performance is judged is based on the scores obtained by hundreds, perhaps even thousands, of students of the same age and school grade level who have taken the test. These test results are reported as averages, or *norms*, and you can use them to determine whether an individual student's score is less than, equal to, or greater than that of the population for which the test data were obtained. Scores for groups, such as a class or a single grade in an entire school or school district, can also be compared with the scores obtained by the norming population.

Standardized tests are norm-referenced tests available for various subjects and skills from commercial test publishers. In many states, the state departments of education have produced their own standardized tests for basic school subjects. Standardized-test results constitute a useful tool for you in revealing general strengths or weaknesses in the achievement of individuals or of an entire class. As instruments of summative evaluation, you ordinarily administer them near the end of the school year.

Standardized tests can be an objective yardstick to assess children's achievement. However, they do have limitations and have, in recent years, come under increased criticism. The following are frequently cited objections to the use of standardized tests:

1. They can be misused by educators who believe that all children must attain the average score and by teachers who teach specifically for the test content.
2. They rely on reading skill and therefore often do not provide good measures of concept attainment and knowledge of informational content.
3. They may be used to label children as high or low achievers and may thereby create self-fulfilling prophecies.
4. They may have the effect of limiting or "freezing" the curriculum to the content of the tests.
5. They are not able to accommodate adequately the local variations found in the curricula of U.S. schools.
6. They test not only school achievement but life experiences and out-of-school learning of all types; that is, the tests have a sociocultural bias favoring children who come from middle and upper socioeconomic levels and whose families have an above-average formal education.
7. They focus on measuring easily identified objectives dealing with subject matter and information and often do not evaluate the broader goals of education.
8. If the test measures for traditional outcomes—as many do—their use maintains the inertia of traditional instruction, thereby impeding adoption of educational reform.
9. Tests in specific subject fields, such as mathematics, are not always consistent with the most current research on what understandings should be expected of children at various grade levels.

Criterion-referenced tests are those that establish specific levels of expected performance. The best example is a learning situation in which you expect mastery.

You may expect children to learn all the spelling words, and they continue to study them until they are able to spell them all correctly. Or you may expect a certain level of quality of handwriting, and students do not complete the requirement until they meet that quality (or "criterion") level. Criterion-referenced tests are often used to evaluate the performance of motor skills, such as those associated with physical education. Any pass–fail test is an example of a criterion-referenced test. Criterion-referenced tests should always be used to assess learning in which less than an adequate performance would result in potentially disastrous consequences. Such learning includes (a) the administration of first aid; (b) fire drills or earthquake alert routines; (c) use of potentially hazardous tools, materials, or equipment; and (d) procedures, such as experiments, that could injure participants if not performed correctly.

Readiness Testing

A *readiness test* is used to determine whether learners have the prerequisite knowledge, skills, and interest to learn new material. Readiness testing is also referred to as *diagnostic assessment* or *preassessment*. Readiness may also have to do with learners' physical maturity. For example, if you expect children to learn a skill that involves complex eye–hand coordination, you would need to ascertain whether they are sufficiently mature physically to perform the task. In the area of physical education, certain learning experiences are referred to as *lead-up activities* and are intended to build the needed readiness for a forthcoming major activity, such as a team game.

Preassessment is also a way of determining students' misconceptions (naïve theories) about a topic you plan to study. At any grade level, you must determine what children already know or think they know about a subject or skill to set new instruction at the appropriate level of difficulty. If instruction is too simple, you are only reviewing what children already know or are proficient in doing. If too difficult, they cannot learn it successfully because it will not be linked psychologically to their existing intellectual framework. Gauging the appropriate level of difficulty for learners is an ability that good teachers are able to apply masterfully. They develop informal evaluation techniques and procedures to establish the degree of readiness. Then they build readiness for new material by using appropriate "lead-up" or "lead-in" activities. Interest building is necessarily an important part of this process. It is critical that you make good decisions at this stage of instructional planning if new learning is to result.

Validity and Reliability

The degree to which a measuring instrument actually measures what it is intended to measure is that instrument's *validity*. For example, when we ask if a test has validity, we are asking the following key questions concerning that test: Does it adequately sample the intended content? Does it measure the cognitive, affective, and psychomotor knowledge and skills that are important to the unit of content being tested? Does it sample all the instructional objectives of that unit of content?

The accuracy with which a technique consistently measures what it is intended to measure is its *reliability*. If, for example, you know that your body weight is 135 pounds, and a scale consistently records 135 pounds when you stand on it, then that scale has reliability. However, if the same scale consistently records 200 pounds when you stand on it, we can still say the scale has reliability. By this example, then, it should be clear to you that an instrument could be reliable (it produces similar results when used again and again) although *not* necessarily valid. In this second instance, the scale is not measuring what it is supposed to measure—that is, rather than 135 pounds it is showing 200 pounds—so although it is reliable, it is not valid. Although a technique might be reliable but not valid, it *must* have reliability before it can have validity. The greater the number of test items or situations measuring for a particular content objective, the higher the reliability. The higher the reliability, the more consistently students' scores will measure their understanding of that particular objective.

ASSESSMENT IN THE CONTEXT OF INSTRUCTION

Assessment is an essential part of teaching and learning because it focuses learners' attention on their need to improve their performance. Furthermore, the more precisely the assessment tells learners what they are doing well and what less well, the easier it will be for them to improve. Just as goals and objectives point students in desired directions, assessment lets them know whether and how well they are proceeding toward attaining them. Assessment helps clarify goals and objectives for students and helps define for them what you, the teacher, believe to be important. Assessment, therefore, is an inseparable part of teaching and learning, and whatever the school accepts as part of its teaching responsibility needs to be evaluated.

It is important for you to understand that the object of assessment in schools is learner *performance* and not to evaluate individuals as human beings. Often these two become confused, and we find ourselves judging the value of people on the basis of their school performance. Thus, there is the ever-present danger that children who do poorly in school may feel as a result that they are not adequate human beings. Teachers and schools must be careful not to encourage or reinforce any notion that the only worthwhile people are those who do well in school. The world is full of creative and successful people who at one time or another did not do well in school.

As we have stated several times in this book, your assessment should properly take place in terms of established goals and objectives. You must align your assessment with your anticipated outcomes. That means that (a) you must know what children are supposed to learn and (b) you must be able to identify behavior that indicates they have learned it. If you use measurable instructional objectives, as explained in Chapter 5, these two dimensions of assessment are embodied in the objective itself. Table 7.1 lists commonly used assessment procedures, along with some of the purposes each can serve.

Table 7.1 includes eight assessment procedures that elementary school teachers commonly use. These appear in the leftmost column. Notice that you may use any one of these eight procedures to assess learning that falls in the three domains discussed in Chapter 5. Because the nature of learning is different in each of the three domains you would of necessity use the assessment procedures differently. Take, for example, the first listed procedure "Group Discussion." You might be *primarily* interested in assessing one of the following:

1. How have children expanded their knowledge of the substantive content of the topic studied? (In this case, the suggestions in the column "Assessment of Cognitive Gain" would be appropriate.) *Or* . . .

2. How have children's feelings or attitudes been affected by studying the topic? (Here the suggestions in the column "Assessment of Attitude and Value Change" would apply.) *Or* . . .

3. How well have children learned certain skills associated with their study of the topic? (For this purpose, you should use the suggestions in the column "Assessment of Skill Development.")

Go through the entire table and try to visualize how you could use each of the eight assessment procedures. As you study the suggestions in the columns, notice what different kinds of learner behaviors they assess.

TABLE 7.1
Procedures commonly used by elementary school teachers to assess student progress

Procedure	Assessment of Cognitive Gain	Assessment of Attitude and Value Change	Assessment of Skill Development
Group Discussion	*Things to note:* How well do the children use the appropriate vocabulary? Are the essential concepts understood? Are the important relationships understood? Are there important concepts needing further study? Is the factual base adequate for the ideas being discussed?	*Things to note:* Extent to which the children express like or dislike of a topic. Presence or absence of comments suggesting racism, sexism, or prejudice. Extent of openness to new ideas. Evidence of responsible self-evaluation.	*Things to note:* Ability to express ideas. Contributions to discussion. Ability to use standards in evaluating work. Evidence of being informed on the topic.
Observation	*Do the children:* Talk with understanding about the topics under study? Cite examples of out-of-school applications of the ideas studied? Propose new plans of action based on the information gained?	*Do the children:* Show respect for the ideas and feelings of others? Carry a fair share of the workload? Show evidence of responsible habits of work?	*Do the children:* Use relevant skills independently when they are needed? Have apparent deficiencies in skills? Avoid using certain important and needed skills?

(Continued)

TABLE 7.1
Continued

Procedure	Assessment of Cognitive Gain	Assessment of Attitude and Value Change	Assessment of Skill Development
Checklists	*Used to:* Indicate mastery, as on a pass–fail performance. Record specific areas of strength or weakness in the knowledge of a subject. Report student progress, as on report cards.	*Used to:* Record observations of specific behaviors of students—such as attitudes toward class-mates, toward authority, or toward attending school.	*Used to:* Evaluate the use of a specific skill, such as giving an oral report, clarity of speaking, or use of references.
Conferences	*Used to:* Examine children orally who may not be able to read or write. Discover evidence of confusion or misunderstanding of ideas. Clarify the kinds of assistance needed by the child. Discover the nature of the needed corrective work.	*Used to:* Learn specific interest of individual children—likes, dislikes, preferred activities, books, topics, and so on.	*Used to:* Diagnose specific problems. Check the proficiency of skill use on an individual basis.
Anecdotal Records	Items listed under Group Discussion and Observation are appropriate here.	Items listed under Group Discussion and Observation are appropriate here.	Items listed under Group Discussion and Observation are appropriate here.
Work Samples and Portfolios	*Used to:* Note qualitative differences in the child's work products over time: a written report, booklet, map, or a classroom test. Show ability to apply, analyze, or summarize ideas.	*Used to:* Note greater sensitivity to others in written work and artwork. Note increased concern for neatness of work; concern for punctuality in completing assigned work. Note originality and creative abilities.	*Used to:* Note qualitative differences in proficiency in use of specific skills. Illustrate student's ability to structure responses.
Diaries and Logs	*Used to:* Help the children recall what has been learned.	*Used to:* Remind the children of the gap between intentions and behavior.	*Used to:* Show improvement in skill use over time.

TABLE 7.1
Continued

Procedure	Assessment of Cognitive Gain	Assessment of Attitude and Value Change	Assessment of Skill Development
Teacher-made Tests	*Used to:* Evaluate understanding of concepts, generalizations, trends, and informational content through the use of such exercises as the following: Matching causes and effects. Arranging events in order or arranging steps in a sequence. Providing reasons or explanations for events. Selecting the best explanations from a list of options. Determining the truth or falsity of statements. Providing examples of concepts. Supplying a generalization based on given facts. Being able to use key terms correctly. Providing ends to unfinished stories or situations based on facts. Placing events on a time line.	*Used to:* Find out about likes, dislikes, interests, and preferences for activities through the use of such exercises as the following: From a list, select the things you liked best, liked least. Check what you like to do during your free time. Write ends to unfinished stories that deal with emotions, prejudice, and discrimination. Select words from a narrative that engender strong feelings.	*Used to:* Check the proficiency of skill use or to diagnose specific difficulties through the use of exercises such as the following: Locating places on a map. Reading to find the main idea. Making an outline of material read, or finishing a partially completed outline. Using an index to find information. Skimming to find specific facts. Writing an ending to a story.

Keeping samples and exhibits of children's work for purposes of assessing progress is something many teachers have been doing for generations. In recent years, however, students have acquired more responsibility for assembling and maintaining such samples, and the term *portfolio* is now applied to this technique. This usage derives from the adult world, where commercial artists, architects, technical writers, portrait photographers, advertising executives, and others whose careers involve developing products prepare a professional portfolio that they then use to document their background when they apply for new positions or seek clients. The use of student portfolios can vividly highlight both progress and

Activity 7.1: Make It Right, *Write*!

Megan Nalley remembered that her university language arts methods instructor said, "Children who learn to write well are those who do a whole lot of writing and are provided critical feedback on their writing efforts." This made a lasting impression on Megan, and now, in her initial year as an employed sixth-grade teacher, she has her students write one-page essays each week. Additionally, she requires them to write lengthy answers to their assigned work. She goes over these papers carefully and writes numerous comments on them. Her problem now is that she has time to do little else but read and correct children's written work. The task is overwhelming! After about 6 weeks, she complains about it to her mentor, an experienced teacher, and asks her what she should do. The mentor offers Megan the following advice:

• Reduce the *length* of the written assignments. In many cases, a single paragraph might be adequate to build a specific writing skill.

• Teach students to edit their own papers for such items as spelling and basic punctuation.

• From time to time, have students work in pairs and edit each other's papers.

• Identify common errors that students make, and comment to the entire class, rather than writing the same comment on 25 separate papers.

• Divide the class into groups of four and have students read their essays aloud to each other. In the process, they also can edit their papers.

• Select specific items for evaluation rather than identifying all the errors in every paper.

Questions for Individual Thought and Group Discussion

1. If Megan uses some of these suggestions, will it be possible for her to attain her objective of improving the writing skills of her sixth graders?
2. In addition to creating an impossible workload for herself, what other detrimental effects might flow from the amount of writing Megan is requiring her students to do?
3. Can you add other helpful suggestions to the six that Megan's mentor offered?

deficiencies in learning. Moreover, the display of written work, creative endeavors, and science and social studies projects illustrates clearly students' progress over time and shows parents and guardians how their children are progressing. Seeing children's actual work over time is much more meaningful to most parents and guardians than is a letter grade alone. We discuss self-assessment and portfolios later in this chapter.

ASSESSMENT IN THE CLASSROOM

If the elementary school experience is to help the children achieve a range of learning goals, it follows that teachers must use a variety of assessment techniques and procedures to evaluate those outcomes. As is evident from Table 7.1, your assessment of student learning can take many forms. These are often informal techniques that rely mainly on your professional judgment and thoughtful observation of student behavior. When you become involved in the preparation of formal tests, however, it is important to ensure that such instruments are technically correct. This demands specialized knowledge usually covered in a course dealing with testing, measurement, and evaluation, a standard requirement in most teacher certification programs. It is in such a course that you, the prospective teacher, should learn about constructing and using such item types as (a) alternative response (true-false, yes-no, agree-disagree, etc.; also called *selected response*), (b) multiple choice, (c) matching, (d) short answer, (e) completion, and (f) essay. It is beyond the purpose of this text to provide detail on such topics, but we do refer you to sources in the suggested readings at the end of this chapter.

Considering that elementary school students range in age from 5 to 13 years old and are in the process of mastering some of the basic learning of our culture, it makes sense to use classroom assessment to measure what they can do after instruction as compared with what they could do prior to it. A few examples will clarify this point. If your class has spent 20 minutes each day for a week learning to spell 20 words, the appropriate test at the end of the week would involve having them write the words and spell them correctly. If you are teaching children how to add three-digit whole numbers, your test should require them to add some three-digit whole numbers to see if they can do it correctly. If children have been learning in social studies about causes and effects, give them a list of causes and a list of effects to see if they can correctly match the items with each other. This is the essence of authentic assessment.

Testing techniques of this type can be misused when teachers exercise flawed judgment in selecting either what is to be learned or the specific testing technique. Let us return to the spelling example in the preceding paragraph. If you *only* have students memorize the words in rote fashion and write them from memory when you dictate them and do not have students use the words in purposeful written communication, one could hardly defend such a procedure as an appropriate performance test. The performance test of any skill or the application of newly learned knowledge should always take place in a context as close to the "real thing" as classroom conditions will allow. This is what the term *authentic* means with reference to evaluating learning.

The following suggestions are intended to help you construct classroom tests for determining students' learning achievement. To confirm your full understanding of each we suggest that you discuss the 12 items with others in your class.

1. When constructing knowledge-based tests, emphasize ideas and concepts requiring reflective thinking rather than focusing solely on recall of information. Remember that students believe that the test defines what is important for them to learn.
2. Select and state items in ways that will encourage good study habits. For example, it is *not* considered good practice to create test items that require children to memorize lengthy text passages.
3. Cast test items in a practical, functional context, that is, close to the "real thing." This includes spelling words. Words on spelling tests should be from the context of the unit of study, not from isolated, disconnected word lists.
4. Be sure that the test relates to what you have taught; do not teach for one set of objectives and test for another.
5. Be aware of the readability factor in *any* performance test that requires students to read. (The test may simply be a reading test rather than a test of science, social studies, current events, or literature.)

6. Do not use textbook language or quote directly from the text in constructing, for example, true–false or completion items.
7. If you require a factual response, do not ask for students' opinions, such as by asking "What do you think . . . ?" "Why do you suppose . . . ?" "When do you believe . . . ?"
8. To the extent possible, be sure the test is at the appropriate level of difficulty for students.
9. Check to see that each test item clearly states what you are asking students to do; also make sure you clearly state the test directions.
10. Avoid providing clues to answers in the statement, stem, or format of the question (e.g., grammatical clues; length of blanks to fill in; mixing names, events, and places; providing the answer to one question in the stem of another).
11. Sample a large enough portion of students' behavior to accurately draw conclusions about the adequacy of their performance.
12. To make assessment consistent with the instruction on which it is based, teach from measurable instructional objectives whenever possible, that is, from an aligned curriculum.

Helping Children Deal with Test Anxiety

Test taking is becoming an increasingly complex and important facet in the educational lives of children and begins at an increasingly younger age. For example, as early as grade 3, children in many states must pass tests in reading and mathematics to be promoted to the next grade level. Children who are still preteens are now taking the Scholastic Aptitude Test (SAT), an entrance examination requirement for many colleges and universities and usually taken in the junior year of high school. Some young adolescent children take the SAT for the practice, whereas others take it to qualify for talent search programs such as the California State University at Sacramento Talent Search Program or the Johns Hopkins University Center for Talented Youth. Because of increased pressures on young people, you may have children in your classroom who knowingly or unknowingly experience and indicate symptoms of text anxiety, symptoms such as sleeplessness, nausea, and headaches. As can be expected from the increased amount of standardized testing nationwide, overall test anxiety in youth of all grade levels, K–12, is reported to be on the increase (Casbarro, 2004; McDonald, 2001). Test anxiety today is a major factor contributing to a variety of negative outcomes (Harris & Coy, 2003). You can help alleviate students' test-related stress by learning and teaching both test-taking strategies and techniques that your students can use to manage their anxiety.

Potential causes of test anxiety in children include: (a) expectations of the adults in their lives, and the child's fear of not meeting those expectations, (b) peer pressures, and (c) the feeling of lack of control and/or the inability to change one's current life situation.

When working with an anxious student, you can help by (a) establishing a rapport with the student whereby the student has confidence in your suggestions and (b) giving specific suggestions to the student such as being positive about the outcomes, using test time efficiently and wisely, being prepared, reading directions carefully, making an outline before answering a performance or essay type question, and to use practice testing.

Finally, to further assist in the learner's control of his/her anxiety, help the child learn relaxation techniques, such as deep breathing while counting to 10, stretching out and then contracting body muscles and then relaxing, and thinking of a happy memory. Some school districts provide counseling intervention services for the most serious cases of test anxiety (Cheek, Bradley, Reynolds, & Coy, 2002).

Before leaving this topic of anxiety, we must mention that teachers, too, are experiencing "test anxiety," not necessarily from having to take the mandated test but from having to administer the test and the accompanying concern or fear that the students will not do well (Terzian, 2002). Thus, our advice is for you to learn and to practice techniques for stress management, such as

1. Breathing exercise: Inhale and hold breath while counting to 10, then exhale slowly. Repeat 10 times.
2. Change your environment for a few minutes, either actually by taking a walk or by closing your eyes and imagining yourself in a relaxing place.
3. Do stretching exercises for 5 to 10 minutes, stretching legs, arms, back, shoulders, and neck.

STUDENT PARTICIPATION IN ASSESSMENT

You should plan students' continuous self-assessment as an important component of your assessment program. If students are to improve their *metacognition* (their thinking about and understanding of their own thinking) and continue to develop intellectually, then they must receive instruction and guidance in how to become more responsible for their own learning. You must help teach them the processes of self-understanding and self-assessment. They must experience success to achieve this self-understanding; to do this they must know how to measure their own achievement. This empowerment raises students' self-esteem and teaches them to think better of their individual capabilities.

To meet these goals, provide opportunities for students to think about what they are learning, how they are learning it, and how far they have progressed. As stated previously, one good procedure is to have students maintain portfolios of their work, using rating scales or checklists periodically to self-assess their progress.

Using Student Portfolios

Teachers use portfolios as a means of instruction, and teachers and students both use them as one means of assessing student learning. Although there is little research evidence to support or to refute the claim, educators believe that the instructional value comes from the process of assembling and maintaining a personal portfolio. During this creative process, you can expect students to self-reflect, to think critically about

Teachers meet periodically with individual students to discuss their self-assessments to reinforce and guide student learning and development. Such individual conferences provide children with understandable and achievable short-term goals and help them develop and maintain positive self-esteem.

Anne Vega/Merrill

what they are learning, and to assume some responsibility for their own learning. Some teachers recently have found renewed interest in student portfolios via the use of electronic portfolios, seemingly because it is done with modern technology, it can be published on the Internet, saved on a CD, and built on over a student's school career (Diehm, 2004).

Educators have invented various categories or types of portfolios, each with a unique purpose, such as *growth portfolio* (to document improvement over a period of time), *proficiency portfolio* (to document mastery of content and skills), or *showcase portfolio* (to document a student's best work over time) (see, for example, Roe & Vukelich, 1998). Elementary-school teachers most commonly use combined growth and proficiency portfolios, but portfolios clearly should not be simply collections of *everything* students have done over time.

Although you and your students should make the final decision jointly as to content, you must ensure that students organize their portfolios well, exhibiting their efforts, progress, and achievements in a way that clearly tracks their learning successes. Generally, portfolios should contain such items as assignment sheets, class worksheets, the results of homework, project binders, and forms for student self-assessment and reflection. As a model of a *career portfolio*, you can show students your personal professional career portfolio (see Activity 2.4 in Chapter 2).

Before using portfolios as an alternative to traditional assessment and instruction, you must carefully consider and clearly understand your reasons for doing so and determine whether they are practical for your situation. Then decide carefully on portfolio content, establish rubrics or expectation standards, anticipate grading problems, and consider and prepare for parent/guardian reactions.

Although *portfolio assessment* as an alternative to traditional methods of evaluating student progress has gained momentum in recent years, establishing standards has been difficult. Research on the use of portfolios for assessment indicates that validity and reliability of teacher evaluation are often quite low. In addition, it is not always practical for every teacher to use portfolio assessment.

Using Checklists and Scoring Rubrics

Students periodically should assess themselves and reflect on their work to maintain a basis by which to measure their progress. You will need to help them learn how to analyze these comparisons. Although students can use almost any assessment instrument for self-assessment, in some cases you may wish to construct specific instruments designed to aid students' self-understanding. These instruments should provide students with new information about their progress and growth.

Elementary-school teachers often employ a series of checklists to assess children's learning. Students can maintain these checklists in their portfolios and may thus easily compare current with previous self-assessments. Items on the checklist will vary depending on your purpose, subject, and grade level (Figure 7.2). Students indicate for each skill whether they currently can demonstrate it satisfactorily by filling in the appropriate blanks. Open-ended questions allow students to provide additional information as well as to do some expressive writing. After a student

---

Checklist: Oral Report Assessment

Student _____   Date _____

Teacher _____   Time _____

Did the student	Yes	No	Comments
1. Speak so that everyone could hear?	_____	_____	_____
2. Finish sentences?	_____	_____	_____
3. Seem comfortable in front of the group?	_____	_____	_____
4. Give a good introduction?	_____	_____	_____
5. Seem well informed about the topic?	_____	_____	_____
6. Explain ideas clearly?	_____	_____	_____
7. Stay on the topic?	_____	_____	_____
8. Give a good conclusion?	_____	_____	_____
9. Use effective visuals to make the presentation interesting?	_____	_____	_____
10. Give good answers to questions from the audience?	_____	_____	_____

FIGURE 7.2

Sample checklist: Assessing a student's oral report

has demonstrated each skill satisfactorily, you would note this next to the student's name in your gradebook.

While emphasizing your assessment criteria, rating scales and checklists provide students with means of expressing their feelings and give you still another source of assessment data. In addition, you should meet periodically with individual students and discuss their self-assessments to reinforce and guide their learning and development. Such conferences provide students with understandable and achievable short-term goals and help them develop and maintain adequate self-esteem (Sylwester, 1997).

TEACHER PREP
MERRILL
PRENTICE HALL

TPW Video Classroom

Series: Classroom Management

Module 6: Communicative Skills for Teaching

Video 1: Documenting Learning

FIGURE 7.3
Checklist and scoring rubric compared

Sample scoring rubric for assessing a student's skill in listening.

Score Point 3—Strong listener:
• Responds immediately to oral directions
• Focuses on speaker
• Maintains appropriate attention span
• Listens to what others are saying
• Is interactive

Score Point 2—Capable listener:
• Follows oral directions
• Usually attentive to speaker and to discussions
• Listens to others without interrupting

Score Point 1—Developing listener:
• Has difficulty following directions
• Relies on repetition
• Often inattentive
• Has short attention span
• Often interrupts the speaker

Sample checklist for assessing a student's skill in map work.

Check each item if the map comes up to standard in this particular category.
_____ 1. Accuracy
_____ 2. Neatness
_____ 3. Attention to details

As you can see from the scoring rubric and checklist shown in Figure 7.3, there is little difference between a rubric and a checklist; the difference is that rubrics show degrees of satisfactory completion for the desired characteristics, whereas checklists usually show only their completion. You easily may turn a checklist into a scoring rubric or vice versa.

Guidelines for Using Portfolios for Instruction and Assessment

Use the following general guidelines when employing student portfolios to assess student learning.

1. Children should understand that the dual purpose of the portfolio is to illustrate their growth in learning and to showcase their finest work.
2. Contents of the portfolio should reflect goals and objectives.
3. Students should have some say in what goes into their portfolios.
4. Students should date everything that goes into their portfolios.
5. After determining what materials students are to keep in their portfolios, announce clearly (post schedule in room) when, how, and by what criteria you will review portfolios. Stress the word *review*. The purpose of this review is to determine growth and areas for continued focus (see item 8).
6. Students are responsible for maintaining their own portfolios.
7. Portfolios should stay in the classroom.
8. Do *not* grade or compare in any way students' portfolios with each other. They exist for student self-assessment and for showing progress in learning. For this to happen, students should keep in their portfolio all papers, or major sample papers. For grading purposes, simply record whether students are maintaining their portfolios and by checking that all required materials are present.

DIAGNOSTIC ASSESSMENT AND CORRECTIVE INSTRUCTION

The challenge of teaching is to secure a best "fit" between individual learner interests, capabilities, and learning styles and the instructional mode—and to do this in the setting of a classroom group. But no matter how well you personalize instruction and how sensitive you are to individual students' needs, learners will respond differently to presentations, and some will need corrective instruction to enable them to progress. A relatively minor learning problem or a missed lesson because of inattentiveness or absence may, if left unattended, escalate into a serious learning handicap for a child. You must, therefore, be alert and able to spot difficulties and correct them before they take on serious proportions. As a teacher, you must see yourself as being in a continuous mode of diagnostic and formative assessment.

In this discussion of diagnostic assessment and corrective instruction, we are not referring to children with special needs. We are, rather, referring to ordinary boys and girls who, for one reason or another, are not progressing as well as you expect. Such children usually respond well to corrective instruction because their learning problem is not related to serious psychological or physical impairment.

The Teacher as Diagnostician

A competent teacher is constantly assessing children's learning in terms of both specific expected outcomes and the school's overall goals, basing most of these assessments on astute observations of children's behavior. The teacher notices that a child is not able to use recently taught word-attack skills; another is unable to compute simple problems in mathematics; a third is losing interest in school. It is from these observations that the teacher forms judgments about an appropriate program of corrective instruction.

Competent teachers do not assume that children learn new concepts and skills simply because they have been taught. They teach and reteach as needed. If one presentation is not clear, good teachers will try another approach. They present complex concepts in varied settings, and they provide adequate drill and practice when teaching skills. Teachers are as much diagnosticians as presenters in the day-to-day work of the classroom. Their assessment of children's behavior is critical to the many decisions they must make each day: how to group, what materials and media to use, which children need more practice, and which ones need special help. Much of what we call effective teaching consists of diagnosing learner needs and shaping the instructional program in accordance with them. Your insight and judgment are critical in doing this well. (See as an illustration the special feature, "What Went Wrong for Antoine?" in Chapter 8.)

Avoid Labeling

In taking a diagnostic approach to teaching, you must avoid labeling children. Labels are of dubious value and often detrimental to children's learning. Quite clearly, labels mark children with stereotypical characteristics that may or may not be appropriate to specific cases. Besides, attaching a label to a behavior does not in and of itself do anything to correct it. In fact, identifying a child as being "aphasic," "dyslexic," "autistic," "mentally retarded," or "a stutterer" may contribute to the complexity of the problem. What *is* important is to know enough about any child's learning problem to be able to develop a suitable program of instruction that will enable the child to progress.

Diagnostic and Corrective Procedures

Teachers oriented to diagnostic assessment and corrective instruction are constantly monitoring children's responses and adjusting their instruction in accordance with such observations. As you become involved in more formal diagnostic work, three questions will guide you: (a) What evidence is there that a learning problem exists? (b) What is the *specific* learning difficulty the child is encountering?

and (c) What level of corrective work is required? Let us examine each of these questions carefully in turn.

What Evidence Is There That a Learning Problem Exists?

Assume that while examining your students' test scores you discover that, with one exception, mathematics, their scores are consistently high. Assuming the problem is not with your tests, this is, then, a clear indicator that a learning problem exists in the mathematics area. If the test results are reported as mean scores, it may be that the scores of a few low-achieving children are depressing the average for the entire group. On the other hand, most children may, in fact, have scored relatively lower on math than they did on the other parts of the test battery. You will need to explore this situation in detail.

Assume further that your case is different from that of another class, in which the teacher finds children's achievement scores low in *all* subjects. This teacher will need to know if this happened because the group as a whole is less capable than an average class, whether the children received poor instruction in prior years, whether the test was given under adverse conditions or at the wrong time of the year, or for some other reason. In any case, the low test scores will alert the teacher to the possibility of learning problems that seem pervasive among those children.

Activity 7.2: Selecting the Right One

For each listed situation, suggest a specific appropriate assessment procedure. Use Table 7.1 to help you make your suggestions.

Grade: 1
Subject: Reading
Objective: Children will be able to use the word-attack skills appropriate for first graders as defined by the curriculum guide.

Assessment:

Grade: 2
Subject: Social Skills
Objective: Children will be able to work with other children in cooperative learning assignments.

Assessment:

Grade: 3
Subject: Science
Objective: Children will learn the similarities and differences among states of matter (i.e., solid, liquid, and gas).

Assessment:

Grade: 4
Subject: Social Studies
Objective: Children will learn the origin of selected place names in their home state.

Assessment:

Grade: 5
Subject: Physical Education
Objective: Children will be able to execute safely each of the following partner and group stunts: Eskimo roll, pyramids, angel balance, and lap-sit.

Assessment:

Grade: 6
Subject: Mathematics
Objective: Children will understand the meaning and function of place value.

Assessment:

Standardized achievement tests are only one method—and perhaps not even the most important one—that may alert you to the presence of learning problems. Your best and most reliable tool for this purpose is skillful observation of children's behavior. To aid your observation, make careful notes, record each child's progress, and systematically keep samples of children's work. A child's progress in learning subject matter and skills is likely to progress in spurts from one week to the next. But over a period of several weeks or months, each child should show signs of improvement. Failure to do so indicates a problem affecting a child's progress. Similarly, if a child is showing no interest in schoolwork, does not pay attention, or has behavioral difficulties, you must suspect and begin a search for a lurking problem.

You should be particularly observant of children's responses when introducing skills. Skills competence is built on practice, and if children are not initially performing the skill properly, they will be practicing it incorrectly. It is not uncommon to find children in the upper grades who are handicapped in their use of skills because they are performing them inefficiently or incorrectly: simple mechanical errors in handwriting, inability to write a single complete sentence, incorrect spelling of most commonly used words, inability to do simple mathematics problems, faulty methods of work (e.g., adding when they should subtract), and so on.

What *Specific* Learning Difficulty Is the Child Encountering?

After you have identified a child's general area of learning difficulty, you must locate as precisely as possible the limitations and deficiencies that child is experiencing. It is insufficient to know that a child is a "poor reader." Anyone off the street could quickly make that determination. What separates professional teachers from "anyone off the street" is their ability to go beyond mere description of behavior, to diagnose the nature of a difficulty, and to prescribe corrective instruction.

So, to provide corrective instruction for a child with a reading difficulty, for example, you must diagnose the precise nature of the problem. For example, does the child have limited word-recognition techniques? Does the child not comprehend the reading? Is the child unable to use reading aids? Does the child have a limited sight vocabulary? If children do not progress rapidly when given corrective instruction, it may be because the instruction does not focus on the precise learning problem. No amount of drill and practice on sentence comprehension, for example, is going to help a child who does not have a repertoire of word-attack skills.

What Level of Corrective Work Is Required?

After identifying the learning problem, you should try to determine its probable cause. There are many; some reside within learners, some are with the classroom and school, and others are external to school. You need to recognize this, without at the same time using it as an excuse to justify continued poor achievement.

Generally speaking, we may sort children's learning problems into three levels of complexity. The simplest are those that you can handle within the classroom.

For instance, a child is absent from school just as you are teaching the class how to multiply fractions. When the child returns, spend some individual time with him, and he will soon be multiplying fractions as well as his classmates. Most learning difficulties are of this level of complexity. All that is required is that you be alert and observant, and that you care enough about individual children to help them overcome minor hurdles in their learning.

A second level of complexity of learning problems requires more time or more specialized instruction than you are able to provide in the classroom. Children with such specific learning difficulties have, for one reason or another, not been able to respond satisfactorily to regular classroom group instruction. For example, a child may have a vision problem, partially corrected by special lenses. Because the child has experienced the problem all her life, however, she has accumulated learning deficits that she now needs to overcome. You do not have time to provide such corrective instruction in class. Thus, the child is pulled out of the regular class for special instruction targeted on the needed work. When she is able to function on a par with her classmates, the corrective work is terminated.

Occasionally, you will encounter children with learning difficulties that far exceed the complexity of the previous two types. In these cases, the learning problem is often a symptom of some deeply rooted physical, neurological, or psychological disorder. Problems of this type may often exceed the professional competence of both you and your school's remedial teacher. Intensive one-to-one tutoring is not likely to be fruitful because such instruction targets the symptoms rather than the cause of the difficulty. That is, the learning problem is a manifestation of some other, less-apparent problem. Children with learning difficulties of this magnitude require the highly specialized psychological, diagnostic, and corrective services of a psychoeducation clinic.

It is your responsibility, therefore, to diagnose learning difficulties in accordance with their complexity and to act appropriately in each case. You will attend to by far the greatest number of learning difficulties in class on an ongoing basis. A few children may need more intensive corrective work than you have time or skills to provide. You would refer these children to the school remedial teacher for special tutoring for a short time each day until they have overcome their problem. If such teachers are not available, you must make some other arrangement to provide these children with the needed individual help—perhaps by contacting parents or guardians, aides, or volunteers. Your responsibility to children with the most severe learning difficulties is to see that an appropriate referral is made. This involves consulting with the principal, parents or guardians, and the person in charge of your district's special services.

Your professional judgment and competence as a reflective decision maker are always tested in sorting out the severity of learning difficulties. You cannot assume that you can attend to all learning problems in the context of your busy classroom. On the other hand, you cannot refer all children with learning problems to someone else. You develop your skills of diagnostic assessment and corrective instruction through experience, technical preparation, and maturity as a professional.

GRADING AND MARKING

If conditions were ideal (which they are not), and if teachers did their job perfectly well (which many of us do not), then all students would receive top marks (the ultimate in mastery or quality learning). Were that the case, then there would be less need to talk here about grading and marking. [Believing that letter grades do not reflect the nature of young children's developmental progress, most school districts hold off using letter grades until children are in at least the third grade or even the sixth grade, and instead favor using developmental checklists and narratives (Lake & Kafka, 1996).] Mastery learning implies that some end point of learning is attainable, but there probably is no end point. In any case, because conditions for teaching are never ideal and we teachers are mere humans, let us discuss this topic of grading.

The term *achievement* appears frequently throughout this text. What exactly does this term mean? Achievement means *accomplishment*, but which—accomplishment of anticipated outcomes (that is, instructional objectives) against preset standards, or simply any accomplishment? Most teachers probably choose the former, where they subjectively establish a standard that students must meet to receive a certain mark or grade for an assignment, project, test, quarter, semester, or course. Such teachers, then, measure achievement by degrees of accomplishment.

Preset standards are usually expressed in percentages (degrees of accomplishment) needed for marks or A-B-C grades. If no student achieves the standard required for the top mark, an A, for example, then no student receives an A. On the other hand, if all students meet the preset standard, then all receive As. Determining student marks and grades on the basis of preset standards is referred to as *criterion-referenced grading,* and for elementary school teaching it is the *only* sensible basis by which to arrive at student marks or grades.

Although criterion-referenced (or competency-based) grading is based on preset standards, norm-referenced grading measures the relative accomplishment of individuals in the group (e.g., one classroom of fourth graders) or in a larger group (e.g., all fourth graders) by comparing and ranking students. This is commonly known as "grading on a curve." Because it encourages competition and discourages cooperative learning, *most educators now do not recommend using norm-referenced grading* to determine student grades. Norm-referenced grading is educationally dysfunctional. For your personal interest, after several years of teaching, you can produce frequency-distribution studies of grades you have given over a period of time, but *do not* base student grades on such a curve. That you should *always* grade and report in reference to learning criteria, and never "on a curve," is well supported by research studies and authorities on the matter (Guskey, 1996; Stiggins, 2001). Tie grades for student achievement to performance levels and determine them on the basis of each student's achievement toward preset standards, that is, on your anticipated outcomes or objectives (as discussed in Chapter 5). This approach implies that effective teaching and learning result in high grades ("A"s) or marks for most students. In fact, when using a mastery concept, students must accomplish the objectives before being allowed to proceed to the next learning task (or to the next grade level). *The philosophy of teachers who favor criterion-referenced procedures recognizes individual potential.* Such teachers accept the challenge of finding learning strategies to help children progress from where they are to the next designated level. Instead of wondering how Juan compares with Sean, you instead compare what Juan could do yesterday and what he can do today and how well these performances compare to your preset standard.

Most school districts use some sort of combination of norm-referenced and criterion-referenced data. Sometimes both kinds of information are useful. For example, students' sixth-grade report cards might indicate how they are meeting certain criteria, such as mastering addition of fractions. Another entry might show that this mastery is expected, however, in the fifth grade. Both criterion- and norm-referenced data may be communicated to parents or guardians as well as to students. Use appropriate procedures: a criterion-referenced approach to show whether students can accomplish a task, and if so, to what degree, and a norm-referenced approach to show how well they perform compared to the larger group to which they belong.

Determining Grades

When determining achievement grades for student performance, you must make several important and professional decisions. Although in a few schools, and for certain classes or assignments, only marks such as E, S, and I or "pass/no pass" are used, percentages of accomplishment and letter grades are used for most intermediate grades and higher (Lake & Kafka, 1996). To reflect each student's progress toward meeting state curriculum standards, many elementary schools now use numeral marks (see Figure 7.4).

At the start of the school term, explain your marking and grading policies *first to yourself,* then to your students, and to their parents and guardians either at "back-to-school night" or by a written explanation students take home, or both. Share sample scoring and grading rubrics with both students and parents/guardians.

Be as objective as possible when converting your interpretation of a student's accomplishments to a letter grade. For criteria for A-B-C grades (or for 1-2-3 numerical marks), select a percentage standard, such as 90 percent for an A, 80 percent for a B, 70 percent for a C, and 60 percent for a D. Cutoff percentages used are your decision, although the school may have established guidelines you are expected to follow.

FIGURE 7.4
Sample rubric for numerical reporting of grade-level standards

5 = exceeds grade-level standards proficiency expectation

4 = proficiency level expectation

3 = basic proficiency expectation

2 = below basic performance expectation

1 = far below basic performance expectation

The parent/guardian and teacher conference allows parents to ask questions of the teacher and for the teacher to convey what their children are actually doing, what their needs seem to be, and what the adults might do at home to assist. The conference also enables the teacher to become aware of the adult's attitudes toward their children, the home, and the school. Some teachers, usually later in the school year, incorporate the use of student-planned and -led three-way conferences that, as shown in the photograph, involve the student, the child's parents or guardians, and the teacher.

Krista Greco/Merrill

Build your grading policy around degrees of accomplishment rather than failure, where students proceed from one accomplishment to the next. This is continuous promotion, not necessarily the promotion of students from one grade level to the next, but within the classroom. (However, some schools have eliminated grade-level designations and, instead use the concept of continuous promotion from the time students enter the school through their graduation or exit from it.)

Assessment and Grading: Not Synonymous Terms

Remember that "assessment" and "grading" are *not* synonymous. Assessment implies collecting information from a variety of sources, including measurement techniques and subjective observations. These data, then, become your basis for arriving at a final grade, which in effect is a final value judgment. Grades are one aspect of evaluation only and are intended to communicate educational progress to students and to their parents or guardians. To validly indicate that progress, you *must* use a variety of sources of data to determine a student's final mark or grade.

Decide beforehand your policy about makeup work. Students will be absent and will miss assignments and tests, so it is best to clearly communicate to students and to their parents or guardians your policies about late assignments and missed tests.

REPORTING STUDENT PROGRESS IN ACHIEVEMENT

One of your responsibilities as a classroom teacher is to report student progress in achievement to parents or guardians as well as to the school administration for record keeping. As stated earlier, some schools report student progress and effort as well as achievement. As described in the discussions that follow, reporting is done in at least two, and sometimes more than two, ways.

Schools periodically issue progress reports generally from four to six times a year, depending on the school, its purpose, and its type of scheduling. Progress and grade reports may be distributed during an advisory period or may be mailed to students' homes, or parents and guardians may pick them up from the school or online. This report represents an achievement report and grade (formative assessment). The final report of the semester is also the semester grade, and for courses only one semester long, it also is the final grade (summative assessment). In essence, the first and sometimes second reports are progress notices, with the semester grade being transferred to students' permanent records.

In addition to academic achievement in the various subject areas, you must report students' social behaviors (classroom conduct) while in your classroom. Whichever reporting form you use, you must separate your assessment of students' social behaviors from their academic achievement. In most instances, there may be a location on the reporting form for you to check whether students have met basic grade-level standards.

TEACHING IN PRACTICE The Experience of Two Teachers in Planning for the First Student-Progress Report and Parent/Guardian Conferences

With the school year barely under way, first-year teachers Ms. Baxter and Mr. Bond were confronted with the task of preparing student-progress reports, popularly known as *report cards*. They were aware that elementary school teachers across the nation were also involved in this process, which has become almost a ritual during early November. Because a considerable amount of emphasis had been placed on the importance of reporting student progress, they were fully aware of its major purposes:

1. To inform children of their progress.
2. To provide parents and guardians with an assessment of children's learning strengths and weaknesses.
3. To serve as a two-way mode of communication between home and school.

They were also aware of the several basic types of student-progress reports used in elementary schools. The most common are numerical or alphabetical ratings, written narratives, checklists, portfolios, and parent/guardian–teacher conferences. In actual practice, most schools use a combination of all of these.

Establishing Parent and Guardian Contacts

Both Ms. Baxter and Mr. Bond were glad to have had the opportunity to meet most of their students' parents and guardians at the "Back to School" night held a month ago in their respective schools. Having had that experience makes them now feel a little less trepidation about communicating with parents and guardians about their children's progress.

Ms. Baxter Prepares for Her First Parent/Guardian Conference

The parent/guardian conference is more prevalent as a way of reporting to parents and guardians of children of grades K–3 than it is for children of grade 4 and beyond. This is partly because it is easier to explain progress in beginning reading in a conference setting than on a report card. You can do a better job of conveying to parents and guardians what their children are actually doing, what their needs are, and what the adults can do at home to assist. The conference also enables you to become aware of parents' and guardians' attitudes toward their children, the home, and the school. This information helps you establish the best possible learning program for children and select appropriate materials for individuals.

Many primary-grades teachers conduct parent/guardian conferences during the first student-progress reporting period and write narrative reports during the remainder of the school year. Some teachers alternate parent/guardian conferences and written reports. Frequently, the first parent/guardian conference follows an "open house," when parents and guardians are invited to attend school, meet the teachers, and listen to an explanation of the school program. This was the procedure at Westhill Elementary School, where Ms. Baxter taught. The school principal began planning with the teachers early in September for the November open house and parent/guardian conferences. She stressed the importance of involving parents and guardians in their children's education. She made the following points:

1. Have children prepare and maintain a portfolio with samples of their schoolwork. Include for each subject representative products that show children's progress over time.
2. Write anecdotes that objectively describe children's behavior.
3. Interpret children's performance on readiness and achievement tests. Be sure to specify children's performance level in terms of their potential.

The school's principal also offered helpful hints on conducting a parent/guardian conference:

1. Begin on a positive note.
2. Try to make parents and guardians feel comfortable.
3. Emphasize children's strengths.
4. Be specific about any learning difficulties children may be experiencing.
5. Provide constructive suggestions about ways parents and guardians can assist in helping their children learn. To this end the principal ensured that relevant materials and resources for materials were available and posted in the teacher's lounge.
6. Listen to what parents and guardians have to say; be receptive to their suggestions.
7. *Never* compare one child with another.
8. Close on a positive note and with a plan of action.

Ms. Baxter discovered that her parent/guardian conferences were very rewarding. The conferences were scheduled over a period of 2 weeks, during which the children were dismissed an hour early. The open house had tested her ability to describe for parents and guardians the type of work the children would be doing that year. She began to appreciate the time she had spent in determining goals for the school year and in getting acquainted with the textbooks and other instructional resources. These early planning activities had provided her with a frame of reference that made her reporting task much easier than it otherwise would have been. As a result, she felt more secure in arranging for parents' and guardians' constructive involvement in their children's learning program.

Mr. Bond Prepares for His First Student-Progress Report

Mr. Bond received student-progress report forms early in September. The school principal emphasized that teachers should keep a work folder for every child. He also suggested that in certain instances, teachers might find it useful to schedule a parent/guardian conference to inform the parents/guardians of children's progress. The work samples would prove worthwhile in such instances.

Mr. Bond was disappointed that the form did not provide for student self-assessment. He made the decision to improvise his own system for this purpose. He developed a simple report form that would allow children to self-assess their "school habits" Figure 7.5). He began discussing self-assessment with children as soon as they had demonstrated that they could work together as a group. He told them that he would discuss the form with each of them personally, at which time he would ask them to complete it. He prepared an enlargement of the form for a wall chart, and gave all students a copy for their notebooks.

When he began to confer with the children about their self-assessments, he learned that some of them were realistic in their ratings and others were not. In each instance, Mr. Bond was able to have a candid discussion with the child about behavior that is important to personal, social, and academic development. He felt much closer to each child following the discussion. He also spent a few minutes each week discussing the student-progress report form with them. He wanted them to know ahead of time the standards on which he was evaluating them.

Mr. Bond found that the planning he had done at the beginning of the year had been of great value to

My School Habits				
	Always	Usually	Seldom	Never
I assume responsibility.				
I contribute to the group.				
I work well with others.				
I play well with others.				
I do my best in my studies.				
I take care of materials.				
I follow school rules.				

FIGURE 7.5
Mr. Bond's form for student self-assessment

him in completing the student-progress reports. He followed the advice of a colleague and began writing the reports a couple of weeks before they were due. He was very glad he had followed this advice instead of waiting until the last minute.

Mr. Bond sent the student-progress reports home on schedule and was pleasantly surprised to learn that many parents and guardians were pleased with their children's performance. He formed this conclusion on the basis of adults' written remarks on the returned forms. Two parents requested follow-up conferences; Mr. Bond scheduled them during after-school hours. He found that these personal contacts helped him establish a closer rapport with the parents. By the end of the year, he knew all of his students' parents or guardians, many of them on a first-name basis. Mr. Bond made a mental note to himself to look into the prospect for next year of having student-led three-way (that is, student–parent/guardian–teacher) conferences.

SUMMARY

Assessment of student learning is an integral and ongoing factor in teaching and learning; consequently, in this chapter we have emphasized the importance of including the following in your teaching:

- Use a variety of instruments to collect a body of evidence to most reliably assess children's learning, focusing on their individual development.
- Involve students in self-assessment; keep children informed of their progress.
- Be sure to base your assessments only on material you have actually taught.
- Strive to assess all students objectively and impartially.

The exponential rate of advances taking place in technology is creating rapid changes in assessment practices. As a classroom teacher, to keep your own program of assessment of student learning most effective and efficient, you will need to actively plan to stay abreast of the developments.

STUDY QUESTIONS AND ADDITIONAL ACTIVITIES

1. The practice of kindergarten retention seems to be increasing. Find research evidence that indicates that the retention of a child in kindergarten has any positive value. Are there options to retention? Share your findings with others in your class. Do you believe there is value in retention of any child in any grade? Share your opinion with others.

2. During a parent/guardian conference, how would you respond to a parent or guardian who is critical of a teacher colleague, critical of the school, or critical of other children in your class? Or, one who is critical of you? Invite two or three experienced elementary school teachers to your class and have them share difficult questions they have received from parents and guardians and how they responded. Role-play a parent/guardian conference with one of your classmates. Include parent/guardian questions that challenge the teacher to provide a thoughtful, discreet response.

3. For a specific unit of study, develop the tools for the diagnostic, formative, and summative assessment of student learning of that unit, using some of the assessment techniques and procedures found in Table 7.1. Include at least one tool that assesses each of the following three categories of outcomes: cognitive gain, affective change, and psychomotor development.

4. If you are now student teaching or a teacher-intern, or if you have contact with a classroom teacher, ask that teacher to explain to you the local policies regarding the use of standardized tests. Find out when they are given, which tests are used, what procedures the teacher uses in administering the tests, how they are scored, and what use is made of the results. Share your findings in your methods class.

5. Assume that you are the teacher of a child who has been achieving satisfactorily in mathematics. In correcting the child's written work, you notice that the child answered incorrectly every problem involving dividing fractions. How would you go about finding out what the difficulty is? How would your approach differ if you discovered that *all* your students answered such problems incorrectly?

6. Visit an elementary school in your area to become familiar with the kinds of educational and psychological referral services available for children with learning problems.

7. Should teachers' effectiveness be judged by the scores that their students obtain on standardized tests near the end of the school year? Should their salaries be dependent on their student's scores on the state tests? Explain your response.

8. Describe any student learning activities or situations that you believe should *not* be graded but should or could be used for assessment of student learning.

9. One recent study reports that 29 percent of teachers surveyed included "effort" when assigning grades, 8 percent included "behavior," 4 percent included "cooperation," and 8 percent included "attendance" (Marzano, 2002). Explain why you believe that a teacher should or should not include these factors when determining and reporting a student's academic grades or marks.

10. Investigate various ways that schools housing some combination of grades K–8 are experimenting with assessing and reporting student achievement. Share and critique your findings with your classmates.

WEB SITES RELATED TO CONTENT OF THIS CHAPTER

- Academy for Educational Development *www.aed.org*
- ASPIRA Parents for Educational Excellence *www.aspira.org/Apex.html*
- Family Support America *www.familysupportamerica.org*
- Federal Citizen Information Center *www.pueblo.gsa.gov*
- *Grady Profile www.aurbach.com*
- Institute for Educational Leadership *www.iel.org*
- Mexican American Legal Defense and Educational Fund *www.maldef.org*
- National Coalition of Parental Involvement *ncpie.org*
- Reading Is Fundamental, Inc. *www.rif.org*
- Spelling program at *www.spellingtime.com*
- Writing assessment Toolkit98 *www.nwrel.org/assessment/ToolKit98.asp*

FOR FURTHER READING

Baldwin, D. (2004). A guide to standardized writing assessment. *Educational Leadership, 62*(2), 72–75.

Benson, B. P., & Barnett, S. P. (2005). *Student-led conferencing using showcase portfolios* (2nd ed.). Thousand Oaks, CA: Corwin Press.

Bielenberg, B., & Fillmore, L. W. (2005). The English they need for the test. *Educational Leadership, 62*(4), 45–49.

Brookhart, S. M. (2004). *Grading.* Upper Saddle River, NJ: Merrill/Prentice Hall.

Diehm, C. (2004). From worn-out to web-based: Better student portfolios. *Phi Delta Kappan, 85,* 792–795.

Elmore, R. F. (2004). Performance vs. attainment. *Harvard Education Letter, 20*(5), 7–8.

Glanfield, F., Bush, W. S., & Stenmark, J. K. (Eds.) (2003). *Mathematical assessment: A practical handbook for grades K–2.* Reston, VA: National Council of Teachers of Mathematics.

Hong, G., & Raudenbush, S. (2005). Effects of kindergarten retention policy on children's cognitive growth in reading and mathematics. *Educational Evaluation and Policy Analysis, 27*(3), 205–224.

Jacksec, C. M., III (2005). *The difficult parent.* Thousand Oaks, CA: Corwin Press.

Lantz, H. B., Jr. (2004). *Rubrics for assessing student achievement in science grades K–12.* Thousand Oaks, CA: Corwin Press.

Reeves, D. B. (2004). The case against the zero. *Phi Delta Kappa, 84,* 324–325.

Rothman, R. (2006). (In)formative assessments. *Harvard Education Letter, 22*(6), 1–3.

Sadker, D., & Zittleman, K. (2004). Test anxiety: Are students failing tests—or are tests failing students? *Phi Delta Kappan, 85,* 740–744, 751.

Sadler, B., & Andrade, H. (2004). The writing rubric. *Educational Leadership, 62*(2), 48–52.

Stenmark, J. K., & Bush, W. S. (Eds.). (2001). *Mathematical assessment: A practical handbook for grades 3–4.* Reston, VA: National Council of Teachers of Mathematics.

Stevens, B. A., & Tollafield, A. (2003). Creating comfortable and productive parent/teacher conferences. *Phi Delta Kappan, 84*(7), 521–524.

Wherry, J. H. (2005). Working with parents: New teachers' greatest challenge. *Principal, 85*(2), 6.

Chapter 8

Organizing and Grouping Children for Quality Learning

INTASC Principles	PRAXIS III Domains	NBPTS Standards
• The teacher uses an understanding of individual and group motivation and behavior to create a learning environment that encourages positive social interaction, active engagement in learning, and self-motivation. (Principle 5)	• Creating an Environment for Student Learning (Domain B)	• Multiple Paths to Knowledge • Respect for diversity

Rather than diluting standards and expectations, believing in the learning potential of every student, exemplary elementary schools and teachers are those who are able to effectively modify the key variables of time, methodology, and grouping to help each individual student achieve mastery of the curriculum. These variables can be attuned or modified to better accommodate each learner's needs. One advantage of the self-contained classroom is that the teacher is in control of the time spent on a given lesson or unit of study and basically is free to modify time however the teacher deems necessary. Ways of varying the methodology are addressed throughout the book. In this chapter, the focus is on ways of grouping children to enhance positive interaction and quality learning for each child.

In the most effective instructional environments, during any given week or even day of school, a student might experience a succession of group settings. Ways of grouping students for quality instruction is the general topic of this chapter, from personalized and individualized instruction to working with dyads, small groups, and large groups. You also will learn more on how to ensure equality in the classroom, how to use assignments and homework, and how to coordinate various forms of independent and small-group, project-based study. The chapter ends with the presentation of a collection of motivational teaching strategies with ideas for lessons, interdisciplinary teaching, transcultural studies, and student projects.

Project-based learning teaches kids the collaborative and critical thinking abilities they'll need to compete.

Source: Bob Pearlman (2006, p. 51)

In the most effective learning environment, during any given school day, an individual child might experience a succession of settings, from whole groups and small groups to dyads and learning alone. Using small groups, as shown here, can enhance children's opportunities to learn group-work skills and assume greater control over their own learning.

Anne Vega/Merrill

ANTICIPATED OUTCOMES

Specifically, upon completion of this chapter you should be able to:

1. Describe the meaning of *mastery (quality) learning* and its implications for elementary school teaching.
2. Explain the advantages and disadvantages of various ways of grouping children for quality learning.
3. Explain how the teacher can personalize the instruction to ensure success for each student.
4. Demonstrate an understanding of the meaning and importance of equity in the classroom and how it can be achieved and maintained.
5. Demonstrate an awareness of appropriate curriculum options and instructional practices for specific groups of learners.
6. Demonstrate a theoretical and practical understanding of how to effectively use each of these instructional strategies: assignments, homework, written and oral reports, cooperative learning, learning centers, problem-based learning, and projects.
7. Demonstrate your developing understanding of the meaning of *developmentally appropriate practice*.
8. Demonstrate developing skills in recognizing, celebrating, and building on student diversity.

MASTERY LEARNING AND PERSONALIZED INSTRUCTION

Learning is an individual or personal experience. Yet as a classroom teacher you will be expected to work effectively with students on other than an individual basis—perhaps 25 or more at a time. Much has been written on the importance of *differentiating the instruction*—of individualizing or personalizing the instruction for learners. Virtually all the research concerning effective instructional practice emphasizes greater individualization of instruction (Carroll, 1994). We know of the individuality of the learning experience, and we know that although some children of elementary school age are primarily verbal learners, many more are primarily visual, tactile, or kinesthetic learners. As the teacher, though, you find yourself in the difficult position of simultaneously ministering to many separate and individual learners with individual learning capacities, styles, challenges, and preferences.

To individualize the instruction, exemplary schools and teachers use a variety of strategies—small learning communities, advisories, exploratory programs, cooperative learning groups, project-based learning, personalized learning plans, and independent study—to respond to individual student competencies, interests, needs, and abilities. They may also use nonconventional scheduling so that teaching teams can vary the length of time in instructional periods and also vary the size of instructional groups and the learning strategies within a given time period.

Common sense tells us that student achievement in learning is related to both the quality of attention and the length of time given to learning tasks. Building on a model developed earlier by John Carroll (1963), Benjamin Bloom (1987) developed the concept of individualized instruction called *mastery learning*, saying that students need sufficient time on task (i.e., engaged time) to master content before moving on to new content.

Today's Emphasis: Quality Learning for Every Child

Emphasis today is on mastery of content, or quality learning, for every child. By mastery of content, we mean that the student demonstrates his or her use of what has been learned. Because of that emphasis and research that indicates that quality learning programs positively affect achievement, the importance of the concept of mastery learning has resurfaced and is becoming firmly entrenched. For example, the nationwide approach of standards-based instruction relies on a goal-driven curriculum model with instruction that focuses on the construction of individual knowledge through mastery and assessment of student learning against the anticipated outcomes. In some instances, unfortunately, attention may be on the mastery of only minimum competencies; thus, in those instances students may not always be encouraged to work and learn to the maximum of their talents and abilities.

Assumptions about Mastery, or Quality, Learning

Today's concept of mastery, or quality, learning is based on certain assumptions (Battistini, 1995; Horton, 1981):

1. Mastery learning can ensure that students experience success at each level of the instructional process—experiencing success at each level provides incentive and motivation for further learning.
2. Mastery of content, or quality learning, is possible for each learner.
3. Most learning is sequential and logical.
4. Most desired learning outcomes can be specified in terms of observable and measurable performance.
5. Although all students can achieve mastery, to master a particular content some may require more time than others—the teacher and the school must provide for this difference in time need to complete a task successfully.
6. For quality learning to occur, it is the instruction that must be modified and adapted, not the students—traditional tracking or ability grouping do not fit.

Elements of Any Mastery Learning Model: The Cycle of Teaching

The essence of mastery (quality) learning is the *cycle of teaching* and contains the following elements:

1. Clearly defined target learning objectives with preset mastery performance expectations

2. Preassessment of the learner's present knowledge
3. Instructional component, with a rich variety of choices and options for students
4. Frequent practice, reinforcement, and comprehension checks (a form of *formative assessment*), with corrective instruction at each step of the way to keep the learner on track
5. Postassessment (*summative assessment*) to determine the extent of student mastery of the learning objectives.

Strategies for Personalizing the Instruction Now!

You can immediately provide personalized instruction by:

- Starting study of a topic from where the students are in terms of what they know (or think they know) and what they want to know about the topic (see "think-pair-share" discussed in Chapter 2; see also KWL and similar strategies in Chapter 5)
- Providing students with choices from a rich variety of learning pathways, resources, and hands-on experiences to learn more about the topic
- Providing multiple instructional approaches (i.e., using multilevel instruction in a variety of settings, from learning alone to whole-class instruction)
- Empowering students with responsibility for decision making, reflection, and self-assessment

> *As long as we let students define what is achievable on their own terms, almost anything is possible.*
>
> **—Katie Wood Ray (2004)**

ACCOMMODATING STUDENT DIFFERENCES: RECOGNIZING AND WORKING WITH SPECIFIC LEARNERS

You are probably quite aware that the variety of individual differences among students in your classroom requires that you use teaching strategies that to some degree or another accommodate those differences. To do that well, you should be able to answer yes to each of the four questions of Figure 8.1.

The importance of building your skills in each of the four areas or categories represented by those questions is likely now quite apparent to you and is a process that begins now during your teacher training and will continue unceasingly throughout your professional career. Specific guidelines that follow will serve as helpful reminders, but are only that—reminders. More detailed instruction will likely follow in special courses during your teacher training. If by then you are still

> • Do I establish a classroom climate in which *all* children feel welcome, that they can learn, and that I support them in doing so?
> • Do I use techniques that emphasize cooperative and social–interactive learning?
> • Do I build on students' individual experiences, conceptions, learning styles, learning capacities, and learning modalities?
> • Do I use techniques that have proven successful for students of specific differences?

FIGURE 8.1
Questions for teacher reflection about planning and accommodating for student differences for personalizing instruction

unclear as to the meaning of any of the four questions, then you need to investigate the topic to a depth beyond that provided by this book (see the suggested readings, for example, at the end of this chapter).

Children with Special Needs

Children with special needs (referred to also as children with exceptionalities) include those with disabling conditions or impairments in any one or more of the following categories: mental, hearing, speech or language, visual, emotional, orthopedic, autism, traumatic brain injury, other health impairment, or specific learning disabilities. To receive special education services, a child must have a disability in one or more of the categories, and by reason thereof, the child needs special education and related services. In other words, not all children who have a disability need services available via special education. For example, a child with a hearing impairment would be entitled to special services when the impairment is so severe that the child cannot understand what is being said, even when the child is equipped with a hearing aid.

Although the guidelines represented by the paragraphs that follow are important for teaching all students, they are especially important for working with special-needs children.

• Adapt and modify materials and procedures to the special needs of each student. For example, a student who has extreme difficulty sitting still for more than a few minutes will need planned changes in learning activities. When establishing student seating arrangements in the classroom, give preference to students according to their special needs. Try to incorporate into lessons activities that engage all learning modalities—visual, auditory, tactile, and kinesthetic. Be flexible in your classroom procedures.
• Exercise your withitness, monitoring students for signs of restlessness, frustration, anxiety, and off-task behaviors. Be ready to reassign individual learners to different activities as the situation warrants.

- Familiarize yourself with exactly what the special needs of each learner are.
- Have all students maintain assignments for the week or some other period of time in an assignment book or in a folder kept in their notebooks. Post assignments in a special place in the classroom (and perhaps on the school's Web site) and frequently remind students of assignments and deadlines.
- Maintain consistency in your expectations and in your responses. Special-needs learners, particularly, can become frustrated when they do not understand a teacher's expectations and when they cannot depend on a teacher's reactions.
- Plan interesting activities to bridge learning, activities that help students connect what is being learned with their real-world experiences.
- Provide for and teaching toward student success. Offer students activities and experiences that ensure each learner's success and mastery at some level. Use of student portfolios can give evidence of progress and help in building student confidence and self-esteem.
- Provide help in the organization of students' learning. For example, give instruction in the organization of notes and notebooks. Have a three-hole punch available in the classroom so students can place their papers into their notebooks immediately, thus avoiding disorganization and the loss of papers. Ask students to read their notes aloud to each other in small groups, thereby aiding their recall and understanding and encouraging them to take notes for meaning rather than for rote learning. Encourage and provide for peer support, peer tutoring or coaching, and cross-age teaching. Ensure the special-needs learner is included in all class activities to the fullest extent possible.
- Provide high structure and clear expectations by defining the learning objectives in behavioral terms. Teach your students the correct procedures for everything. Break complex learning into simpler components, moving from the most concrete to the abstract, rather than the other way around. Check frequently for student understanding of instructions and procedures and for comprehension of content.
- Provide scaffolded instruction, that is, give each student as much guided or coached practice as time allows. Provide time in class for students to work on assignments and projects. During this time, you can monitor the work of each student while looking for misconceptions, thus ensuring students get started on the right track.

TEACHING IN PRACTICE Help! No Aide Today

Of the 25 children in Hannah's kindergarten class, one, Aliya, is a special-needs child with multiple disabilities, including Down's syndrome and severe hearing loss. On this day, Aliya's aide failed to come to school. The aide also failed to notify the school that she would be absent. Today, Hannah is the only adult in class. Aliya needs to go to the bathroom now! What would you do if you were Hannah?

CLASSROOM VIGNETTE A Teachable Moment

While Elina was reciting, she had a little difficulty with her throat (due to a cold) and stumbled over some words. The second-grade teacher jokingly said, "That's okay Elina, you must have a frog in your throat."

Quickly, Mariya, a recent immigrant from the Ukraine, asked, "How could she have a frog in her throat?" Missing this teachable moment, the teacher ignored Mariya's question and continued with the lesson.

Children of Diversity and Differences

You must quickly determine the language and ethnic groups represented by the students in your classroom. A major problem for recent newcomers, as well as some ethnic groups, is learning a second (or third or fourth) language. Although in many schools it is not uncommon for more than half the students to come from homes where the spoken language is not English, standard English is a necessity in most communities of this country if a person is to become vocationally successful and enjoy a full life. Learning to communicate reasonably well in English can take an immigrant child at least a year and probably longer and from 3 to 7 years to catch up academically in English. By default, then, an increasing percentage of public school teachers in the United States are teachers of English language learning (ELL). Helpful to the success of teaching students who are ELLs are the demonstration of respect for students' cultural backgrounds, long-term teacher–student cohorts (such as in looping), and the use of active and cooperative learning.

Specific techniques recommended for teaching ELL students include (Curtin, 2006; Fitzgerald & Graves, 2005; Gray & Fleischman, 2004):

- Assisting the child in learning how to deal with the anxiety caused by "language shock," that is, from not knowing or understanding well the language of the child's new country.
- Allowing more time for learning activities than one normally would.
- Allowing time for translation by a classroom aide or by a classmate and allowing time for dialogue to clarify meaning, encouraging the students to transfer into English what they already know in their native language.
- Avoiding jargon or idioms that might be misunderstood.
- Building on what the students already have experienced and know.
- Dividing complex or extended language discourse into smaller, more manageable units.
- Encouraging student writing, such as by using student journals or by using blogs.
- Giving directions in a variety of ways.
- Giving special attention to keywords that convey meaning and writing them on the board.
- Helping students learn the vocabulary. Assist the ELL student in learning two vocabulary sets: the regular English vocabulary needed for learning and the new vocabulary introduced by the subject content. For example, while learning science a student is dealing with both the regular English language vocabulary and the special vocabulary of science.

- Involving parents or guardians or siblings. Students whose primary language is not English may have other differences about which you will also need to become knowledgeable. These differences are related to culture, customs, family life, and expectations. To be most successful in working with language-minority students, you should learn as much as possible about each student. Parents (or guardians) of new immigrant children are usually truly concerned about the education of their children and may be very interested in cooperating with you in any way possible.

TPW Video Classroom

Series: General Methods

Module 2: Student Learning in Diverse Classrooms

Video 1: Incorporating the Home Experience of Culturally Diverse Students

---

- Planning for and using all learning modalities, by using auditory, visual, tactile, and kinesthetic learning activities.
- Presenting instruction that is concrete (least abstract), and that includes the most direct learning experiences possible.
- Providing scaffolded reading experiences, that is, a framework of activities for use in prereading (such as preteaching vocabulary and predicting outcomes), during-reading (such as guided reading and silent reading activities), and postreading (such as playacting and writing), of any genre of text.
- Reading written directions aloud, and then writing the directions on the board.
- Reducing the cognitive load while still maintaining high expectations for the learning of each child.
- Speaking clearly and naturally but at a slower than normal pace.
- Treating ELLs, their homes and communities, and their primary languages and cultures with respect and as important resources.
- Using a variety of examples and observable models.
- Using simplified vocabulary without talking down to students.
- Using small-group cooperative learning. Cooperative learning strategies are particularly effective with language-minority students because they provide opportunities for students to produce language in a setting less threatening than speaking before the entire class.
- Using the benefits afforded by modern technology. For example, computer networking allows students to write and communicate with peers from around the world as well as participate in "publishing" their classroom work.

Little Wonder That English Is _Not_ an Easy Language to Learn

Consider the paradoxes found in the following sentences.

A bass was hanging from the top of the bass violin.

Can you see what is wound around the wound?

She was too close to the window to close it.

Since there is not time like the present, we decided it was time to present the present.

The nomad decided to desert his dessert in the desert.

To lead one might need to get the lead out.

When we walked by, the dove dove into the bushes.

With a garden, one can produce produce.

Can you think of or offer others?

How does a teacher help children handle these discrepancies in meanings of words that are spelled identically?

Additional Guidelines for Working with Students of Diverse Backgrounds

To be compatible with, and be able to teach, students who come from backgrounds different from yours, you need to believe that, given adequate support, all children *can* learn—regardless of gender, social class, physical characteristics, language, religion, and ethnic or cultural backgrounds. You also need to develop special skills that include those in the following guidelines.

- Build the learning around students' individual learning styles. To the extent possible, personalize learning for each student, much like what is done by using the IEP with special-needs learners.
- Establish and maintain high expectations, although not necessarily the same expectations, for each child. Both you and your students must understand that intelligence is not a fixed entity, but a set of characteristics that—through a feeling of "I can" and with proper coaching—can be developed.
- Teach individuals by using a variety of strategies to achieve an objective or by using a number of different objectives at the same time (multilevel teaching).
- Use techniques that emphasize collaborative and cooperative learning—that deemphasize competitive learning.

Children Who Are Gifted

Historically, educators have used the term *gifted* when referring to a person with identified exceptional ability in one or more academic areas and *talented* when referring to a person with exceptional ability in one or more of the visual or performing arts (Clark & Zimmerman, 1998). Today, however, the terms more often are used interchangeably (Callahan, 2001), which is how they are used for this book, that is, as if they are synonymous.

Sometimes, unfortunately, in the regular classroom gifted students are neglected (Feldhusen, 1998; Gross, 2000). At least some of the time, it is probably because there is no singularly accepted method for identification of these students. In other words, students who are gifted in some way or another may go unidentified as such. For placement in special classes or programs for the gifted, school districts traditionally have used grade point averages and standard intelligence quotient (IQ) scores. On the other hand, because IQ testing measures linguistic and logical/mathematical aspects of giftedness, it does not account for others and thus gifted students sometimes are unrecognized. They also are sometimes among the students most at risk of eventually dropping out of school (Saunders, 2003).

To work most effectively with gifted learners, their talents first must be identified. This can be done not only by using tests, rating scales, and auditions, but also by observations in the classroom, out of the classroom, and from knowledge about the student's life away from school. With those information sources in mind, indicators of superior intelligence are (Schwartz, 1997):

- A strong sense of self, pride, and worth
- Ability to assume adult roles and responsibilities at home or at work
- Ability to cope with school while living in poverty
- Ability to cope with school while living within dysfunctional families
- Ability to extrapolate knowledge to different circumstances
- Ability to lead others
- Ability to manipulate a symbol system
- Ability to reason by analogy
- Ability to retrieve and use stored knowledge to solve problems
- Ability to think and act independently
- Ability to think logically
- An understanding of one's cultural heritage
- Creativity and artistic ability

Guidelines for Working with Students with Special Gifts and Talents

When working in the regular classroom with a student who has special gifts and talents, you are advised to:

- Collaborate with the children in some planning of their personal objectives and activities for learning.
- Emphasize skills in critical thinking, problem solving, and inquiry.
- Identify and showcase the student's special gift or talent, while being careful to not embarrass the child.
- Involve the student in selecting and planning activities, encouraging the development of the child's leadership skills.
- Plan assignments and activities that challenge the children to the fullest of their abilities. This does not mean overloading them with homework or giving identical assignments to all students (see "tiered assignments" later in this chapter). Rather, carefully plan so students' time spent on assignments and activities is quality time spent on meaningful learning.
- Provide in-class seminars for students to discuss topics and problems they are pursuing individually or as members of a learning team.

- Provide independent and self-paced learning and dyad learning opportunities.
- Use curriculum compacting, a process that allows a student who already knows the material to pursue enriched or accelerated study (Willard-Holt, 2003). Plan and provide optional and voluntary enrichment activities. Learning centers, special projects, learning contracts, and computer and multimedia activities are excellent tools for provision of enriched learning activities.
- Use diagnostic assessments for reading level and subject content achievement so you are better able to prescribe objectives and activities for each student.

Meaningful Curriculum Options: Multiple Pathways to Success

Every child needs a challenging academic environment. Although grouping and tracking children based on interest and demonstrated ability is still practiced (such as reading groups, grade-level retention, accelerated groups, and special education placement), an overwhelming abundance of sources in the literature adamantly opposes the homogeneous grouping of students according to ability, or *curriculum tracking*, as it has long been known. Grouping and tracking do not seem to increase overall achievement of learning, but they do promote inequity (Schwartz, 2000). Tracking is acceptable when it is based on grouping students according to their interests or later on their vocational aspirations, but tracking students on the basis of race, intelligence, or social class is *not* acceptable and should not be practiced, in the classroom or schoolwide.

Because of what is now known about learning and intelligence, the trend today is to assume that every child, to some degree and in some area of learning and doing, has the potential for giftedness and to provide sufficient curriculum options, or multiple pathways, so each child can reach those potentials. That is the reason why, for example, in schools' mission statements (see Chapter 5) today there is usually reference to the school's belief that *all* students can succeed. Clearly, achievement in school increases, children learn more, enjoy learning, and remember more of what they have learned when the instruction is developmentally appropriate for the needs of the particular students and when individual learning capacities, styles, and modalities are identified and accommodated.

To provide relevant curriculum options, a trend in schools is to eliminate from the school curriculum what have traditionally been the lower and general curriculum tracks and instead provide curriculum options to ensure a positive environment with success for each and every child. While attempting to diminish the discriminatory and damaging effects on students believed caused by tracking and homogeneous ability grouping, educators have devised and are refining numerous other seemingly more productive ways of attending to student differences, of providing a more challenging but supportive learning environment, and of stimulating the talents and motivation of each and every student. Because the advantage gained from utilizing a combination of responsive practices concurrently is generally greater

- Adult advocacy relationships for each child
- Ensuring bilingual programs are intellectually stimulating and designed for integration with mainstream education
- Collaborative and cooperative learning opportunities in the classroom and school community
- Community service learning that is connected in some way to the academic program
- Curriculum compacting (an enriched or an accelerated study of the curriculum)
- Flexible block scheduling
- High expectation for each student
- Integration of appropriate technology into the curriculum
- Interdisciplinary learning and teaming
- Looping
- Mastery learning with instructional scaffolding
- Nongraded school
- Opportunity for academic help for every child
- Opportunity to skip a traditional grade level
- Peer and cross-age instruction or tutoring
- Personal problems assistance
- Personalized education planning and instruction
- Recovery opportunities
- Smaller learning communities
- Thematic instruction
- Ungraded or multiage grouping
- Within-class and across-discipline student-centered projects

FIGURE 8.2
Multiple pathways to success: Productive ways of attending to student differences, of providing a positive and challenging learning environment, and of stimulating the talents, interests, and motivation of each and every student

than is the gain from using any singular practice by itself, in many instances in a given school the practices overlap and are used simultaneously. These practices are shown in Figure 8.2

Children Who Take More Time but Are Willing to Try

Students who are slower to learn typically fall into one of two categories: (a) those who try to learn but simply need more time to do it, and (b) those who do not try, referred to variously as underachievers, recalcitrant, or reluctant learners. Practices that work well with students of one category are often not those that work well with those of the second—making life difficult for a teacher of 28 students, half who try and half who don't (Kellough, 1970). It is worse still for a teacher of a group of 25 or so students, some who try but need time, one or two who learn regardless, two or three who have special needs but not the same special needs, a few LEP students, and several who not only seem unwilling to try but who are also disruptive in the classroom. And, by the way, this last example is probably closer to reality for the vast majority of today's teachers.

> Just because a student is slow to learn doesn't mean the student is less intelligent; some students just plain take longer, for any number of reasons.

The following guidelines may be helpful when working with a child who is slow but willing to try:

- Adjust the instruction to the student's preferred learning style, which may be different from yours and from other students in the group.
- Being less concerned with the amount of content coverage than with the student's successful understanding of content that is covered. Teach toward mastery (although this may be antagonistic to modern emphasis on improved student scores on high-stakes assessment tests).
- Discover something the student does exceptionally well, or a special interest, and try to connect the child's learning with that.
- Emphasize basic communication skills, such as speaking, listening, reading, and writing, to ensure the child's skills in these areas are sufficient for learning the intended content.
- Get to know each student, at least well enough that you have understanding and empathy for where the child is coming from. For example, many children from high-poverty inner-city neighborhoods feel hopeless that they will be able to improve their lives (Bolland, 2003). Commit yourself to helping them understand the power of education in finding their way out of such feelings of hopelessness.
- Help the student learn content in small sequential steps with frequent checks for comprehension. Use instructional scaffolding.
- If necessary, help the child to improve his or her reading skills, such as pronunciation and word meanings.
- If using a single textbook be certain the reading level is adequate for the student; if it is not, then for that student use other more appropriate reading materials. Many exemplary teachers maintain a variety of optional texts in their classroom just for this purpose.
- Maximize the use of in-class, on-task work and cooperative learning, with close monitoring of the student's progress.

- Vary the instructional strategies, using a variety of activities to engage the visual, verbal, tactile, and kinesthetic modalities.
- When appropriate, use frequent positive reinforcement, with the intention of building the child's confidence and self-esteem.

Recalcitrant Learners

For working with recalcitrant learners, you can use many of the same guidelines from the preceding list, except you should understand that the reasons for these students' behaviors may be quite different from those for the other category of slow learners. Slower-learning students who are willing to try may be slow because of their learning style, because of genetic factors, or a combination of those and any number of other reasons. They are simply slower at learning. But they can and will learn. Recalcitrant learners, on the other hand, may be generally quick and bright thinkers but reluctant even to try because of improper support from home, a history of failure, a history of boredom with school, low confidence level for academic work, a poor self-concept, severe personal problems that distract from school, or any variety and combination of these and other reasons, many of which are emotional/psychological in nature.

Whatever the case, a child identified as being a slow or recalcitrant learner might, in fact, be quite gifted or talented in some way, but because of personal problems, have a history of increasingly poor school attendance, poor attention to schoolwork, poor self-confidence, and an attitude problem. With those factors in mind, consider the following guidelines when working with recalcitrant learners:

- As the school year begins, learn as much about each student as you can. Be cautious in how you do it, though, because many of these students, especially the older ones, will be suspicious of any interest you show in them. Be businesslike, trusting, genuinely interested, and patient. A second caution: although you learn as much as possible about each student, what has happened in the past is history. Use the information not as ammunition, something to be held against the student, but as insight to help you work more productively with the child.
- Avoid lecturing to these students; it won't work, at least not for a while.
- Early in the school term, preferably with the help of adult volunteers (e.g., using professional community members as mentors has worked well at helping change the student's attitude from rebellion to one of hope, challenge, and success), work out a personalized education program with each student.
- Engage the students in learning by using interactive media, such as the Internet.
- Engage the students in active learning with real-world problem solving and perhaps community service projects (see the many examples later in this chapter in the list of motivational strategies).
- Forget about trying to "cover the subject matter," concentrating instead on student learning of some things well. Practice mastery (although this may go against the grain of modern emphasis on improved student scores on high-stakes

achievement tests). A good procedure is to use thematic teaching and divide the theme into short segments. Because school attendance for these children is sometimes sporadic, and increasingly so as they get older, try personalizing their assignments so they can pick up where they left off and move through the academic work in an orderly fashion, even when they have been absent excessively. Try ensuring some degree of success for each child.

- Help students develop their studying and learning skills, such as concentrating, remembering, and comprehension. Mnemonics, for example, is a device these students respond to positively, often quick and creative in inventing their own.
- If using a single textbook, see if the reading level is appropriate; if it is not, then allow that student to discard the book and select other, more appropriate, reading materials.
- Make sure your classroom procedures and rules are understood at the beginning of the school term and be consistent about following them.
- Maximize the use of in-class, on-task work and cooperative learning, with close monitoring of the student's progress. Be cautious about relying much on successful completion of traditional out-of-class assignments unless the student receives coached guidance before leaving your classroom and unless you are confident that there is support at home.
- Use simple language in the classroom. Be concerned less about the words the students use and the way they use them and more about the ideas they are expressing. Let the students use their own idioms without carping too much on grammar and syntax. Always take care, though, to model proper and professional English yourself.
- When appropriate, using frequent positive reinforcement, with the intention of increasing the student's sense of personal worth. When using praise for reinforcement, however, try always to direct your praise to the deed rather than the individual.

LEARNING ALONE

Although some children learn well in pairs (dyads), and others learn well with their peers in groups—collaboratively, cooperatively, or competitively—or collaboratively with adults, and others learn well in combinations of these patterns, researchers tell us that more than 10 percent of students learn best alone (Dunn, 1995). Learning-alone students often are gifted, nonconforming, able to work at their own pace successfully, comfortable using media, or seemingly underachieving but potentially able students for whom unconventional instructional strategies, such as *contract learning packages*—that is, agreements between the teacher and individual students to proceed with tasks appropriate to their readiness, interests, or learning profiles in a sequence and at a pace each student selects—are often successful. For an alone-learning student, instructional packages utilizing a multisensory approach are most apt to encourage and ensure academic success.

Activity 8.1 Preparing A Self-Instructional Module*

Instructions: The purpose of this activity is to guide you through the process of preparing a self-instructional module for use in your own teaching. The exercise continues for several pages; it is important that you follow it step by step, beginning with the following "cover page."

Self-Instructional Module Number: 1
Instructor's Name: Professor Richard D. Kellough
School: California State University, Sacramento
Course: Methods of Teaching
Intended Students: Students in Teacher Preparation
Topic: How to Write a Self-Instructional Module
Estimated Working Time: 10 hours

For the challenge of today's classroom . . .

The Self-Instructional Module

You are about to embark on creating and writing a perfect lesson plan. The result of your hard work will be an instructional module in which you will take a lot of pride. More important, you will have learned a technique of teaching that ensures learning takes place. For what more could you ask?

Let us get to the essence of what this self-instructional module (SIM) is: This SIM is about how to write a SIM. The general objective is to guide you

gently through the process of preparing and writing your first SIM. Let's begin the experience with background about the history of the SIM.

A History

Research evidence indicates that student achievement in learning is related to time and to the *quality of attention* being given to the learning task. You knew that already! In 1968, Benjamin Bloom developed a concept of individualized instruction called mastery learning, based on the idea that students need sufficient time on task to master content before moving on to new content. Did you know that? _____. (Please read along with a pencil, and fill in the blanks as you go.)

Although Bloom is usually given credit for the concept of mastery learning, the idea did not originate with him. He reinforced and made popular a model developed earlier by John Carroll. In 1968, Fred Keller developed a similar model called the Keller Plan, or the Personalized System of Instruction (PSI). The PSI quickly became a popular teaching technique in the community and four-year colleges. In about 1972, enter Johnson and Johnson (not of the Band-Aid family, but Rita and Stuart Johnson), who developed their model of mastery learning and called it the Self-Instructional Package (SIP). Since 1972, I (Richard D. Kellough) have been developing my version, the Self-Instructional Module, which you are now experiencing. As you will learn, *frequent comprehension checks and corrective instructions* are important to the effectiveness of the SIM.

One other thing. There are several devices available to individualize instruction, but the SIM has the flexibility to be adaptable for use at all grade levels, from kindergarten through college. I believe the following to be the reasons for the popularity of this strategy:

• The SIM allows the teacher to *create an experience that ensures learning.* Creating makes you feel good; when your students learn, you feel good—two reasons for the SIM's popularity.

• The SIM is truly *individualized,* because it is a module written for an individual student, with that student in mind as it is being written.

• Although it takes time to prepare, the SIM *requires little financial expenditure,* a fact important to today's teacher.

• Once you have prepared your first SIM, you might see that you have begun a series. Subsequent modules are easier to do, and you may see the value in having a series available.

• With today's emphasis on the *basics*, the SIM is particularly helpful for use in remediation.

• When you finish your SIM, you will have collected the content that could be used for a computer program

• With today's *large and mixed-ability classes*, teachers need help! Here is time- and cost-effective help!

• With emphasis today on competency-based instruction, the SIM makes sense.

How are we doing so far? _____
Are your interests and curiosity aroused? _____
_____ Do you have questions? _____
If so, write them down (on separate paper), then continue.

What Is the Self-Instructional Module and Why Use It?

The SIM is a learning module designed for an individual student; it is self-instructional (i.e., if you, the teacher, drop dead—heaven forbid—the student can continue to learn), and *it requires about 30 minutes of learning time*. The final module can be recorded on tape, video, or computer disc; it can be written in booklet form; or it can exist in any combination of these.

Here are ways that teachers have found the SIM to be useful:

• As an *enrichment* activity for an accelerated student.

• As a strategy for makeup for a student who has been absent.

• As a strategy for a student in need of *remediation*.

• As a strategy for introducing basic information to an entire class, freeing the teacher to work with individual students, making the act of teaching more *time-efficient*, a particularly significant value of the SIM.

• As a learning experience especially coordinated with manipulatives, perhaps in connection with a science experiment, library work, a computer, a recording, hands-on materials for an activity, or any combination of these.

One other point before we stop and check your comprehension: *The single most important characteristic of the SIM is that is uses small sequential steps followed by immediate and corrective feedback to the learner*. In that respect, the SIM resembles programmed instruction.

Stop the action!

Let's check your learning with the review questions and instructions that follow.

Comprehension Check 1

Answer the following three questions (on separate paper), then check your responses by reviewing Feedback Check 1. If you answer all three questions correctly, continue the package; otherwise, back up and review.

1. How would you define a SIM?
2. What is the single most important characteristic of the SIM?
3. What is one way that the SIM could be used in your own teaching, a way that currently stands out in your thinking?

Feedback Check 1

1. Although we will continue development, of the definition, at this point it should resemble this: The SIM is an individualization of learning–teaching strategy that teaches toward mastery learning of one relatively small bit of content by building on small, sequential steps and providing corrective feedback throughout.
2. Referring to the small, sequential steps, followed by immediate and corrective feedback.
3. Your answer is probably related to one of those listed earlier but it could differ.

How Does the SIM Differ from Other Kinds of Learning Packages?

Another characteristic of the SIM is the *amount of learning contained in one module*. Each SIM is designed to teach a relatively small amount of material, but to do it well. *This is a major difference in the SIM from other types of learning activity packages.*

And, in case you have been wondering about what the SIM can be designed to teach, I want to emphasize that it *can be designed*

- For any topic,
- At any grade level,
- In any discipline,
- For cognitive understanding,
- For psychomotor development, and
- For affective learning.

That probably brings to your mind all sorts of thoughts and questions. Hold them for a moment, and let's do another comprehension check.

Stop the action and check your learning.

Comprehension Check 2

Answer the following two questions (on separate paper), then check your responses in Feedback Check 2 that follows.

1. How does the SIM differ from other self-contained learning packages?
2. Although teachers frequently emphasize learning that falls within the cognitive domain, is it possible for the SIM to be written to include learning in the psychomotor and affective domains? Yes or no?

Feedback Check 2

1. Length of learning time is shorter for the SIM, and it is written with an individual student in mind. It is written to teach one thing well, to one student.

2. The SIM *can* be written for any domain, although evaluation is trickier for the affective and for the highest-level psychomotor.

Perhaps we should now say a word about what we mean when we use the expression *teach one thing well*—that is, to explain what is meant by mastery learning. Theoretically, if the package is being used by an individual student, performance level expectation is 100%. In reality, performance level will most likely be between 85 and 95%, particularly if you are using the SIM for a group of students rather than an individual. That 5–15% difference allows for human errors that can occur in written communication.

Now that you have learned what the SIM is—and how this learning strategy differs from other learning activity packages—it is time to concentrate on developing your SIM. Please continue.

SIM Development

How Do I Develop a SIM?

As with any good lesson plan, it takes time to develop an effective SIM. Indeed, preparation of your first SIM will test your imagination and writing skills! Nevertheless, it will be time well spent; you will be proud of your product. *It is important that you continue following this module, step by step; do not skip parts.* Development of your SIM emphasizes the importance of

- Writing the learning objectives clearly, precisely, and in behavioral terms.
- Planning the learning activities in small, sequential steps.
- Providing frequent practice and learning comprehension checks.
- Providing immediate feedback, corrective instruction, and assurance to the learner.
- Preparing evaluative questions that measure against the learning objectives.

As you embark on preparing what may be the perfect lesson plan, keep in mind the following two points:

1. Prepare your first SIM so it will take no more than
   10–15 minutes for children of grades K–3
   30 minutes for children of grades 4–8

2. Use a *conversational tone* in your writing. Write in the first person, as though you are talking directly to the student for whom it is intended. For example, when speaking of the learning objectives, use *You will be able to* rather than *The student will be able to*. Keep in mind that you are communicating with one person rather than with an entire class (even though you may be preparing your package for entire class use). It helps to pretend that you are in a one-on-one situation tutoring the student at the writing board.

Stop the action, and again check your learning.

Comprehension Check 3

Answer the following two questions (on separate paper); then check your responses in Feedback Check 3.

1. What maximum learning-time duration is recommended?
2. What major item of importance has been recommended for you to keep in mind as you write your SIM?

Feedback Check 3

1. Approximately 10–30 minutes, depending on the age of the student.
2. Write in the first person, as if you are speaking directly to the student.

Now that I have emphasized the *length of learning time* and *the personalization of your writing,* here are other important reminders.

1. Make your SIM attractive and stimulating. Consider using cartoons, puns, graphics, scratch-and-sniff stickers, and interesting manipulatives. Use your creative imagination! Use both cerebral hemispheres!

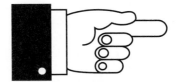

Add sketches, diagrams, modules, pictures, magazine clippings, humor, and a conversational tone, as students appreciate a departure from the usual textbooks and worksheets.

2. Use colleagues as resource persons, brainstorming ideas as you proceed through each step of module production.

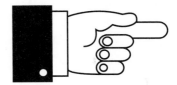

During production, use your best cooperative learning skills.

3. The module should not be read (or heard) like a lecture. It *must* involve small sequential steps with frequent practice and corrective feedback instruction (as modeled in this module).

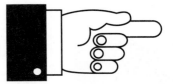

". . . and with the course material broken down into small self-instructional units, students can move through at individual rates."

4. The module should contain a variety of activities, preferably involving all four learning modalities—*visual, auditory, tactile,* and *kinesthetic.*

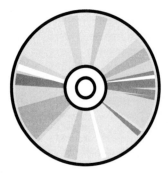

packet that you are using has been "toned down" and modified for practical inclusion in this textbook.

6. Your SIM does not have to fit the common $8\frac{1}{2}''\times11''$ size. You are encouraged to be creative in the design of your SIM's shape, size, and format.

7. Like all lesson plans, the SIM is subject to revision and improvement after use. Use your best creative writing skills. *Write, review, sleep on it, write more, revise, test, revise. . . .*

5. Vary margins, indentations, and fonts so the final module does not have the usual textbook or worksheet appearance with which students are so familiar. Build into your module the "Hawthorne effect."

Perhaps before proceeding, it would be useful to review the preceding points. Remember, too, the well-written module *will ensure learning.* Your first SIM will take several hours to produce, but it will be worth it!

Proceed with the steps that follow.

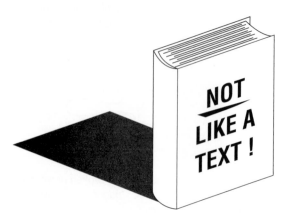

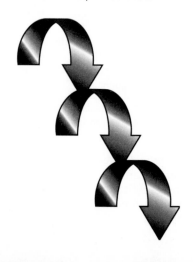

Note about the cosmetics of your SIM: My own prejudice about the SIM is that it should be spread out more than the usual textbook page or worksheet. Use double-spaced lines, varied margins, and so on. Make cosmetic improvements after finishing your final draft. Write, review, sleep on it, write more, revise, add that final touch. This modular

Steps for Developing Your SIM

Instructions: It is important that you proceed through the following module development step by step.

One thing you will notice is that immediately after writing your learning objectives, you will prepare the evaluative test items; both steps precede the preparation of the learning activities. That is not the usual order followed by a teacher when preparing lessons, but it does help to ensure that test items match objectives. Now, here we go! *Step-by-step, please.*

Note: Write on separate paper for draft planning.

Step 1: Prepare the cover page

It should include the following items:

- Instructor's name (that is you)
- School (yours)
- Class or intended students (whom it's for)
- Topic (specific but not wordy)
- Estimated working time

For a sample, refer to the beginning of this module. You can vary the design of the cover page according to your needs.

Step 2: Prepare the instructional objectives

For now, these should be written in specific behavioral terms. Later, when writing these into your module introduction, you can phrase them in more general terms.

Recommended is the inclusion of at least one attitudinal (affective) objective, such as "Upon completion of this module, you will tell me your feelings about this kind of learning."

Step 3: Comprehension Check 4

Share with your colleagues what you have accomplished (with steps 1 and 2) to solicit their valuable feedback and input.

Step 4: Depending on feedback (from step 3), *modify items 1 and 2,* if necessary. For example, after listing the learning instructions, you may find that you really have more than one module in preparation, and within the list of objectives you may find a natural cutoff between modules 1 and 2. You may discover that you have a *series* of modules begun.

Step 5: Prepare the pretest

If the learner does well on the pretest, there may be no need for the student to continue the module. Some modules (like this one) may not include a pretest, though most will. And if this is your first SIM writing experience, I think you *should* include a pretest.

Suggestion: The pretest need not be as long as the posttest but should include a limited sample of questions to determine whether the student already knows the material and need not continue with the module. A pretest also serves to set the student mentally for the SIM.

Step 6: Prepare the posttest

The pretest and posttest could be identical, but usually the pretest is shorter. It is important that both pretest and posttest items actually test against the objectives (of step 2). Try to keep the items objective (e.g., multiple-choice type), avoiding as much as possible the use of subjective test items (e.g., essay type), but do include at least one item measuring an affective objective (see second paragraph in step 2).

Important reminder: If your module is well written, the student should achieve 85–100% on the posttest.

Step 7: Comprehension Check 5

Share with colleagues your pretest and posttest items (providing a copy of your objectives) for suggested improvement changes before continuing to the next step.

Use a special place to write notes to yourself about ideas you are having and regarding any materials you may need to complete your module.

Good work so far! Before continuing, take a break.

It is time to stop working for a while . . .   *. . . and go play!*

Step 8: Okay, enough play; it is time to prepare the text of your SIM

This is the "meat" of your module—what goes between the pretest and the posttest. It is the IN-STRUCTION. *Reminder:* For the SIM to be self-instructional, the learner should be able to work through the module with little or no help from you.

An important ingredient in your module is the *directions*. The module should be self-directed and self-paced. Therefore, each step of the module should be clear to the learner, making you, the instructor, literally unnecessary. *Everything needed by*

the learner to complete the module should be provided with the module.

Use small, sequential steps with frequent practice cycles, followed by comprehension checks and corrective feedback. Make it fun and interesting with a variety of activities for the student, activities that provide for learning in several ways, from writing to reading, from viewing a video to drawing, from listening to a tape recording to doing a hands-on activity. And be certain the activities correlate with the learning objectives. The learning cycles should lead to satisfaction of the stated objectives, and the posttest items *must* measure against those objectives.

Step 9: Comprehension Check 6

Test your package. Try it out on your colleagues as they look for content errors, spelling and grammar errors, and clarity, as well as offer suggestions for improvement. Duplicate and use the SIM Assessment Form provided at the end of this activity.

Stop the Action!
Congratulations on the development of your first SIM. However, two additional steps need your consideration.

Step 10: Revise if necessary

Make appropriate changes to your SIM as a result of the feedback from your colleagues. Then you are ready to give your SIM its first real test—try it out on the student for whom it is intended.

Step 11: Further revisions

This comes later, after you have used it with the student for whom it was originally intended. Like any other well-prepared lesson or unit plan, it should always be subject to revision and to improvement, never "set in concrete."

SIM Assessment Questions

(Use separate paper, as space is not provided here)

1. Module identification
   Author
   Title of SIM

2. Module Objectives
   Do they tell the student
      a. What the student will be able to do?
      b. How the student will demonstrate this new knowledge or skill?
   Is there a clear statement (overview or introduction) of the importance, telling the learner what will be learned from completion of the module?
3. Pretest
4. Activities (practice cycles)
   Are small sequential steps used?
   Are there frequent practice cycles, with comprehension checks and corrective feedback to the learner?
5. Posttest: Does it test against the objectives?
6. Clarity and continuity of expression.
7. Is the module informative, attractive, and enjoyable?
8. Additional comments useful to the author of the SIM.

LEARNING IN PAIRS

It is sometimes advantageous to pair children (dyads) for learning. Four types of dyads are described as follows.

TPW Video Classroom

Series: Language Arts Methods

Module 3: Writing

Video 2: Peer Editing

Peer Tutoring, Mentoring, and Cross-Age Coaching Peer mentoring, *peer tutoring*, or peer-assisted learning (PAL) is a strategy whereby one student tutors another. It is useful, for example, when one student helps another who has limited proficiency in English or when a student skilled in math helps another whom is less skilled. It has been demonstrated repeatedly that peer tutoring is a significant strategy for promoting active learning (Bacon, 2005; Thrope & Wood, 2000). Cross-age coaching is a strategy whereby one student coaches another from a different, and sometimes lower, grade level (Jacobson et al., 2001; Potenza, 2003). This is similar to peer tutoring, except that the coach is from a different age/grade level than the student being coached.

Paired Team Learning Paired team learning is a strategy whereby students study and learn in teams of two. Students identified as gifted work and learn

Peer tutoring is a significant strategy for promoting active learning.

Barbara Schwartz/Merrill

especially well when paired. Specific uses for paired team learning include drill partners, science buddies, reading buddies, book report pairs, summary pairs, homework partners, project assignment pairs, and elaborating and relating pairs.

Think-pair-share, in which students are asked to think about an idea, share thoughts about it with a partner, and then share the pair's thoughts with the entire class; *think-write-pair-share*, in which each student writes his or her ideas about the new word and then shares in pairs before sharing with the entire class; and *jigsaw*, in which individuals or small groups of students are given responsibilities for separate tasks lead to a bigger task or understanding, thereby putting together parts to make a whole.

The Learning Center

Another significantly beneficial way of pairing students for instruction (as well as of individualizing the instruction and learning alone and integrating the learning) is by using the *learning center (LC)* or *learning station*. (*Note:* Whereas each learning center is distinct and unrelated to others, learning stations are sequenced or in some way linked to one another, as discussed in the TEAMS approach that follows.) The LC is a special area located in the classroom where one student (or two, if student interaction is necessary or preferred at the center; or as many as four or five students in the case of learning stations) can quietly work and learn at the student's own pace more about a special topic or to improve specific skills. All materials needed are provided at that center, including clear instructions for operation of the center.

Whereas the LC used to be thought of as belonging to the domain of primary-grades teachers with self-contained classrooms, now, with block scheduling and longer class periods in many middle-level schools the LC has special relevance and

The learning center is a special station located in the classroom where an individual student (or a pair of students, if student interaction is necessary for the center) can quietly work and learn at his or her own pace.

Tom Watson/Merrill

usefulness for all teachers, regardless of grade level. In the words of a teacher of French and Spanish at Bailey Middle School (Austin, TX),

> As other teachers in our district have begun to use center techniques, I hear comments such as, "The students are so excited," and "There was none of the chaos I was afraid of." In using centers as a teaching tool, I have found that students are eager to participate in all class work and excited about speaking a new language both inside and outside the classroom. (Voelzel, 2000)

The value of learning centers as instructional devices undoubtedly lies in the following facts. LCs can provide instructional diversity. While working at a center, the student is giving time and quality attention to the learning task (learning toward mastery) and is likely to be engaging his or her most effective learning modality, or integrating several modalities or all of them.

Learning centers are of three types. In the *direct-learning center*, performance expectations for cognitive learning are quite specific, and the focus is on mastery of content. In the *open-learning center*, the goal is to provide opportunity for exploration, enrichment, motivation, and creative discovery. In the *skill center*, as in a direct-learning center, performance expectations are quite specific, but the focus is on the development of a particular skill or process.

In all instances, the primary reason for using a learning center is to individualize—that is, to provide collections of materials and activities adjusted to the various readiness levels, interests, and learning profiles of students. Other reasons to use a LC are to provide (a) a mechanism for learning that crosses discipline boundaries; (b) a special place for a student with exceptional needs; (c) opportunities for creative work, enrichment experiences, and (d) multisensory experiences and the opportunity to learn from learning packages that utilize special equipment or media of which only one or a limited supply may be available for use in the classroom (e.g., science materials, a microscope, a computer, a DVD player, or some combination of these).

> Learning centers should be used for educational purposes, *never* for punishment.

To adapt instruction to the curriculum and to students' individual needs and preferences, it is possible to design a learning environment that includes several learning stations, each of which uses a different medium and modality or focuses on a special aspect of the curriculum. Students then rotate through the various stations according to their needs and preferences (Reiser & Butzin, 2000).

Guidelines for Setting up a Learning Center

To construct an LC you can be as elaborate and as creative as your time, imagination, and resources allow. Children can even help you plan and set up learning centers, which will relieve some of the burden from your busy schedule. The following paragraphs present guidelines for setting up and using this valuable instructional tool.

The center should be designed with a theme in mind, preferably one that integrates the students' learning by providing activities that cross discipline boundaries. Decide the purpose of the center and give the center a name, such as "the center for the study of wetlands," "walking tour of Jerusalem," "our state capitol," "the center for worldwide communication," "history of the overseas highway," and so on. The purpose of the center should be clearly understood by the students.

The center should be designed to be attractive, purposeful, and uncluttered and should be identified with an attractive sign. Engage the children in the design and construction of the sign. Learning centers should be activity oriented (i.e., dependent on the student's manipulation of materials, not just paper-and-pencil tasks).

Topics for the center should be related to the instructional program—for review and reinforcement, remediation, or enrichment. The center should be self-directing (i.e., specific instructional objectives and procedures for using the center should be clearly posted and understandable to the student user). The center should also be self-correcting (i.e., student users should be able to tell by the way they have completed the task whether or not they have done it correctly and have learned).

The center should contain a variety of activities geared to the varying abilities and interest levels of the children. A choice of two or more activities at a center is one way to provide for this.

Materials to be used at the center should be maintained at the center, with descriptions for use provided to the students. Using SIMs (Activity 8.1) with LCs works well. Materials should be safe for student use, and you or another adult should easily supervise the center. Some centers, such as the "reading center," may become more or less permanent centers, that is, remain for the school term or longer, whereas others may change according to what is being studied at the time.

LEARNING IN SMALL GROUPS

Small groups are those involving three to five students, in either a teacher- or a student-directed setting. Using small groups for instruction, including the *cooperative learning group* (CLG), enhances the opportunities for students to assume greater control over their own learning, sometimes referred to as *empowerment*.

Purposes for Using Small Groups

Small groups can be formed to serve a number of purposes. They might be useful for a specific learning activity (e.g., *literature circles*, where students who have read the same self-selected story or novel discuss their reading [Scott, 1994]), or *reciprocal reading groups*, where students take turns asking questions, summarizing, making predictions about, and clarifying a story (Slater & Horstman, 2002). Or they might be formed to complete an activity that requires materials that are of short supply or to complete a project, only lasting as long as the project does. Teachers have various rationales for assigning students to groups. Groups can be formed by grouping students according to (a) personality type (e.g., sometimes a teacher may want to team less-assertive children together to give them the opportunity for greater management of their own learning), (b) social pattern (e.g., sometimes it may be necessary to break up a group of rowdy friends, or it may be desirable to broaden the association among students), (c) common interest, (d) learning styles (e.g., forming groups of either mixed styles or of styles in common), or (e) according to their abilities in a particular skill or their knowledge in a particular area. One specific type of small-group instruction is the cooperative learning group.

COOPERATIVE LEARNING

More than a century ago, Lev Vygotsky studied the importance of a learner's social interactions in learning situations, concluding that learning is most effective when learners cooperate with one another in a supportive learning environment under the careful guidance of a teacher. Cooperative learning, group problem solving, problem-based learning, and cross-age tutoring are instructional strategies used by teachers that have grown in popularity as a result of research evolving from the work of Vygotsky (1962, 1978).

The Cooperative Learning Group (CLG)

The *cooperative learning group* is a heterogeneous group (i.e., mixed according to one or more criteria, such as ability or skill level, ethnicity, learning style, learning capacity, gender, and language proficiency) of three to five students who work together in a teacher- or student-directed setting, emphasizing support for one another.

Oftentimes, a CLG consists of four students of mixed ability, learning styles, gender, and ethnicity, with each member of the group assuming a particular role. Teachers usually change the membership of each group several to many times during the year.

TPW Video Classroom

Series: General Methods

Module 9: Cooperative Learning and the Collaborative Process

Video 1: Cooperative Learning

The Theory and Use of Cooperative Learning

The theory of cooperative learning is that when small groups of students of mixed backgrounds and capabilities work together toward a common goal, members of the group increase their friendship and respect for one another. As a consequence, each individual's self-esteem is enhanced, students are more motivated to participate in higher-order thinking, and academic achievement is accomplished. In short, the effective use of heterogeneous cooperative learning helps students grow academically, socially, and emotionally (Schniedewind & Davidson, 2000).

There are several techniques for using cooperative learning (see, for example, Coelho, 1994; Johnson, Johnson, & Holubec, 1998; Sharan & Sharan, 1992). Yet the primary purpose of each is for the groups to learn—which means, of course, that individuals within a group must learn. Group achievement in learning, then, is dependent on the learning of individuals within the group. Rather than competing for rewards for achievement, members of the group cooperate with one another by helping one another learn so that the group reward will be a good one. Normally, the group is rewarded on the basis of group achievement, though individual members within the group can later be rewarded for individual contributions. Because of peer pressure, when using CLGs you must be cautious about using group grading. For grading purposes, bonus points can be given to all members of a group; individuals can add to their own scores when everyone in the group has reached preset standards. The preset standards must be appropriate for all members of a group. Lower standards or improvement criteria could be set for students with lower ability so everyone feels rewarded and successful. To determine each student's term grades, individual student achievement is measured later through individual students' results on tests and other criteria, as well as through each student's performance in the group work.

TPW Video Classroom

Series: Classroom Management

Module 4: Managing Cooperative Learning Groups

Video 1: Collaborative Grouping

Roles Within the Cooperative Learning Group

It is advisable to assign roles (specific functions) to each member of the CLG. (The lesson plan shown in the unit plan of Figure 6.14 shows the use of a CLG activity using assigned roles for a lesson in science.) These roles should be rotated, either during the activity or from one time to the next. Although titles may vary, five typical roles are

- *Group facilitator*—role is to keep the group on task.
- *Materials manager*—role is to obtain, maintain, and return materials needed for the group to function.
- *Recorder*—role is to record all group activities and processes and perhaps to periodically assess how the group is doing.
- *Reporter*—role is to report group processes and accomplishments to the teacher and/or to the entire class. When using groups of four members, the roles of recorder and reporter can easily be combined.
- *Thinking monitor*—role is to identify and record the sequence and processes of the group's thinking. This role encourages metacognition and the development of thinking skills.

It is important that students understand and perform their individual roles, and that each member of the CLG performs her or his tasks as expected. No student should be allowed to ride on the coattails of the group. To give significance to, to reinforce the importance of each role, and to be able to readily recognize the role any student is playing during CLG activity, one teacher made a trip to an office supplier and had permanent badges made for the various CLG roles. During CLGs, then, each student attached the appropriate badge to her or his clothing.

What Students and the Teacher Do When Using Cooperative Learning Groups

Actually, for learning by CLGs to work, each member of the CLG must understand and assume two roles or responsibilities—the role he or she is assigned as a member of the group and that of making sure all others in the group are performing their roles. Sometimes this requires interpersonal skills that children have yet to learn or to learn well. This is where the teacher must assume some responsibility, too. Simply placing students into CLGs and expecting each member and each group to function and to learn the expected outcomes may not work. In other words, skills of cooperation must be taught, and if all your students have not yet learned the skills of cooperation, then you will have to teach them. This doesn't mean that if a group is not functioning you immediately break up the group and reassign members to new groups. Important to group learning is learning the process of how to work out conflict. For a group to work out a conflict may require your attention and assistance. With your guidance, the group should be able to discover the problem that is causing the conflict, then identify some options and mediate at least a temporary solution. If a particular skill is needed, students identify and learn that skill with your assistance.

When to Use Cooperative Learning Groups

CLGs can be used for discussion and review, problem identification, problem solving, investigations, experiments, review, project work, or almost any other instructional purpose. Just as you would for small-group work in general, you can use CLGs for most any purpose at any time.

Cooperative Group Learning, Assessment, and Grading

Normally, the CLG is rewarded on the basis of group achievement, though individual members within the group can later be rewarded for individual contributions (see Figure 8.3). Because of peer pressure, when using CLGs you must *be cautious about using group grading* (Guskey, 1996; Kagan, 1995). Some teachers give bonus points to all members of a group to add to their individual scores when everyone in the group has reached preset criteria. In establishing preset standards, the standards can be different for individuals within a group, depending on each member's ability and past performance. It is important that each member of a group feel rewarded and successful. For determination of students' report card grades, individual student achievement is measured later through individual results on tests and other sources of data.

Why Some Teachers Experience Difficulty Using CLGs

Sometimes, when they think they are using CLGs, teachers have difficulty and either give up trying to use the strategy or simply tell students to divide into groups for an activity and call that cooperative learning. As emphasized earlier, for the strategy to work, each student must be given training in and have acquired basic skills in interaction and group processing and must realize that individual achievement rests with that of their group. And, as is true for any other strategy, the use of CLGs must not be overused—teachers must vary their strategies.

For the use of CLGs to work well, advanced planning and effective management are a must. Each student must be assigned a responsible role within the group and be held accountable for fulfilling that responsibility. And, when a CLG activity is in process, groups must be continually monitored by the teacher for possible breakdown of this process within a group. In other words, while students are working in groups, the teacher must exercise withitness. When a potential breakdown is noticed, the teacher quickly intervenes to help the group get back on track.

	9–10	8	7	1–6
Goals	Consistently and actively helps identify group goals; works effectively to meet goals.	Consistently communicates commitment to group goals; carries out assigned roles.	Sporadically communicates commitment to group goals; carries out assigned role.	Rarely, If ever, works toward group goals or may work against them.
Interpersonal Skills	Cooperates with group members by encouraging, compromising, and/or taking a leadership role without dominating; shows sensitivity to feelings and knowledge of others.	Cooperates with group members by encouraging, compromising, and/or taking a leadership role.	Participates with group, but has own agenda; may not be willing to compromise or to make significant contributions.	May discourage others, harass group members, or encourage off-task behavior. Makes significant changes to others' work without their knowledge or permission.
Quality Producer	Contributes significant information, ideas, time, and/or talent to produce a quality product.	Contributes information, ideas, time, and/or talent to produce a quality product.	Contributes some ideas, though not significant; may be more supportive than contributive; shows willingness to complete assignment but has no desire to go beyond average expectations.	Does little or no work toward the completion of group product; shows little or no interest in contributing to the task; produces work that fails to meet minimum standards for quality.
Participation	Attends daily; consistently and actively utilizes class time by working on the task.	Attends consistently; sends in work to group if absent; utilizes class time by working on the task.	Attends sporadically; absences/tardies may hinder group involvement; may send in work when absent; utilizes some time; may be off task by talking to others, interrupting other groups, or watching others do the majority of the work.	Frequent absences or tardies hinder group involvement; fails to send in work when absent; wastes class time by talking, doing other work, or avoiding tasks; group has asked that member be reproved by teacher or removed from the group.
Commitment	Consistently contributes time out of class to produce a quality product; attends all group meetings as evidenced by the group meeting log.	Contributes time out of class to produce a quality product; attends a majority of group meetings as evidenced by the group meeting log.	Willing to work toward completion of task during class time; attends some of the group meetings; may arrive late or leave early; may keep inconsistent meeting log.	Rarely, if ever, attends group meetings outside of class or may attend but hinders progress by the group; fails to keep meeting log.

FIGURE 8.3

Sample scoring rubric for assessing individual students in cooperative learning group project. Possible score = 50. Scorer marks a relevant square in each of the five categories (horizontal rows), and the student's score for that category is the small number in the top right corner within that square.

Source: Courtesy of Susan Abbott and Pam Benedetti, Elk Grove School District, Elk Grove, CA.

LEARNING IN LARGE GROUPS

As defined for purposes of this book, large groups are those that involve more than five students, usually the entire class. Most often, they are teacher directed. Student presentations and whole-class discussions are two techniques that involve the use of large groups.

Student Presentations

Students should be encouraged to be presenters for discussion of the ideas, opinions, and knowledge obtained from their own independent and small-group study. Several techniques encourage the development of certain skills and intelligent behaviors, such as the skills of studying and organizing material, discovery, discussion, rebuttal, listening, analysis, suspending judgment, and critical thinking. Possible forms of discussions involving student presentations are described as follows:

- *Debate*. The debate is an arrangement in which oral presentations are made by members of two opposing teams on topics preassigned and researched. The speeches are followed by rebuttals from each team.
- *Jury Trial*. The jury trial is a discussion approach in which the class simulates a courtroom, with class members playing the various roles of judge, attorneys, jury members, bailiff, and court recorder.
- *Panel*. The panel is a setting in which four to six students, with one designated as the chairperson or moderator, discuss a topic about which they have studied, followed by a question-and-answer period involving the entire class. The panel usually begins with each panel member giving a brief opening statement.
- *Research Report*. One or two students or a small group of students gives a report on a topic that they investigated, followed by questions and discussion by the entire class.
- *Roundtable*. The roundtable is a small group of three to five students who sit around a table and discuss among themselves (perhaps with the rest of the class listening and later asking questions) a problem or issue that they have studied. One member of the panel may serve as moderator.

To use these techniques effectively, students may need to be coached by you—individually, in small groups, or in whole-class sessions—on how and where to gather information; how to listen, take notes (Marzano, Pickering, & Pollock, 2001), select major points, organize material, and present a position succinctly and convincingly (see Figure 8.4); how to play roles; and how to engage in dialogue and debate with one another.

Whole-Class Discussion

Direct, whole-class discussion is a teaching technique used frequently by most or all teachers. On this topic, you should consider yourself an expert. Having been a student in formal learning for at least 15 years, you are undoubtedly knowledgeable

GROUP PRESENTATION SCORING RUBRIC

5. Presentation was excellent. Clear understanding of their project and organized in delivery.
   - Made eye contact throughout presentation
   - Spoke loud enough for all to hear
   - Spoke clearly
   - Spoke for time allotted
   - Stood straight and confidently
   - Covered at least five pieces of important information
   - Introduced project
   - All members spoke

4. Presentation was well thought out and planned.
   - Made eye contact throughout most of presentation
   - Spoke loud enough and clearly most of the time
   - Spoke for almost all of time allotted
   - Covered at least four pieces of important information
   - Introduced project
   - All members spoke

3. Adequate presentation. Mostly organized.
   - Made eye contact at times
   - Some of audience could hear the presentation
   - Audience could understand most of what was said
   - Spoke for about half of time allotted
   - At least half of team spoke
   - Covered at least three pieces of important information
   - Project was vaguely introduced

2–1. Underprepared presentation. Disorganized and incomplete information.
   - No eye contact during presentation
   - Most of audience was unable to hear presentation
   - Information presented was unclear
   - Spoke for only a brief time
   - Covered less than three pieces of information
   - Project was not introduced or only vaguely introduced

FIGURE 8.4
Sample scoring rubric for small-group or individual presentation

about the advantages and disadvantages of whole-class discussions, at least from your personal vantage point.

EQUALITY IN THE CLASSROOM

Especially when conducting direct, whole-group discussions, it is easy for a teacher to fall into the trap of interacting with only "the stars," or only those in the front of the room or on one side, or only the most vocal and assertive. You must exercise caution and avoid falling into that trap. To ensure a psychologically safe and effective environment for learning for every person in your classroom, you must attend to all students and try to involve all students equally in all class activities. You must avoid any biased expectations about certain students, and you must avoid discriminating against students according to their gender or some other personal characteristic.

To guarantee equity in interaction with students, many teachers have found it helpful to ask someone (perhaps a member of your teaching team) secretly to tally

Activity 8.2: Whole-Class Discussion as a Teaching Strategy

Part A: What do I already know?

This activity allows you to build your knowledge base about using whole-class discussions by sharing experiences and knowledge with your classmates. Answer each of the following 19 questions, and then share your responses with classmates, perhaps first in small discussion groups and then in the larger group. After doing that, proceed to Part B.

1. Your grade level (primary, intermediate, middle level) and, if relevant, your subject field of interest.
2. For what reasons would you hold a whole-class discussion?
3. Assuming that your classroom has movable seats, how would you arrange them for a whole-class discussion? (for example: linear rows, circle, rectangle)
4. What would you do if seats were fixed (not movable)?
5. What rules would you have established before discussion begins?
6. Should student participation be forced? Why or why not? If so, how?
7. How would you discourage a few students from dominating the discussion, or would you?
8. What preparation, if any, should the students and teacher be expected to make prior to beginning the discussion?
9. How would you handle digression from the topic?
10. Should children serve as discussion leaders? Why or why not? If so, what training, if any, should they receive, and how would they receive it?
11. What teacher roles are options during the class discussion? And when is each of these roles most appropriate?
12. When, if ever, is it appropriate to hold a whole-class class meeting for a discussion of class procedures, rather than subject matter?
13. Can brainstorming be a form of whole-class discussion? Explain.
14. What follow-up activities would be appropriate after a whole-class discussion? On what basis would you decide to use each?
15. What sorts of activities should precede a whole-class discussion?
16. Should a discussion be given a set length? Explain why or why not, and if so, how it is decided.
17. Should students be graded for their participation in a whole-class discussion? Why or why not? If so, how and by whom? What would be the criteria?
18. For effective whole-class discussions, 10 to 12 feet is the maximum recommended distance between participants. During a teacher-led discussion, what can the teacher do to keep within this limit?
19. Are there any pitfalls or other points of importance that a teacher should be aware of when planning and implementing a whole-class discussion? If so, explain them and how to protect against them.

Part B: Building on what I already know

Now that you have shared your responses to the 19 questions, in Part A, first as an individual answer the first two questions that follow. Then, in a small group, use all three questions to guide you as you generate a list of five general guidelines for using whole-class discussions as a strategy for teaching in the elementary school. Share your small group's guidelines with the whole class. Then, finally, as a whole class, derive a final list of general guidelines.

1. How effective was your small-group discussion in Part A of this activity?
2. What allowed for or inhibited the effectiveness of that small-group discussion?
3. How effective was this small-group discussion? Explain.

FIVE GENERAL GUIDELINES GENERATED FROM YOUR SMALL-GROUP DISCUSSION

GENERAL GUIDELINES FOR USING WHOLE-CLASS DISCUSSION: FINAL LIST DERIVED FROM WHOLE-CLASS DISCUSSION classroom interactions between the teacher and students during a class discussion. After an analysis of the results, the teacher arrives at decisions about his or her own attending and facilitating behaviors. Such an analysis is the purpose of Activity 8.3.

In addition to the variables mentioned at the beginning of Activity 8.3, the activity can be modified to include responses and their frequencies according to other teacher–student interactions, such as your calling on all students equally for responses to your questions or to assist you with classroom helping jobs, or your chastising students for their inappropriate behavior.

Ensuring Equity

In addition to the advice given in Chapter 3 about using questioning, there are many other ways of ensuring that students are treated fairly in the classroom, including the following:

- During whole-class instruction, insist that the students raise their hands and be called on by you before they speak.
- Have and maintain high expectations, although not necessarily identical expectations, for all students.
- Insist on politeness in the classroom. For example, a student can be shown appreciation—such as with a sincere "thank you" or "I appreciate your contribution," with whole-class applause, or with a handshake or a genuine smile—for her or his contribution to the learning process.
- Insist children be allowed to finish what they are saying without being interrupted by others. Be certain that you model this behavior yourself.
- Keep a stopwatch handy to unobtrusively control the wait time given for each student. Although at first this idea may sound impractical, it does work.
- Use a seating chart attached to a clipboard, and next to each student's name, make a tally for each interaction you have with a student. This also is a useful way to maintain records of students' contributions to class discussion. The seating chart can be laminated so it can be used day after day simply by erasing the marks of the previous day.

LEARNING FROM ASSIGNMENTS AND HOMEWORK

An *assignment* is a statement of what the student is to accomplish and is tied to a specific instructional objective. Assignments, whether completed at home or at school, can ease a child's learning in many ways, but when poorly planned, they can discourage the child and upset an entire family. *Homework* can be defined as any out-of-class task that a student is assigned as an extension of classroom learning. Like all else that you do as a teacher, it is your professional responsibility to think about and plan carefully any and all homework assignments you give to your students.

Activity 8.3: Teacher Interaction with Students According to Student Gender (or Other Student Differences)

Instructions: The purpose of this exercise is to provide a tool for the analysis of your own interactions with students according to gender. To become accustomed to the exercise, you should do a trial run in one of your university classes, then use it during your student teaching, and again during your first years of teaching. The exercise can be modified to included (a) the amount of time given for each interaction, (b) the response time given by the teacher according to student gender, and (c) other student characteristics, such as ethnicity.

Prior to class, select a student (this will be you during the trial run recommended above) or an outside observer, such as a colleague, to do the tallying and calculations as follows. Ask the person to tally secretly the interactions between you and the students by placing a mark after the name of each student (or on the student's position on a seating chart) with whom you have verbal interaction. If a student does the tallying, that student should not be counted in any of the calculations.

Exact time at start: _____
Exact time at end: _____
Total time in minutes: _____

Total in class today = _____	Girls = _____	Boys = _____
	% Girls = _____	% Boys = _____

Tally of Interactions	
With girls	With boys
Total Interactions = _____	
% with girls = _____	% with boys = _____

Teacher Reflections and Conclusions:

Before giving students any assignment, consider how you would feel were you given the assignment, how you would feel were your own child given the assignment, about how much out-of-class time you expect the assignment to take, and to what extent, if any, parents and guardians and other family members should or could be involved in assisting the child with the assignment.

The time a student needs to complete assignments beyond school time will vary depending on many variables; the *very general rule of thumb* has been to expect a child to spend 4 nights a week (Monday through Thursday) doing roughly 10 minutes of homework per grade level, which means, for example, a first grader would spend about 10 minutes a night doing homework, a third grader about 30 minutes, and a sixth grader about 60 minutes. During your student teaching and later as an employed teacher you will want to check with your school about its particular expectations regarding this matter.

Purposes for Assignments

Purposes for giving homework assignments can be any of the following: to constructively extend the time that students are engaged in learning, to help students to develop personal learning, to help students develop their research skills, to help students develop their study skills, to help students organize their learning, to individualize the learning, to engage parents and guardians in their children's learning, to provide a mechanism by which students receive constructive feedback, to provide students with the opportunity to review and practice what has been learned, to reinforce classroom experiences, and to teach new content.

Guidelines for Using Assignments

To use assignments, consider the guidelines in the following paragraphs. An *assignment* is a statement of what the student is to accomplish, and *procedures* are statements of how to do something. Although students may need some procedural guidelines, especially with respect to your expectations on an assignment, generally, you will want to avoid supplying too much detail on how to accomplish an assignment.

Plan early and thoughtfully the types of assignments you will give (e.g., daily and long-range; minor and major; in class, out of class, or both; individual, paired, or group), and prepare assignment specifications. Assignments must correlate with specific instructional objectives and should *never* be given as busywork or as punishment. For each assignment, let students know what the purposes are; for example, whether the assignment is to prepare the student for what is to come in class, to practice what has been learned in class, or to extend the learning of class activities.

Use caution in giving assignments that could be controversial or could pose a hazard to the safety of students. In such cases (especially if you are a newcomer to the community), before giving the assignment, it is probably a good idea to talk it over with members of your teaching team or an administrator. Also, for a particular assignment, you may need to have parental or guardian permission and/or support for students to do it or be prepared to give an alternate assignment for some students.

Provide differentiated, tiered, or optional assignments—assignment variations given to students or selected by them on the basis of their interests and learning capacities (Willard-Holt, 2003). Students can select or be assigned different activities to accomplish the same objective, such as read and discuss, or they can participate with others in a more direct learning experience. After their study, as a portion of the assignment, students share what they have learned. This is another example of using multilevel teaching.

Sometimes teachers find it beneficial to prepare personalized study guides with questions to be answered and activities to be completed by the student while reading textbook chapters as homework. One advantage of a study guide is that it can make the reading more than a visual experience. A study guide can help to organize student learning by accenting instructional objectives, emphasizing important points to be learned, providing a guide for studying for tests, and encouraging the student to read the homework assignment.

Teachers need to understand that not only can homework help students learn factual information, develop study skills, and involve parents or guardians as facilitators in their child's education, but it can also overwhelm students and cause them to dislike learning, encourage them to take shortcuts, such as copying others' work, and prevent them from participating in extracurricular activities. Teachers sometimes underestimate just how long it will take a student to complete a homework assignment or how a particular assignment can disrupt the relationships in the child's home. With these considerations in mind, and as we said at the beginning of this section, think carefully about all homework assignments before making them.

Some students find homework and assignments very difficult, especially those children who have limited English proficiency, special needs, and little to no support from home. As an aid to these children in particular and to any student in general, many teachers use student volunteers to serve as *homework helpers* to assist other students both during class and after school, perhaps by exchanging telephone numbers or e-mail addresses. In some schools, teachers also use older students and even paid college students and adults as mentors.

As a general rule, homework assignments should stimulate thinking by arousing a student's curiosity, raising questions for further study, and encouraging and supporting the self-discipline required for independent study.

Determine the resources that students will need to complete assignments, and check the availability of these resources. This is important; students can't be expected to use that which is unavailable to them. Many will not use that which is not readily available.

Avoid yelling out assignments as students are leaving your classroom. When giving assignments in class, you should write them on a special place on the writing board, give a copy to each student, require that each student write the assignment into his or her assignment folder (an expectation in many schools), or include them in the course syllabus, taking extra care to be sure that assignment specifications are clear to students and to allow time for students to ask questions about an assignment. It's important that your procedure for giving and collecting assignments be consistent throughout the school year.

Students should be given sufficient time to complete their assignments. In other words, avoid announcing a new assignment that is due the very next day. As a general rule, assignments should be given much earlier than the day before they are due.

Although not always possible, try to avoid changing assignment specifications after they are given. Especially avoid changing them at the last minute, such as changing an assignment that is due tomorrow but was made weeks ago. Changing specifications at the last minute can be very frustrating to students who have already completed the assignment, and it shows little respect for those individuals.

We believe that time in class should be provided for students to begin work on homework assignments, so the teacher can give them individual attention (called *guided or coached practice*). The benefits of this coached practice include being able to monitor student work so that a student does not go too far in a wrong direction; help students reflect on their thinking; assess the progress of individual students; and discover or create a "teachable moment." For example, while monitoring students doing their work, you might discover a commonly shared student misconception. Then, taking advantage of this teachable moment, you stop and talk about that and attempt to clarify the misconception.

If the assignment is important for students to do, then you must give your full and immediate attention to the product of their efforts. Read almost everything that your students write. Students are much more willing to do homework when they believe it is useful, when it is treated as an integral component of instruction, when it is read and evaluated by the teacher, and when it counts in the grading. See "How to Avoid . . ." that follows, on the next page.

Provide feedback about each child's work, and be positive and constructive in your comments. Always think about the written comments that you make to be relatively certain they will convey your intended message to the student. When writing comments on student papers, consider using a color other than red, such as green or blue. Although to you this may sound trite, to many people red brings with it a host of negative connotations (e.g., blood, hurt, danger, stop), and children may perceive it as punitive.

Most routine homework assignments should not be graded for accuracy, only for completion. Rather than giving a percentage or numerical grade, with its negative connotations, teachers often prefer to mark assignment papers with constructive and reinforcing comments and symbols they have created for this purpose.

Regardless of subject being taught, you must give attention to the development of students' reading, listening, speaking, and writing skills. Attention to these skills must also be obvious in your assignment specifications and your assignment grading policy. Reading is crucial to the development of a person's ability to write. For example, to foster higher-order thinking, students in any subject can and should be encouraged to write (in their journals, as discussed later in this chapter) or draw representations of their thoughts and feelings about the material they have read.

Opportunities for Recovery

Using the concept of mastery (quality) learning would seem to us to dictate the need for a policy whereby students are able to revise and resubmit assignments for reassessment and grading. Although it is important to encourage positive initial efforts by students, sometimes, for a multitude of reasons, a student's first effort is inadequate or is lacking entirely. Perhaps the student is absent from school without legitimate excuse, or the student does poorly on an assignment or fails to turn in an assignment on time or at all. Although accepting late work from students is extra work for the teacher, and although allowing the resubmission of a marked or tentative-graded paper increases the amount of paperwork, many teachers report that it is worthwhile to give students the opportunity for recovery and a day or so to make corrections and resubmit an assignment for an improved score. However, out of regard for students who do well from the start and to encourage a best first effort, it is probably unwise to allow a resubmitted paper to receive an *A* grade (unless, of course, it was an *A* paper initially).

Students sometimes have legitimate reasons for not completing an assignment by the due date. It is our opinion that the teacher should listen and exercise professional judgment in each instance. As someone once said, there is nothing democratic about treating unequals as equals. The provision of recovery options seems a sensible and scholastic tactic.

How to Avoid Having So Many Papers to Grade That Time for Effective Planning Is Restricted

A Waterloo for some beginning teachers is that of being buried beneath mounds of homework to be read and marked, leaving less and less time for effective planning. To keep this from happening to you, consider the following suggestions. Although, in our opinion, the teacher should read almost everything that students write, papers can be read with varying degrees of intensity and scrutiny, depending on the purpose of the assignment. For assignments that are designed for learning, understanding, and practice, you can allow students to check them themselves using either self-checking or peer checking. During the self- or peer checking, you can walk around the room, monitor the activity, and record whether a student did the assignment or not, or after the checking, you can collect the papers and do your recording. Besides reducing the amount of paperwork for you, student self- or peer checking provides other advantages: It allows students to see and understand their errors, it encourages productive peer dialogue, and it helps them develop self-assessment techniques and standards. If the purpose of the assignment is to assess mastery competence, then the papers should be read, marked, and graded only by you or by you and members of your teaching team.

Caution about Using Peer Checking   Peer checking can, however, be a problem. Sometimes during peer checking of student work, students may spend more time watching the person checking their paper than they do accurately checking the one given to them. And use of peer checking does not necessarily allow a student to see or understand his or her mistakes.

Of even greater concern is the matter of privacy. Even though the U.S. Supreme Court (on February 19, 2002) ruled unanimously that students may grade each other's work in class without violating federal privacy law, still when Student A becomes knowledgeable of the academic success or failure of Student

B, Student A, the "checker," could cause emotional or social embarrassment to Student B. It is our opinion that peer checking of papers should be done only for the editing of classmates' drafts of stories or research projects, making suggestions about content and grammar, but not assigning a grade or marking answers right or wrong.

PROJECT-CENTERED LEARNING: GUIDING LEARNING FROM INDEPENDENT AND GROUP INVESTIGATIONS, PAPERS, AND ORAL REPORTS

For the most meaningful student learning to occur, independent study, individual writing, student-centered projects, and oral reports should be major features of your instruction. There will be times when the students are interested in an in-depth inquiry of a topic and will want to pursue a particular topic for study. This undertaking of a learning project can be flexible—an individual student, a team of two, a small group, or the entire class can do the investigation. The *project* is a relatively long-term investigative study from which students produce something called the culminating presentation. It is a way for students to apply what they are learning. The *culminating presentation* is a final presentation that usually includes an oral and written presentation accompanied by a hands-on item of some kind (e.g., a display, play or skit, book, song or poem, multimedia presentation, diorama, poster, maps, charts, and so on).

Values and Purposes of Project-Centered Learning

The values and purposes of encouraging project-centered learning are to develop individual skills in cooperation and social interaction; develop student skills in writing, communication, and in higher-level thinking and doing; foster student engagement and independent learning and thinking skills; optimize personal meaning of the learning to each student by considering, valuing, and accommodating individual interests, learning styles, learning capacities, and life experiences; provide an opportunity for each student to become especially knowledgeable and experienced in one area of subject content or in one process skill, thus adding to the students' knowledge and experience base and sense of importance and self-worth; provide an opportunity for students to become intrinsically motivated to learn because they are working on topics of personal meaning, with outcomes and time lines that are relatively open-ended; provide an opportunity for students to make decisions about their own learning and to develop their skills in managing time and materials; and provide an opportunity for students to make an important contribution. As has been demonstrated time and again, when students choose their own projects, integrating knowledge as the need arises, motivation and learning follow naturally (Tassinari, 1996; McCullen, 2000).

Guidelines for Guiding Students in Project-Centered Learning

In collaboration with the teacher, students select a topic for the project. Some experts suggest planning projects backward, that is, by first identifying the desired results (the objectives), then determining acceptable evidence, followed lastly by planning the learning experience (Fagan & Sherman, 2002). Regardless, what you can do is to stimulate ideas and provide anchor studies (also called model or benchmark examples). You can stimulate ideas by providing lists of things students might do, by mentioning each time an idea comes up in class that this would be a good idea for an independent, small-group, or class project, by having former students tell about their projects, by showing the results of other students' projects, by suggesting Internet resources and readings that are likely to give students ideas, and by using class discussions to brainstorm ideas.

Sometimes a teacher will write the general problem or topic in the center of a graphic web and ask the students to brainstorm some questions. The questions will lead to ways for students to investigate, draw sketches, construct models, record findings, predict items, compare and contrast, and discuss understandings. In essence, this kind of brainstorming is the technique often used by teachers in collaboration with students for the selection of an interdisciplinary thematic unit of study.

Allow students to individually choose whether they will work alone, in pairs, or in small groups. If they choose to work in groups, then help them delineate job descriptions for each member of the group. For project work, groups of four or less students usually work better than groups of more than four. Even if the project is one the whole class is pursuing, the project should be broken down into parts with individuals or small groups of students undertaking independent study of these parts.

You can keep track of the students' progress by reviewing weekly updates of their work. Set deadlines with the groups and meet with groups daily to discuss any questions or problems they have. Based on their investigations, the students will prepare and present their findings in culminating presentations.

Provide coaching and guidance. Work with each student or student team in topic selection, as well as in the processes of written and oral reporting. Allow students to develop their own procedures, but guide their preparation of work outlines and preliminary drafts, giving them constructive feedback and encouragement along the way. Aid students in their identification of potential resources and in the techniques of research. Assist the students, for example, in their understanding of the concepts of accuracy and reliability.

Your coordination with the library and other resource centers is central to the success of project-centered teaching. Frequent drafts and progress reports from the students are a must. With each of these stages, provide students with constructive feedback and encouragement. Provide written guidelines and negotiate time lines for the outlines, drafts, and the completed project.

Promote sharing by insisting that students share both the progress and the results of their study with the rest of the class. The amount of time allowed for this sharing will, of course, depend on many variables. The value of this type of instructional strategy comes not only from individual contributions but also from the learning that results from the experience and the communication of that experience with others. For project work and student sharing of the outcomes of their study, some teachers have their students use the KWHLS strategy (see Chapter 5), where the student identifies what he/she already *K*nows about the topic of study, *W*hat he/she wants to learn, *H*ow the student plans to learn it, then what he/she *L*earned, and how the student will *S*hare with others what was learned from the study.

Without careful planning, and unless students are given steady guidance, project-based teaching can be a frustrating experience for both the teacher and the students, and especially for a beginning teacher who is inexperienced in such an undertaking. Students should do projects because they want to and because the project seems meaningful. Therefore, students with guidance from you should decide what project to do and how to do it. Your role is to advise and guide students so they experience success. If the teacher or teaching team lays out a project in too much detail, that then is a procedure rather than a student-centered project. There must be a balance between structure and opportunities for student choices and decision making. Without frequent progress reporting by the student and guidance and reinforcement from the teacher, a student can become frustrated and quickly lose interest in the project. What do we mean when we say "frequent"? In our opinion, as a general rule, progress reports from students should be weekly.

Writing as a Required Component of Project-Centered Learning

Provide options but insist that writing be a component of each student's work. Research examining the links among writing, thinking, and learning has helped emphasize the importance of writing. Writing is a complex intellectual behavior and process that helps the learner create and record his or her understanding—that is, to construct meaning.

When teachers use project-centered teaching, a paper and an oral presentation are usually automatically required of all students. It is recommended that you use the *I-Search paper* strategy: Under your careful guidance, the student: (a) lists things that he/she would like to know, and from the list selects one, which becomes the research topic; (b) conducts the study while maintaining a log of activities and findings, which becomes a process journal; (c) prepares a booklet that presents the student's findings, and that consists of paragraphs and visual representations; (d) prepares a summary of the findings, including the significance of the study and the student's personal feelings; and (e) shares the project as a final oral report with the teacher and classmates.

Assessing the Final Product

The final product of the project, including papers, oral reports, and presentations, should be graded. The method of determining the grade should be clear to students from the beginning, as well as the weight of the project grade toward each student's term grade. Provide students with clear descriptions (*rubrics*) of how evaluation and grading will be done. Evaluation should include meeting deadlines for drafts and progress reports. The final grade for the study should be based on four criteria: (a) how well it was organized, including meeting draft deadlines; (b) the quality and quantity of both content and procedural knowledge gained from the experience; (c) the quality of the student's sharing of that learning experience with the rest of the class; and (d) the quality of the student's final written or oral report.

WRITING: EVERY TEACHER'S RESPONSIBILITY

Because writing is a discrete representation of thinking, every teacher should consider himself or herself to be a teacher of writing. In exemplary schools, using multiple technologies to teach writing—paper and pencil, e-mail, listservers, and software packages (Yancey, 2004)—student writing is encouraged in all subjects, at all grade levels, across the curriculum. For example, Burns (2004) suggested that a teacher of mathematics give writing assignments that fall into these four categories: maintaining journals or logs, solving problems, explaining mathematical ideas, and writing about learning processes. Oftentimes, and especially with the current prominence of standardized writing assessments, all teachers of a particular school, and even district, are expected to assess students' papers using the same scoring rubric (Baldwin, 2004).

TPW Video Classroom

Series: Language Arts Methods

Module 3: Writing

Video 1: Prewriting in Sixth Grade

Kinds of Writing

A student should experience a variety of kinds of writing rather than the same form, class after class, year after year. Perhaps most important is that writing should be emphasized as a process that illustrates one's thinking, rather than solely as a product completed as an assignment. Writing and thinking develop best when a student experiences, during any school day, various forms of writing to express their ideas, such as the following.

Autobiographical Incident   The writer narrates a specific event in his or her life and states or implies the significance of the event.

Evaluation   The writer presents a judgment on the worth of an item—book, movie, artwork, consumer product—and supports this with reasons and evidence.

Eyewitness Account   The writer tells about a person, group, or event that was objectively observed from the outside.

Firsthand Biographical Sketch   Through incident and description, the writer characterizes a person he or she knows well.

Interpretation   The writer conjectures about the causes and effects of a specific event.

Problem Solving   The writer describes and analyzes a specific problem and then proposes and argues for a solution.

Report of Information   The writer collects data from observation and research and chooses material that best represents a phenomenon or concept.

Story   Using dialogue and description, the writer shows conflict between characters or between a character and the environment.

Student Journals

Many teachers have their students maintain journals in which the children keep a log of their activities, findings, and thoughts (i.e., *process journal*) and write their thoughts about what it is they are studying (*response journal*). Actually, commonly used are two types of response journals: dialogue journals and reading-response journals. *Dialogue journals* are used for students to write anything that is on their minds, perhaps on a Web site (see sample entries in the boxed scenario on page 336), or in a written binder on the right-side page, whereas peers, teachers, and parents or guardians respond on the left-side page, thereby "talking with" the journal writer (Werderich, 2002). *Response journals* are used for students to write (and perhaps draw—a "visual learning log") their reactions to whatever is being studied.

Purpose and Assessment of Student Journal Writing   Normally, academic journals are *not* the personal diaries of the writer's recollection of daily events and the writer's thoughts about the events. Rather, the purpose of journal writing is to encourage students to write, to think about their writing, to record their creative thoughts about what they are learning, and to share their written thoughts with an audience—all of which help in the development of their thinking skills, in their learning, and in their development as writers. Students are encouraged to write about experiences, both in school and out, that are related to the topics being studied. They should be encouraged to record their feelings about what and how they are learning.

Journal writing provides practice in expression and should *not* be graded by the teacher. Negative comments and evaluations from the teacher will discourage creative and spontaneous expression by students. Teachers should read the journal

TEACHING IN PRACTICE Students Who Supposedly Can't Write, Try— and They Can! Mr. Mayo Uses Blogs to Encourage Student Writing[*]

Last year, I set up blogs for eight students in a remediation class I teach. The students in this class had failed one or more parts of the fifth-grade Standards of Learning state test. They lose an elective in sixth grade and have to take this remediation class to work on their reading and writing skills. These are the students who supposedly can't write. Well, they can, and they did. They wrote a lot once they had their own blogs.

Each student assumed a nickname for an online blog identity. My first assignment: Write about your favorite hobby. It ended up being the most productive writing day of the entire semester.

Here's Shiloh, a.k.a. Kangaroo, on her favorite hobby, canoeing:

"Whin I cone whith my dad in his cone he sters and I have to whouch for rocks. He gets rilly mad if we hit one. You may not think it is easy to brake a cone, but this one man hit a rock on one of the tuffest rivers and the cone got raped aroun a ruck. It was cool looking. My dad jumd on it and poped the dint rit out."

Here's another sample from Cody, a.k.a. Fox. He's writing about his favorite hobby, BMX biking:

"My favorite thing to do is bikeing. I like to bike that I have a biking club. My biking clubs name is The Ghost Rider Kings. We are very good. We can do some good tricks. We can do indos, ghost riders, skids, Biddle caps, snakes. I can do the Biddle cap very good."

When asked to write about something they love to do, the students wrote enthusiastically. The writing was fun and purposeful. Blogs make student writing more accessible. With blogs, students know that what they write is going to be immediately published. They take their writing more seriously.

Here's a quote from, Todd, a.k.a. Giraffe, about writing on his blog:

"I used to hate writing but now I like it the day I came I was angry that I was in remediation and knew it would be boring but I was wrong and

waited until we actually started the class. Now I know that if I am here for the rest of the year I will just learn more and more."

My remediation students were amazed at the amount of writing they did on their blogs. They regularly scrolled up and down the screen reading and marveling at everything they had written. They talked to each other about what they had written, and compared entries.

As students begin to accumulate a large amount of writing, they begin to feel more confident. They also begin to see themselves as writers. Not only were they interested in their own blogs, they became curious about what others were up to. The clean and accessible format of the writing naturally builds curiosity. Students talk spontaneously to each other about their writing and their ideas. They actually start to point out sentence-level errors to each other as they discuss their writing.

Student blogs help create a sense of community by making student writing accessible to anyone who has Internet access. With blogs, a student's peers, relatives, teachers, and administrators are invited to watch a student's growth. The more people who read a student's work, the more likely they are to talk to that student about their writing. This helps create a sense of community that is otherwise hard to imagine. Parents can check in whenever they feel like it to see what their kids are doing in school, and interested parties get a candid sense of student writing in their true voices. This helps establish a dialogue between parent and child and draws parents into the classroom in a new way. With blogs, students are more likely to care about what they write because they have a built-in audience.

This experience has convinced me that blogs can be a powerful motivator to get students to write and to take their writing more seriously. For the next school year, I am setting up blogs for all 120 of my students and will ask my students to write on their blogs as much as possible.

[*] Courtesy of George Mayo.

writing and then offer constructive and positive feedback, but avoid negative comments or grading the journals. For grading purposes, most teachers simply record whether or not a student does, in fact, maintain the required journal.

A COLLECTION OF ANNOTATED MOTIVATIONAL TEACHING STRATEGIES WITH IDEAS FOR LESSONS, INTERDISCIPLINARY TEACHING, TRANSCULTURAL STUDIES, AND STUDENT PROJECTS

Today's young people are used to multimillion-dollar productions on television, stage, CDs and DVDs, arcade games, and the movie screen. When they come to school, into your classroom, and are subjected each day to something short of a high-budget production, it is little wonder that they sometimes react in a less than highly motivated fashion. No doubt, today's children are growing up in a highly stimulating instant-action society, a society that has learned to expect instant electronic communication, instant information retrieval, instant pain relief, instant meals, instant gratification, instant replays, and perhaps, in the minds of many youth, instant high-paying employment with signing bonuses for jobs that entail more fun than hard work. In light of this cultural phenomenon, we are on your side: The classroom teacher is on the firing line each day and is expected to perform—perhaps instantly and entertainingly, but most certainly in a highly competent and professional manner—in situations that are far from ideal. In any case, you must gain your students' attention before you can teach them.

In this, the final section of this chapter, you will find the presentation of an annotated list of ideas, many of which have been offered over recent years by classroom teachers. (See also Web site listings at the conclusion of this chapter.) Although the ideas are organized according to discipline, and some may be more appropriate for one group of children or grade level than another, you may profit from reading all entries for each field. Although a particular entry might be identified as specific to one discipline, it might also be useful in others (many of them can be used in interdisciplinary teaching—for example, number one can clearly be combined with mathematics and science, as well as art), or it might stimulate a creative thought for your own stock of motivational techniques, such as an idea for a way to utilize the theory of multiple learning capacities, to incorporate technology, or to emphasize the multicultural aspect of a lesson in math, social studies, or whatever the central discipline or theme of a lesson or unit of instruction.

The Visual and Performing Arts

1. As part of a unit combining design or creativity with science, have students design, construct, and decorate their own kites. Designate a launch date, location, and time.

2. Use lyrics from popular music to influence student work in class, such as putting the lyrics into pictures or movement.

3. Utilize the outdoors or another environment, such as a shopping mall, for a free drawing experience.

4. Invite a local artist who has created a community mural to speak to the class about the mural. Plan and create a class mural, perhaps on a large sheet of plywood or some other location approved by the school administration. For example, at Chartiers Valley Intermediate School (Pittsburgh, PA), for a number of years, as a culminating project in the school's visual arts program, each fifth-grade class has contributed its own section to a growing mural in the school cafeteria.

5. Create a mandala to demonstrate the importance of individual experience, as in interpreting paintings and interpreting poetry.

6. Study masks. Collect books, magazines, posters, films, videos, computer software programs, and other sources that show different kinds of masks work by people from around the world. Ask students to identify the similarities and differences in the masks. Have them research the meanings that mask characters have in various cultures. Have students design and create their own masks to illustrate their own personalities, cultures, and personal characteristics.

7. As portion of a unit on the creative process, have each student draw or sketch on a piece of paper, then pass it on to the next person, and that person will make additions to the drawing. Instructions could include "improve the drawing," "make the drawing ugly," "make the drawing 17th century," and "add what you think necessary to complete the composition."

8. Imagine that you're a bird flying over a large city you have visited. Draw a "sensory" map of what you see, hear, smell, feel, and taste.

9. Assign each student a different color. Have the students arrange themselves into warm and cool colors and explain their decisions (why blue is cool, etc.). Discuss people's emotional responses to each of the colors.

10. Watch a video of dances from various countries and cultures. Invite students to identify similarities and differences. Ask them to research the meanings and occasions of particular dances.

11. Challenge students to discover ways that music, art, and dance are used in their community.

12. Find a popular song liked by the students. Transpose the melody into unfamiliar keys for each instrument. This makes the student want to learn the song, but in the process the student will have to become more familiar with the instrument.

13. Play a group-activity rhythm game, one such as the "Dutch Shoe Game," to get students to cooperate, work together, and enjoy themselves using rhythm. Participants sit in a circle, and as the song is sung, each person passes one of his or her shoes to the person on the right in rhythm to the music. Shoes continue to be passed as long as verses are sung.

14. Choose a rhythmical, humorous poem or verse to conduct as if it were a musical work. The students read the poem in chorus while you stand before them and

conduct. Students must be sensitive to the intonation, speed, inflection, mood, and dynamics that you expect them to convey in their reading.

15. Organize a Retired Senior Citizens Volunteer Program (RSCVP) with senior citizens presenting folk art workshops with students, where the children and seniors work together to create artwork for the school and community.

16. Students from Elkhorn Area Middle School (Elkhorn, WI) organized an Improv Troupe, which creates and performs unscripted, improvisational skits about social issues relevant to today's youth (Reedy, 2001).

English, Languages, and the Language Arts

17. Organize a paper or electronic letter-writing activity between senior citizens and your students.

18. On a U.S. road map, have students find the names of places that sound "foreign" and categorize the names according to nationality or culture. Students could research when and how places got their names.

19. Set up this problem to enhance understanding of parts of speech. Provide several boxes (shoe boxes work fine) containing different parts of speech. Each student is to form one sentence from the fragments chosen from each box, being allowed to discard only at a penalty. The students then nonverbally make trades with other students to make coherent and perhaps meaningfully amusing sentences. A student may trade a noun for a verb but will have to keep in mind what parts of speech are essential for a sentence. Results may be read aloud as a culmination to this activity.

20. Students can match American English and British English words (or any other combination of languages), such as cookies and biscuits, hood and bonnet, canned meat and tinned meat, elevator and lift, flashlight and torch, subway and tube, garbage collector and dustman, undershirt and vest, sweater and jumper, and gasoline and petrol. Have students compare pronunciations and spellings.

21. English words derive from many other languages. Have students research and list some, such as ketchup (Malay), alcohol (Arabic), kindergarten (German), menu (French), shampoo (Hindi), bonanza (Spanish), piano (Italian), kosher (Yiddish), and smorgasbord (Swedish).

22. Read a story to the class but without ending. Then ask the students (as individuals or in think-write-share-pairs) to invent and write their own endings or conclusions.

23. Challenge students to create an advertisement (decide for radio, TV, Internet, or print medium) using a propaganda device of their choice.

24. Invite students (individually or in pairs) to create and design an invention and then to write a "patent description" for their invention.

25. Using think-write-share-pair, invite students to write a physical description of some well-known public figure, such as a movie star, politician, athlete, or musician. Other class members may enjoy trying to identify the "mystery" personality from the written description.

26. Everyone has heard of or experienced stereotyping. Ask students to list stereotypes they have heard and examples they find in media. Have students discuss these questions: Have you ever felt stereotyped? How do you suppose stereotypes come to be? Does stereotyping have any useful value? Can it be harmful?

27. Remove the text from a newspaper comic strip and have the students work in pairs to create the storyline; or, give each pair a picture from a magazine and have the pair create a story about the picture.

28. Invite students to choose a short story from a text and write it into a play and perform the play for their family members.

29. To begin a poetry unit, ask students to bring in the lyrics to their favorite songs. Show how these fit into the genre of poetry.

30. Invite students to analyze commercial advertisements and search for ads for a product that is potentially damaging to the natural environment.

31. Have students analyze commercial advertisements for the emotions to which they appeal, for the techniques used, and for their integrity. Try the same thing with radio, youth magazines, theater advertisements, Web sites, and other media.

32. Change the learning environment by moving to an outdoor location, and ask students to write poetry to see if the change in surroundings stimulates or discourages their creativeness. Discuss the results. For example, take your class to a large supermarket, a mall, a lake, a forest, or an athletic stadium to write.

33. Use your state's seal to initiate the study of the concept of interpretations. Have students analyze the seal for its history and the meaning of its various symbols. Do the same with a dollar bill.

34. Provide puppets in native costume for students to use in practicing dialogue when learning a language or in developing language skills.

35. Have students use the Internet to establish communication with students from another place in the world.

36. As a class or small-group project, design a page on your school Web site.

37. Use drama to build language arts and thinking skills. Have students write dialogue, set scenes, and communicate emotions through expressive language and mime.

38. One teacher uses a digital camera to take pictures of her students acting out scenes from a book being read in class. She puts the photos on slides and asks the students to describe their actions in words. From this activity, the students then create their own books.

39. Invite students to create and write a movie script by viewing any five- to ten-minute scene taken from a film and then writing a script for that scene.

40. Students from a school in Arizona became pen pals with inner-city students from Toledo, OH. Not only did the experience prove beneficial for their lessons in language arts, but it also promoted their knowledge about their city and state, resulting in cross-curricular learning (Lemkuhl, 2002).

41. Challenge students to look for, create, and collect *palindromes*, a series of words or sentences, or numbers, that read the same backward or forward. Examples are the names *Ava* and *Otto*, the words *racecar* and *solos*, the date *6.06.06*, and the year 2002.

Mathematics

42. Collaboratively plan with students a role-play unit where members role-play the solar system. Students calculate their weights, set up a proportion system, find a large field, and as a culmination to the project actually simulate the solar system, using their own bodies to represent the sun, planets, and moons. Notify local media of the culminating event.

43. Encourage students to look for evidence of the (Leonardo Pisano) Fibonacci number series (i.e., 1, 1, 2, 3, 5, 8, 13, 21, etc., where each number is gotten by adding the two previous numbers), both within and outside mathematics, such as in nature and in manufactured objects. Perhaps your students might like to organize a Fibonacci Club and through the Internet establish communication with similar clubs around the world.

44. Have students research the history of the cost of a first-class, U.S. postage stamp, and then ask them to devise ways of predicting its cost by the year they graduate from high school, the year they become grandparents, or some other target year.

45. Provide students a list of the frequencies of each of the 88 keys and strings on a piano (a local music store can provide the information). Challenge students to derive an equation to express the relation between key position and frequency. After they have done this, research and tell them about the Bösendorfer piano (Germany) with its nine extra keys at the lower end of the keyboard. See if students can predict the frequencies of those extra keys.

46. Using a light sensor to measure the intensity of a light source from various distances, have students graph the data points and then find the relevant equation.

47. Students at George Washington Middle School (Alexandria, VA) participate in a parachute creation contest. Using plastic from trash bags, string, and a bobby pin as the skydiver, the challenge is to design a parachute with the least surface area and longest hang time (Mann, 2000).

48. Establish a service-learning project, mentoring children of lower grades.

49. Invite your students to survey and map the school grounds.

50. Invite your students to research, design, build, and decorate their own kayaks or canoes.

Physical Education

51. Ask students to choose individually (or in dyads) a famous athlete they most (or least) admire. A short report will be written about the athlete. The student will then discuss the attributes and/or characteristics that they admire (or dislike) in the athlete and how they feel they can emulate (or avoid) those qualities. After all pairs of students have made their presentations, as a class devise two lists, one of common attributes admired, the other of qualities to avoid.

52. Challenge students, in small learning groups, to create an exercise routine to their favorite music recording and share it with the class. Have them discuss how they arrived at decisions along the way.

A science program that provides for a heavy loading of hands-on, minds-on activities is a valuable segment of the elementary school curriculum. Notice in this photograph that the children have been provided safety eyewear to protect against accidental injury while conducting their science investigation.

Anthony Megnacca/Merrill

Science

53. Challenge students to create and test their own science tools and materials, such as microscopes using stems of bamboo with a drop of water in each end, or litmus indicators made from the petals of flowers.

54. Record sounds of the environment. Compare and write about day versus night sounds, fall versus spring sounds, foggy day versus sunny day sounds, busy mall versus residential backyard sounds, single residential dwelling versus multiple residential dwelling sounds.

55. Plan a yearlong project where each student, or small group of students, must develop knowledge and understanding of some specific piece of technology. Each project culmination presentation must have five components: visual, oral, written, artistic, and creative.

56. For a life science class, on the first day of class give each student one live guppy in a test tube and one live cactus plant in a three-inch pot. Tell the students that the minimum they each need to pass the course is to bring their pet plant and fish back to you during the final week of school—alive.

57. If you are a life science teacher, make sure your classroom looks like a place for studying life rather than a place of death, that is it contains living plants and animals, rather than only preserved ones.

58. With each student playing the role of a cell part, have students set up and perform a role-play simulating parts of cells.

59. Divide your class into groups, and ask each group to create an environment for an imaginary organism using discarded items from the environment. By asking

questions, each group will try to learn about the other groups' "mystery" organisms.

60. Have each student, or student pair, "adopt" a chemical element. The student then researches that element and becomes the class expert whenever that particular substance comes up in discussion. There could be a special bulletin board for putting up questions on interesting or little-known facts about the elements.

61. You gotta have milk! Challenge your students to make their own buttons from milk. Milk can be precipitated, separated, and the solid product dried to form a very hard substance that was, in the days before plastic, used to make buttons.

62. As a class or interdisciplinary team project, obtain permission and "adopt" a wetland area or some other environmental project that is located near the school.

63. Invite students to research the composition and development of familiar objects. For example, the ordinary pencil is made of cedar wood from the forests of the Pacific Northwest. The graphite is often from Montana or Mexico and is reinforced with clays from Georgia and Kentucky. The eraser is made from soybean oil, latex from trees in South America, reinforced with pumice from California or New Mexico and sulfur, calcium, and barium. The metal band is aluminum or brass, made from copper and zinc, and mined in several states of the United States and in several provinces of Canada. The paint to color the wood and the lacquer to make it shine are made from a variety of different minerals and metals, as is the glue that holds the wood together.

64. Invite students to locate and design large posters to hang on the classroom walls that show the meaning of words used in science that are not typical of their meaning in everyday language usage—the words *theory* and *Spanish moss* are examples.

65. With your students, plan a community service project. For example, students of the Powder River County School District (Broadus, MT) adopted community flower gardens and conduct an annual food drive for the needy. At Great Falls Middle School (Montague, MA), students research and produce television documentaries on subjects related to energy. The documentaries are broadcast on the local cable channel to promote energy literacy in the school and community.

66. Sometimes projects become ongoing, permanent endeavors with many spinoff projects of shorter duration. For example, what began as a science classroom project at W. H. English Middle School (Scottsburg, IN) has become what is perhaps the largest animal refuge shelter in the Midwest, and students at Baldwyn Middle School (Baldwyn, MS) plan and care for the landscaping of the local battlefield/museum.

67. Invite students to research and produce TV documentaries on subjects related to energy, fuel consumption, or on a health-related topic. To promote topic literacy in the school and surrounding community, a local TV channel might be willing to broadcast the documentaries.

About SCIENCE, MAGIC, AND SHOWMANSHIP

A Personal Story from
Author Richard Kellough

If you ever have attended a local, regional, or national meeting for science teachers, you are undoubtedly aware of the popularity of sessions that include "magic" in their titles. Two popular presenters of such sessions have been Alan McCormack and the late Tik Liem. Besides their magical presentation ability, at least two other reasons explain this popularity: the mystique and natural interest in magic and the continuing needs of teachers to find ways of turning their students on.

When I was a child, my Uncle Raymond Stephens was a professional magician, whose stage performances and personal presentations to me were always a source of fascination, a man whose magic and showmanship never failed to set my brain into gear. During my professional years of working with science teachers, their one need that seems always to stand out is their insatiable appetite for finding ways of presenting science that will make learning for students exciting and lasting—learning that sets the students' brains into gear. Perhaps in today's electronic age the need is greater than ever, as youth seem to need and to expect steady stimulation. Many seem as if they are addicted to an ongoing adrenaline high.

The first time I saw the phrase, "science, magic, and showmanship," I was curious, curious because I had always believed that science and magic were mutually exclusive, as being, so to speak, from different camps. My attention was further captured by the marriage of the terms "science" and "magic" with the term "showmanship." What follows, then, is my explanation of that significance as I have learned it to be.

We all know the meaning of the noun "science." Science is several things—a way of thinking, a body of knowledge, a way of investigating, an active process that can be carried on by anyone trained in the skills and attitude of sciencing. (*Note:* "Sciencing" is a word used to emphasize the importance of process when talking about what it is a scientist does [Victor and Kellough, *Science K–8*, Merrill Prentice Hall, 10th edition, 2004, p. 15].)

"Magic," however can be defined as either a noun or as an adjective. As a noun it means having an overpowering influence or seeming control over natural phenomena. There is *black magic*, or sorcery, that has to do with invoking supernatural powers for sinister purposes, and there is *white magic*, that has to do with the study of natural phenomena. The natural sciences have evolved from white magic. As an adjective, magic means mysteriously impressive or beautiful. That is the definition being used when we use the phrase "science, magic, and showmanship."

"Showmanship," a noun, is the ability to present or to demonstrate something in a dramatic and favorable manner.

So, you see, using the terms together does make sense. The phrase "science, magic, and showmanship" refers to the presentation of science in an impressively (even beautifully) dramatic and favorable fashion. As with my Uncle Raymond, the magician, the vehicle for catching student attention and getting the student to science (here being used as a verb) is by showing the student something that is contrary to the student's experience and expectation.

Situations that are contrary to what the student thinks and expects create cognitive disequilibria and are known as *discrepant events*. Discrepant events naturally cause the student to wonder and to hypothesize an explanation. When one observes a discrepant event, not unlike watching a magic show, hypothesizing an explanation is an immediate and unavoidable mental phenomenon. The brain attempts to make sense from the observed discrepancy. When the student finds a tentative, but acceptable explanation, the student is at a new cognitive level and is ready to focus on other situations that cause even further curiosity, excitement, and motivation to do science—to learn.

Perhaps many of the best science teachers, indeed best of teachers of any subject or grade level, are those who knowingly or unknowingly are able to incorporate a bit of magic and showmanship into their teaching. It is never too late to begin your own collection of ideas.

68. Have a group of students research from the Internet and library the literature and report on the plant *Morinda citrifolia*. Have them share their findings with the rest of the class.
69. Have students use bobblehead toys to explore force and motion (Foster, 2003).
70. Engage your students in planning and implementing a family science night at school [see Lundeen in the suggested readings at the end of the chapter].

Social Studies/History

71. Invite the students to organize an improvisation troupe to create and perform skits about social issues relevant to today's youth. Perform the skits at school events, parent–teacher organization meetings, and for community groups.
72. Organize an Intergenerational Advocacy program, in which students and senior citizens work together to make a better society for both groups (MacBain, 1996).
73. Initiate a service-learning project where, for an extended period of time, students work directly with community organizations and agencies. For example, at John Ford Middle School (St. Matthews, SC) students incorporate the Constitutional Rights Foundation "City Youth" program into the curriculum, helping to make decisions about areas of the community that need improvement.
74. During their study of Ancient Egypt or Central America, invite students to create and build their own model pyramids; in science, students could study simple machines that will help in their pyramid building.
75. Invite students to plan how they would improve their living environment, beginning with the classroom, moving out to the school, home, community, state, country, and finally the global level.
76. Start a pictorial essay on the development and/or changes of a given area in your community, such as a major corner or block adjacent to the school. This is a study project that could continue for years and that has many social, political, and economic implications.

77. Invite your students in small groups or as a class project to design and build a model of their community.

78. Start a folk hero study. Each year ask, "What prominent human being who has lived during (a particular period of time) do you most (and/or least) admire?" Collect individual responses to the question, tally results, and discuss. After doing this for several years, you may wish to share with your class for comparison and discussion purposes the results of your surveys of previous years.

79. Start a sister class program. Establish a class relationship with another similar class from another school from your district, a neighboring district, or from around the country or the world, perhaps by using the Internet.

80. During their study of westward expansion, challenge students to organize a role-play of a simulated family movement to the West in the 1800s. What items would they take? What would they toss out of the wagon to lighten the load? Where would they stop and settle? Or would they stop, turn around, and return to their point of origin? What issues would enter into their decision making?

81. Invite students to collect music, art, or athletic records from a particular period of American history. Have them compare their collections with the music, art, or recordings of today and predict the music, art, or recordings of the future.

82. Using play money, establish a capitalistic economic system within your classroom. Salaries may be paid for attendance and bonus income for work well done, taxes may be collected for poor work, and a welfare section established somewhere in the room.

83. Divide your class into small groups, and ask that each group make predictions as to what world governments, world geography, world social issues, world health, world energy, or some other related topic will be like some time in the future. Let each group give its report, followed by debate and discussion. With guidance from the school administration, plant the predictions in some secret location on the school grounds for a future discovery.

84. As an opener to a unit on the U.S. Constitution, have students design their own classroom (or school) "Bill of Rights."

85. Using Legos or sugar cubes as construction blocks, and with assigned roles, challenge students to simulate the building of the Great Wall of China.

86. At Indian Trail Junior High School (Addison, IL), all eighth graders and teachers from not only social studies but various other content areas, including English, mathematics, physical education, and science, work together on a "real-world," problem-based project titled the Inspector Red Ribbon Unit. The unit focuses on a social problem that has truly occurred too many times—the prom night automobile accident.

87. Challenge students to establish a caring and antibullying or antiviolence program.

88. During an interdisciplinary thematic unit of study of the medieval period of Europe, have students study and build model castles.

89. With guidance from three teachers using a common philosophical approach based on Glasser's Choice Theory, Reality Therapy, and ideas from his book *The Quality School*, students of history at Longfellow Middle School

(La Crosse, WI) designed and built their own middle school nation (Frost, Olson, & Valiquette, 2000).

90. Plan time each week for students to comment on the week's classroom activities and to compliment a peer.

91. Organize a study to determine how well children who have arrived in the United States from other countries are integrated into your community and school's culture.

92. Invite students to research, identify, and discuss current plagiarism and copyright issues, particularly pertaining to Internet and recorded music.

SUMMARY

This chapter has continued the development of your repertoire of teaching strategies. As you know, children can be quite peer-conscious, can have relatively short attention spans for experiences in which they are uninterested, and prefer experiences that are multisensory and require activity. Most are intensely curious about things of interest to them. Cooperative learning, student-centered projects, and teaching strategies that emphasize shared discovery and inquiry (discussed in the next and final chapter) within a psychologically safe environment encourage the most positive aspects of thinking and learning. Central to your strategy selection should be those strategies that encourage students to become independent thinkers and skilled learners who can participate in the planning, structuring, regulating, and assessing of their own learning and learning activities.

STUDY QUESTIONS AND ADDITIONAL ACTIVITIES

1. Using modern software to enhance their project presentations, students are learning to put their presentations on computerized visual shows that they fill with colorful animation, bold topic headings and neat rows of points they wish to make, each introduced with a highlight mark. Some educators are concerned that too often young people become fixated on fonts and formats and other aspects of the technology without actually giving much deep thought to the content of their presentations. Share your experiences and opinions about this.

2. Do you have concerns about using project-based teaching and not being able to cover all the content you believe should be covered? Think back to your own schooling. What do you really remember? Most likely you remember projects, yours and other students' presentations, the lengthy research you did, and your extra effort for the artwork to accompany your presentation. Maybe you remember a compliment by a teacher or a pat on the back by peers. Most likely you do not remember the massive amount of content that was covered. Discuss your feelings about this with your classmates. Share experiences and concerns.

3. It is an aphorism that to learn something well, students need time to practice it. There is a difference, however, between solitary practice and coached practice. Describe the difference and conditions in your teaching where you would use each.

4. Divide into teams of four, and have each team develop one learning center for a specified use in a particular subject and group of children. Set up and share the LCs in your college classroom.

5. Explain how a teacher can tell when he or she is truly using cooperative learning groups for instruction as opposed to traditional, small-group learning.

6. When a student is said to be on task, does that necessarily imply that the student is mentally engaged? Is it possible for a student to be mentally engaged although not on task? Explain your answers.

7. What concerns you most about teaching the diversity of students you are likely to have in a classroom? Share those concerns with others in your class. Categorize your group's concerns. By accessing an Internet teacher bulletin board, see what kinds of problems classroom teachers are currently concerned about. Are assessment practices, curriculum expectations, scheduling, grading, group learning, and classroom management high in frequency of concern? Are the concerns of teachers as expressed on the Internet similar to yours? As a class, devise a plan and time line for attempting to ameliorate your concerns.

8. For a specific grade level (identify it, K–8) and subject (identify), what classroom activities would be particularly well suited to a whole-class configuration? Which ones are best suited for small groups? For each, explain why.

9. Describe three things you will do to help children develop their writing skills.

10. Of the more than 90 motivational ideas listed in this chapter, identify five that you would most like to try in your teaching. Share your list with others in your class, discussing what most interests you about each of your selections. Did certain of the ideas show up frequently? If so, what about them do you believe caused that? Discuss your conclusion with your colleagues.

WEB SITES RELATED TO CONTENT OF THIS CHAPTER

Miscellaneous

- Digital cameras *members.ozemail.com.au/~cumulus/digcam.htm*
- Gender bias *www.american.edu/sadker*
- *Global Schoolhouse www.gsh.org*
- *globalEDGE globaledge.msu.edu*
- *Intercultural E-Mail Classroom Connections www.iecc.org/*
- Learning theories *tip.psychology.org/theories.html*
- *PBS Teacher Source www.pbs.org/teachersource*
- *Teachers Net Lesson Bank teachers.net/lessons*
- Teachers Pay Teachers (for lesson plans) *www.teacherspayteachers.com*
- *The Library in the Sky www.nwrel.org/sky*

- Weblogging service *www.typepad.com*
- Web page creation *www.marshall-es.marshall.k12.tn.us*
- *What Kids Can Do* wkcd.org

Arts
- *American Alliance for Theatre & Education www.aate.com*
- *The Hip-Hop Circuit www.hiphopcircuit.com*
- *Music Education Resource Links K-12Music.com*
- TheatreLink *www.theatrelink.com*

Environmental Issues
- World Bank *www.worldbank.org/depweb*

History/Social Studies
- *American Women's History frank.mtsu.edu/~kmiddlet/history/women.html*
- Best of History Web Sites *www.besthistorysites.net*
- Choices Program *www.choices.edu*
- Civics Online *civics-online.org*
- Facing History and Ourselves *facinghistory.org*
- *FedWorld www.fedworld.gov*
- *Historical Text Archive historicaltextarchive.com*
- *History Net www.thehistorynet.com*
- *Houghton Mifflin Social Studies Center www.eduplace.com/ss/*
- Links to lesson plans, unit plans, thematic units, and resources *www.csun.edu/~hcedu013/index.html*
- *Mexico Online www.mexonline.com*
- National Council for the Social Studies *www.socialstudies.org*
- U.S. History, *From Revolution to Reconstruction grid.let.rug.nl/~welling/usa/usa.html*

Language and Literacy
- Early literacy training for Latino children *www.leeysearas.net*
- Language links *www.langlink.net/langlink*
- Literacy Network *http://literacynetwork.verizon.org*
- National Clearinghouse for English Language Acquisition & Language Instruction Education Programs *www.ncela.gwu.edu*

Mathematics
- Math Activities *www.klll.k12.il.us/king/math.htm*
- *Math Archives archives.math.utk.edu*
- *Math Forum www.mathforum.org*
- *Mega Mathematics www.c3.lanl.gov/mega-math*
- *PlaneMath www.planemath.com*
- Show-Me Project *www.showmecenter.missouri.edu*

Science, Food, and Health
- Centers for Disease Control and Prevention; National Center on Birth Defects and Developmental Disabilities *www.cdc.gov/ncbddd*
- *Columbia Education Center* lesson plan collection *www.coled.org/cur/science.html#scil*

- *Dive and Discover* *www.divediscover.whoi.edu*
- The Edible Schoolyard *www.edibleschoolyard.org*
- *Electric Universe* *ameren.electricuniverse.com*
- *Electronic Zoo* *netvet.wustl.edu/e-zoo.htm*
- EXCITE (Excellence in Curriculum Integration through Teaching Epidemiology *www.cdc.gov/excite*
- Stanford Solar Center *solar-center.stanford.edu*
- Windows to the Universe *www.windows.umich.edu*

Publishers of Children's Writing
- *New Moon* (for girls ages 8–14) *www.newmoon.org*
- *Potato Hill Poetry* *www.potatohill.com*
- *Stone Soup* *www.stonesoup.com*
- *What If* (for Canadians) *www.whatifmagazine.com*

Service Learning
- Learning In Deed *www.learningindeed.org*
- National Service-Learning Clearinghouse *www.servicelearning.org*
- National Service-Learning Exchange *www.nslexchange.org*

FOR FURTHER READING

Bacon, S. (2005). Reading coaches: Adapting an intervention model for upper elementary and middle school readers. *Journal of Adolescent and Adult Literacy, 48,* 416–427.

Bailey, L. (2005). Understanding Chris to teach him more effectively. *Middle School Journal, 37*(2), 37–46.

Bernt, P. W., Turner, S. V., & Bernt, J. P. (2005). Middle school students are co-researchers of their media environment: An integrated project. *Middle School Journal, 37*(1), 38–44.

Blackburn, M. V. (2006). Risky, generous, gender work. *Research in the Teaching of English, 40,* 262–271.

Brown, T. E. (2007). A new approach to attention deficit disorder. *Educational Leadership, 64*(5), 22–27.

Buck, F. S. (2005). The basics of blogging. *Principal, 85*(2), 54–55.

Carrier, K. A. (2005). Key issues for teaching English language learners in academic classrooms. *Middle School Journal, 37*(2), 4–9.

Clark, K. F., & Graves, M. F. (2005). Scaffolding students' comprehension of text. *Reading Teacher, 58,* 570–580.

Connor, C. M., Morrison, F. J., Fishman, B. J., Schatschneider, C., & Underwood, P. (2007). Algorithm-guided individualized reading instruction. *Science, 26,* 464–465.

Cushman, K. (2005). It takes a village. *Edutopia.* Online at http://edutopia.org/magazine/ed1article.php?id=Art_1396&issue=nov_05

Daniel, V. A. H., Stuhr, P. L., & Ballengee-Morris, C. (2006). Suggestions for integrating the arts into the curriculum. *Art Education, 59*(1), 6–11.

Dunton, S. (2006). Building a microsociety. *Educational Leadership, 63*(8), 56–60.

Faden, M., & Christopher, A. (2005). Play with food [a card game for children ages 7-10]. *Edutopia, 1*(5), 32.

Fairbanks, E. K., Clark, M., & Barry, J. (2005). Developing a comprehensive homework policy. *Principal, 84*(3), 36–39.

Garbe, G., & Guy, D. (2006). No homework left behind. *Educational Leadership, 63,* 1–6. In *Helping All Students Succeed,* ASCD online journal at www.ascd.org:80/portal/site/ascd.

Grandin, T. (2007). Autism from the inside. *Educational Leadership, 64*(5), 29–32.

Gray, T., & Fleischman, S. (2005). Successful strategies for English language learners. *Educational Leadership, 62*(4), 84–85.

Harqis, C. H. (2006). *Teaching low achieving and disadvantaged students* (3rd ed.). Springfield, IL: Charles C Thomas.

Johnson, C. (2005). Making instruction relevant to language minority students at the middle level. *Middle School Journal, 37*(2), 10–14.

Klingner, J. K., Vaughn, S., & Boardman, A. (2007). *Teaching reading comprehension to students with learning difficulties. What works for special-learners.* New York: Guilford.

Kveven, A. (2007). Snapshots of science in practice. *Educational Leadership 64*(4), 48–51.

Lundeen, C. (2005). So, you want to host a family science night? *Science and Children, 42*(8), 30–35.

Margolis, H. (2005). Resolving struggling learners' homework difficulties: Working with elementary school learners and parents. *Preventing School Failure, 50*(1), 5.

Mastropieri, M. A., Scruggs, T. E., & Berkeley, S. L. (2007). Peers helping peers. *Educational Leadership, 64*(5), 54–58.

McNary, S. J., Glasgow, N. A., & Hicks, C. D. (2005). *What successful teachers do in inclusive classrooms.* Thousand Oaks, CA: Corwin Press.

Ohl, T., & Cates, W. (2006). The nature of groups: Implications for learning design. *Journal of Interactive Learning Research, 17*, 71–89.

Olshansky, B. (2006). Teaching the art of writing. *Educational Leadership, 63*, 1–9. In *Helping All Students Succeed*, ASCD online journal at www.ascd.org:80/portal/site/ascd.

Pugh, K. H. (2005). *Peer tutoring do's and don'ts.* Fastback 528. Bloomington, IN: Phi Delta Kappa Educational Foundation.

Reyes, S. A. (2007). Beetles and butterflies: Language and learning in a dual language classroom. *Journal of Latinos & Education, 6*(1), 81–92.

Roush, B. E. (2005). Drama rhymes: An instructional strategy. *The Reading Teacher, 58*, 584–586.

Sadker, D., & Sadker, E. S. (Eds.). (2007). *Gender in the Classroom: Foundations, skills, methods, and strategies across the curriculum.* Mahwah, NJ: Lawrence Erlbaum.

Short, D., & Echevarria, J. (2005). Teacher skills to support English language learners. *Educational Leadership, 62*(4), 8–13.

Taylor, R. T. (2005). Using literacy leadership to improve the achievement of struggling students. *Middle School Journal, 36*(1), 26–31.

Walpole, S., & McKenna, M. C. (2007). *Differentiated reading instruction: Strategies for the primary grades.* New York: Guilford.

Walser, N. (2007). Response to intervention. *Harvard Education Letter 23*(1), 1–3.

Wanket, M. O. (2005). Building the habit of writing. *Educational Leadership, 63*(1), 74–76.

Chapter 9

Additional Strategies and Strategy Integration

INTASC Principles	PRAXIS III Domains	NBPTS Standards
• The teacher understands and uses a variety of instructional strategies to encourage students' development of critical thinking, problem solving, and performance skills. (Principle 4)	• Organizing Content Knowledge for Student Learning (Domain A)	• Multiple Paths to Knowledge

Perhaps no other strategy is used more by teachers than is teacher talk, so we begin this final chapter with a presentation of guidelines for using that vital and significant instructional strategy.

A strategy related to teacher talk is the demonstration, which is addressed later in the chapter, followed by guidelines for other important strategies, namely, inquiry, discovery, and games. Finally, in keeping with the important practice of integrating the learning for your students, we cap the book with a discussion of ways of doing that.

Whether you are a beginning or an experienced teacher, one way to collect data and improve your effectiveness is through periodic assessment of your teaching performance. This can be done either by an evaluation of your teaching in the real classroom or, if in a teacher education program, by a technique called micro peer teaching. The latter is the final activity of this chapter, indeed of this book, a type of summative performance assessment for your study of this book, especially of the final two chapters.

ANTICIPATED OUTCOMES

Specifically, upon your completion of this chapter you should be able to:

1. Make an effective demonstration performed either by yourself, by some students, or collaboratively between you and students.
2. Demonstrate an understanding of the relationship among problem solving, discovery, and inquiry.
3. Explain ways of integrating strategies for integrated learning.
4. Demonstrate when and how to use inquiry for student learning.
5. Describe when and how to use teacher talk for instruction.
6. Demonstrate your knowledge of advantages and disadvantages of each of seven categories of games for learning.

TEACHER TALK: FORMAL AND INFORMAL

Teacher talk encompasses both lecturing *to* students and talking *with* students. A lecture is considered formal teacher talk, whereas a discussion with students is considered informal teacher talk.

Cautions in Using Teacher Talk

Whether your talk is formal or informal, you need to be mindful of certain cautions. Perhaps the most important is that of *talking too much*. If a teacher talks too much, the significance of the teacher's words may be lost because some children will tune the teacher out.

Another caution is to avoid *talking too fast*. Children can hear faster than they can process into comprehension of what they hear. It is a good idea to remind yourself to talk at a reasonable pace and to check frequently for student comprehension of what you are talking about. And, when working with English language learning (ELL) students, you will want to talk even more slowly and do more frequent checks for comprehension. It is also important to remember that your one brain is communicating with many student brains, each of which responds to sensory input (auditory in this instance) at varying rates. Because of this, you will need to pause to let words sink in, and you will need to pause during transitions from one point or activity to the next.

A third caution is to be sure you are being *heard and understood*. Sometimes teachers talk in too low a pitch, use words that are not understood by many of the students, or both. You should vary the pitch of your voice, and you should stop and help students with their understanding of vocabulary that may be new to them.

A fourth caution is to remember that *just because students have heard something before does not necessarily mean that they understand it or learned it*. From the earlier discussions of learning experiences (such as "The Learning Experiences Ladder" in Chapter 6), remember that although verbal communication is an important form of communication, because of its reliance on the use of abstract symbolization, it is not a very reliable form of communication. Teacher talk relies on words and on skill in listening, a skill that is not mastered by many elementary-school children (or many adults, for that matter). For that and other reasons, to ensure student understanding, it is good to reinforce your teacher talk with either direct or simulated learning experiences.

A related caution is to *resist believing that students have attained a skill or have learned something that was taught previously by you or by another teacher*. During any discussion (formal or informal), rather than assuming that your students know something, you should ensure they know it. For example, if the discussion and student activity involve a particular math skill or thinking skill, then you will want to make sure that students understand how to use that skill.

Still another problem is *talking in a humdrum monotone*. Children need teachers whose voices exude enthusiasm and excitement (although not to be overdone) about the subject and about teaching and learning. Such enthusiasm and excitement for learning are contagious. A voice that demonstrates genuine enthusiasm for teaching and learning is more likely to motivate students to learn.

A final caution is *just because your speaking (auditory output) channel is engaged doesn't mean that you should disengage your sensory input channels*. This is another time when the competent teacher's skills of withitness and overlapping are apparent. While a competent teacher is talking, that teacher is still seeing and listening and is capable of changing her or his physical location in the classroom.

Keep those cautions in mind as you study the general principles and specific guidelines for the productive and effective use of teacher talk.

Teacher Talk: General Guidelines

Certain general guidelines should be followed whether your talk is formal or informal. First, begin the talk with an advance organizer. *Advance organizers* are introductions that mentally prepare students for a study by helping them make connections with material already learned or experienced—a *comparative organizer*—or by providing students with a conceptual arrangement of what is to be learned—an *expository organizer* (Ausubel, 1963). The value of using advance organizers is well documented by research (Good & Brophy, 2003). An advance organizer can be a brief introduction or statement about the main idea you intend to convey and how it is related to other aspects of the students' learning (an expository organizer), or it can be a presentation of a discrepancy to arouse curiosity (a comparative organizer, in this instance causing students to compare what they have observed with what they already knew or thought they knew). Preparing an organizer helps you plan and organize the sequence of ideas, and its presentation helps students organize their own learning and to become motivated about it. An advance organizer can also make their learning meaningful by providing important connections between what they already know and what is being learned.

Second, *your talk should be planned so that it has a beginning and an end, with a logical order between*. During your talk, you should reinforce your words with visuals (discussed in the specific guidelines that follow). These visuals may include writing unfamiliar terms on the board (helping students learn new vocabulary), visual organizers, and prepared graphs, charts, photographs, and various audiovisuals.

Third, *pacing is important*. Your talk must move briskly, although not too fast. For many beginning teachers, the ability to pace the instruction is a difficult skill (the tendency among many beginning teachers is to talk too fast and too much), but one that improves with experience. Until you have developed your skill in pacing lessons, you may need to remind yourself during lessons to slow down and provide silent pauses (allowing for *think time*) and frequent checks for student comprehension. Specifically, your talk should

- Be brisk, though not too fast, but with occasional slowdowns to change the pace and to check for student comprehension. Allow students time to think, to ask questions, and to make notes (Marzano, Pickering, & Pollock, 2001).
- Have a time plan. A talk planned for, say, 10 minutes, if interesting to children, will probably take longer. If not interesting to them, it will probably take less time.
- Always plan with careful consideration given for the characteristics of the students. For example, if you have a fairly high percentage of ELL students or of students with exceptionalities, then your teacher talk may be less brisk, sprinkled with even more visuals, repeated statements and simpler word use, and frequent checks for student comprehension.

Fourth, *encourage student participation*. Their active participation enhances their learning. This encouragement can be planned as questions that you ask or as time allowed for students to comment and ask questions or as some sort of a visual and conceptual outline that students complete during the talk.

Fifth, *plan a clear ending (closure)*. Be sure your talk has a clear ending, followed by another activity (during the same or subsequent instructional period) that will help secure the learning. As for all lessons, you want to strive for planning a clear and mesmerizing beginning, an involving lesson body, and a firm and meaningful closure.

Teacher Talk: Specific Guidelines

Specific guidelines for using teacher talk are presented in the following paragraphs.

Understand the Various Reasons for Using Teacher Talk

Teacher talk, formal or informal, can be useful to discuss the progress of a unit of study, explain an inquiry, introduce a unit of study, present a problem, promote student inquiry or critical thinking, provide a transition from one unit of study to the next, provide information otherwise unobtainable to students, share the teacher's experiences, share the teacher's thinking, summarize a problem, summarize a unit of study, and teach a thinking skill by modeling that skill.

Clarify the Objectives of the Talk

Your talk should center on one idea. The learning objectives, which should not be too numerous for one talk, should be clearly understood by the students.

Choose between Informal and Formal Talk

Although an occasional formal cutting-edge lecture may be appropriate for some upper-grade elementary-school children, spontaneous, interactive informal talks of 5 to 12 minutes are preferred. You should *never* give long lectures with no teacher–student interaction. A formal period-long noninteractive lecture, common in some college teaching, is developmentally inappropriate when teaching elementary-school children of any grade level. On the other hand, to arouse student interest and to provide new information in relatively small and intellectually digestible chunks, a lecture of 5 to 12 minutes duration may be appropriate. If, during your student teaching, you have doubts or questions about your selection and use of a particular instructional strategy, discuss it with your cooperating teacher or your university supervisor, or both. When you have doubts about the appropriateness of a particular strategy, trust your intuition—without some modification, the strategy probably is inappropriate.

TEACHING IN PRACTICE When Student Attention Begins to Drift

Today's youth are used to electronic interactions as well as "commercial breaks," and the capacity to "surf channels" to find something of personal interest. For many lessons, especially those that are teacher centered, after about 8 minutes student attention is quite likely to begin to waft, to begin to "channel surf." For that eventuality, you need lesson elements planned to recapture student attention. These planned elements can include

- Analogies to help connect the topic to students' experiences
- Humor
- Pauses for emphasis and to allow information to register

- Sensory cues, such as eye contact and proximity (as in your moving around the room)
- Verbal cues, such as voice inflections and name dropping
- Visual cues, such as the use of overhead displays, charts, board drawings, excerpts from CDs, realia, and body gestures.

Question for Class Discussion

Can you think of other elements or techniques that could be used to recapture waning student attention, perhaps specific to a subject field? Share and discuss your ideas with your classmates.

Vary Strategies and Activities Frequently

Perhaps most useful as a strategy for recapturing student attention is to change to an entirely different strategy or learning modality. For example, from teacher talk (a teacher-centered strategy) you would change to a student activity (a student-centered strategy). Notice that changing from a lecture (mostly teacher talk) to a teacher-led discussion (mostly more teacher talk) would not be changing to an entirely different modality. Figure 9.1 provides a comparison of different changes.

As a generalization, when using teacher-centered direct instruction, with most groups of students you will want to change the learning activities about every 8 to 15 minutes. (That is one reason that in the preferred lesson plan format we offer in Chapter 6, you find space for at least four activities, including the introduction and closure.) This means that in a 50- or 60-minute time block, for example, you should probably plan three or four *sequenced* learning activities, with some that are teacher centered and many others that are more student centered. In a 90-minute block, plan five or six learning activities.

In exemplary classrooms, rather than using teacher-centered direct instruction, teachers often have several activities *concurrently* being performed by individuals, dyads, and small groups of students (i.e., the teachers use multitasking or multilevel instruction). Multilevel instruction is particularly important for use during long block periods, sometimes called *macroperiods*, typically a couple hours in length.

Prepare and Use Notes as a Guide to Yourself for Your Talk

Planning your talk and preparing notes to be used during formal and informal teacher talk is important—just as important as is implementing the talk with visuals. There is absolutely nothing wrong with using notes during your teaching. You can carry

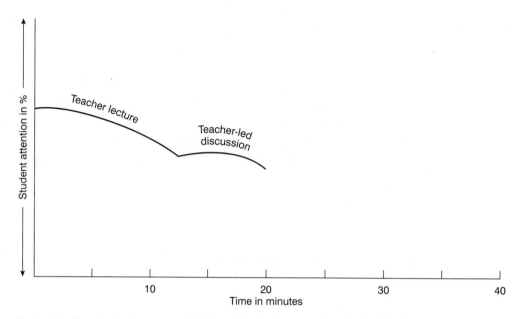

Example 1: Changing from teacher talk (lecture) to more teacher talk (e.g., teacher-led discussion).

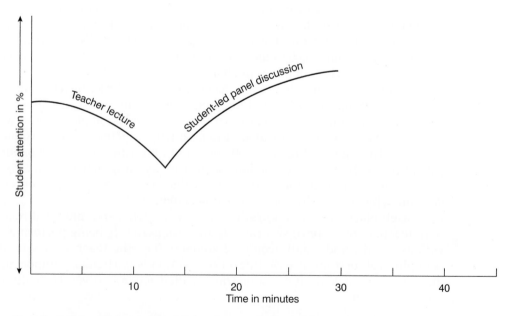

Example 2: Changing from teacher talk (teacher-centered activity) to student-led panel discussion (student-centered activity).

FIGURE 9.1
Recapturing student attention by changing the instructional strategy

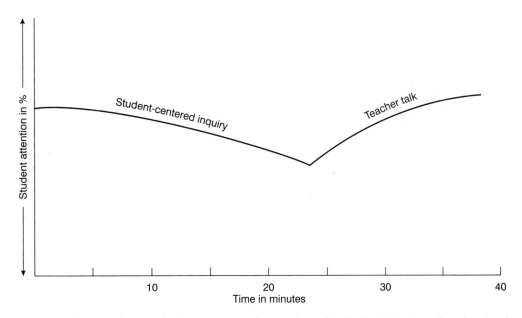

Example 3: Changing from inquiry (student-centered) to teacher-talk fueled by student questions from inquiry.

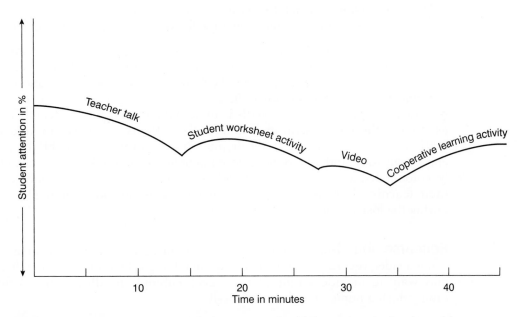

Example 4: Changing from teacher talk (teacher-centered activity) to cooperative learning activity (student-centered activity).

FIGURE 9.1
Continued

them on a clipboard, perhaps a neon-colored one that gives students a visual focus as you move around the room. Your notes for a formal talk can first be prepared in narrative form; for class use, though, they should be reduced to an outline form. *Talks to students should always be from an outline, never read from prose.* The only time that a teacher's reading from prose aloud to students is appropriate is when reading a brief, published article (such as in science or social studies) or portions of a story or a poem (such as in reading/English/language arts).

In your outline, use color coding with abbreviated visual cues to yourself. You will eventually develop your own coding system, though keep whatever coding system you use simple lest you forget what the codes are for. Consider these examples of coding:

- Where media will be used, mark *M* or *V* for *visual* or *PP* for *PowerPoint.*
- Where transitions of ideas occur and you want to allow silent moments for ideas to sink in, mark *P* for *pause,* *T* for a *transition,* and *S* for moments of *silence.*
- Where you intend to stop and ask a question, mark *TQ* for *teacher question,* or *TQ (student name)* when you intend to ask the question of a particular student.
- Where you plan *reviews* and *comprehension checks,* mark *R* and *CS.*
- Where you plan *small-group work,* mark *SG,* or for *cooperative learning group work,* mark CLG.
- Where you plan to have a *discussion,* mark *D.*
- Where you plan to switch to an *investigatory* activity, mark *I.*
- Where you want to stop and allow time for *student questions,* mark *SQ* or *?.*

Share your note organization with your students. Sharing with them how you organize for your work is important modeling for them for their organization of their own learning and doing. Teach the students how to take notes and what kinds of things they should write down, including how to summarize. Teaching students note-taking and summarizing skills is to help them with what researchers refer to as "two of the most useful academic skills students can have" (Marzano et al., 2001, p. 29). Use colored chalk or markers to outline and highlight your talk; encourage your students to use colored pencils for note taking, so their notes can be color coded to match your writing board notes. This serves not only to enhance their learning but also keeps them productively and kinesthetically occupied during the instruction.

Rehearse Your Talk Using your lesson plan as your guide, rehearse your talk using a video recorder, or rehearse it while talking into a mirror or to a friend. You may want to include a time plan for each subtopic to allow you to gauge your timing during implementation of the talk.

Avoid Racing Through the Talk Solely to Complete It by a Certain Time

It is more important that students understand some of what you say than that you cover it all and they understand little or none of it. If you do not finish, continue it later.

Augment Your Talk with Multisensory Stimulation and Allow For Think Time　Your presentation should not rely too much on verbal communication. When using visuals, do not think that you must be constantly talking; after clearly explaining the reason for using a particular visual, give students sufficient time to look at it, think about it, and ask questions about it. The visual is new to the students, so give them time to take it in.

Carefully Plan the Content of Your Talk　The content of your talk should supplement and enhance that found in the student textbook rather than simply rehash content from the textbook. Students may never read their book if you tell them in an interesting and condensed fashion everything that they need to know from it.

Monitor Your Delivery　Your voice should be pleasant and interesting to listen to rather than a steady, boring monotone or a constantly shrieking, irritating, high pitch. On the other hand, it is good to show enthusiasm for what you are talking about, for teaching and learning. Occasionally use dramatic voice inflections to emphasize important points and meaningful body language to give students a visual focus. So as not to appear phony, practice these skills so they become second nature.

When teaching a large group of students (by "large group," we mean more than 8 students), *avoid standing in the same spot for long periods of time.* (When teaching elementary school children of any age or grade level, we consider 10 minutes in the same spot to be a long time.) Be mobile! Even during direct instruction, you need to monitor student behavior and to engage occasional signal interference (eye contact, hand gesturing, proximity). As a matter of fact, it is especially during extended periods of direct instruction that a beginning teacher's skills in withitness and overlapping behaviors are likely to be most put to task.

View the Vocabulary of the Talk as an Opportunity to Help Students with Their Word Morphology　Words you use should be easily understood by the students, though you should still model professionalism and help students develop their vocabulary—both the vocabulary of your special discipline and the more general vocabulary of the English language. During your lesson planning, predict when you are likely to use a word that is new to most students, and plan to stop to ask a student to explain its meaning and perhaps demonstrate its derivation. Help students with word meaning. This assists students with their remembering. Remember, regardless of subject or grade level, *every teacher is a teacher of language arts.* Knowledge of word morphology is an important component of skilled reading and includes the ability to generate new words from prefixes, roots, and suffixes. For some students, nearly every subject in the curriculum is basically a foreign language. That is certainly true for some ELLs, for whom teacher talk, especially formal teacher talk, should be used sparingly, if at all. As we have repeated often throughout this book, every teacher of grades K–8 has the responsibility of helping students learn how to learn, and that includes helping students develop their word comprehension skills, reading skills, thinking and memory skills, and motivation for learning.

Give Thoughtful and Intelligent Consideration to Student Diversity

While preparing your talk (during the preactive phase of your instruction), consider students in your classroom who are culturally and linguistically different and those who have special needs. Personalize the talk for them by choosing your vocabulary carefully and appropriately, speaking slowly and methodically, repeating often, and planning meaningful analogies and examples and relevant audio and visual displays.

Use Familiar Examples and Analogies to Help Students Make Relevant Connections (Bridges)

Although this sometimes takes a great deal of creative thinking as well as action during the planning phase of instruction, it is important that you do your best to connect the talk with ideas and events with which the students are already familiar. The most effective talk is one that makes frequent and meaningful connections between what students already know and what they are learning, which bridges what they are learning with what they have experienced in their lives. Of course, to do this well means you need to "know" your students.

Establish Eye Contact Frequently

Your primary eye contact should be with your students—always! That important point cannot be overemphasized. Only momentarily should you look at your notes, your visuals, the projection screen, media equipment, the writing board, and other adults or objects in the classroom. Although you may raise your eyebrows in doubt when you read this, it is true, and it is important that with practice you can learn to scan a classroom of 25 students, establishing eye contact with each student about once every 60 seconds. To "establish" eye contact means that the student is aware that you are looking at him or her. Frequent eye contact can have two major benefits. First, as you "read" a student's body posture and facial expressions, you obtain clues about that student's attentiveness and comprehension. Second, eye contact helps to establish rapport between you and a student. A look with a smile or a wink from the teacher to a student can say so much! Be alert, though, for students who are from cultures where eye contact is infrequent or unwanted and could have negative consequences. In other words, don't push it!

Frequent eye contact is easier when using a screen display (such as with the overhead projector or a PowerPoint presentation) than when using the writing board. When using a writing board, you have to turn at least partially away from your audience; you may also have to pace back and forth from the board to the students to retain that important proximity to them.

As said at the start of the discussion of teacher talk, while lecturing on a topic, you must remain aware and attentive to everything that is happening in the classroom (i.e., to student behavior as well as to the content of your lecture). No one truly knowledgeable about it ever said that good teaching is easy. But don't dismay; with the knowledge of the preceding guidelines and with practice, experience, and intelligent reflection, you will in time develop the skills.

DEMONSTRATIONS

Most elementary school children like demonstrations because the person doing the demonstration is actively physically engaged in a learning activity rather than merely verbalizing about it. Demonstrations can be used to teach any topic in any discipline and for a variety of reasons. The teacher demonstrates role-playing in preparation for a social studies simulation. Select students demonstrate how they solved a mathematics problem. A language arts/English teacher demonstrates clustering to students ready for a creative writing assignment. A life science teacher demonstrates the focus adjustments when using a microscope. The physical education teacher or student volunteer demonstrates the proper way to serve in volleyball.

Reasons for Using Demonstrations

A demonstration can be designed to serve any of the following functions, and the reason(s) for using a particular demonstration should be communicated to the students.

- Assist in recognizing a solution to an existing problem; to bring an unusual closure to a lesson or unit of study
- Conservation of time and resources (as opposed to the entire class doing that which is being demonstrated)
- Establish discrepancy recognition
- Establish problem recognition
- Give students an opportunity for vicarious participation in active learning
- Illustrate a particular point of content
- Introduce a lesson or unit of study in a way that grabs the students' attention
- Model or demonstrate a skill, such as a skill in sports, inquiry, thinking, note taking, summarizing, social behavior, library use, or a skill useful in conflict resolution
- Model or demonstrate proper use of equipment, such as a microscope or a trampoline
- Reduce potential safety hazards (where the teacher demonstrates with materials that are too dangerous for students to handle)
- Review or summarize a topic or unit of study
- Test a hypothesis

Guidelines for Using Demonstrations

When planning a demonstration, consider the following guidelines.

Decide the most effective way to conduct the demonstration. It might be a verbal or a silent demonstration by a student or the teacher, by the teacher with a student helper, by a student with the teacher as helper, to the entire class or to small groups, or by some combination of these, such as first by the teacher followed by a repeat of the demonstration by a student or a succession of students.

Be sure that the demonstration is visible to all students. Unless your class is equipped with overhead mirrors or video cameras connected to large-screen television monitors, a raised demonstration table will probably suffice. This reminds us of the sixth-grade teacher we have long known who had built in the front-center of his classroom a raised platform or stage, about 10 feet square. We have always been impressed with the positive usefulness that permanent classroom stage seemed to provide, mostly as a center of visual focus for the students.

Practice with the materials and procedure before demonstrating to the students. During your practice, try to prepare for anything that could go wrong during the real demonstration; if you don't, as Murphy's Law states, if anything can go wrong, it probably will. Then, if something does go wrong during the live demonstration, use that as an opportunity for a teachable moment; engage the students in working with you to try to figure out what went wrong, or if that isn't feasible, then go to Plan B (an *emergency alternate plan* that you made during lesson planning, always a good idea when planning a demonstration or the use of media).

Consider your pacing of the demonstration, allowing for enough student wait-see-and-think time. At the start of the demonstration, explain the learning objectives. Remember this familiar adage: Tell them what you are going to do, show them, and then help them understand what they saw. As with any lesson, plan your closure and allow time for questions and discussion. During the demonstration, as in other types of teacher talk, use frequent stops to check for student understanding.

Consider using special lighting to highlight the demonstration. (One teacher uses a "recycled" slide projector as a spotlight.) And finally, be sure the demonstration table and area are free of unnecessary objects that could distract, be in the way, or pose a safety hazard.

With potentially hazardous demonstrations, such as might occur in physical education or science classes, you must *model* proper safety precautions.

INQUIRY TEACHING AND DISCOVERY LEARNING

Intrinsic to the effectiveness of both inquiry and discovery is the assumption that students would rather actively seek knowledge than receive it through traditional direct instruction (i.e., information delivery) methods such as lectures, demonstrations, worksheets, and textbook reading. Although inquiry and discovery are important teaching tools, there is sometimes confusion about exactly what inquiry teaching is and how it differs from discovery learning. The distinction should become clear as you study the following section discussing these two important tools for teaching and learning.

Although inquiry and discovery are well recognized as valuable teaching tools, they do tend to consume more instructional time than do traditional methods of information delivery (direct instruction). Coupled with that and the current emphasis on standardized testing, classroom use of inquiry and discovery methods may be in jeopardy (Jorgenson & Vanosdall, 2002).

Experiences afforded by inquiry help students understand the importance of suspending judgment and also the tentativeness of answers and solutions to problems. With those intelligent understandings, students eventually are likely better able to deal with life's ambiguities.

Problem Solving

Perhaps a major reason why inquiry and discovery are sometimes confused is that in both, students are actively engaged in problem solving. *Problem solving* can be thought of as the ability to recognize, identify, define, or describe a problem, determine the preferred resolution, identify potential solutions, select strategies, test solutions, evaluate outcomes, and revise any of these steps as necessary (Costa, 1985).

Children need to learn the skills of problem solving, and how to do it in groups as well as alone. Real-world problem solving has become so complex that seldom can any person do it alone.

Anne Vega/Merrill

TABLE 9.1
Levels of Inquiry

	Level I (not true inquiry)	Level II	Level III
Problem identification	Identified by teacher or textbook	Identified by teacher or textbook	Identified by student
Process of solving problem	Decided by teacher or textbook	Decided by student	Decided by student
Identification of tentative solution to problem	Resolved by student	Resolved by student	Resolved by student

Source: Adapted from Schwab, 1962, p. 55.

Inquiry versus Discovery

Problem solving is *not* a teaching strategy but a high-order intellectual behavior that facilitates learning. What a teacher can and should do is provide opportunities for students to identify and tentatively solve problems. Experiences in inquiry and discovery can provide those opportunities. With the processes involved in inquiry and discovery, teachers can help children develop the skills necessary for effective problem solving. Two major differences between discovery and inquiry are (a) who identifies the problem and (b) the percentage of decisions that are made by the students. Table 9.1 shows three levels of inquiry, with each level defined according to what the student does and decides.

It should be evident from Table 9.1 that what is called *Level I inquiry* is actually traditional, didactic, workbook and "cookbook" teaching, where both the problem and the process for resolving it are identified and defined *for* the student. The student then works through the process to its inevitable resolution. If the process is well designed, the result is inevitable, because the student "discovers" what was intended by the writers of the program. This level is also called *guided inquiry* or *discovery*, because the students are carefully guided through the investigation to (the predictable) "discovery."

TPW Video Classroom

Series: Science Methods

Module 1: The Nature of Science

Video 1: Questioning, Investigating, and Observing

Level I is, in reality, a strategy within the delivery mode, the advantages of which were described in Chapter 6. Because Level I "inquiry" is highly manageable and the learning outcome is predictable, it is probably best for teaching basic concepts and principles. Students who never experience learning beyond Level I

FIGURE 9.2
The inquiry cycle

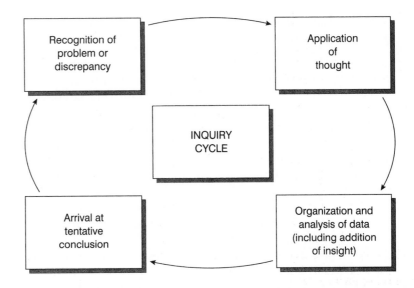

are missing an opportunity to engage their highest mental operations, and they seldom (or never) get to experience more motivating, real-life problem solving. Furthermore, those students may come away with the false notion that problem solving is a linear process, which it is not. As illustrated in Figure 9.2, true inquiry is cyclical rather than linear. For that reason, Level I is not true inquiry because it is a linear process. Real-world problem solving is a cyclical rather than linear process. One enters the cycle whenever a discrepancy or problem is observed and recognized, and that can occur at any point in the cycle.

If thinking is to be the central purpose of U.S. education, as many believe it should be, then teachers must devise ways to help individual children develop their thinking skills. One such way is through inquiry, where the teacher's role is to both challenge and assist learners by helping them recognize problems and questions and by guiding their inquiry.

Anne Vega/Merrill

True Inquiry

By the time children are in the intermediate grades, they should be provided school experiences for true inquiry, which begins with *Level II inquiry*, where students actually decide and design processes for their inquiry. In true inquiry there is emphasis on the tentative nature of conclusions, which makes the activity more like real-life problem solving, where decisions are always subject to revision if and when new data so prescribe.

At *Level III inquiry*, students recognize and identify the problem as well as decide the processes and reach a conclusion. In project-centered teaching, students are usually engaged at this level of inquiry. By the time students are in middle grades, Level III inquiry should be a major strategy for instruction, which is often the case in schools that use cross-age teaching and interdisciplinary thematic instruction. But it is not easy; like most good teaching practices, it is a lot of work. But also like good teaching, the intrinsic rewards, concomitant with the fact that students achieve meaningful learning, make the effort worthwhile. As exclaimed by one teacher using interdisciplinary thematic instruction with student-centered inquiry, "I've never worked harder in my life, but I've never had this much fun, either."

The Critical Thinking Skills of Discovery and Inquiry

In true inquiry, students generate ideas and then design ways to test those ideas. The various processes used represent the many critical thinking skills. Some of those skills are concerned with generating and organizing data; others are

---

Activity 9.1: Does It Really Matter What It's Called?

From the time of her first brush with the classroom as a student teacher, it was clear that Ms. Marsh had a knack for asking questions that sparked children's thinking. And they loved it! She would rarely come right out and tell them much of anything. She would rephrase and clarify what they said and, in the process, would provide a cue or two that led them in the direction of what they wanted and needed to know. Now, in her seventh month as a contracted teacher, her classroom was something of a science laboratory, a museum, a "fix-it" shop, an art gallery, and a learning resources center all wrapped into one. Her students seemed always to be talking interestedly about what was going on in the classroom and would often ask each other questions about projects and activities. A colleague told her one day, "How lucky you are to have such a curious and interested group of children. They've changed so this past year."

"Yes, they do seem interested in what we are doing, and they learn a great deal on their own. But I must get back to school this summer and broaden my knowledge of inquiry teaching," replied Ms. Marsh.

1. Is there anything about this sketch that suggests that Ms. Marsh is already making effective use of the inquiry mode of teaching?
2. Are the terms *discovery learning* and *inquiry teaching* referring to the same thing? Explain why they are or are not.
3. What do you think of her colleague's comment that Ms. Marsh is "lucky to have such a curious and interested group of children"?

FIGURE 9.3
Inquiry cycle processes

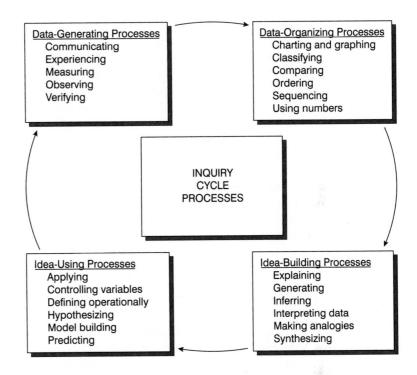

concerned with building and using ideas. Figure 9.3 provides four main categories of these thinking processes and illustrates the place of each within the inquiry cycle.

Some processes in the cycle are discovery processes, and others are inquiry processes. Inquiry processes include the more complex mental operations (including all of those in the idea-using category). Project-centered teaching provides an avenue for doing that, as does problem-centered teaching.

Inquiry learning is a higher-level mental operation that introduces the concept of the discrepant event, something that establishes *cognitive disequilibrium* (using the element of surprise to challenge students' prior notions, sometimes called *naïve theories*) to help students develop skills in observing and being alert for discrepancies (Echevarria, 2003). Such a strategy provides opportunities for students to investigate their own ideas about explanations. Inquiry, like discovery, depends on skill in problem solving; the difference between the two is in the amount of decision-making responsibility given to students. Experiences afforded by inquiry help students understand the importance of suspending judgment and also the tentativeness of answers and solutions. With those intelligent understandings, students eventually are better able to deal with life's ambiguities. When students are not provided these important educational experiences, their education is incomplete.

One of the most effective ways of stimulating inquiry is to use materials that provoke students' interest. These materials should be presented in a nonthreatening, noncompetitive context, so students think and hypothesize freely. The teacher's role is to encourage students to form as many hypotheses as possible and then support their hypotheses with reasons. After the students suggest several ideas, the teacher should begin to move on to higher-order, more abstract questions that involve the development of generalizations and evaluations. True inquiry problems have a special advantage in that they can be used with almost any group of students. Members of a group approach the problem as an adventure in thinking and apply it to whatever background they can muster. Background experience may enrich a student's approach to the problem, but is not crucial to the use or understanding of the evidence presented to that student. Locating a colony, Figure 9.4, is a Level II inquiry. As a class, we suggest that you do the inquiry.

INTEGRATING STRATEGIES FOR INTEGRATED LEARNING

In today's exemplary classrooms, instructional strategies are combined to establish the most effective teaching–learning experience. For example, in an integrated language arts program, teachers are interested in their students' speaking, reading, listening, thinking, study, and writing skills. These skills (and not textbooks) form a holistic process that is the primary aspect of integrated language arts.

In the area of speaking skills, oral discourse (discussion) in the classroom has a growing research base that promotes methods of teaching and learning through oral language. These methods include cooperative learning, instructional scaffolding, and inquiry teaching.

In *cooperative learning* groups, students discuss and use language for learning that benefits both their content learning and skills in social interaction. Working in heterogeneous groups, students participate in their own learning and can extend their knowledge base and cultural awareness with students of different backgrounds. When students share information and ideas, they are completing difficult learning tasks, using divergent thinking and decision making, and developing their understanding of concepts. As issues are presented and responses are challenged, student thinking is clarified. Students assume the responsibility for planning within the group and for carrying out their assignments. When needed, the teacher models an activity with one group in front of the class, and when integrated with student questions, the modeling can become inquiry teaching. Activities can include any from a variety of heuristics (a *heuristic* is a tool used in solving a problem or understanding an idea), such as the following:

Brainstorming. Members generate ideas related to a keyword and record them. Clustering or chunking, mapping, and the Venn diagram (all discussed in the following paragraphs) are variations of *brainstorming*.

Presentation of the Problem. In groups of three or four, students receive the following information.

Background. You (your group is considered as one person) are one of 120 passengers on the ship *Prince Charles.* You left England 12 weeks ago. You have experienced many hardships, including a stormy passage, limited rations, sickness, cold and damp weather, and hot, foul air below deck. Ten of your fellow immigrants to the New World, including three children, have died and been buried at sea. You are now anchored at an uncertain place, off the coast of the New World, which your captain believes to be somewhere north of the Virginia Grants. Seas are so rough and food so scarce that you and your fellow passengers have decided to settle here. A landing party has returned with a map they made of the area. You, as one of the elders, must decide at once where the settlement is to be located. The tradesmen want to settle along the river, which is deep, even though this seems to be the season of low water levels. Within 10 months they expect deep-water ships from England with more colonists and merchants. Those within your group who are farmers say they must have fertile, workable land. The officer in charge of the landing party reported seeing a group of armed natives who fled when approached. He feels the settlement must be located so that it can be defended from the natives and from the sea.

Directions, step one: You (your group) are to select a site on the attached map that you feel is best suited for a colony. Your site must satisfy the different factions aboard the ship. A number of possible sites are already marked on the map (letters A–G). You may select one of these locations or use them as reference points to show the location of your colony. When your group has selected its site, list and explain the reasons for your choice. When each group has arrived at its tentative decision, these will be shared with the whole class.

Directions, step two: After each group has made its presentation and argument, a class debate is held about where the colony should be located.

Notes to teacher: For the debate, have a large map drawn on the writing board or on an overhead transparency, where each group's mark can be made for all to see and discuss. After each group has presented its argument for its location and against the others, we suggest that you then mark on the large map the

two, three, or more hypothetical locations (assuming that, as a class, there is no single favorite location yet). Then take a straw vote of the students, allowing each to vote independently rather than as members of groups. At this time you can terminate the activity by saying that if the majority of students favor one location, then that, in fact, is the solution to the problem—that is, the colony is located wherever the majority of class members believe it should be. No sooner will that statement be made by you than someone will ask, "Are we correct?" or "What is the right answer?" They will ask such questions because, as students in school, they are used to solving problems that have right answers (Level I inquiry teaching). In real-world problems, however, there are no "right" answers, though some answers may seem better than others. It is the process of problem solving that is important. You want your students to develop confidence in their ability to solve problems and understand the tentativeness of "answers" to real-life problems.

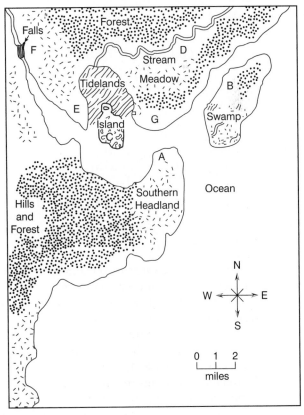

FIGURE 9.4

Locating a colony: a Level II inquiry

Source: Adapted by permission from unpublished material provided by Jennifer Devine and Dennis Devine.

Chunking or clustering. Groups of students apply mental organizers by clustering information into chunks for easier manipulation and remembering.

Comparing and contrasting. Similarities and differences between items are found and recorded.

Inferring. For instance, students assume the roles of different people (real or fictional) and infer their motives, personalities, and thoughts.

Memory strategies. The teacher and students model the use of acronyms, mnemonics, rhymes, or clustering of information into categories to promote learning. Sometimes, such as in memorizing the Social Security number, one must learn by rote information that is not connected to any prior knowledge. To do that, it is helpful to break the information to be learned into smaller chunks, such as dividing the eight-digit Social Security number into smaller chunks of information (with, in this instance, each chunk separated by a hyphen). Learning by rote is also easier if one can connect that which is to be memorized to some prior knowledge. Strategies such as these are used to bridge the gap between rote learning and meaningful learning and are known as *mnemonics* (Mastropieri & Scruggs, 1998; Raschke, Alper, & Eggers, 1999; van Hell & Mahn, 1997). Sample mnemonics are

- The notes on a treble staff are *FACE* for the space notes and *Empty Garbage Before Dad Flips* (*EGBDF*) for the line notes. The notes on the bass staff are *All Cows Eat Granola Bars* for space notes and *Grizzly Bears Don't Fly Airplanes* (*GBDFA*) for line notes.
- The names of the Great Lakes are HOMES for *H*uron, *O*ntario, *M*ichigan, *E*rie, and *S*uperior.
- To remember when to use "affect" versus "effect," remember RAVEN for *R*emember *a*ffect (is a) *v*erb, *e*ffect (is a) *n*oun.
- To remember when a vowel is not pronounced, use "When vowels go walking, the first one does the talking."
- To remember when to use "principle" versus "principal," remember "The principal is your pal."
- Visual mnemonics are useful too, such as remembering that Italy is shaped in the form of a boot.

Outlining. Each group completes an outline that contains some of the main ideas but with subtopics omitted.

Paraphrasing. In a brief summary, each student restates a short selection of what was read or heard.

Reciprocal teaching. In classroom dialogue, students take turns at summarizing, questioning, clarifying, and predicting (Carter, 1997; Marzano et al., 2001; Palincsar & Brown, 1984).

Review. Although frequent review of material being learned is essential, it is most effective when the students are actively involved in planning and implementing the review as opposed to their being passive respondents to a review conducted by the teacher (Wolfe, 2001).

Study strategies. Important strategies that should be taught explicitly include vocabulary expansion, reading and interpreting graphic information, locating resources, using advance organizers, adjusting one's reading rate, and skimming, scanning, and study reading (Choate & Rakes, 1998).

Visual tools. A variety of terms for visual tools useful for learning have been invented (some of which are synonymous), such as brainstorming web, cluster, cognitive map, conflict map, graphic organizer, mind mapping web, semantic map, spider map, thinking process map, Venn diagram, and visual scaffold. Visual tools are separated into three categories according to purpose: (a) *brainstorming tools* (such as mind mapping, webbing, and clustering) for the purpose of developing one's knowledge and creativity; (b) *task-specific organizers* (such as life cycle diagrams used in life science, decision trees used in mathematics, and text structures in reading); and (c) *thinking process maps* for encouraging cognitive development across disciplines (Hyerle, 1996). It is the latter about which we are interested here.

Based on Ausubel's (1963) theory of meaningful learning, thinking process mapping has been found useful in helping students change prior notions (i.e., their misconceptions or naïve views). It can help students in their ability to organize and to represent their thoughts, as well as to help them connect new knowledge to their past experiences and precepts (Novak, 1990, 1998; Plotnick, 1997; van Boxtel, van der Linden, Roelofs, & Erkens, 2002). Simply put, concepts can be understood as classifications that attempt to organize the world of objects and events into a smaller number of categories. In everyday usage, the term concept means idea, as when someone says, "My concept of love is not the same as yours." Concepts embody a meaning that develops in complexity with experience and learning over time. For example, the concept of love that is held by a second grader is unlikely to be as complex as that held by an eleventh grader. Thinking process mapping is a graphical way of demonstrating the relationship between and among concepts.

Typically, a thinking process map refers to a visual or graphic representation of concepts with bridges (connections) that show relationships. Figure 9.5 shows a partially complete thinking process map done by an integrated science and social studies class, where students have made connections of concept relationships related to fruit farming and marketing. The general procedure for thinking process mapping is to have the students: (a) identify important concepts in materials being studied, often by circling those concepts; (b) rank the concepts from the most general to the most specific; and (c) arrange the concepts on a sheet of paper, connect related ideas with lines, and define the connections between the related ideas.

One specific type of thinking process map is the *vee map* (Figure 9.6). This is a V-shaped road map completed by students, as they learn, showing the route they follow from prior knowledge to new and future knowledge.

Venn diagramming is a thinking process mapping tool for comparing concepts or, for example, two stories, to show similarities and differences. Using stories as an example, a student is asked to draw two circles that intersect and to mark the circles one and two and the area where they intersect three. In circle one, the student lists characteristics of one story, and in circle two she or he lists the

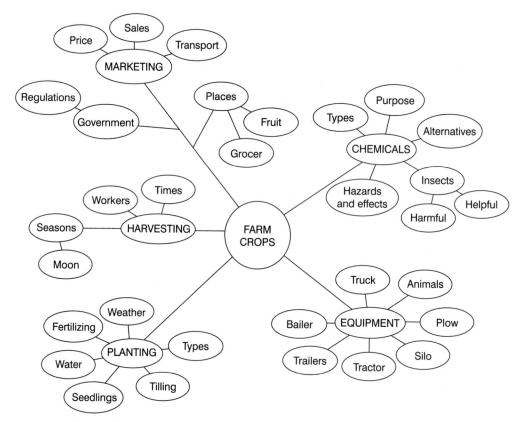

FIGURE 9.5
Sample partially completed thinking process map

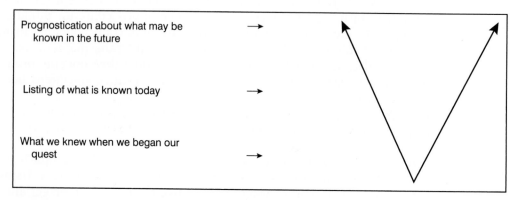

FIGURE 9.6
Vee map

FIGURE 9.7
Venn diagram

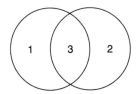

characteristics of the second story. In the area of the intersection, marked three, the student lists characteristics common to both stories (Figure 9.7).

Venn diagrams can be useful for assessing for higher-order thinking. For example, the sample assessment item in Figure 9.8 assesses for the student's understanding of the concepts of the universe, planets, and the Earth's moon. For scoring or marking the student's response, each possible response has a maximum score of 3, one point for three distinct responses that are obvious elements of the item.

Instructions: From the diagram write down all you can tell from the diagram about planet Earth.

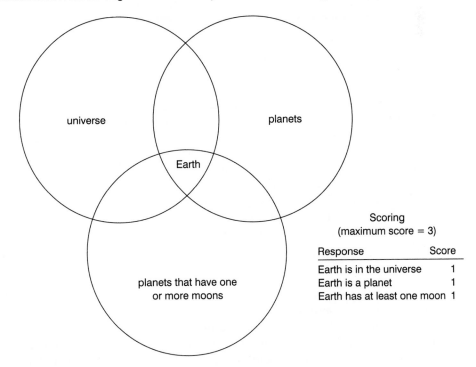

Scoring
(maximum score = 3)

Response	Score
Earth is in the universe	1
Earth is a planet	1
Earth has at least one moon	1

FIGURE 9.8
Sample assessment item using Venn diagramming

Activity 9.2: A Study of Inquiry and Strategy Integration

Instructions: The purpose of this activity is to analyze the Locating a Colony Inquiry (the Level II inquiry of Figure 9.4 that you did with your classmates) and the discussion in the text about integrating strategies and then synthesizing that information for use in your own teaching. We suggest that you first answer the questions of this activity and then share your answers with others in your discipline (in groups of about four). Finally, share your group's collective responses with the entire class.

1. My grade level interest (K–8):
2a. How I could use the Locating a Colony inquiry (for what purpose, goals, or objectives)?
2b. Content in my class that students might be expected to learn from doing the Locating a Colony inquiry:
3. In what way could I involve my students in reciprocal teaching while doing the Locating a Colony inquiry?

4. How brainstorming could be used while doing the Locating a Colony inquiry:
5. How clustering could be used while doing the Locating a Colony inquiry:
6. How thinking process mapping could be used while doing the Locating a Colony inquiry:
7. How outlining could be used while doing the Locating a Colony inquiry:
8. How comparing and contrasting could be used while doing the Locating a Colony inquiry:
9. How paraphrasing could be used while doing the Locating a Colony inquiry:
10. How reviewing and summarizing could be used while doing the Locating a Colony inquiry:
11. How memory strategies could be used while doing the Locating a Colony inquiry:
12. How inferring could be used while doing the Locating a Colony inquiry:
13. What other skills could be taught while doing the Locating a Colony inquiry? For each, describe how.

The *visual learning log* (VLL) is another kind of road map completed by students showing the route they follow from prior knowledge to new and future knowledge, except that the VLL consists of pictograms (free-form drawings) that each student makes and that are maintained in a journal.

The value of the previously discussed representations is believed to be because they engage what psychologists refer to as the "dual-coding" theory of information storage (Pavio, 1971, 1990); that knowledge is stored in the brain in two forms, a linguistic form and a nonlinguistic form, the latter of which is stored as mental pictures and as sensory sensations (Marzano, Pickering, & Pollock, 2001). Again, the oft-repeated message and central theme of this edition of our book is that when teaching elementary-school children, the most effective and longest-lasting learning is not that of verbiage alone but that which engages most or all of their senses.

EDUCATIONAL GAMES

Devices classified as educational games include a wide variety of learning activities, such as simulations, role-play and sociodrama activities, mind games, board games, computer games, and sporting games—see section that follows—all of which provide valuable learning experiences for participants. That is, they are experiences that tend to involve several senses and involve several learning modalities, tend to engage higher-order thinking skills, and tend to be quite effective as learning tools.

Of all the arts, drama involves the learner–participant most fully—intellectually, emotionally, physically, verbally, and socially. Interactive drama, which is role-playing, a simplified form of drama, is a method by which students can become involved with literature.

Simulations, a more complex form of drama, serve many of the developmental needs of elementary-school children. They provide for interaction with peers and allow students of differences to work together on a common project. They engage

---

CLASSROOM SCENARIO

Science Students Write and Stage a One-Act Play

Early in the year, in preparation for a unit on the study of oxygen and other gases, Robert told the 28 students in his seventh-grade physical science class that, if they were interested, he would like for them to plan, write, and stage a one-act play about the life of Joseph Priestley, the theologian and scientist who in 1774 discovered what he called "dephlogisticated air," later named *oxygen* by Lavoisier. Furthermore the students would be given one week to plan. The play would be presented and videotaped in class. The students accepted Robert's idea with enthusiasm and immediately went about the task of organizing and putting their ideas into motion. They took on the challenging task with such vigor and seriousness that they asked Robert for an additional three days to prepare. Sean, a bright student who was really more interested in theatre than science, was selected by the students to play the role of Priestley and to be the producer. Other students played lesser roles. Students with special interest in writing wrote the play. Those with interest in art and stagecraft assumed the task of designing and preparing the set, while another assumed the role of sound stage manager. The resulting 60-minute presentation was more successful than Robert, and perhaps the students, could ever have anticipated. By request of the school principal, the students put on the play two more times, once for the entire student body, and a second time for the school's parent–teacher–student organization. Both performances resulted in standing ovations. During the performance before the PTO, the student production was simultaneously recorded by the local cable television network and later played several times over the community cable channel. Robert later said that during this experience the students learned far more content than they ever would have via his traditional approach to the topic. In addition, these students were highly motivated in learning science for the entire rest of the year. Several years later, Sean graduated with honors from the University of California with a degree major in theatre and a minor in chemistry.

TEACHING IN PRACTICE Games in the Classroom
and the Underperforming Student*

High-stakes state assessments have recently spot-lighted the underperforming student. One teacher found a unique way to get students excited about studying the language arts and math skills required for the state tests.

The teacher was assigned to teach a special class for those students who were likely to fail the state test. The students, including a good number of special-needs students and English language learn-ers, were generally apathetic toward trying again to learn what they had failed to learn in math and English class.

They were apathetic, that is, until their teacher told them, "Put away your pencils and notebooks. Today we're going to play a video game!" After a demonstration by the teacher of how the game worked, the students, every one of them, were con-centrating hard on achieving the best score in the class . . . on a video game. In a few minutes, Jacinto, one of the more competitive students,

exclaimed, "I beat the game!" The teacher recorded Jacinto's score and encouraged Jacinto to try to beat the game in fewer than 100 seconds. Jacinto accepted the challenge.

Did the students know that they were learning math? Certainly. The goal of the game was to state the range and domain (e.g., $22 < y < 97$ and $65 < x < 144$) of 10 randomly displayed functions. Once a student earned an A for "beating the game," they were encouraged to earn another A by turning in a time of under 100 seconds. Toward the end of the period, Jacinto and four other students were vying for the lowest time. When the dismissal bell rang, Ana had beaten Jacinto by 1 second, but the real reward was when they were asked to express the range and domain of a function on the state math assessment test.

*Source: The teacher Mark Greenberg, now an English teacher at Phoenix Union Cyber High School (Phoenix, AZ). By permission.

students in physical activity and provide them the opportunity to try out different roles, which help them better understand themselves. Role-play simulations can provide concrete experiences that help students to understand complex concepts and issues, and they provide opportunities for exploring values and developing skill in decision making. Indeed, in the not-so-distant future because it involves a learning that is powerfully effective, that young people are familiar with, and that is based on the best of what we know about how children learn, we are likely to see greater use of technology-based simulation games in teaching (Foreman, 2004).

Educational games can play an integral role in interdisciplinary teaching and as indicated above serve as valuable resources for enriching the effectiveness of stu-dents' learning. As with any other instructional strategy, the use of games should follow a clear educational purpose, have a careful plan, and be congruent with the instructional objectives.

Classification of Educational Games

What are educational games? Seven types of games fall under the general heading of "educational games." Table 9.2 shows the seven types, with characteristics and examples of each.

TABLE 9.2
Classification of Educational Games

Type	Characteristics	Examples
1. Pure game*	Fun	*Ungame, New Games*
2. Pure contest	Stimulates competition; built-in inefficiency[‡]	Political contests, e.g., U.S. presidential race
3. Pure simulation*	Models reality	Toddler play
4. Contest/game	Stimulates competition; fun; built-in inefficiency	Golf; bowling; *Trivial Pursuit*
5. Simulation/game*	Models reality; fun	*SIMCITY; Our Town's Planning Commission Meeting*[§]
6. Contest/simulation	Stimulates competition; models reality; built-in inefficiency	Boxcar Derby of Akron, OH
7. Simulation/game/contest	Models reality; fun; stimulates competition; built-in inefficiency	*Monopoly, Life, Careers*

*These game types do not emphasize competition and thus are particularly recommended for use in the classroom as learning tools.

[‡]Rules for accomplishing the game objective make accomplishment of that objective less than efficient. For example, in golf the objective is to get the ball into the hole with the least amount of effort, but to do that, one has to take a peculiarly shaped stick (the club) and hit the ball, find it, and hit it again, continuing that sequence until the ball is in the hole. Yet, common sense tells us that the best way to get the ball into the hole with the least amount of effort would be simply to pick up the ball and place it by hand into the hole.

[§]See Vort, J. V. "Our town's planning commission meeting," *Journal of Geography,* 96(4), 183–190 (July–August 1997).

Functions of Educational Games

Games can be powerful tools for teaching and learning. A game can serve several of the following functions, and the function(s) of a particular game being used should be communicated to the students.

- Add variety and change of pace, providing a break from the usual rigors of learning
- Assess student learning
- Encourage lateral thinking
- Encourage learning through peer interaction
- Enhance student self-esteem
- Enhance student social relationships
- Motivate students
- Offer learning about real-life issues through simulation and role-playing
- Provide learning through tactile and kinesthetic modalities, as well as through linguistics
- Provide problem-solving situations and experiences
- Provide skill development and motivation through computer usage

Activity 9.3: Developing a Lesson Using Inquiry Level II, Thinking Skill Development, A Demonstration, or an Interactive Lecture

Instructions: The purpose of this activity is to provide the opportunity for you to create a brief lesson (about 20 minutes of instructional time, but to be specified by your instructor) designed for a specific grade level and subject and to try it out on your peers for their feedback in an informal (i.e., non-graded) micro peer teaching demonstration.

Divide your class into four groups. The task of members of each group is to prepare lessons (individually) that fall into one of the four categories: Level II inquiry, thinking level, demonstration, or interactive lecture. Schedule class presentations so that each class member has the opportunity to present her or his lesson and to obtain feedback from class members about it. For feedback, class members who are the "teacher's" audience can complete the assessment rubric shown below (by circling one of the three choices for each of the 10 categories) and give their completed form to the teacher for use in analysis and self-assessment. Before your class starts this activity, you may want to review the scoring rubric and make modifications to it with the class's input.

To structure your lesson plan, use one of the sample lesson plan formats presented in Chapter 6; however, each lesson should be centered around one major theme or concept and be planned for about 20 minutes of instructional time.

Group 1: Develop a Level II inquiry lesson.

Group 2: Develop a lesson designed to raise the level of student thinking.

Group 3: Develop a lesson that involves a demonstration.

Group 4: Develop a lesson that is an interactive lecture.

Peer and Self-Assessment Rubric for Use with Activity 9.3 [May Be Copied for Class Use]

For:		Group:	
	1	0.5	0
1. Lesson beginning Comment:	effective	less effective	not effective
2. Sequencing Comment:	effective	less effective	rambling
3. Pacing of lesson Comment:	effective	less effective	too slow or too fast
4. Audience involvement Comment:	effective	less effective	none
5. Motivators (e.g., analogies, verbal cues, humor, visual cues, sensory cues) Comment:	effective	less effective	not apparent
6. Content of lesson Comment:	well chosen	interesting	boring or inappropriate
7. Voice of teacher Comment:	stimulating	minor problem	major problems
8. Vocabulary used Comment:	well chosen	appropriate	inappropriate
9. Eye contact Comment:	excellent	average	problems
10. Closure Comment:	effective	less effective	unclear/none

Other Comments:

- Provide skill development in inductive thinking
- Provide skill development in verbal communication and debate
- Reinforce convergent thinking
- Review and reinforce subject-matter learning
- Stimulate critical thinking
- Stimulate deductive thinking
- Teach both content and process

Sources for useful educational games include professional journals and the Internet. Web sources of commercially available educational games for use in teaching are shown at the end of the chapter.

SUMMARY

Central to your selection of instructional strategies for teaching should be those that encourage children to become independent thinkers and skilled learners who can help in the planning, structuring, regulating, and assessing of their own learning and learning activities. This final chapter has presented guidelines for some of the most frequently used and useful ways of helping children become independent thinkers and skilled learners.

This final chapter ushers in an important transition in your professional career, a career that as emphasized in the introduction of the final activity is really only a beginning. Throughout your teaching career, you will continue improving your knowledge and skills in all aspects of teaching and learning.

We wish you the very best in what is to be the first chapter in your new career. Be the very best teacher that you can be. The nation, indeed the world, and its children need you.

—Richard Kellough
—John Jarolimek

STUDY QUESTIONS AND ADDITIONAL ACTIVITIES

1. Many cognitive researchers agree that students should spend more time actively using knowledge to solve problems and less time reading introductory material and listening to teachers. Describe the meaning of this statement and how you now feel about it with respect to your decision to become a teacher. Do you expect to act on their suggestion? Explain why not, or how you will do it.
2. Explain the meaning of *integrating strategies for integrated learning.*
3. Are there any cautions that, as a teacher, you need to be aware of when using games for teaching? If there are, describe them.

4. Explain some specific ways you can help students develop their skills in thinking and learning. Explain how you will determine that students have raised their skill level in thinking and in learning.

5. Select one of the characteristics of intelligent behavior and (for a grade level of your choice and time limit as decided by your class) write a lesson plan for helping students develop that behavior. Share or teach your lesson to others in your class for their analysis and suggestions.

6. Test scores typically do not measure skills and intelligent behaviors such as critical thinking, persistence, cooperation, ingenuity, patience, creativity, originality, and flexibility in thinking. How should students who demonstrate achievement in intelligent behaviors be recognized?

7. Return to your response to question number 3 at the end of Chapter 2. Modify it if necessary. Share your modifications with those of your classmates.

8. Recent years have seen a tremendous growth in gaming, and for many young people, technology-centered games are a component of their everyday lives. Explain the impact of games, if any, in your own life. Considering these facts, what do you predict for the near future in public school teaching for the use of video, computer, or online games for teaching?

9. Think back about your own schooling. What is one demonstration that you observed that stands out as being most impressive to you, in either a negative or a positive way? Identify one or two characteristics of that demonstration that made it so. Share your conclusion with your classmates. From your sharing, what conclusions can be made about using demonstrations for teaching and learning.

10. It is often claimed that "teaching is *not* telling." If this is true, why do so many teachers continue to do a great deal of "telling"? For a specific grade level (K–8), describe with examples when telling by the teacher is okay and when it is not okay.

WEB SITES RELATED TO CONTENT OF THIS CHAPTER

- Ampersand Press *www.ampersandpress.com/*
- Aristoplay *www.aristoplay.com/*
- Creative Teaching Associates *www.mastercta.com/*
- Dawn publications *www.dawnpub.com/*
- Harcourt Brace School Publishers *www.harcourtbrace.com/*
- Novostars Designs *www.novostar.com/*
- Prufrock Press *www.prufrock.com*
- Summit Learning *www.summitlearning.com/pg1.htm*
- Teacher Created Materials *myconsumerguide.com/teacher_created_materials.htm*
- *The Sims www.maxis.com*
- Visual learning mapping software *www.ihmc.us* and *www.inspiration.com*

FOR FURTHER READING

Chapko, M. A., & Buchko, M. (2004). Math instruction for inquiring minds. *Principal, 84*(2), 30–33.

Dass, P. M., Kilby, D., & Chappell, A. (2005). Scientific inquiry and real-life applications bring middle school students up to standards. *Middle School Journal, 36*(5), 20–29.

Hallett, R. (2005). They dig it [an on-campus simulation paleontological dig]. *Science & Children, 42*(8), 22–25.

Hibbing, A. N., & Rankin-Erickson, J. L. (2003). A picture is worth a thousand words: Using visual images to improve comprehension for middle school struggling readers. *The Reading Teacher 56*, 758–770.

Jenkins, H. (2005). Getting into the game. *Educational Leadership, 62*(7), 48–51.

Lobman, C., & Lundquist, M. (2008). *Unscripted Learning: Using Improv Activities Across the K–8 Curriculum.* New York: Teachers College Press.

MacKinnon, G. R., & MacKenzie, C. (2005). Take the eco-challenge [a board game]. *Science and Children, 42*(8), 18–21.

Moyer, P. S., & Bolyard, J. J. (2003). Classify and capture: Using Venn diagrams and tangrams to develop abilities in mathematical reasoning and proof. *Mathematics Teaching in the Middle School, 8*, 325–330.

Pogrow, S. (2004). Supermath: An alternative approach to improving math performance in grades 4 through 9. *Phi Delta Kappan, 86*, 297–303.

Shaffer, D. W., Squire, K. R., Halverson, R., & Gee, J. P. (2005). Video games and the future of learning. *Phi Delta Kappan, 87*, 104–111.

Shreve, J. (2005). Let the games begin. Video games, once confiscated in class, are now a key teaching tool. If they're done right. *Edutopia, 1*(4), 29–31.

Tower, C. (2000). Questions that matter: Preparing elementary students for the inquiry process. *The Reading Teacher, 53*, 550–557.

Van Eck, R. (2006). The effect of contextual pedagogical advisement and competition on middle-school students' attitude toward mathematics and mathematics instruction using a computer-based simulation game. *Journal of Computers in Mathematics and Science Teaching, 25*, 165–195.

Wormeli, R. (2004). *Summarization in any subject: 50 techniques to improve student learning.* Alexandria, VA: Association for Supervision and Curriculum Development.

Glossary

ability grouping The assignment of students to separate classrooms or to separate activities within a classroom according to their perceived academic abilities. *Homogeneous grouping* is the grouping of students of similar abilities; *heterogeneous grouping* is the grouping of students of mixed abilities.

accountability Reference to the concept that an individual is responsible for his or her own behaviors and should be able to demonstrate publicly the worth of the activities carried out.

active learning See *hands-on learning*.

adolescence The period of life from the onset of puberty to maturity, terminating legally at the age of majority, generally the ages of 12 to 20, although young or early adolescence may start as soon as age 9.

advance organizer Preinstructional cues that encourage a mental set; used to enhance retention of content to be studied.

advisor-advisee Common to many middle schools, the (sometimes referred to as *homebase* or *advisory*) program that provides each student the opportunity to interact with peers about school and personal concerns and to develop a meaningful relationship with at least one adult.

affective domain The area of learning related to interests, attitudes, feelings, values, and personal adjustment.

alternative assessment Assessment of learning in ways different from traditional paper-and-pencil objective testing, such as a portfolio, project, or self-assessment. See *authentic assessment*.

anticipatory set See *advance organizer*.

articulation Term used when referring to the connectedness of the various components of the formal curriculum—*vertical articulation* refers to the connectedness of the K–12 curriculum, and *horizontal articulation* refers to the connectedness across a grade level.

assessment The relatively neutral process of finding out what students are or have learned as a result of instruction.

assignment A statement telling the student what he or she is to accomplish.

at risk General term given to a student who shows a high potential for not completing school.

authentic assessment The use of assessment procedures (usually portfolios and projects) that are compatible with the instructional objectives. Also referred to as *accurate, active, aligned, alternative, direct,* and *performance assessment*.

basal reader A reading textbook designed for a specific grade level.

behavioral objective A statement of expectation describing what the learner should be able to do on completion of the instruction.

behaviorism A theory that equates learning with changes in observable behavior.

block scheduling The school programming procedure that provides large blocks of time (e.g., 2 hours) in which individual teachers or teacher teams can organize and arrange groupings of students for varied periods of time, thereby more effectively individualizing the instruction for students with various needs and abilities.

brainstorming An instructional strategy used to create a flow of new ideas, during which judgments of the ideas of others are forbidden.

CD-ROM (compact disc–read only memory) Digitally encoded information (up to 650 MB of data that can include animation, audio, graphics, text, and video) permanently recorded on a compact (4.72 inch 12 cm in diameter) disc.

character education Focuses on the development of the values of honesty, kindness, respect, and responsibility.

classroom control The process of influencing student behavior in the classroom.

classroom management The teacher's system of establishing a climate for learning, including techniques for preventing and handling student misbehavior.

closure   The means by which a teacher brings the lesson to an end.

coaching   See *mentoring*.

cognition   The process of thinking.

cognitive disequilibrium   The mental state of not yet having made sense out of a perplexing (discrepant) situation.

cognitive domain   The area of learning related to intellectual skills, such as retention and assimilation of knowledge.

cognitive psychology   A branch of psychology devoted to the study of how individuals acquire, process, and use information.

cognitivism   A theory that holds that learning entails the construction or reshaping of mental schemata and that mental processes mediate learning. Also known as *constructivism*.

common planning time   A regularly scheduled time during the school day when teachers who teach the same students meet for joint planning, parent conferences, materials preparation, and student evaluation.

competency-based instruction   See *performanced-based instruction*.

comprehension   A level of cognition that refers to the skill of understanding.

computer-assisted instruction (CAI)   Instruction received by a student when interacting with lessons programmed into a computer system. Known also as computer-assisted learning (CAL).

computer literacy   The ability at some level on a continuum to understand and use computers.

computer-managed instruction (CMI)   The use of a computer system to manage information about learner performance and learning-resources options to prescribe and control individual lessons.

constructivism   See *cognitivism*.

continuous progress   An instructional procedure that allows students to progress at their own pace through a sequenced curriculum.

convergent thinking   Thinking that is directed to a preset conclusion.

cooperative learning   A genre of instructional strategies that use small groups of students working together and helping each other on learning tasks, stressing support for one another rather than competition.

core curriculum   Subject or discipline components of the curriculum considered as being absolutely necessary. Traditionally these are English/ language arts, mathematics, science, and social science. However, the No Child Left Behind legislation of 2001 includes these as the core subjects: English, reading or language arts, mathematics, science, foreign language, civics and government, economics, arts, history, and geography.

covert behavior   A learner behavior that is not outwardly observable.

criterion   A standard by which behavioral performance is judged.

criterion-referenced assessment   Assessment in which standards are established and behaviors are judged against the present guideline, rather than against the behaviors of others.

critical thinking   The ability to recognize and identify problems, to propose and to test solutions, and to arrive at tentative conclusions based on the data collected.

curriculum   Originally derived from a Latin term referring to a racecourse for the chariots, the term still has no widely accepted definition. As used in this text, curriculum is that which is planned and encouraged for teaching and learning. This includes both school and nonschool environments, overt (formal) and hidden (informal) curriculums, and broad as well as narrow notions of content—its development, acquisition, and consequences.

curriculum standards   Statements of the essential knowledge, skills, and attitudes to be learned.

deductive learning   Learning that proceeds from the general to the specific. See also *expository learning*.

detracking   An effort to minimize or eliminate separate classes or programs for students who are of differing abilities.

developmental characteristics   A set of common intellectual, psychological, physical, and social characteristics that, when considered as a whole, indicate an individual's development relative to others during a particular age span.

developmental needs A set of needs that are unique and appropriate to the developmental characteristics of a particular age span.

diagnostic assessment See *preassessment*.

didactic teaching See *direct instruction*.

differentiated instruction Varying the methods and content of instruction according to individual student differences and needs.

direct experience Learning by doing (applying) that which is being learned.

direct instruction Teacher-centered expository instruction, such as lecturing or a teacher-guided group discussion.

direct intervention Teacher use of verbal reminders or verbal commands to redirect student behavior, as opposed to nonverbal gestures or cues.

direct teaching See *direct instruction*.

discipline The process of controlling student behavior in the classroom. The term has been largely replaced by the terms *classroom control* or *classroom management*. It is also used in reference to the subject taught (e.g., language arts, science, mathematics, and so forth).

discovery learning Learning that proceeds from identification of a problem, through the development of hypotheses, the testing of the hypotheses, and the arrival at a conclusion. See also *critical thinking*.

divergent thinking Thinking that expands beyond original thought.

downshifting Reverting to earlier learned, lower-cognitive-level behaviors.

DVD (digital versatile disc) Like a CD-ROM but with a much greater storage capacity.

early adolescence The developmental stage of young people as they approach and begin to experience puberty. This stage usually occurs between 10 and 14 years of age and deals with the successful attainment of the appropriate developmental characteristics for this age span.

eclectic Utilizing the best from a variety of sources.

effective school A school where students master basic skills, seek academic excellence in all subjects, demonstrate achievement, and display good behavior and attendance. Known also as an *exemplary school*.

elective High-interest or special-needs courses that are based on student selection from various options.

elementary school Any school that has been planned and organized especially for children of some combination of grades kindergarten through six. There are many variations, though; for example, a school might house children of preschool through grades seven or eight and still be called an elementary school.

empathy The ability to understand the feelings of another person.

equality Considered to be same in status or competency level.

equity Fairness and justice, that is, impartiality.

evaluation Like assessment, but includes making sense out of the assessment results, usually based on criteria or a rubric. Evaluation is more subjective than is assessment.

exceptional child A child who deviates from the average in any of the following ways: mental characteristics, sensory ability, neuromotor or physical characteristics, social behavior, communication ability, or multiple handicaps. Also known as a *special-needs child* and *special education student*.

exemplary school See *effective school*.

exploratory An experience designed to help students explore curriculum based on their felt needs, interests, and abilities.

expository learning The traditional classroom instructional approach that proceeds as follows: presentation of information to the learners, reference to particular examples, and application of the information to the learner's experiences.

extended-year school Schools that have extended the school-year calendar from the traditional 180 days to a longer period, such as 200 days.

extrinsic motivators Motivation of learning by rewards outside the learner, such as parent and teacher expectations, gifts, certificates, stamps, and grades.

facilitating behavior Teacher behavior that makes it possible for students to learn.

facilitative teaching See *indirect instruction*.

family See *school-within-a-school*.

feedback Information sent from the receiver to the originator that provides disclosure about the reception of the intended message.

flexible scheduling Organization of classes and activities in a way that allows for variation from day to day, as opposed to the traditional, fixed schedule that does not vary from day to day.

formative assessment Evaluation of learning in progress.

goal, course A broad generalized statement about the expected outcomes of a course.

goal, educational A desired instructional outcome that is broad in scope.

goal, student A statement about what the student hopes to accomplish.

goal, teacher A statement about what the teacher hopes to accomplish.

hands-on learning Learning by actively doing.

Hawthorne effect Says that no matter what, if you try something new, it will show positive effects at first simply because of the interest demonstrated when something new is tried. Name derived from the first notice of the effect in 1962 at the Hawthorne plant of Western Electric in Cicero, IL.

heterogeneous grouping A grouping pattern that does not separate students into groups based on their intelligence, learning achievement, or physical characteristics.

high school A school that houses students in any combination of grades 9 to 12.

high-stakes assessment An assessment is called high stakes if use of the assessment's results carry serious consequences, such as a student's grade promotion rests on the student's performance on one test, or the student's graduation from high school rests on the student's performance on a single test.

holistic learning Learning that incorporates emotions with thinking.

homogeneous grouping A grouping pattern that separates students into groups based on common characteristics, such as intelligence, achievement, or physical characteristics.

house See *school-within-a-school*.

inclusion The commitment to the education of each special-needs learner, to the maximum extent appropriate, in the school and classroom the student would otherwise attend.

independent study An instructional strategy that allows a student to select a topic, set the goals, and work alone to attain them.

indirect instruction Student-centered teaching using discovery and inquiry as learning strategies.

individualized instruction See *individualized learning* and *differentiated instruction*.

individualized learning The self-paced process whereby individual students assume responsibility for learning through study, practice, feedback, and reinforcement with appropriately designed instructional modules.

inductive learning Learning that proceeds from specifics to the general. See also *discovery learning*.

inquiry learning Like discovery learning, except the learner designs the processes to be used in resolving the problem.

in-service teacher Term used when referring to credentialed and employed teachers.

instruction Planned arrangement of experiences to help a learner develop understanding and to achieve a desirable change in behavior.

instructional module Any freestanding instructional unit that includes these components: rationale, objectives, pretest, learning activities, comprehension checks with instructive feedback, and posttest.

integrated (interdisciplinary) curriculum Curriculum organization that combines subject matter traditionally taught independently.

interdisciplinary instruction Instruction that combines subject matter disciplines traditionally taught independently.

interdisciplinary team An organizational pattern of two or more teachers representing different subject areas. The team shares the same students, schedule, areas of the school, and the opportunity for teaching more than one subject.

interdisciplinary thematic unit (ITU) A thematic unit that crosses boundaries of two or more disciplines.

intermediate grades Term sometimes used to refer to grades 4 to 6.

internalization The extent to which an attitude or value becomes a part of the learner. That is, without having to think about it, the learner's behavior reflects the attitude or value.

interscholastic sports Athletic competition between teams from two or more schools.

intervention A teacher's interruption to redirect a student's behavior, either by direct intervention (e.g., by a verbal command) or by indirect intervention (e.g., by eye contact or physical proximity).

intramural program Organized activity program that features events between individuals or teams from within the school.

intrinsic motivation Motivation of learning through the student's internal sense of accomplishment.

intuition Knowing without conscious reasoning.

junior high school A school that houses grades 7 to 9 or 7 to 8 and that has a schedule and curriculum that resemble those of the senior high school (grades 9 to 12 or 10 to 12) more than they do those of the elementary school.

lead teacher The member of a teaching team who is designated to facilitate the work and planning of that team.

leadership team A group of teachers and administrators, and sometimes students, designated by the principal or elected by the faculty (and student body) to assist in the leadership of the school.

learning The development of understandings and the change in behavior resulting from experiences. For different interpretations of learning, see *behaviorism* and *cognitivism*.

learning center (LC) An instructional strategy that utilizes activities and materials located at a special place in the classroom and is designed to allow a student to work independently at his or her own pace to learn one area of content. See also *learning station*.

learning modality The way a person receives information. Four modalities are recognized: visual, auditory, tactile (touch), and kinesthetic (movement).

learning resource center The central location in the school where instructional materials and media are stored, organized, and accessed by students and staff.

learning station (LS) Like a learning center, except that where each learning center is distinct and unrelated to others, learning stations are sequenced or in some way linked to one another.

learning style The way a person learns best in a given situation.

literacy The ability to read, write, speak, listen, and think critically.

looping An arrangement in which the cohort of students and teachers remain together as a group for several or for all the years a child is at a particular school. Also referred to as multiyear grouping, multiyear instruction, multiyear placement, and teacher–student progression.

magnet school A school that specializes in a particular academic area, such as science, mathematics and technology, the arts, or international relations. Also referred to as a *theme school*.

mainstreaming Placing an exceptional child in regular education classrooms for all (inclusion) or part (partial inclusion) of the school day.

mandala A diagram, usually circular, with spiritual and ritual significance.

mastery learning The concept that a student should master the content of one lesson before moving on to the content of the next.

measurement The process of collecting and interpreting data.

mentoring One-on-one coaching, tutoring, or guidance to facilitate learning.

metacognition Planning, monitoring, and evaluating one's own thinking. Known also as *reflective abstraction*.

middle grades   Grades 5 to 8.

middle level education   Any school unit between elementary and high school.

middle school   A school that has been planned and organized especially for students of ages 10 to 14.

minds-on learning   Learning in which the learner is intellectually active, thinking about what is being learned.

misconception   Faulty understanding of a major idea or concept. Also known as a naïve theory and conceptual misunderstanding.

modeling   The teacher's direct and indirect demonstration, by actions and by words, of the behaviors expected of students.

multicultural education   A deliberate attempt to help students understand facts, generalizations, attitudes, and behaviors derived from their own ethnic roots as well as others. In this process, students unlearn racism and biases and recognize the interdependent fabric of society, giving due acknowledgment for contributions made by its members.

multilevel instruction   See *multitasking*.

multilevel teaching   See *multitasking*.

multimedia   The combined use of sound, video, and graphics for instruction.

multiple intelligences   A theory of several different intelligences, as opposed to just one general intelligence; intelligences that have been described are verbal/linguistic, musical, logical/mathematical, naturalist, visual/spatial, bodily/kinesthetic, interpersonal, and intrapersonal.

multipurpose board   A writing board with a smooth plastic surface used with special marking pens rather than chalk. Sometimes called a visual aid panel, the board may have a steel backing and then can be used as a magnetic board as well as a screen for projecting visuals.

multitasking   The simultaneous use of several levels of teaching and learning in the same classroom, with students working on different objectives or different tasks leading to the same objective. Also called *multilevel teaching*.

naïve theory   See *misconception*.

norm-referenced   Individual performance is judged relative to overall performance of the group (e.g., grading on a curve), as opposed to being criterion referenced.

orientation set   See *advance organizer*.

overlapping   A teacher behavior where the teacher is able to attend to more than one matter at a time.

overt behavior   A behavior that is outwardly observable.

peer tutoring   An instructional strategy that places students in a tutorial role in which one student helps another learn.

performance assessment   See *authentic assessment*.

performance-based instruction   Instruction designed around the instruction and assessment of student achievement against specified and predetermined objectives.

performance objective   See *behavioral objective*.

phonemic awareness   The ability to identify, isolate, and manipulate the individual sounds, or phonemes, in words.

phonics   The application of sound-symbol relationships to the teaching of reading.

phonological awareness   The knowledge of the sounds of language, including the ability to hear syllables in words, hear the parts of words, hear individual sounds in words, and identify and make rhymes.

portfolio assessment   An alternative approach to evaluation that assembles representative samples of a student's work over time as a basis for assessment.

positive reinforcer   A means of encouraging desired student behaviors by rewarding those behaviors when they occur.

preassessment   Diagnostic assessment of what students know or think they know prior to the instruction.

preservice   Term used when referring to teachers in training, as opposed to in-service teachers, teachers who are employed.

probationary teacher An untenured teacher. After a designated number of years in the same district, usually three, upon rehire the probationary teacher receives a tenure contract.

procedure A statement telling the student how to accomplish a task.

psychomotor domain The domain of learning that involves locomotor behaviors.

realia Real objects used as visual props during instruction, such as political campaign buttons, plants, memorabilia, art, balls, and so forth.

reciprocal teaching A form of collaborative teaching where the teacher and the students share the teaching responsibility and all are involved in asking questions, clarifying, predicting, and summarizing.

reflection The conscious process of mentally replaying experiences.

reflective abstraction See *metacognition*.

reliability In measurement, the consistency with which an item or instrument is measured over time.

rubric An outline of the criteria used to assess a student's work.

rules In classroom management, rules are the standards of expectation for classroom behavior.

schema (plural: schemata) A mental construct by which the learner organizes his or her perceptions of situations and knowledge.

school-within-a-school Sometimes referred to as a *house, cluster, village, pod,* or *family,* it is a teaching arrangement where one team of teachers is assigned to work with the same group of about 125 students for a common block of time, for the entire school day or, in some instances, for all the years those students are at that school.

secondary school Traditionally, any school housing students for any combination of grades 7 to 12.

self-contained classroom Commonly used in the primary grades, it is a grouping pattern where one teacher teaches all or most all subjects to one group of children.

self-paced learning See *individualized learning.*

sequencing Arranging ideas in logical order.

simulation An abstraction or simplification of a real-life situation.

special-needs student See *exceptional child.*

standards See *curriculum standards.*

student teaching A field experience component of teacher preparation, traditionally the culminating experience, where the teacher candidate practices teaching children while under the supervision of a credentialed teacher and a university supervisor.

summative assessment Assessment of learning after instruction is completed.

teacher leader See *lead teacher.*

teaching See *instruction.*

teaching style The way teachers teach; their distinctive mannerisms complemented by their choices of teaching behaviors and strategies.

teaching team A team of two or more teachers who work together to provide instruction to the same group of students, either alternating the instruction or team teaching simultaneously.

team teaching Two or more teachers working together to provide instruction to a group of students.

tenured teacher After serving a designated number of years in the same school district (usually three) as a probationary teacher, on rehire the teacher receives a tenure contract, which means that the teacher is automatically rehired each year thereafter unless the contract is revoked by either the district or the teacher and for specific and legal reasons.

terminal behavior That which has been learned as a direct result of instruction.

thematic unit A unit of instruction built on a central theme or concept.

theme school See *magnet school.*

think time See *wait time.*

tracking The practice of the voluntary or involuntary placement of students in different programs or courses according to their ability and prior academic performance. See also *ability grouping.*

traditional teaching Teacher-centered direct instruction, typically using lectures, discussions, textbooks, and worksheets.

transition In a lesson, the planned procedures that move student thinking from one idea to the next or that move their actions from one activity to the next. With reference to schooling, transitions are the times when a student moves from one level of school to the next.

untracking See *detracking*.

validity In measurement, the degree to which an item or instrument measures that which it is intended to measure.

village See *school-within-a-school*.

wait time In the use of questioning, the period of silence between the time a question is asked and the inquirer (teacher) does something, such as repeats the question, rephrases the question, calls on a particular student, answers the question him- or herself, or asks another question. Also referred to as *think time*.

whole-language learning A point of view with a focus on seeking or creating meaning that encourages language production, risk taking, independence in producing language, and the use of a wide variety of print materials in authentic reading and writing situations.

withitness The teacher's timely ability to intervene and redirect a student's inappropriate behavior.

year-round school A school that operates as is tradition, which is with 180 school days, but the days are spread over 12 months rather than the usual 10. Most common is the nine-weeks on, three-weeks off format.

young adolescent The 10- to 14-year-old experiencing the developmental stage of early adolescence.

References

Albert, L. (1989, rev. 1996). *A teacher's guide to cooperative discipline: How to manage your classroom and promote self-esteem.* Circle Pines, MN: American Guidance Service.

Allen, R. (2003, Winter). Civic virtue in the schools. *Curriculum Update,* 1–3, 6–8.

Amrein, A. L., & Berliner, D. C. (2003). The testing divide: New research on the intended and unintended impact of high-stakes testing. *Peer Review, 5*(2), 21–32.

Armstrong, T. (1998). *Awakening genius in the classroom.* Alexandria, VA: Association for Supervision and Curriculum Development.

Ashton, P., & Webb, R. (1986). *Making a difference: Teacher's sense of efficacy and student achievement.* New York: Longman.

Astington, J. W. (1998). Theory of mind goes to school. *Educational Leadership, 56*(3), 46–48.

Ausubel, D. P. (1963). *The psychology of meaningful learning.* New York: Grune & Stratton.

Bacon, S. (2005). Reading coaches: Adapting an intervention model for upper elementary and middle school readers. *Journal of Adolescent and Adult Literacy, 48,* 416–427.

Baker, J. C., & Martin, F. G. (1998). *A neural network guide to teaching,* Fastback 431. Bloomington, IN: Phi Delta Kappa Educational Foundation.

Baldwin, D. (2004). A guide to standardized writing assessment. *Educational Leadership, 62*(2), 72–75.

Barojas, J., & Dehesa, N. (2001). Mathematics for social scientists: Learning cycles and teaching strategies. *Industry & Higher Education, 15,* 269–277.

Barron, J. B., & Sternberg, R. J. (Eds.). (1987). *Teaching thinking skills: Theory and practice.* New York: W. H. Freeman.

Battistini, J. (1995). *From theory to practice: Classroom application of outcome-based education.* Bloomington, IN: ERIC Clearinghouse on Reading, English, and Communication.

Becker, R. R. (2000). The critical role of students' questions in literacy development. *Educational Forum, 64,* 261–272.

Bevevino, M. M., Dengel, J., & Adams, K. (1999). Constructivist theory in the classroom: Internalizing concepts through inquiry learning. *Clearing House, 72,* 275–278.

Black, S. (2002). Starving in silence. *American School Board Journal, 189,* 334–337.

Black, S. (2004). All together now. *American School Board Journal, 191*(3), 40–42.

Bloom, B. S. (Ed.). (1984). *Taxonomy of educational objectives, book 1, cognitive domain.* White Plains, NY: Longman.

Bloom, B. S. (1987). *Human characteristics and school learning.* New York: McGraw-Hill.

Bolak, K., Bialach, D., & Dunphy, M. (2005). Standards-based, thematic units integrate the arts and energize students and teachers. *Middle School Journal 36*(5), 9–19.

Bolland, J. M. (2003). Hopelessness and risk behaviour among adolescents living in high-poverty inner-city neighbourhoods. *Journal of Adolescence, 26,* 145–158.

Bomer, R. (2004). Speaking out for social action. *Educational Leadership, 62*(2), 34–37.

Boyer, E. (1995). *The basic school: A community for learning.* San Francisco: Jossey-Bass.

Brand, S., Dunn, R., & Greb, F. (2002). Learning styles of students with attention deficit hyperactivity disorder: Who are they and how can we teach them? *Clearing House, 75,* 268–273.

Brandt, R. (2000). On teaching brains to think: A conversation with Robert Sylwester. *Educational Leadership, 57*(7), 72–75.

Brogan, B. R., & Brogan, W. A. (1995). The Socratic questioner: Teaching and learning in a dialogical classroom. *The Educational Forum, 59,* 288–296.

Brown, J. (2005). *Edutopia, 1*(8), 43–44.

Bruner, J. S. (1960). *Process of education.* Cambridge, MA: Harvard University Press.

Burns, M. (2004). Writing in math. *Educational Leadership, 62*(3), 30–33.

Burrett, K., & Rusnak, T. (1993). *Integrated character education*. Fastback 351. Bloomington, IN: Phi Delta Kappa Educational Foundation.

Caine, R. N., & Caine, G. (1997). *Education on the edge of possibility*. Alexandria, VA: Association for Supervision and Curriculum Development.

Callahan, C. M. (2001). Beyond the gifted stereotype. *Educational Leadership, 59*(3), 42–46.

Campbell, L., & Campbell, B. (1999). *Multiple intelligences and student achievement: Success stories from six schools*. Alexandria, VA: Association for Supervision and Curriculum Development.

Canter, L., & Canter, M. (1992). *Assertive discipline: Positive behavior management for today's schools*. Santa Monica, CA: Lee Canter & Associates.

Carroll, J. (1963). A model of school learning. *Teachers College Record, 64*, 723–733.

Carroll, J. M. (1994). The Copernican plan evaluated. *Phi Delta Kappan, 76*(2), 105–113.

Carter, C. J. (1997). Why reciprocal teaching? *Educational Leadership, 54*(6), 64–68.

Carter, P. (2005). The modern multi-age classroom. *Educational Leadership 63*(1), 54–58.

Casbarro, J. (2004). Reducing anxiety in the era of high-stakes testing. *Principal, 83*(5), 36–38.

Cheek, J. R., Bradley, L. J., Reynolds, J., & Coy, D. (2002). An intervention for helping elementary students reduce test anxiety. *Professional School Counseling, 6*, 162–164.

Choate, J. S., & Rakes, T. A. (1998). *Inclusive instruction for struggling readers*. Fastback 434. Bloomington, IN: Phi Delta Kappa Educational Foundation.

Clark, G., & Zimmerman, E. (1998). Nurturing the arts in programs for gifted and talented students. *Phi Delta Kappan, 79*, 747–751.

Coelho, E. (1994). *Learning together in the multicultural classroom*. Portsmouth, NH: Heinemann.

Combs, A. W. (Ed.). (1962). *Perceiving, behaving, becoming: A new focus for education*. Alexandria, VA: Association for Supervision and Curriculum Development.

Conley, D. T. (1993). Restructuring: In search of a definition. *Principal, 72*(3), 12.

Costa, A. L. (Ed.). (1985). *Developing minds: A resource book for teaching thinking*. Alexandria, VA: Association for Supervision and Curriculum Development.

Costa, A. L. (Ed.). (1991a). *Developing minds: A resource book for teaching thinking* (3d ed.). Alexandria, VA: Association for Supervision and Curriculum Development.

Costa, A. L. (1991b). *The school as a home for the mind*. Palatine, IL: Skylight.

Costa, A. L., & Kallick. B. (2000). *Discovering and exploring habits of mind*. Book 1 of Habits of Mind: A Developmental Series. Alexandria, VA: Association for Supervision and Curriculum Development.

Cruickshank, D. R. (1990). *Research that informs teachers and teacher educators*. Bloomington, IN: Phi Delta Kappa.

Curtin, E. M. (2006). Lessons on effective teaching from middle school ESL students. *Middle School Journal, 37*(3), 38–45.

Danielson, C. (1996). *Enhancing professional practice: A framework for teaching*. Alexandria, VA: Association for Supervision and Curriculum Development.

Danielson, C., & McGreal, T. I. (2000). *Teacher evaluation to enhance professional practice*. Alexandria, VA: Association for Supervision and Curriculum Development, and Princeton, NJ: Educational Testing Service.

Davis, A. K. (2001). The politics of barking and the state of our schools. *Phi Delta Kappan, 82*, 786–789.

De Bono, E. (1970). *Lateral thinking: Creativity step by step*. New York: Harper & Row.

DeLay, R. (1996). Forming knowledge: Constructivist learning and experiential education. *Journal of Experiential Education, 19*(2), 76–81.

Diehm, C. (2004). From worn-out to web-based: Better student portfolios. *Phi Delta Kappan, 85*, 792–794.

Dreikurs, R., & Cassel, P. (1972). *Discipline without tears*. New York: Hawthorne Books.

Dreikurs, R., Grunwald, B. B., & Pepper, F. C. (1982). *Maintaining sanity in the classroom: Classroom management techniques* (2nd ed.). New York: Harper & Row.

Dunn, R. (1995). *Strategies for educating diverse learners*. Fastback 384. Bloomington, IN: Phi Delta Kappa Educational Foundation.

Echevarria, M. (2003). Anomalies as a catalyst for middle school students' knowledge construction and scientific reasoning during science inquiry. *Journal of Educational Psychology, 95*, 357–374.

Educational Leadership. (1999). The constructivist classroom, the entire November theme issue, *Educational Leadership, 57*.

Egley, A. (2002). *National youth gang survey trends from 1996 to 2000. OJJDP Fact Sheet.* Washington, DC: U.S. Department of Justice, Office of Justice Programs, Office of Juvenile Justice and Delinquency Prevention.

Eisner, E. W. (1979). *The educational imagination*. New York: Macmillan.

Elder, L., & Paul, R. (1998). The role of Socratic questioning in thinking, teaching, and learning. *Clearing House, 71*, 297–301.

Elias, M. J. (2001). Easing transitions with social-emotional learning. *Principal Leadership, 1*, 1–4. Retrieved April 1, 2001, from http://www. nassp.org/news/pl_soc_emo_lrng_301.htm

Englert, C. S., & Mariage, T. V. (1991). Making students partners in the comprehension process: Organizing the reading "POSSE." *Learning Disability Quarterly, 14*(1), 123–138.

English, L. (1998). Uncovering students' analytic, practical, and creative intelligences: One school's application of Sternberg's triarchic theory. *School Administrator, 55*(1), 28–29.

Esbensen, F., & Osgood, D. W. (1997). *National evaluation of G.R.E.A.T. research in brief.* Washington, DC: U.S. Department of Justice, Office of Justice Programs, National Institute of Justice.

Fagan, H., & Sherman, L. (2002). Starting at the end: Alaska project-based learning expert Helena Fagan insists that good projects are designed "backward"—that is, what do we want kids to know when they're done? *Northwest Education, 7*(3), 30–35.

Feldhusen, J. F. (1998). Programs for the gifted few or talent development for the many? *Phi Delta Kappan, 79*, 735–738.

Findley, N. (2002). In their own ways. *Educational Leadership, 60*(1), 60–63.

Fischer, P. (2002). Wow! Kindergarten/first grade inquiry. *Primary Voices K–6, 10*(3), 9–15.

Fitzgerald, J., & Graves, M. F. (2005). Reading supports for all. *Educational Leadership, 62*(4), 68–71.

Foreman, J. (2004). Game-based learning: How to delight and instruct in the 21st century. *Educause Review, 39*. Retrieved online October 14, 2004.

Foster, A. S. (2003). Let the dogs out: Using bobble head toys to explore force and motion. *Science Scope, 26*(7), 16–19.

Franklin, J. (2002). Taking up the challenge: Safeguarding the shelves of school libraries. *Curriculum Update, 44*(8), 1, 3, 8.

Freiberg, H. J. (Ed.). (1997). *Beyond behaviorism: Changing the classroom management paradigm*. Boston: Allyn & Bacon.

Freiberg. H. J. (Ed.). (1999). *Perceiving behaving becoming: Lessons learned*. Alexandria, VA: Association for Supervision and Curriculum Development.

Frost, R., Olson, E., & Valiquette, L. (2000). The wolf pack: Power shared and power earned—building a middle school nation. *Middle School Journal, 31*(5), 30–36.

Gagné, R. M., Briggs, L. J., & Wager, W. W. (1994). *Principles of instructional design* (4th ed.). New York: Holt, Rinehart and Winston.

Gardner, H. (1996). Multiple intelligences: Myths and messages. *International Schools Journal, 15*(2), 8–22.

Gathercoal, F. (1997). *Judicious discipline* (4th ed.). San Francisco: Caddo Gap Press.

Geelan, D. R. (1997). Epistemological anarchy and the many forms of constructivism. *Science and Education, 6*(1–2), 15–28.

Ginott, H. G. (1971). *Teacher and child.* New York: Macmillan.

Glasser, W. (1965). *Reality therapy: A new approach to psychiatry.* New York: Harper & Row.

Glasser, W. (1969). *Schools without failure.* New York: Harper & Row.

Glasser, W. (1986). *Control theory in the classroom.* New York: Harper & Row.

Glasser, W. (1990). *The quality school: Managing students without coercion.* New York: Harper & Row.

Glasser, W. (1993). *The quality school teacher.* Harper-Perennial.

Glasser, W. (1997). A new look at school failure and school success. *Phi Delta Kappan, 78,* 597–602.

Glod, M. (November 10, 2004). High achievers leaving schools behind. *Washington Post.*

Goleman, D., Boyatzis, R., & McKee, A. (2002). *Primal leadership: Realizing the power of emotional intelligence.* Boston: Harvard Business School Press.

Good, T. L., & Brophy, J. E. (2003). *Looking in classrooms* (9th ed.). New York: Allyn & Bacon.

Goos, M., & Galbraith, P. (1996). Do it this way! Metacognitive strategies in collaborative mathematics problem solving. *Educational Studies in Mathematics, 30,* 229–260.

Gordon, D. T. (2002). Curriculum access in the digital age. *Harvard Education Letter, 18*(1), 1–5.

Gordon, T. (1989). *Discipline that works: Promoting self-discipline in the classrooms.* New York: Penguin.

Gray, T., & Fleischman, S. (2004). Successful strategies for English language learners. *Educational Leadership, 62*(4), 84–85.

Gross, M. U. M. (2000). Exceptionally and profoundly gifted students: An underserved population. *Understanding Our Gifted, 12*(2), 3–9.

Guskey, T. R. (Ed.). (1996). *Communicating student learning.* Alexandria, VA: Association for Supervision and Curriculum Development.

Gustafson, C. (1998). Phone home. *Educational Leadership, 56*(2), 31–32.

Harrington-Lueker, D. (1997). Emotional intelligence. *High Strides, 9*(4), 1, 4–5.

Harris, H. L., & Coy, D. R. (2003). *Helping students cope with test anxiety.* Greensboro, NC: ERIC Clearinghouse on Counseling and Student Services. (ERIC Document Reproduction Service No. ED479355)

Harrison, G., Andrews, J., & Saklofske, D. (2003). Current perspectives on cognitive and learning styles. *Education Canada, 43*(2), 44–47.

Harrow, A. J. (1977). *Taxonomy of the psychomotor domain.* New York: Longman.

Haynes, C. C., Chaltain, S., Ferguson, J. E., Jr., Hudson, D. L., Jr., & Thomas, O. (2003). *The First Amendment in schools.* Alexandria, VA: Association for Supervision and Curriculum Development and Nashville, TN: First Amendment Center.

Helfand, D., & Rubin, J. (online Nov. 8, 2004). Few parents move their children out of failing schools. *Los Angeles Times.* Retrieved November 8, 2004, from www.latimes.com

Henry J. Kaiser Family Foundation. (September 2004). Children, the digital divide, and federal policy. *Issue Brief.*

Hewit, J. S., & Whittier, K. S. (1997). *Teaching methods for today's schools: Collaboration and inclusion.* Boston: Allyn & Bacon.

Hitz, R., & Driscoll, A. (1989). *Praise in the classroom.* ED313108. Washington, DC: ERIC Clearinghouse on Assessment and Evaluation.

Hopping, L. (2000). Multi-age teaming: A real-life approach to the middle school. *Phi Delta Kappan, 82,* 270–272, 292.

Horton, L. (1981). *Mastery learning.* Fastback 154. Bloomington, IN: Phi Delta Kappa Educational Foundation.

Howell, J. C. (1998). *Youth gangs: An overview.* Washington, DC: U.S. Department of Justice, Office of Justice Programs, Office of Juvenile Justice and Delinquency Prevention.

Howell, J. C. (2000). *Youth gangs: Programs and strategies. OJJDP Summary.* Washington, DC: U.S. Department of Justice, Office of Justice

Programs, Office of Juvenile Justice and Delinquency Prevention.

Hunkins, F. P. (1995). *Teaching thinking through effective questioning.* (2nd ed.). Boston: Christopher-Gordon.

Hyerle, D. (1996). *Visual tools for constructing knowledge.* Alexandria, VA: Association for Supervision and Curriculum Development.

Jacobson, J., Thrope, L., Fisher, D., Lapp, D., Frey, N., & Flood, J. (2001). Cross-age tutoring: A literacy improvement approach for struggling adolescent readers. *Journal of Adolescent & Adult Literacy, 44,* 528–536.

Jensen, E. (1998). *Teaching with the brain in mind.* Alexandria, VA: Association for Supervision and Curriculum Development.

Johnson, D. W., & Johnson, R. T. (1995). *Reducing school violence through conflict resolution.* Alexandria, VA: Association for Supervision and Curriculum Development.

Johnson, D. W., Johnson, R. T., & Holubec, E. (1998). *Cooperation in the classroom* (3rd ed.). Edina, MN: Interaction Book Co.

Joiner, L. L. (2003). Where did we come from? *American School Board Journal, 190*(4), 30–34.

Jones, F. (1987). *Positive classroom discipline.* New York: McGraw-Hill.

Jorgenson, O., & Vanosdall, R. (2002). The death of science? What we risk in our rush toward standardized testing and the three R's. *Phi Delta Kappan, 83,* 601–605.

Jung, C. G. (1923). *Psychological types.* New York: Harcourt Brace.

Kagan, S. (1995). Group grades miss the mark. *Educational Leadership, 52*(8), 68–71.

Kahlenberg, R. D. (2006). The new integration. *Educational Leadership 63*(8), 22–25.

Karplus, R. (1974). *Science curriculum improvement study,* teacher's handbook. Berkeley: University of California.

Kellough, R. D. (1970). The humanistic approach: An experiment in the teaching of biology to slow learners in high school—an experiment in classroom experimentation. *Science Education, 54,* 253–262.

Kellough, R. D. (1994). *A resource guide for teaching K–12.* New York: Macmillan.

Kellough, R. D., & Kellough, N. G. (1999). *Middle school teaching: A guide to methods and resources* (3rd ed.). Upper Saddle River, NJ: Merrill/Prentice Hall.

Kellough, R. D., & Roberts, P. L. (1994). *A resource guide for elementary school teaching: Planning for competence* (3rd ed.). New York: Macmillan.

Kelly, E. B. (1994). *Memory enhancement for educators.* Fastback 365. Bloomington, IN: Phi Delta Kappa Educational Foundation.

Kim, E. C., & Kellough, R. D. (1991). *A resource guide for secondary school teaching: Planning for competence* (5th ed.). New York: Macmillan.

Kohlberg, I. (1981). *The meaning and measurement of moral development.* Worcester, MA: Clark University Press.

Kolb, D. A. (1984). *Experiential learning: Experience as a source of learning and development.* Upper Saddle River, NJ: Prentice Hall.

Kounin, J. S. (1970). *Discipline and group management in classrooms.* New York: Holt, Rinehart & Winston.

Krank, H. M., Moon, C. E., & Render, G. F. (2002). Inclusion and discipline referrals. *Rural Educator, 24*(1), 13–17.

Krathwohl, D. R., Bloom, B. S., & Masia, B. B. (1964). *Taxonomy of educational goals, handbook 2, affective domain.* New York: David McKay.

Lake, K., & Kafka, K. (1996). Reporting methods in grades K–8. In T. R. Guskey (Ed.), *Communicating student learning: 1996 yearbook* (Chapter 9). Alexandria, VA: Association for Supervision and Curriculum Development.

Lemkuhl, M. (2002). Pen-pal letters: The cross-curricular experience. *Reading Teacher, 55,* 720–722.

Lennon, P. A., & Middlemas, D. (2005). The cultural maelstrom of school change. *School Administrator, 62*(3), 32.

Littky, D. (2004). *The big picture.* Alexandria, VA: Association for Supervision and Curriculum Development.

Long, D., Drake, K., & Halychyn, D. (2004). Go on a science quest. *Science & Children, 42*(2), 40–45.

Lumsden, L. (2002). *Preventing bullying.* ED463563. Eugene, OR: ERIC Clearinghouse on Educational Management.

MacBain, D. E. (1996). *Intergenerational education programs.* Fastback 402. Bloomington, IN: Phi Delta Kappa Educational Foundation.

Mann, L. (2000). Recalculating middle school math. *Education Update, 42*(1), 2–3, 8.

Manning, M. L., & Bucher, K. T. (2001). Revisiting Ginott's congruent communication after thirty years. *Clearing House, 74*(4), 15–18.

Marzano, R. J. (1992). *A different kind of classroom: Teaching with dimensions of learning.* Alexandria, VA: Association for Supervision and Curriculum Development.

Marzano, R. J. (2002). In search of the standardized curriculum. *Principal, 8*(3), 6–9.

Marzano, R. J., Pickering, D. J., & Pollock, J. E. (2001). *Classroom instruction that works: Research-based strategies for increasing student achievement.* Alexandria, VA: Association for Supervision and Curriculum Development.

Mastropieri, M. A., & Scruggs, T. E. (1998). Constructing more meaningful relationships in the classroom: Mnemonic research into practice. *Learning Disabilities Research & Practice, 13*(1), 138–145.

McCarthy, B. (1990). Using the 4MAT system to bring learning styles to schools. *Educational Leadership, 48*(2), 33.

McCarthy, B. (1997). A tale of four learners: 4MAT's learning styles. *Educational Leadership, 54*(6), 47–51.

McCarthy, M. H., & Corbin, L. (2003). The power of service-learning. *Principal, 82*(3), 52–54.

McCullen, C. (2000). In project-based learning, technology adds a new twist to an old idea. *Middle Ground, 3*(5), 7–9.

McDonald, S. (2001). The prevalence and effects of test anxiety in school children. *Educational Psychology: An International Journal of Experimental Educational Psychology, 21*(1), 89–101.

McEwan, B., & Gathercoal, P. (2000). Creating peaceful classrooms: Judicious discipline and class meetings. *Phi Delta Kappan, 81,* 450–454.

McEwin, C. K., Jenkins, D., & Dickinson, T. S. (1996). *America's middle schools: A 25-year perspective.* Columbus, OH: National Middle School Association.

Meier, D. (2005). *Harvard Education Letter, 21*(3), 7.

Mesmer, H. A. E., & Hutchins. E. J. (2002). Using QARs with charts and graphs. *Reading Teacher, 56*(1), 21–27.

Miller, W. B. (2001). *The growth of youth gang problems in the United States: 1970–98.* Washington, DC: U.S. Department of Justice, Office of Justice Programs, Office of Juvenile Justice and Delinquency Prevention.

Mulholland, L. A., & Bierlein, L. A. (1995). *Understanding charter schools.* Fastback 383. Bloomington, IN: Phi Delta Kappa Educational Foundation.

Nansel, T. R., Overpeck, M. D., Haynie, D. L., Ruan, W. J., & Scheidt, P. C. (2003). Relationships between bullying and violence among US youth. *Archives of Pediatrics & Adolescent Medicine, 157,* 348–353.

National Law Center on Homeless and Poverty. Retrieved January 10, 2003, from http://www.nlchp.org/FA_HAPIA

National PTA. (1997). *National standards for parent/family involvement programs.* Chicago: Author.

Nelsen, J. (1987). *Positive discipline.* New York: Ballantine Books.

Nelsen, J., Lott, L., & Glenn, H. S. (1993). *Positive discipline in the classroom: How to effectively use class meetings and other positive discipline strategies.* Rocklin, CA: Prima Publishing.

Novak, J. D. (1990). Concept maps and vee diagrams: Two metacognitive tools to facilitate meaningful learning. *Instructional Science, 19*(1), 29–52.

Novak, J. D. (1998). *Learning, creating, and using knowledge: Concept maps as facilitative tools in schools and corporations.* Mahwah, NJ: Lawrence Erlbaum.

Ogle, D. M. (1986). K-W-L: A teaching model that develops active reading of expository text. *Reading Teacher, 39*(6), 564–570.

Otten, E. H. (2000). *Character education.* ED444932. Bloomington, IN: ERIC Clearinghouse for Social Studies/Social Science Education.

Pai, Y., & Adler, S. A. (2001). *Cultural foundations of education.* (3rd ed.). Upper Saddle River, NJ: Merrill Prentice Hall.

Palincsar, A. S., & Brown, A. L. (1984). Reciprocal teaching of comprehension—fostering and comprehension-monitoring activities. *Cognition and Instruction, 1,* 117–175.

Pardini, P. (2002). Revival of the K–8 school. *School Administrator, 59*(3), 6–12.

Pavio, A. (1971). Imagery and verbal processing. New York: Holt, Rinehart & Winston.

Pavio, A. (1990). Mental representations: A dual coding approach. New York: Oxford University Press.

Pearlman, B. (2006). New skills for a new century. *Edutopia, 2*(4), 50–53.

Phillips, C. (2000). A sense of wonder: Young philosophers in San Francisco ponder age-old questions. *Teaching Tolerance, 17,* 36–39.

Piaget, J. (1972). *The psychology of intelligence.* Totowa, NJ: Littlefield Adams.

Plotnick, E. (1997). *Concept mapping: A graphical system for understanding the relationship between concepts.* ED407938. Syracuse, NY: ERIC Clearinghouse on Information and Technology.

Popham, W. J. (2006). Those [fill-in-the-blank] tests! *Educational Leadership, 63*(6), 85–86.

Potenza, S. A. (2003). Science buddies. *Science and Children, 40*(4), 40–43.

Protheroe, N. (2005). Learning and the teacher–student connection. *Principal, 85*(1), 50–52.

Queen, J. A., Blackwelder, B. B., & Mallen, L. P. (1997). *Responsible classroom management for teachers and students.* Upper Saddle River, NJ: Merrill Prentice Hall.

Rakow, S. J. (1992). Assessment: A driving force. *Science Scope, 15*(6), 3.

Raschke, D., Alper, S., & Eggers, E. (1999). Recalling alphabet letter names: A mnemonic system to facilitate learning. *Preventing School Failure, 43*(2), 80–83.

Ray, K. W. (2004). When kids make books. *Educational Leadership, 62*(2), 14–18.

Rayneri, L. J., Gerber, B. L., & Wiley, L. P. (2003). Gifted achievers and gifted underachievers: The impact of learning style preference in the classroom. *Journal of Secondary Gifted Education, 14*(4), 197–204.

Rea, P. J., McLaughlin, V. L., & Walther-Thomas, C. (2002). Outcomes for students with learning disabilities in inclusive and pullout programs. *Exceptional Children, 68,* 203–222.

Reedy, P. A. (2001). Improv and the middle school. *Principal, 80*(4), 52.

Reiser, R. A., & Butzin, S. M. (2000). Using teaming, active learning, and technology to improve instruction. *Middle School Journal, 32*(2), 21–29.

Renard, L. (2005). Teaching the DIG generation. *Educational Leadership, 62*(7), 44–47.

Robb, L. (2002). Multiple texts: Multiple opportunities for teaching and learning. *Voices from the Middle, 9*(4), 28–32.

Robinson, F. P. (1961). *Effective study* (Rev. ed.). New York: Harper & Brothers.

Roe, M. F., & Vukelich, C. (1998). Literacy portfolios: Challenges that affect change. *Childhood Education, 74,* 148–153.

Rothman, R. (2005). Is history . . . history? *Harvard Education Letter, 21*(6), 1–3.

Rowe, M. B. (1974). Wait time and reward as instructional variables. Their influence on language, logic, and fate control: Part 1. Wait time. *Journal of Research in Science Teaching, 11*(2), 81–94.

Rubenstein, G. (2006). World party. *Edutopia, 2*(2), 22–25.

Rumberger, R. W. (2002). *Student mobility and academic achievement.* ED466314. Champaign, IL: ERIC Clearinghouse on Elementary and Early Childhood Education.

Sadowski, M. (2006). Making schools safer for LGBT youth. *Harvard Education Letter, 22*(3), 1–3,

Salcido, R. M., Omelas, V., & Garcia, J. A. (2002). A neighborhood watch program for inner-city school children. *Children & Schools, 24*, 175–187.

Saunders, C. L. (2003). Case study: A gifted child at risk. *Journal of Secondary Gifted Education, 14*(2), 100–106.

Schneider, E. (2000). Shifting into high gear. *Educational Leadership, 58*(1), 57–60.

Schniedewind, N., & Davidson, E. (2000). Differentiating cooperative learning. *Educational Leadership, 58*(1), 24–27.

Schon, D. A. (1983). *The reflective practitioner: How professionals think in action.* New York: Basic Books.

Schonfeld, D. J., & Quackenbush, M. (2000). Teaching young children about AIDS. *Principal, 79*(5), 33–35.

Schumaker, J. B., Denton, P. H., & Deshler, D. D. (1984). *The paraphrasing strategy.* Lawrence, KS: Edge Enterprises.

Schwab, J. J. (1962). *The teaching of science as enquiry.* Cambridge, MA: Harvard University Press.

Schwartz, S. (1997). *Strategies for identifying the talents of diverse students.* ED410323. New York: ERIC Clearinghouse on Urban Education.

Schwartz, W. (1999). *Preventing violence by elementary school children.* New York: ERIC/CUE Digest Number 149, ERIC Clearinghouse on Urban Education.

Schwartz, W. (Ed.). (2000). *New trends in language education for hispanic students.* ED442913. New York: ERIC Clearinghouse on Urban Education.

Scott, J. E. (1994). Literature circles in the middle school classroom: Developing reading, responding, and responsibility. *Middle School Journal, 26*(2), 37–41.

Senesac, B. V. K. (2002). Two-way bilingual immersion: A portrait of quality schooling. *Bilingual Research Journal, 26*(1), 85–101.

Sharan, Y., & Sharan, S. (1992). *Cooperative learning through group investigation.* New York: Teachers College Press.

Simpson, E. J. (1972). *The classification of educational objectives in the psychomotor domain. The psychomotor domain: Volume 3.* Washington, DC: Gryphon House.

Skinner, B. F. (1968). *The technology of teaching.* New York: Appleton-Century-Crofts.

Skinner, B. F. (1971). *Beyond freedom and dignity.* New York: Knopf.

Slater, W. H., & Horstman, F. R. (2002). Teaching reading and writing to struggling middle school and high school students: The case for reciprocal teaching. *Preventing School Failure, 46*(4), 163–166.

Sosniak, L. (2001). The 9% challenge: education in school and society. *Teachers College Record* (Online only, 2001; retrieved May 7, 2001, from http://www.tcrecord.org, ID Number: 10756).

Sowell, J. E. (1993). Approach to art history in the classroom. *Art Education, 46*(2), 19–24.

Sternberg. R. J. (1998). Teaching and assessing for successful intelligence. *School Administrator, 55*(1), 30–31.

Sternberg, R. J., Grigorenko, E. L., & Jarvin, L. (2001). Improving reading instruction: The triarchic model. *Educational Leadership, 58*(6), 48–51.

Stevenson, C., & Carr, J. F. (Eds.). (1993). *Integrated studies in the middle grades.* New York: Teachers College Press.

Stiggins, R. J. (2001). *Student-involved classroom assessment* (3rd ed.). Upper Saddle River, NJ: Merrill Prentice Hall.

Stright, S. D., & Supplee, L. H. (2002). Children's self-regulatory behaviors during teacher-directed, seat-work, and small-group instructional contexts. *Journal of Educational Research, 95*(4), 235–244.

Sunderman, G. L., & Kim, J. (2004). Inspiring vision, disappointing results: Four studies on implementing the No Child Left Behind Act. *The Civil Rights Project of Harvard University.* Retrieved February 6, 2004, from http://www.civilrightsproject.harvard.edu

Sylwester, R. (1997). The neurobiology of self-esteem and aggression. *Educational Leadership, 54*(5), 75–79.

Tai, R. H., Liu, C. Q., Maltese, A. V., & Fan, X. (2006). Planning early for careers in science. *Science, 312*, 1143–1144.

Tassinari, M. (1996). Hands-on projects take students beyond the book. *Social Studies Review, 34*(3), 16–20.

Terry, M. (2004). One nation, under the designer. *Phi Delta Kappan, 86*(4), 265–270

Terzian, S. (2002). On probation and under pressure: How one fourth-grade class managed high-stakes testing. *Childhood Education, 78*(5), 282–284.

Thames, D. G., & York, K. C. (2003). Disciplinary border crossing: Adopting a broader, richer view of literacy. *The Reading Teacher, 56*, 602–609.

Thomas, W. P., & Collier, V. P. (December 1997–January 1998). Two languages are better than one. *Educational Leadership, 55*(4), 23–26.

Thomas, W. P., & Collier, V. P. (2003). The multiple benefits of dual language. *Educational Leadership, 61*(2), 61–64.

Thrope, L., & Wood, K. (2000). Cross-age tutoring for young adolescents. *Clearing House, 73*, 239–242.

Tiegerman-Farber, E., & Radziewicz, C. (1998). *Collaborative decision making: The pathway to inclusion.* Upper Saddle River, NJ: Merrill Prentice Hall.

Tomlinson, C. A. (2000). Reconcilable differences? Standards-based teaching and differentiation. *Educational Leadership, 58*(1), 6–11.

Tomlinson, C. A. (2002). Invitations to learn. *Educational Leadership, 60*(1), 8.

Trump, K. S. (2002). Be prepared, not scared. *Principal, 81*(5), 10–12, 14.

U.S. Department of Education. (1997). *A study of charter schools: First-year report 1997.* Washington, DC: Office of Educational Research and Improvement.

U.S. Department of Education. (1997). *Tried and true: Tested ideas for teaching and learning from the regional educational laboratories.* Washington, DC: Office of Educational Research and Improvement, U.S. Department of Education.

Vail, K. (2003). Where the heart is. *American School Board Journal, 190*(6), 12–17.

van Boxtel, C., van der Linden, J., Roelofs, E., & Erkens, G. (2002). Collaborative concept mapping: Provoking and supporting meaningful discourse. *Theory into Practice, 41*(1), 40–46.

van Hell, J. G., & Mahn, A. C. (1997). Keyword mnemonics versus rote rehearsal: Learning concrete and abstract foreign words by experienced and inexperienced learners. *Language Learning, 47*, 507–546.

Vars, G. F., & Beane, J. A. (2000). *Integrative curriculum in a standards-based world.* ED441618. Champaign, IL: ERIC Clearinghouse on Elementary and Early Childhood Education.

Victor, E., & Kellough, R. D. (2004). *Science K–4: An integrated approach.* Upper Saddle River, NJ: Pearson Merrill Prentice Hall.

Villa, R. A., & Thousands, J. S. (Eds.). (1995). *Creating an inclusive school.* Alexandria, VA: Association for Supervision and Curriculum Development.

Voelzel, L. (2000). Making foreign language instruction the center of attention. *Middle Ground, 4*(2), 44–46.

Vygotsky, L. (1962). *Thought and language.* Cambridge, MA: MIT Press.

Vygotsky, L. (1978). *Mind in society: The development of higher psychological processes* (M. Cole, V. John-Steiner, S. Scribner, & E. Souberman, Eds.). Cambridge, MA: Harvard University Press.

Walker, M. L. (1995). Help for the "fourth-grade slump"—SRQ2R plus instruction in text structure or main idea. *Reading Horizons, 36*(1), 38–58.

Want, M. C., Haertel, G. D., & Walberg, H. J. (December 1993–January 1994). What helps students learn? *Educational Leadership, 51*(4), 74–79.

Wassermann, S. (1999). Shazam! You're a teacher. *Phi Delta Kappan, 80*, 464, 466–468.

Weasmer, J., & Woods, A. M. (2000). Shifting classroom ownership to students. *Middle School Journal, 32*(2), 15–20.

Werderich, D. E. (2002). Individualized responses: Using journal letters as a vehicle for differentiated reading instruction. *Journal of Adolescent & Adult Literacy, 4*(8), 5, 746–754.

Whiteford, T. (1998). Math for Moms and Dads. *Educational Leadership, 55*(8), 64–66.

Wiggins, G., & McTighe, J. (1998). *Understanding by design.* Alexandria, VA: Association for Supervision and Curriculum Development.

Wilen, W. (1991). *Questioning skills for teachers: What research says to the teacher* (3rd ed.). Washington, DC: National Education Association.

Willard-Holt, C. (1999). *Dual exceptionalities.* ERIC Digest E574. Reston, VA: ERIC Clearinghouse on Disabilities and Gifted Education.

Willard-Holt, C. (2003). Raising expectations for the gifted. *Educational Leadership, 61*(2), 72–75.

Wimer, J. W., Ridenour, C. S., Thomas, K., & Place, W. A. (2001). Higher order teaching questioning of boys and girls in elementary mathematics classrooms. *Journal of Educational Research, 95*(1), 84–92.

Wolfe, P. (2001). *Brain matters.* Alexandria, VA: Association for Supervision and Curriculum Development.

Wynne, E. A., & Ryan, K. (1997). *Reclaiming our schools: Teaching character, academics, and discipline* (2nd ed.). Upper Saddle River, NJ: Prentice Hall.

Yancey, K. B. (2004). Using multiple technologies to teach writing. *Educational Leadership, 62*(2), 38–40.

Name Index

Subject Index